The South, the Nation, and the World

The South, the Nation, and the World

PERSPECTIVES ON SOUTHERN ECONOMIC DEVELOPMENT

David L. Carlton and Peter A. Coclanis

University of Virginia Press
Charlottesville and London

University of Virginia Press

Printed in the United States of America on acid-free paper

First published 2003

1 3 5 7 9 8 6 4 2

Library of Congress Cataloging-in-Publication Data

Carlton, David L. (David Lee), 1948–
The South, the nation, and the world : perspectives on southern economic development / David L. Carlton and Peter A. Coclanis.
p. cm.
Includes bibliographical references and index.
ISBN 0-8139-2184-8 (cloth : perm. paper) — ISBN 0-8139-2185-6 (pbk. : perm. paper)
1. Southern States — Economic conditions. I. Coclanis, Peter A., 1952– II. Title
HC107.A13 C33 2003
330.975'04—dc21

2002151566

To

John Christopher Marlow, June 20, 1949–March 25, 2000

George David Terry, August 23, 1950–October 20, 2001

Two Southern Historians Who Died Too Soon

Contents

Acknowledgments

The authors have incurred so many intellectual debts over the years that it would be presumptuous to try to identify them all, much less to repay them. Many individuals (and institutions) are thanked in the notes to the essays included in *The South, the Nation, and the World,* and we are pleased to refer readers there. In putting together this volume, however, we took on more debt (sixteen tons?), which we would like to acknowledge here. First, we would like to thank Richard K. Holway and his staff for their faith in our work and efforts on our behalf. The anonymous referees for the University of Virginia Press provided insightful and extremely helpful criticism for which we are thankful indeed. Matthew Brown at UNC, Chapel Hill, did a fine job helping to prepare our manuscript for publication. Ms. Lori Cohen of the Vanderbilt history department's staff redid figure 9.5; William Nelson of William Nelson Cartography redid figures 9.1, 9.2, 9.3, and 9.4. The VU history department staff, including Ms. Cohen, Ms. Vicki Crowthers, and administrative assistant Brenda Hummel, offered services too numerous to detail.

We shudder to think how many bases we have left untouched in acknowledging aid for work done in bits and pieces over the past decade and a half; we can only hope that those who assisted us know they are appreciated.

David L. Carlton, Nashville, Tennessee
Peter A. Coclanis, Chapel Hill, North Carolina
April 2002

The South, the Nation, and the World

1

Introduction

Our collaboration can fairly be said to date back some twenty years, to a time when the two of us found ourselves working in the same building—the South Caroliniana Library of the University of South Carolina in Columbia. We had taken decidedly different paths to that building—Carlton from a cotton-mill village outside Spartanburg, South Carolina, through college and graduate school in New England, Coclanis from the West Side of Chicago through schooling in the Midwest and New York City. But, once at the Caroliniana, we learned that our interests—Carlton's in industrialization, Coclanis's in agricultural history—potentially complemented each other. We were soon exchanging ideas—and sometimes epithets—in the mornings on the stone benches beneath the portico, over coffee, at lunch, and over barbeque at Ray Lever's in Blythewood. After several years we went off to earn our livings and advance our careers, but we continued to feed off each other intellectually, and by the late 1980s we began to formalize the relationship with a series of collaborations. The collection before you—both the coauthored and the individually authored pieces—is the product of that relationship and the intellectual cross-fertilization that has benefitted us mutually.

What were the concerns that brought us together? They weren't necessarily apparent at first. Carlton, a self-consciously *southern* historian, was seeking to understand a particular time and place; Coclanis, with broader interests in international capitalism, was more concerned with the particular as a piece of a larger whole. Yet Carlton's problem, as it turned out, was one with which Coclanis could help: how does one fit such "modern" behavior as industrialization into the historical narrative of a region commonly conceived as "premodern"? For his part, Coclanis came to rely on Carlton—and other "insiders" such as Lacy Ford, Allen Stokes, and George Terry—to tether his sometimes free-floating abstractions to the admittedly swampy ground of the Carolina low country.

Over time our interests clustered increasingly around two general concerns. First, we both were convinced that the history of the particular should be framed in terms that permit the most fruitful connections with the experiences of other times and places. Second, general explanations of world-historical events should be rooted in the histories of particular times and places, and should take account of the variety of ways in which the imperatives of place and time interact with larger forces.

These grand concerns generated a series of consequences that have provided us with our common research agenda. We decided initially that the best way to approach our project was by focusing not on "snapshots" of particular times and places but on the *process* by which a time or place became something else. We further agreed early on that an understanding of process would require us to reject explanations predicated on cultural exogeneity. Interpretations of the historical path taken by the American South—especially its chronic difficulties with economic development—have long tended to fall back on notions of a persistent "premodern" southern cultural distinctiveness, rooted either in the southern people as a whole or the retrograde interests of designated "ruling classes."[1] Neither of us, though, have found such cultural explanations of southern backwardness convincing. Whether we were looking at Carlton's small-town boosters turned industrialists or Coclanis's low country grandees, we saw men (mostly) in close touch with the intellectual currents of the modern world, oriented to progress and viewing the developed world of their day as the mirror in which they could see their own futures. Such figures, furthermore, seemed to us to behave in ways that could be described as "rational" both in the economic and the Weberian sense: they sought to maximize their material and psychological well-being and minimize their risk and anxiety, and they pursued their goals with discipline and creativity. Finally, the economic record of the South over the past sixty-odd years, with its stunning record of per-capita-income convergence, hardly suggests a region mired in backward mentalité. Given the twists and turns we see in southern economic history, it is clear that cultural explanations too often fall victim to the logical fallacy of attempting to use an alleged constant to explain a variable.

This is not to say that we believe that culture *is* a constant, or that cultural change is irrelevant to the story we sketch out in the following essays. Southern culture has been shaped and reshaped in a complex, dialectical relationship to southern economic life. At times a "backward" economy and culture have been mutually reinforcing; but southern cultural values have also changed over time in ways relevant to the region's ability to generate economic progress, expand economic welfare, and, critically, extend that economic welfare to *all* its people. As Robert Fogel, Seymour Drescher, Thomas Haskell, and others have argued, the abolition of slavery in the Western world was driven emphatically *not* by economics, but by a cultural shift whose material impact can aptly be termed "econocide." Similarly, one should hardly underplay the importance of the civil rights revolution in opening modern southern society to cosmopolitan entrepreneurial influences and in broadening access to economic opportunity. Nor, as first glance might suggest, are the above examples wholly exogenous impositions on a resistant region.[2]

We nonetheless believe that one should look first to economic processes to understand economic change. "Backward" cultures often reflect "backward" economics; more significantly, as Albert Hirschman has sharply noted, "cultural backwardness" itself is often as much constructed from regional economic disparities as "objectively" observed.[3] "Culture" is a slippery concept, not least because, as with subatomic particles, its observed characteristics are so intimately related to the observer and the act of observing. Cultural explanations for southern backwardness lend themselves to selectivity and manipulation; reasoning backward from consequence to cause, they depend as much on the historian's preconceptions about what *should* cause an observed effect as on a demonstrable causative relationship. The approach we take in these essays will not satisfy many; it does not yet wholly satisfy us. But we think the framework we sketch out points the way to a greatly improved understanding of the tangled process of southern economic and cultural change.

While we both feel that the strongest explanation of southern development must embrace both its failures and its successes, we are convinced that the foremost question in southern economic history is, as C. Vann Woodward contended, the exception it has posed to the prevailing narrative of American success.[4] If southerners have achieved striking gains in personal welfare in recent decades, their path to that achievement has been uncommonly tortuous, and their triumph even now is less than complete. Deindustrialization has arguably afflicted the rural and small-town South more than any other part of the nation; among the largest zones of rural poverty remaining in the United States are those of southern Appalachia and the former plantation belt; and even the gloss of such showpieces of southern progress as North Carolina's Research Triangle masks some persistent weaknesses.[5]

How to deal with such tangled paradoxes? We argue that the way to understand southern economic history is by looking first at structure—not only the internal structure of the regional economy but the larger national and international structures in which it has been embedded. We also believe in taking an evolutionary approach, focusing on the array of constraints and opportunities confronting southern economic actors at successive historical moments. How southerners dealt with their economic situation at any given time, and how their solutions to their problems in turn shaped future choices—these questions should be at the heart of any inquiry into the economic history of the region.

These concerns have informed the essays included in this volume. Collectively they cover a broad range of topics over most of the chronological sweep of southern history; most have previously appeared in print, though several have not. In a formal sense, some are Coclanis's alone, some Carlton's, and some coauthored; all, however, are imbued with a joint outlook forged over the past two decades. We offer these pieces in this form because we believe that, while hardly encyclopedic in their coverage, they provide a reasonably consistent and coherent approach to understanding both southern economic history and its broader implications for social developments in the region. We also believe that they fill an important scholarly gap. Except for Gavin Wright, and to a lesser extent Lee Alston and Joseph Ferrie, few modern scholars have attempted to offer a systematic interpretation of southern economic life.[6] While we do not presume to do so here, we nonetheless think that, along with these predecessors, we can provide a set of concepts and critical tools that can point us toward a better understanding of how the struggle against scarcity has shaped southern life.

How do we apply our general approach to the subject at hand—the American South as embedded in the larger nation and world? We can best proceed by starting at the beginning of American, and southern, history, with reference to two starting premises. First, we posit the entrepreneurial, and thus proto-modern, roots of what became "American" culture, regardless of section. Second, we see an emerging structural divergence between "the South" and "the North," resulting from what we consider the fundamental difference between the two: the centrality or absence of the plantation.

With respect to the first premise, English/British expansion into the New World needs to be understood as a manifestation of an "enterprising" spirit. That spirit, while not fully capitalistic in the way we understand that term nowadays, was, in its adventurousness (and, some might add, ruthlessness), fully continuous with the larger project of commercial-imperial expansion that at the same time was dispatching European traders to all the coasts of the world, sending European soldiers to Peru, India, and the North American interior, and devising institutions ranging from the modern nation-state to the first multinational corporations to coordinate the operations. It follows that the central animating purpose behind the founding of all the colonies of British America, from Canada to the Caribbean, was the desire to use the appropriated lands as staging grounds for enterprise, whether corporate or individual.

This is not to say that colonization can be reduced to commercial purpose; the English were, after all, a people emerging from a premodern culture with a rich and complex tradition. Among those venturing to these shores, the lust for personal gain tangled in frequently ironic ways with the nostalgic ache to restore what was slipping away, or the religious aspiration to establish a new Jerusalem. Thus the tense, paradoxical alliance of rural gentry and London tradesmen that created Puritan New England, or the weird amalgam of feudal utopia and land-company prospectus called the Fundamental Constitutions of Carolina. Nonetheless, New England theocrat and Carolina landgrave alike ultimately had to give way to the deeper commercial wellsprings that underwrote and peopled their projects.[7]

By the time the North American colonies were ready to embark on the vaster project of independence, all had converged on a set of basic cultural characteristics. In the public sphere, Americans were broadly tolerant of varied faiths and cultural practices, accommodating toward individual decision making, protective of property rights, and eager both to remove remaining roadblocks to enterprise and to reward innovative contributions to continental development. Privately, while still honoring the old ideal of the disinterested gentleman devoted to the public good, they increasingly reserved their highest rewards, both material and psychic, for those who expanded the material possibilities of American life, even if just for their own race and gender.[8]

Americans were alike, as well, in the fences they erected around their politico-economic "public sphere." White male northerners and southerners alike barred the gates to African Americans and sharply limited access to women and the indigenous peoples. This was attributable in part to "racism," but more deeply it stemmed from one of the great ironies of "free enterprise" in the early modern world: its heavy reliance on forced labor. The early modern age had yet to figure out how to mobilize the free, autonomous individuals that Americans idealized into the work forces that entrepreneurs desired to maximize the scale of their ambitions. The North American landscape was, by European standards, "empty" and needed laborers; but laborers were prevented by distance and poverty from moving to the site of opportunity, or would refuse to move at all if they had their druthers. Thus enterprising colonials had to take charge of moving their own laborers onto the lands they were appropriating, and keeping control of them once they arrived. Because the vastness of the landscape and the very openness and entrepreneurial spirit of the New World societies offered opportunities that undercut labor discipline, and because agriculture required long-term labor commitments, the enterprisers enforced draconian measures to maintain their control of labor.[9]

Thus, well into the early years of the Republic, American enterprise both north and south rested on bondage of various sorts: indentured servitude, apprenticeship, and for that matter family labor on farms and in shops, bound to the patriarch by the proverbial ties of love and fear. And, above all and most rigorously, slavery. Slaves worked alike on plantations and farms; they did much of the rough and menial work that powered commerce in Philadelphia and New York. New England Puritans, Manhattan merchants, Pennsylvania Quakers, Virginia and Carolina planters and backcountry farmers—all found slave property as important an extension of their ambition as property in land, goods, and ships. Only slowly and awkwardly did some begin to see problems with slavery, and such contradictions as were first recognized concerned not economic values but intellectual and moral ones.[10]

Furthermore, it was only in the nineteenth century that the link between labor-mobilizing enterprise and coercion began to weaken. Urbanization and increasingly complex institutions and infrastructure allowed unbound labor to move more fluidly and get better information about the location of opportunities, while the resulting concentrated pools of workers allowed employers to dispense with coercion. Rising incomes and lower transatlantic transportation costs reduced the need for entrepreneurs to finance immigration and increased the numbers of people voluntarily coming to American shores. As David Eltis among others has noted, only at this time did the bulk of immigration to the New World come to be unbound.[11] The shift of labor from agriculture and extractive industry to urban manufacturing and services was accompanied by an increased emphasis by employers in those sectors on mobilizing small, interchangeable units of labor power rather than persons; the process Marx termed "alienation" paradoxically allowed individual workers to liberate their personal lives from the master's grasp. Not only did employers gain greater flexibility in managing labor, but, at least in certain sectors, society could begin to afford a "working class" whose ambitions could be accorded the same scope as those of their "betters." The promise of American life could be broadened and—the new oppressions of industrial capitalism notwithstanding—could begin presenting itself for the first time as a promise for all, a promise that furthermore could mobilize free people of enterprise to pursue levels of material welfare historically available only to an expropriating few. The ultimate triumph of "free labor" remained well in the future, to be sure, and until the Civil War was by no means clear; in the United States it continued to coexist with possibly the most economically dynamic and prosperous bound-labor system the world had ever seen. But its appearance produced an increasingly sharp regional differentiation, as, with regard to their basic economic structures, North and South began decisively to part company.

Why? For all their commonalities, the two ends of the coastal string of British colonies had developed one fundamental difference: the southern colonies had committed themselves to a form of business enterprise—the staple-producing, forced-labor plantation—generally unavailable to the northern settlers. For all their feudal trappings, plantations must be understood not as landed estates affording steady, unearned income to rentier landlords (and certainly not in recompense for service to a lord or king), but as large-scale business enterprises, in which risk-taking entrepreneurs tapped into far-flung markets for purchased workers and sold to equally distant markets for their produce. Indeed, as late as 1860 plantations were the most numerous large-scale business enterprises in the United States, the largest of which dwarfed all but the largest manufacturing enterprises and which collectively wielded the political clout (and drew the resentment) that one would expect of such an enormous interest. The masters of these "firms" were, as we show in chapter 2 ("The Paths before Us/U.S."), as fully entrepreneurial as any Boston Associate or midwestern booster. Chapter 3 ("How the Low Country Was Taken to Task") elaborates the argument with a specific case, showing how a peculiarity of labor organization on plantations in the Tidewater Lower South—the so-called task system—can best be explained not in terms of the cultural preferences of either the European masters or the African slaves, but through economic analysis of the relations between "principals" and "agents."

As chapter 2 also demonstrates, though, the plantation's very success in the South—and its failure in the North—took these two ends of a common culture in very different directions. At the core of the plantation's peculiarity were several structural features of its operations. First, it was able to supply most of its needs internally and rely on a simple and well-established set of mediating institutions to supply the rest. Second, its heavy reliance on long-distance trade for its sales and purchases obviated the need for internal exchange and inhibited the development of the institutional framework needed to further that exchange. Third, its dependence on expropriated labor and ruthless suppression of slave consumption, human-capital development, and autonomy stifled both the development of consumer markets and a potentially important source of entrepreneurial energy. Finally, its extension over huge swaths of the southern landscape, from Virginia to Florida to Texas, left little scope for the development of any nonagricultural enterprise not somehow dependent on the plantation complex.[12]

Some of the consequences for the South of its economic thralldom to the plantation are detailed in chapters 4 and 5. In "Antebellum Southern Urbanization" we see that the plantation complex effectively retarded and distorted the development of cities and urban life in the region. Again, and contrary to commentators who have attributed the peculiarities of a Charleston or a New Orleans to their distinctive cultural traits, we find that southern cities shared many critical qualities with American cities more generally: commercial focus, civic direction by a booster elite, even a large European immigrant working class. The real distinctions were structural; cities were few, largely limited geographically to the edges of the region and functionally to connecting the plantations to the larger Atlantic world. The plantation economy afforded them few opportunities to develop trade with each other, and thus kept markets for manufactured goods below the threshold size needed for industrialization to take hold. The stunted size of these cities made them unattractive destinations for the ambitious and sapped their value as centers for what the geographer Allan Pred has termed "the circulation of information."[13] All this stands in sharp contrast to the North. There, as we show in chapter 2, the lack of a single, dominant form of large-scale enterprise forced settlers to rely instead on a diversity of small-scale enterprise, linked together and to outside markets by a complex web of institutions. These institutions, centered both in cities and proliferating interior towns, were adaptable to internal as well as long-distance exchange, generating large-scale markets that the largely autarchic plantations, with their forcibly under-consuming slave populations, could never offer. The result was that the institutional basis for what came to be called a "free-labor" economy—the next stage in modern development—found its home in the North, effectively bypassing the South, with consequences to which we shall return.

Another consequence of the plantation complex for the fate of the South concerned its lack of control over its place in the larger world—a theme elaborated in chapter 5, "Distant Thunder." By their natures, plantation economies are perfectly adaptable to a highly specialized niche in the world economy, and become slavishly dependent on that niche for access to the goods, services, and, above all, market outlets they need. But what happens when they lose their competitive position? As "Distant Thunder" suggests, low country rice planters enjoyed little control over the organization of their markets and could not adapt to changes in transportation costs and the entry of new competitors, especially from Asia. Moreover, they were unable quickly to alter their own cost structures, and their institutional frameworks lacked the diversity and flexibility that might allow them to move into new enterprises. Such would be the fate of the larger American South in the nineteenth century, not only with respect to rice but, as Gavin Wright has stressed, to the central staple, cotton, as well.[14]

The South's chickens came home to roost in the years following the Civil War and the collapse of the slave regime. About the economic aspects of the war and emancipation, and the long shadows cast by slavery and its white supremacist regime on southern efforts to emerge from the disasters the region brought upon itself in the 1860s, much ink has already been productively spilled, and in the present work we see no point in competing with the likes of Roger Ransom, Richard Sutch, Jay R. Mandle, and Gavin Wright.[15] A truly comprehensive interpretation of southern economic life will incorporate this epic story, and we hope to undertake this at another time.

One consequence of the plantation's hold on the region deserves further exploration, however: its retardation of the region's industrialization. Because the Northeast and Midwest established the institutional basis for an industrial society, while the South continued to rely on outside providers for its nonagricultural needs, the Unionist regions gained a signal advantage over their Civil War adversary. As chapter 11, "The American South and the American Manufacturing Belt," notes, such a manufacturing belt emerged between 1840 and 1880, stretching from southern New England west to St. Louis, south to Baltimore and the Ohio Valley, and north into southern Ontario. While many historians have treated this development as unnatural, even as driven by nefarious imperialistic designs on the part of the victorious North, such regional polarization was in fact a logical outcome of processes outlined by figures as disparate as Albert Hirschman and Paul Krugman.[16] Economic activity not bound to natural resources is inherently gregarious, seeking out locales with the strongest institutional support systems and the most plentiful and adaptable human capital. In turn, the best workers and entrepreneurs (including not a few southerners) were drawn to these enterprise magnets.

That the South was shut out of the process that created the manufacturing belt in the crucial years of its formation left it at a severe disadvantage when the time came to catch up with developments in the rest of the country—a disadvantage not only absolute but also self-reinforcing. The South's troubles became especially acute as the

United States, in the late nineteenth century, completed the process of creating within its territory a continental market. The consequences of southern backwardness imbedded in a much larger, dynamic marketplace are explored in chapters 6 and 7. "The Revolution from Above"—originally conceived in debate with scholars who contended that the South, like post-Napoleonic Prussia stung by defeat, launched a program of "top-down" modernization—uses North Carolina as a case study of how southern entrepreneurs were constrained by the limited opportunities available to them, and were directed into a narrow range of mature industries and technologies. These industries—cotton textiles most especially—were in important respects like the plantation itself. Specialized and technologically mature, reliant on outsiders for critical services from marketing to finance to equipment and design, they were highly portable, and were adaptable to rural as well as urban contexts. At the same time, they developed few linkages to local industries and failed to instill, in either entrepreneurs or workers, the versatile skills appropriate to a truly dynamic industrial society.

Southern entrepreneurial conservatism was deepened by an important heritage from the plantation era: the region's failure to develop the sort of institutional "support network" that could underwrite risk and absorb failure. An example of that institutional failure is investigated in chapter 7, "Capital Mobilization and Southern Industry." Here we argue that the lack of well-developed capital markets forced emerging southern industrialists to rely disproportionately on friends and neighbors in their local communities—local nest eggs whose holders prized stability over risk and whose demands reinforced the propensity of southern entrepreneurs to go for the tried and true, rather than the risky cutting edge.

The consequences of that entrepreneurial caution for southern technology are analyzed in chapter 8, "The Uninventive South?" In this piece, based on a reworking of data from a classic article by the economic historian Robert Higgs, we note a paradox: as the South began to industrialize in the late nineteenth and early twentieth centuries, it failed to make commensurate progress in raising its levels of innovative activity. This deepening retardation, we suggest, can be attributed to the region's industrial structure; those industries (mainly capital-goods industries) most closely associated at the time with innovative drive generally avoided the region. Or, perhaps more to the present point, cautious southern entrepreneurs generally avoided *them.*

But while southerners pursued development warily, the region nonetheless began to industrialize, and after a time its industrial growth, like that of the manufacturing belt, took on a self-reinforcing character. However, that very process imported regional polarization into the region itself. As we show in chapter 9, "Unbalanced Growth and Industrialization," the emerging disparities appeared in especially vivid relief in South Carolina, where the industrializing Piedmont had by the 1920s leaped far ahead of the old plantation belt and low country in the sophistication of its transportation and electric-power infrastructure. This process of self-reinforcing polarization, however, produced increasing political tensions, which in the 1920s and 1930s brought on a fundamental shift in the state's economic development policies. Paradoxically, the new departure was led by the oligarches of the Black Belt, who at this time seized the role of the modernizing Prussian Junker and began using the power of the state to spread development to less favored regions. It was a decidedly conservative, "top-down" form of modernization—the oligarches were obsessed with providing highways and public power to draw enterprise in, but, at least at first, stingy with the public health and education investments necessary to spread opportunity out. Nonetheless, by using government to substitute for the developmental inadequacies of local entrepreneurship—a strategy, as Alexander Gerschenkron famously noted, common among "late-comer" nations—they, along with counterparts in other southern states and the New Dealers who created institutions such as the Tennessee Valley Authority, laid the groundwork for what has been termed the "second wave" of southern development.[17]

The "second wave"—the post–World War II upsurge in southern economic development that decisively broke the region free of its postbellum disabilities and brought its income levels to 90 percent of U.S. levels by the 1990s—was (and continues to be) a complex development. It has involved a deepening and broadening of the southern industrial base, massive shifts from agriculture to manufacturing to services, and, in resource-using industries, movement to a more elaborate, coordinated exploitation of the environment.[18] A key feature in the eyes of many historians, though, has been the enhanced role of government—the most notable aspect of which has been defense spending. A great deal has been written about the fit between the region and the military-industrial complex—about the alleged southern "military tradition," or the use by powerful politicians of federal defense dollars to subsidize the region's development while sapping the economic strength of the "Frostbelt." Chapter 10, "The American South and the U.S. Defense Economy," is an effort to sort out the various claims and assess the role of defense in spurring the second-wave surge. In essence, this chapter concludes, while the contribution of military spending has been significant, it has also been greatly exaggerated. Not only are the totals less than one might expect, but the spending has been directed in ways that largely reinforced older southern development patterns; as one observer aptly put it, the South has been not the arsenal of the military but the commissary. Thus the postwar defense economy, for all its alleged novelty, illustrates at a deeper level the structural continuities of southern economic history.

We place those continuities in a broader historical context in the concluding essay, "The American South and the American Manufacturing Belt." If the South has been a region of poverty in a land of plenty not because of its backward culture but because of structural disability, this essay is a comprehensive effort to come to grips with that disability. As it demonstrates, regions in American economic history cannot be understood in isolation from each other. To the contrary, regions came into existence in relationship with each other. Thus the American South, beginning as a region distinguished from the northerly parts of British North America primarily by its greater reliance on the plantation as its characteristic form of business, became steadily more distinctive as "free-labor" society took hold in the antebellum North. It became more distinctive still (and harshly so) as the collapse of the slave plantation was followed by consolidation of the national market and the regional polarization that created the manufacturing belt.

To be sure, the era of the "second wave" has seen a partial depolarization of the relationship. As the belt reached maturity, its industry acquired more "southern" characteristics, and a broader range of manufacturing and "back office" service industries began to migrate out of the core. In the meantime, the mid-twentieth-century revolution in southern agriculture and the civil rights revolution broke down the major remaining structural and cultural barriers to full southern participation in national economic life. Finally, globalization has increasingly imposed common experiences on both regions: in both the South and the manufacturing belt, mature industries have departed for the less developed world, foreign-based producers have moved in, seeking access to the greatest market on earth, and a new wave of immigration from non-Western nations is profoundly affecting locales from New Jersey to Los Angeles to Chatham County, North Carolina.

But this is not to say that the South has come full circle. The heritage of the plantation complex persists in numerous subtle ways, as development leaders fret about collapsing cotton mills and absconding apparel plants, and as levels of education and health care continue to lag, while non-southern industrial communities from the midwestern machine-tool complex to Silicon Valley continue to display an ability to adapt to currency gyrations and bursting speculative bubbles. At this writing, evidence is appearing that the "second wave" may have spent its force, without solving the remaining problems of southern backwardness. The southern Black Belt and Central Appalachia remain mired in poverty, while much of the remaining rural South maintains a wobbly hold at best on its industrial base. State and local governments are reaching the limits of their revenues, and are encountering growing resistance to improving their services. Plantation culture is gone, Jim Crow is gone, the whole way of life idealized by the Nashville Agrarians has been abandoned even in the countryside—and yet many of the old disabilities remain, resistant to the solutions favored by the post–World War II development establishment. We hope, in the end, that our approach to southern economic history may open up new avenues for understanding not simply the South's past predicaments, but its present and future ones as well.

2

The Paths before Us/U.S.

Tracking the Economic Divergence of the North and the South

PETER A. COCLANIS

This essay revises and extends themes developed originally for the First Annual Alfred D. Chandler, Jr., Lecture in Southern Business History, which was delivered at UNC–Chapel Hill in April 1999. In this piece (and in the last essay of this collection) the interpretive line informing *The South, the Nation, and the World*—which is to say, the importance of structural, institutional, and geo-historical variables to the developmental process—is emphasized. In keeping with this approach, free-floating cultural variables ("the Protestant ethic," for example) have been reined in, embedded, and brought down to earth.

Questions relating to the distinctiveness of the American North and South have intrigued historians and the public for generations. In fact, these questions and broader related controversies have proven among the most long-lived and provocative in the literature of American history. Travelers visiting British North America in the eighteenth century, for example, often commented on the differences between the northern and southern colonies. Such travel commentary grew in both abundance and verve in the first half of the nineteenth century, with Tocqueville's *Democracy in America* being the most notable case in point. Questions relating to regional distinctiveness gained even greater currency with the approach of the Civil War, and many historians since that time, perhaps taking their cue from William Seward's famous "irrepressible conflict" speech of 1858, have sought to interpret the rupture between North and South in schematic, dichotomous terms: a split between two distinct economies, societies, and, at times, even civilizations. It is much easier, after all, to impart meaning to the 620,000 lives lost during the Civil War by arguing that those who died did so in defense of beliefs and values under attack by people with antithetical worldviews.

Despite the power of this appeal to difference and to the idea of the irrepressibility of sectional conflict, this interpretation has not gone unchallenged. In the 1940s and 1950s, a number of Civil War historians sought to downplay differences between North and South by arguing that the war was repressible and targeting one group in particular for blame: the "blundering generation" of politicians holding office in the decades prior to the war. To these revisionists, political fallibility rather than distinctive beliefs and values, chance and circumstance rather than inevitability, best explain the coming of war. Scholars emphasizing difference quickly pointed out that the qualitative differences between the sections far outweighed their similarities, however numerous, and that even if the North and South were more similar than different, it does not necessarily follow that war was repressible. The Civil War revisionists never completely rebutted these arguments, and their interpretation is currently out of favor. Today, most scholars once again stress the differences rather than the similarities between the North and the South, even as they disagree among themselves over the details.[1]

While political historians would doubtless offer alternative chronologies, economic historians commonly trace the roots of regional difference and distinctiveness back to the seventeenth century. The North and the South began to diverge as early as the mid- to late seventeenth century, when the formalization of racial slavery, the production of a staple crop (tobacco), and the rise of a nascent plantation sector set the South down a path never followed in temperate colonies in the North. These divergences were due largely to differences in climate, profit possibilities, and what classical economists called "land"—or natural resources—rather than to any stark contrasts in settlers' backgrounds, culture, or worldviews. Once the South embarked upon this path, inertial forces—what economists call lock-in mechanisms associated with path dependence, or path influence—worked to keep the region on a developmental route distinct from those followed in the North.[2]

Not surprisingly, the materialist argument for path dependence or influence goes against the view that attributes economic differences between North and South predominantly to cultural differences between the dominant groups in the two regions. To downplay the importance of culture and cultural difference as independent variables is not to suggest that from the start the European settlers in the southern colonies were just like those in the northern colonies. Nor is it to privilege in any absolute or universal sense material concerns above all others. What this argument does suggest, however, is a commitment to the idea that by the late seventeenth century—that is to say, after the radical Protestant communities in New England began to backslide into the mainstream—the behavior of most Europeans in what later became the United States is explainable or at least understandable through recourse to an economic logic predicated upon "rational" responses to market signals and signs.

Given the climate, natural resources, and profit possibilities in the southern colonies, such logic tended over time to channel metropolitan capital and Euro-American entrepreneurship down relatively narrow and ultimately sterile lines. During the early modern period, the southern colonies each passed through a rough-and-ready time of economic experimentation of varying lengths followed by a period of more systematic use of natural resources and accumulation of capital before securing sufficient knowledge, order, capital, and labor to get down to the main business at hand: the production by bound laborers on plantations of agricultural staples for export. To be sure, each colony in the South followed its own trajectory, and both North Carolina and backcountry areas throughout the region developed more slowly, replicating this pattern at some remove. Nonetheless, in a broad sense, both the Chesapeake colonies and those of the Lower South were organized—or at least eventually came to be organized—economically, socially, politically, and culturally around the plantation complex more than anything else.[3]

The Chesapeake colonies of Virginia and Maryland were the first southern colonies to go through the process outlined above. Both passed rapidly through phases of experimentation and rudimentary extraction before turning to tobacco, the crop that came to dominate the Chesapeake region's economy from the 1620s through the remainder of the colonial period and beyond. During the second half of the seventeenth century, moreover, supply and demand conditions in Atlantic labor markets led to a momentous shift in labor organization in the Chesapeake. Relatively cheap African and African American slave laborers increasingly replaced relatively expensive European laborers, free or indentured, in tobacco cultivation, and servitude for Africans and African Americans became a permanent rather than temporary condition, as had hitherto often been the case. The link between tobacco and slavery was dependent upon the Chesapeake planters' ability to sell their tobacco, which they did with great success in Europe, via England and Scotland, throughout the early modern era. While wheat was added to the Chesapeake export mix in the middle of the eighteenth century, for all intents and purposes tobacco dominated the Chesapeake economy in the seventeenth and eighteenth centuries.

By substituting the word "rice" for tobacco, we can segue into a discussion of the evolution of British colonies in the lower South, particularly South Carolina. Permanent European and African settlement in this part of British America began much later than in the Chesapeake regions—in the 1670s in the case of the Carolinas and in the early 1730s in that of Georgia.[4] South Carolina in the early eighteenth century was the first of these colonies to establish a plantation economy. Rice proved the state's principal export staple throughout the century, with indigo playing a supplementary role from the 1740s to the 1790s. Georgia's transformation into a plantation economy did not begin until the 1750s, after early legal prohibitions against slavery in the colony were lifted. Once this labor constraint was eased, white Georgians quickly began to replicate developmental patterns in South Carolina, immediately to the north. For a variety of reasons—the colony's initial settlement patterns and its relatively inaccessible coast, for example—North Carolina never developed a widespread plantation economy during the colonial period, although small numbers of planters were operating in the Cape Fear and Albemarle regions by the time of the American Revolution.

Despite the slow development of a plantation economy in North Carolina and the retrograde nature of social development in parts of the southern backcountry, plantations dominated the southern economy by the 1770s: those who controlled them—a relatively small group of white planters and merchants—had decisively shaped the region's economic course and, perhaps, its destiny. By that time both the Chesapeake colonies and those in the Lower South had become wealthy, slave-based economies dependent upon the production of agricultural staples for export, particularly to northern Europe. African and African American slaves constituted roughly 40 percent of the region's one million white and black inhabitants in 1770, and in the heavily commercialized plantation districts near the coast, slaves constituted a much greater proportion of the total population, more than 90 percent in parts of South Carolina.[5]

Given these considerations, it is not surprising that the southern colonies were marked by extreme inequality, not merely inequality in landholding, income, and wealth, but in the political, social, and cultural realms as well. Such inequality was both a function and an expression of the entrepreneurial strategy the white inhabitants of the region had been pursuing for generations. This strategy was as narrowly based as it was initially successful, predicated as it was on the enrichment of a few through the expropriation and exportation of the agricultural staples produced by a large servile labor force. The narrowness of this strategy was suggested as well by the pinched and niggardly institutional development characteristic of the southern colonies: everything from transportation networks to urban systems to educational and religious organization in the region lacked richness and elaboration. This weak institutional development would impede the region's growth over the long run and as early as 1776 had begun to distinguish the southern colonies from their sister colonies in the North.[6]

The Northern Economic Path

The economic history of the British colonies north of the Chesapeake is replete with irony. In comparison to those in the South, let alone those in the West Indies, the northern colonies seemed to lack drama and even economic definition. More to the point, they lacked export staples of great importance to the Crown. To be sure, timber and naval stores from New England proved useful to the Royal Navy, and exports of wheat and other small grains from the Middle Colonies were not insignificant to the Mother Country. Nonetheless, nowhere in the northern colonies could be found an export staple similar in value to the tropical and semitropical dazzlers, sugar, tobacco, and rice.[7]

With no great staples and thus relatively few agricultural slaves, the inhabitants of the northern colonies were forced early on to improvise economically and later to pursue a development strategy based on a mixture of flexible enterprises, quick response times, commercial and shipping services, and local and regional trade. Despite or perhaps because of the lack of staples, this strategy proved quite successful: by some measures, the northern colonies were as wealthy as the southern on the eve of the Revolution.[8] Even more important, the strategy proved not merely conducive to but responsible for the area's precocious industrialization in the nineteenth century. To the "losers," it seems, went the spoils.

Not that the inhabitants of the northern colonies necessarily preferred economic improvisation and constant economic change to the staple path to growth. The difference between North and South turned rather less on matters of ideology, however, than on material factors such as climate and soil. After all, did not the same Puritans who settled Massachusetts Bay in 1630 attempt to establish a slave-based staple-producing colony on Providence Island off the east coast of what is now Nicaragua?[9] And were not Philadelphia and, particularly, New York City home to urban slaves in the eighteenth century? For every opponent of slavery in the North in 1770, for every holdout against the market and market values, there was a budding Yankee sharper, a Newport trader of slaves, a New York land developer, and a Quaker merchant in Philadelphia in pursuit of the main chance.

With the possible exception of the European settlers in parts of Atlantic Canada, the colonists in New England faced the most difficult entrepreneurial problems in all of British America. Simply put, they had somehow to find a way to achieve and sustain economic viability in a region marked by significant resource and climatic limitations, limitations rendered more burdensome still by early modern technological constraints. Over time, New Englanders were able to achieve such viability and then some. By adhering to—or, in the view of some, overcoming—their Puritan belief structure, they created an intricate, rather ingeniously balanced regional economy based on mixed husbandry, small-scale manufacturing, forest industries, fishing, shipping, commerce, and, last but by no means least, the so-called invisible earnings—freighting, insurance, credit services, and the like—associated with the carrying trade. In so doing, New Englanders successfully combined subsistence activities with local, regional, and international trade and, as a result, were able to earn sufficient export credits to sustain the flow of vital imports, achieve steady if modest rates of economic growth, and make possible admirably high living standards for much of the region's population. If per capita income and wealth were not quite as high in New England as in the Middle Colonies or the South, living standards in colonies such as Massachusetts, Rhode Island, and Connecticut compared favorably with those in almost any other part of the early modern world.

Residents of the "Middle Colonies" of British North America fared better still. Over time the colonists in this region, the most ethnically heterogeneous in British America, built an extremely healthy and wealthy economy, one in which agriculture, manufacturing, and trade fit together as hand in glove.[10] Blessed with fertile river valleys and two great natural harbors, the four political units comprising the Middle Colonies—New York, Pennsylvania, New Jersey, and Delaware—offered considerable opportunity to the enterprising Britons, Germans, and Dutch that dominated the region in numerical terms. If no single crop, market, or endeavor dominated the region's economic life, thousands of agricultural, manufacturing, and commercial activities, large and small, were pursued by the "calculating people" who called the Middle Colonies home. However quotidian and prosaic many of these activities may have seemed to the sugar nabobs of the West Indies, the rice grandees of the Lower South, or the tobacco lords of the Chesapeake, they brought broadly based prosperity—the region had the least concentrated wealth distribution in British America—and economic depth, variation, and sophistication to the Middle Colonies that would bode well for the future.

Let me elaborate a bit on the economic benefits associated with the Middle Colonies' structural diversity. By the end of the colonial period, for example, the region's small and medium-sized farms, employing sundry combinations of family, wage, and indentured labor, produced a significant export crop, wheat, that did a nice trade in southern Europe and the West Indies in most years, though the quantities shipped to each of these markets varied considerably from season to season. Exports of wheat and other small grains not only earned the credits necessary for imports to the Middle Colonies but engendered a substantial flour-milling industry in the region, and other related industries such as barrel making and cooperage, wagon and boat building, warehousing, and wholesale and retail baking.[11] The general prosperity of the region meant that domestic demand in the Middle Colonies was robust, which in turn created good opportunities not only for those involved in the activities mentioned above, but for those in a plethora of other craft and artisanal vocations ranging from cordwaining to silversmithing.

Given such developments it is not surprising that the urban systems of the Middle Colonies developed apace, with Philadelphia and New York City, the two largest towns in British America, occupying the top rungs of the region's urban ladder. These two cities, and to a lesser extent Boston, were true entrepôts; the other principal cities in British America—Charleston, Newport, Norfolk, Baltimore, Bridgetown, and Port Royal, for example—were rather more limited transshipment points for exports and imports, as well as sites of cultural productions of one type or another, performed by government, religious bodies, or other "theatrical" groups. In the entrepôts of Philadelphia and New York City, however, the economics of agglomeration at once generated more jobs, particularly in shipping and commercial services; enhanced the flow of information, thereby increasing productivity; and created relatively integrated local and regional markets bursting with entrepreneurial energy.

Not that development in the region was ever easy. Unlike the situation in the southern colonies, no staple market was ever assured to residents of the Middle Colonies, few business strategies proved durable, much less venerable, and few laborers in the region were legally enthralled for life. Entrepreneurial challenges had to be met on a daily basis, and, over time, the inhabitants of the Middle Colonies developed sufficient capacity, flexibility, and resiliency to meet such tests, however stiff.

To reiterate, then, by the time of the Revolution, there were two broad groups of colonies in the North and South respectively, each comprising two subgroups: New England and the Middle Colonies in the former region, and the Chesapeake colonies and those of the Lower South in the latter. Income and wealth levels were high in each of these regions, and both the structures and institutions of their economies, as well as the behavior and values of the participants therein were consistent and consonant with evolving capitalist principles.

There were, however, vivid contrasts between development patterns in the North and South that can be attributed in large part to differences in the resources available in the regions initially and to the resulting entrepreneurial responses. In the temperate North, colonists were unable to produce valuable plantation staples, which limited the value and thus the use of slave labor in the region and compelled the population to pursue developmental strategies that placed premiums on economic balance and diversity, flexibility, rapid response, constant innovation, and creative entrepreneurship. Over time, such strategies led to broad-based prosperity; frequent, organic economic interactions between town and country; a relatively egalitarian distribution of income and wealth (particularly in rural areas); and, concomitantly, broad public access to an array of social, educational, political, cultural, and institutional entitlements.

The economies in the semitropical southern colonies, on the other hand, were early organized around plantation staples and slave labor. Because of the profit possibilities in plantation agriculture, the capitalization of labor via slavery, and the existence of economies of scale in the production of at least some of the southern staples, income and wealth quickly became highly skewed in the Chesapeake and the Lower South. As time passed, this imbalance appeared in other realms as well, and southern society became similarly unequal virtually across the board. Such economic and social inequality in turn helped to confine if not to lock the South into an overly specialized, low-tech, rigid, and inflexible strategy of development predicated on plantation agriculture, relatively unskilled slave labor, and exports. This strategy would increasingly take the region out of the American mainstream.

1789-1860—Towards a Modern Society

In the period between the end of the Revolution in the early 1780s—or, more appropriately, given its importance to American capitalist development, the establishment of the Constitution in 1789—and the coming of the Civil War, the United States extended its political boundaries across the continent, began to industrialize in a major way, and created the necessary underpinnings and conditions for the "national" market that emerged between 1865 and 1920. Moreover, as fierce political battles raged between North and South, between free states and slave, another powerfully important but more insidious development was taking place: the precocious growth of a true business/industrial culture in the North.[12] Although not yet fully established by 1860, this culture arguably made the North and South more distinct economically than they ever were before the Civil War and ultimately would divide the regions at least as much as slavery ever did.

Not surprisingly, this culture emerged out of the vigorous and enterprising business communities of the mid-Atlantic area, especially Pennsylvania and New York, and New England. Having faced formidable entrepreneurial challenges—uncertain, constantly changing markets, most notably—for generations, these communities were more or less inclined to embrace economic change, including the technological and organizational changes associated with the "Industrial Revolution" then transforming parts of northwest Europe. Leveraging their transatlantic contacts and networks with resources of their own, merchants and manufacturers in the Northeast were able by the 1850s to establish the foundations—economic, social, political, institutional, and cultural—for a modern, urban, industrial society.

Such dynamic interactions—often involving what sociologists infelicitously call "identity-inflected networks" (that is, family and friends, kith and kin, and the like)—over time produced hugely important developmental synergies: highly calibrated, deeply articulated networks and markets for information, capital, and innovation. These are precisely the types of synergies that today are said to be so important to the so-called cluster economies in places like Cambridge, Manhattan, and Silicon Valley, and to a lesser extent even in the Sunbelt in such places as Austin, Charlotte, Atlanta, and North Carolina's Research Triangle Park. Or to put all this another way, as Dennis Weatherstone, the former chairman of J. P. Morgan once did: "financial centers couldn't exist without lunch."[13] And neither could centers of innovation or entrepreneurship.

In the mid-nineteenth century, the "networked" Northeast not only played a key role in the development of the interior of the United States, particularly the "Old Northwest" (Ohio, Indiana, Michigan) and the Great Lakes region, but also began incorporating this area into what would later become the industrial core of America, the quadrant east of the Mississippi River and north of the Ohio River, all of which quickly fell under northeastern economic and financial suzerainty.[14] One final result of these initiatives deserves mention: as it willed itself to power, this powerful cultural complex from the Northeast succeeded in both marginalizing and rendering anachronistic the "Old South" and by implication that region's hidebound developmental strategy based on the indefinite expansion of the plantation system and racial slavery.

Not that growth-oriented southerners did nothing to develop their region between the time of the Constitution and the coming of the Civil War. During the first half of the nineteenth century, the agricultural regime established originally in the Chesapeake and the Lower South was successfully transplanted all across the southern interior, only now with short-staple cotton rather than tobacco or rice as the principal market crop. Such success was predicated upon the resolution of numerous entrepreneurial problems: the fertile lands of the southern interior had to be expropriated from Native Americans, significant quantities of labor and capital had to be transferred to the southwest, and the marketing and transportation infrastructure necessary for the long-distance trade of bulky agricultural commodities had to be created. Southerners, by and large, proved up to such tasks and performed most of them with aplomb, if not moral distinction. The economic forms and structures of the Chesapeake and Lower South proved "portable," as economic historian David Weiman has pointed out, and they were largely replicated in the "Old Southwest," which in a developmental sense was both good and bad: the agricultural economy of the South, based as it was on export staples and slaves, was efficient, to be sure, but in a qualitative sense it appeared little different in 1860 than it had a century before.[15]

Unlike the situation in the North, then, southern entrepreneurship tended to follow well-trodden paths. In this the South was by no means unique in the nineteenth century. Most populations throughout history have followed the tried and true. Indeed, as historian James McPherson has suggested, it was in many ways the North, particularly the Northeast, that was peculiar in the nineteenth century in terms of its economic performance and its population's normative behavior and values.[16]

What did regional difference and distinctiveness add up to by 1860? A good question, the answer to which depends in large part on interpretive preferences and point of view. By that time, for example, the "North" included about two-thirds of the 31.4 million white and black inhabitants of the United States, and the "South" about one-third. According to the federal census returns, about 20 percent of Americans lived in "urban" places in 1860— meaning that they lived in areas of relatively dense settlement with populations of 2,500 or more—but this percentage figure masks considerable regional variation. The Northeast was already 36 percent urban by that time, while the corresponding figures for the West and "North Central" (Midwest) census regions were about 16 percent and 14 percent respectively. The South lagged badly according to this index: in 1860 just under 10 percent of the region's population lived in urban places.[17]

Both the North and the South were extremely wealthy in 1860, positioned near the top of world income and wealth tables. Although per capita income in the South was only about 75 to 85 percent of the figure for the North, the South, if considered an independent geopolitical entity, would have trailed only two or three other nations in the world at the time. In terms of per capita income, the South surpassed such places as Canada, the Netherlands, Belgium, France, and the various German states.[18]

As we have already seen, the South's income and wealth were based largely on export agriculture—cotton was by far the greatest single export from the United

States in the antebellum period, for example—but the South also had surprising industrial capacity in 1860, ranking among the world's leaders in railroad mileage and cotton textile production per capita. Nonetheless, the region's industrialization efforts paled in comparison to those of the North. With one-third of the nation's population in 1860, the South was responsible for only 10 percent of U.S. manufacturing output and possessed only 10 percent of the nation's labor force and 11 percent of its manufacturing capital. The South trailed not only New England and the mid-Atlantic region in these manufacturing categories, but also the Midwest, which got a much later start.[19]

These measures are quantitative in nature, but there were also numerous qualitative differences between the northern and southern economies. The most important of these related to economic balance and linkages, investment in human capital (including public education), and agglomeration economies, all of which were present in the North but sadly lacking in the South. Nowhere is the internal imbalance of the southern economy expressed more clearly than in the region's rudimentary "conveyor-belt" transportation system and in its peculiar peripheral pattern of urban development: few cities in the interior of the South, with ports hugging the Atlantic and Gulf coasts and the Ohio and Mississippi rivers. If they did little to connect southerners to one another or to create a cohesive regional economy, the South's transportation and urban systems did perform one function extremely well: getting goods in and out of the region without leaving much of a trail.[20]

Against these quantitative and qualitative differences must be weighed the many similarities between North and South. In 1860 both were predominantly English-speaking regions whose largely Protestant populations lived under a common frame of government, the Constitution, which was the object of widespread veneration on both sides of the Mason-Dixon line. The United States had developed a republican form of government that guaranteed a wide, perhaps unprecedented, range of rights, privileges, and immunities both to individual states and to free individuals; these guarantees were honored and upheld more or less in the same way in the North and South alike. Moreover, northerners and southerners—or at least free male northerners and southerners—shared a common history, had fought side by side against common enemies on more than one occasion, and partook of many of the same ideological traditions, most notably basic commitments to republican conceptions of independence and virtue and to the liberal principles of life, liberty, and property, however much they came to disagree about the proper definition of the last of these. Finally, both North and South were basically organized along capitalist lines, notwithstanding the hold in the latter region of an increasingly anachronistic labor system based on racial slavery.

Where, then, does this leave us? In the last analysis, should we emphasize similarities or differences? A tough question, but "differences" gets the nod. So great were the consequences of the early decision, in one case, to organize economic life around slave labor and, in the other, around free labor that by April 1861 the many similarities uniting North and South were overwhelmed. Lincoln made this same point simply but eloquently in his Second Inaugural Address when he stated that slavery "was, somehow, the cause of the war." The operative word here is "somehow," for by the middle of the nineteenth century, slavery had insinuated itself into virtually every important issue in American life, causing regional fissures and tears of the most brutal and vicious kind.

History is full of ironies, of course. Consider, for example, the possibility that North and South were more distinct from one another in 1900 than they had been at the time of the Civil War. Consider, even, the possibility that their increased distinctiveness was, in fact, a *product* of the war. By 1900 the area north of the Ohio River and east of the Mississippi—the northeastern quadrant of the United States—had been transformed into one of the world's great manufacturing regions.[21] The population of this vast region was increasingly wealthy, largely urban, and, although almost exclusively white, marked by growing ethnic, religious, and cultural heterogeneity, the result of the ongoing New Immigration that had brought millions of southern and eastern Europeans into the region. By 1900 the Northern Plains had been transformed from a frontier into a wealthy and modern agricultural zone, specializing in the export of wheat and other small grains, and in the eastern part of the Plains region the wealthy and heavily commercialized corn-hog complex was in full swing. The West—i.e., the Mountain and Pacific states—was the wealthiest and whitest region of the United States, its economy dominated by mining and modern commercial agriculture and ranching.

Now cut to the South. In 1900 this region, which had once been rich, was poor, its per capita income but half of the U.S. average. Its population was 32 percent black—and 90 percent of the nation's African American population lived in the region. The white population was still composed overwhelmingly of Protestants, the New Immigration having had little impact on the region. Whereas the nation as a whole was 40 percent urban and 25 percent of the U.S. labor force was involved in manufacturing, the South was but 18 percent urban in 1900, with only 10 percent of the region's labor force in manufacturing. Finally, the region's agricultural sector in 1900 seems like a textbook model of agricultural underdevelopment: a bloated, redundant farm population marked by low human capital development, low productivity, and high unemployment and underemployment; undercapitalized and undermechanized farms; subsistence production on tiny holdings, or more or less coerced production of semitropical staples for distant markets.[22] Hardly a pretty picture, and certainly a far cry from agriculture in the North.

Were regional differences and distinctions in the United States in 1900 more remarkable than the differences and distinctions between North and South in 1860, when the Union was "half slave and half free?" Not necessarily, although it is intellectually exciting to entertain the possibility that the Civil War helped to *create* two distinct societies and was not an expression or a reflection of the same. At once unveiling and unleashing the developing business/industrial culture of the North, the Civil War, to employ Marxian terminology, "burst asunder" the "integuments" confining Yankee capital and entrepreneurship, not to mention ingenuity. In the last analysis, it seems clear that capitalism almost from the time of initial settlement has tied together the history of the North and South, albeit in complex, combined, and uneven ways. Certainly a good case can be made that throughout the nineteenth century, northerners and southerners shared a lot more than did Germans and Galicians in Austria-Hungary, Punjabis and Tamils in India, Manchu and Cantonese in China, or Tuscans and Calabrians in Italy. Italy, as the great Austrian statesman Metternich contended, might have been "a mere geographical expression" in the first half of the nineteenth century, but one would be hard pressed to say that about the United States.

3

How the Low Country Was Taken to Task

Slave-Labor Organization in Coastal South Carolina and Georgia

PETER A. COCLANIS

This essay was written for a festschrift published in 2000 honoring Eugene D. Genovese, the great historian of slavery in the Americas. In the essay, recent insights from microeconomics, particularly relating to the economics of information, are brought to bear on a problem that has puzzled students of slavery over the years: how and why slave-labor organization took different forms in different areas, different economic activities, and different periods of time.

The great South Carolina planter-sportsman William Elliott loved Cheeha more than any place else on earth. Located roughly forty miles southwest of Charleston, Cheeha was a low, swampy neck of land between the Ashley and Combahee rivers, a place that Elliott, renowned author of *Carolina Sports by Land and Water,* considered "the best hunting-ground" in the state.[1]

Elliott was also an absentee planter at Cheeha, but his passion for the area clearly owed more to white-tailed deer than to white or golden rice. As Theodore Rosengarten has recently pointed out, Elliott makes four separate trips to Cheeha in *Carolina Sports* but in so doing spends only two hours at his rice plantation there, and even then only rather grudgingly.[2] Nonetheless, one can gain important insights into low-country agriculture from Elliott's 1846 volume. Indeed, the well-educated and highly cultivated author, a man who refers to himself as Piscator and Venator in the book, might well have added Agricola—a pseudonym he used elsewhere.[3]

Not that Elliott goes on at length in *Carolina Sports* about matters agronomic. Moreover, when he does talk about agriculture, he does so rather whimsically, suggesting a certain casualness, if not insouciance. To be sure, much of this is artifice. Yet even after allowing for genre conventions and authorial self-fashioning, it is clear that Elliott illuminates much about the planter's world, whether intentionally or not.

In a chapter entitled "A Business Day at Chee-Ha," Elliott, who claims his motto is "Business before pleasure," makes a rare visit to his plantation to inspect his crops.[4] He arrives at the end of October, when the fetid swamplands at Cheeha are less dangerous to human health; even so, Elliott remarks that his overseer "crawled forth" to greet him, "pale and . . . feeble" with malaria.[5]

Elliott is in a hurry to hunt, but as this visit to Cheeha is his first of the year, he knows that he is obliged to look over his plantation operations. He rides quickly through his cornfield but, finding "that the grain had been gathered," asks, perhaps rhetorically, "Why should I pause to observe it narrowly?" and moves on. A bit later, while riding toward his cotton field, he decides that because "it lies out of [his] way, a distant coup d'oeil must serve" until such time that he can "examine it closely." Better to head home.[6]

Arriving back at the plantation yard, Elliott dismounts from his steed and climbs up into his rice-winnowing house; there his interrogation of his slave driver about the year's rice crop segues neatly into managerial meditation.

> "Have you threshed out a rick?"
> "Yes, sir," says the driver.
> "What was the yield to the acre?"
> "Sixty bushels sir."
> "Was it your best rick?"
> "N-o, sir."
> "Mixed you any of the straw rice with this rick?"
> "Y-es, sir, a lettle; but you kin see, maussa!"
> and the driver brought me a sheaf from a rick hard by—thick, full-grained, heavy; a magnificent sample (if true sample it was) of a crop which was to reward my expectation. Alas, Venator! thou knewest not that the rick was *plated,* or rather gilt; and that while the outward and tangible sheaf was of such satisfactory quality, the light, and the mow-burnt, and the bird-pecked was safely bestowed, far from the reach of inquisitive eyes, in the very centre of those proud looking ricks! How like a honeymoon in the planter's life are the first brief visits of the fall, to the long deserted plantations! All then is bright and full of glorious promise; but winter comes, and at its close—the hours of disenchantment![7]

Then, after a rather awkward—and potentially confrontational—encounter with some of his slaves, Elliott hurries off his plantation to join his hunting group. "It is wonderful," Elliott observes in the chapter, "how we stride over the field of business, when we have hitched to the fence beyond, some favorite hobby which we are impatient to mount and ride!" Indeed.[8]

Now, Elliott was obviously trying to be funny in this chapter, and in many ways he succeeded. He was, of course, more serious about planting than he allows in "A Business Day at Chee-Ha," writing knowledgeably on agriculture throughout the antebellum period and bringing in large crops of rice and Sea Island cotton on a regular basis. According to some scholars, in fact, *Carolina Sports by Land and Water* was intended at least in part as a thinly veiled critique of the desultory practices of other low-country planters.[9] "A Business Day at Chee-Ha" is indispensable for our purposes in any case. In capturing certain raw, spare truths about the low country in slavery times—the highly mortal disease environment, the striking levels of planter absenteeism and inattention, and, perhaps most importantly, the centrality of bound African American labor—it affords a splendid opportunity to employ some relatively new analytical concepts from microeconomics to help reinterpret the low country's agricultural history, dare I say, from the ground up.[10]

To start at ground level in a place like the low country means to start with labor, largely black slave labor, organized for the most part by task rather than in gangs. It is difficult, in fact, to overstate the importance to the low country of tasked labor and the social patterns arising therefrom. Indeed, the so-called task system, which was far less common than the gang system, is frequently considered not merely the "central feature of low country slave life" but the principal reason why slavery in the low country of South Carolina and Georgia seemed so different from slavery in other parts of the South.[11] The tendency of scholars (including this author) to "exoticize" the low country at times seems related, albeit in indirect ways, to the task system as well. For the system seemed to promote greater cultural autonomy and independence among an enslaved majority with non-European historical, if not necessarily genealogical, roots.

Under the task system, of course, a slave was responsible for a set amount of work—a certain number of tasks, as it were—upon the completion of which that slave was "free" to do as he or she so chose. Although some masters expected their slaves to produce part or all of their provisions during their "free" time, many slaves clearly were able to allocate part of their workdays or workweeks to labor for themselves.[12] Compared to the so-called gang system, the principal form of slave-labor organization, the task system allowed those working under it more physical and psychological "space," which at a minimum meant less direct or at least less immediate monitoring and supervision and a greater degree of control over work pace, rhythms, and routines. To be sure, in both the gang and task systems slaves were expected to work hard, but it is probably true that agricultural units organized under the gang system more closely resembled factories in the fields and everything that this nineteenth-century metaphor connoted.

A word of caution should be sounded here, however, for it is both easy and tempting to idealize or reify the task and gang systems of slave-labor organization and to view these systems as not merely antipodal but quite possibly antithetical. In reality, the systems proved both more complex and more indistinct than usually depicted.

The systems, moreover, were sometimes combined, and hybrid organizational forms emerged as a result.[13] Still, the terms *task* and *gang*, however reduced and stylized, serve certain analytical purposes and are retained because the concern here is less with variation than with pattern, less with individual cases than with generalization. This concern leads logically to a consideration of the temporal, spatial, and occupational dimensions of these labor systems. More specifically, what accounts for the employment of one or the other system at certain times and in particular geographical areas or economic activities?

Obviously, one can find some examples of each of these labor systems wherever slavery existed and in virtually all economic activities in which slaves were involved. In several important articles Philip D. Morgan, for example, has documented the existence of tasking not only across the United States South but in both the Caribbean Basin and Brazil as well. Moreover, according to Morgan and others, the task system was sufficiently versatile and adaptable to be used in such diverse agricultural activities as coffee, sugar, hemp, and pimento cultivation, as well as in so-called forest industries such as timbering and naval-stores production.[14] In addition, a number of scholars, Charles B. Dew most recently, have demonstrated that the task system was employed at times in southern manufacturing establishments, and references to the task system can be found for still other activities, including "grass picking" and even weaving and spinning.[15]

On the whole, these efforts have sharpened scholarly understanding of slave-labor organization, but in searching hither and yon for each and every reference to tasking—an exercise somewhat akin to "listing" in the world of bird watching—scholars may lose sight of the fact that the task system informed the economy of only one important region in the Western Hemisphere, the South Carolina–Georgia low country.[16] Elsewhere, the role of the task system was more limited. It was employed, for example, on a part-time basis in the production of minor staples and nonstaples and in marginal parts of the "extended Caribbean." The role of tasking in the Jamaican coffee industry and the Bahamian timber industry are cases in point. Moreover, because of ameliorationist sentiment or changing technology, or both, use of the task system sometimes became common even in major staples during the last years of slavery. For instance, the task system emerged in the 1820s and 1830s in the sugar colonies of Demerara, Essequibo, Berbice, and Martinique and in the 1840s in the cotton state of Mississippi.[17]

Nonetheless, the gang system—closely monitored labor in groups over set periods of time (sunup to sundown)—prevailed in most places and in the most important economic activities most of the time.[18] In light of this fact, one question immediately springs to mind: Why was the low country, in a manner of speaking, taken to task? Both contemporary observers and latter-day scholars have weighed in on this question; and out of a welter of explanations, three or four more or less distinct lines of argumentation can be discerned. According to one, often associated with U. B. Phillips, climate generally and malaria specifically were responsible. An inhospitable disease environment, that is to say, compelled low-country planters—the originators of the task system in this view—to impose a form of labor control that would at once allow for relatively regular and committed work on the part of unskilled slaves and relatively regular bouts of absenteeism on the part of planters.[19]

A second interpretive line, advanced most recently by Philip D. Morgan, attributes the task system's origins in the low country primarily to the technical requirements of rice cultivation. In this view, because rice "was a hardy plant, requiring a few relatively straightforward operations for . . . successful cultivation," and because in rice production the laborers' work efforts were subject to "inexpensive and efficient measurement," conditions were conducive to the emergence of the task system. If several other factors played some part, it was, according to Morgan, the "staple-crop requirements" associated with rice that, by minimizing the need for close managerial supervision, permitted the establishment of a labor regimen predicated largely on the self-paced performance of discrete, readily measurable tasks.[20]

To be sure, Morgan attributes the terms of the system, once established, in large part to the bargaining strategies employed by enslaved African Americans. Nonetheless, he tends to downplay the role of African Americans, let alone Africans, in the genesis of the system, unlike scholars such as Ira Berlin and, especially, Judith Carney.[21] To these scholars, the transfer of African agricultural technology was central not just to the several rice-cropping regimes that developed over time in the low country but to the establishment of the region's system of labor organization as well. Carney makes the fullest case regarding the latter point. After documenting the fact that the task system "was already a pervasive feature of African slavery along the Upper Guinea coast and its hinterland during the Atlantic Slave Trade," she concludes that this system, like other West African knowledge relating to risiculture, probably survived the Middle Passage and was, thus, available for and, in fact, deployed in the low-country rice industry.[22] In this Afro-centered view, then, the principal role of Europeans is to appropriate rather than to initiate a venerable and potentially profitable technology.

A final interpretive line remains to be discussed. Mounting an argument similar to but more theoretically rigorous than that of Morgan, the economist Jacob Metzer contends that the task system owed its origins to the efforts of planters to practice "precise and scientific management" wherever possible when "handling work routines and organizing field work." Given the "technical requirements" of rice cultivation—Metzer describes these requirements in basically the same way as Morgan—economically rational planters, operating with perfect information, are said to have turned, virtually homeostatically, to the incentive-laden task system in order at once to enhance efficiency, reduce shirking, and lessen their supervisory loads.[23] Clearly, complicated questions such as the origins of the task system do not pose much of a problem in the neat and tidy Walrasian world inhabited by Professor Metzer, if not by the rice planters of the low country.

Here, then, are the most important and influential explanations for the origins of the task system. Each of these explanations is the result of first-rate scholarship, yet each is incomplete in my view. One can, however, use the many insights contained in these four frameworks to construct a richer, denser, and more interpretively satisfying framework of our own. Some recent developments in microeconomics, particularly in the economics of information, can show us how.

That ideas have consequences is by now a truism. Just as paranoiacs sometimes do have enemies, however, even truisms can be revealing. Indeed, the contention here is that the most fruitful way to understand the role of the task system in the low country is through a set of ideas developed by economists over the past twenty-five years. These ideas, all of which are related in one way or another to the economics of information, offer us an elegant, even parsimonious way to reconcile hitherto unreconcilable scholarly points of view.

Until relatively recently almost all mainstream economists in the West, economists working, that is to say, from a conventional, neoclassical perspective, held to a rigorous set of assumptions about economic life. These assumptions are often associated in their purest and most insistent form with the French economist Leon Walras. Walras, one of the cofounders in the late nineteenth century of neoclassicism, is frequently disparaged today, somewhat unfairly, for his seemingly reductionistic assumptions that markets were "freely competitive," functioning almost as "organized auctions"; that they were unbounded and thus unaffected by space or time; and that the participants in markets were maximizers with both constant preferences and, more importantly for our purposes, perfect information.[24]

However useful and even necessary such assumptions are—general equilibrium as a theory and comparative statics as an analytical strategy are predicated in large part on these assumptions—both economists and economic historians have long known that they were quite unrealistic. Some of the problems with these assumptions were, in fact, pointed out early on, even in Walras's lifetime. Irving Fisher's suggestion in the 1890s that Walras had failed to consider time in his analysis is a case in point. Other problems, most notably those growing out of the assumption that markets are "freely competitive," have been targeted by economists through much of the twentieth century.[25]

That the Walrasian system was able to withstand such scholarly onslaughts was due in large part to the efforts of future Nobelist Kenneth Arrow. Indeed, Arrow's collaborative work forty-odd years ago with another future Nobelist, Gerard Debreu, work encapsulated in the so-called Arrow-Debreu or A-D model of competitive equilibrium, revivified the Walrasian approach and appeared for a time to settle residual questions about the original formulation. Ultimately, however, the clarity of the A-D model allowed critics to discover its own weaknesses and limitations, including its unrealistic assumptions about perfect information.[26]

Ironically, among the most effective of such critics was Arrow himself, who, along with James Mirrlees, George Akerlof, Stephen Ross, Joseph Stiglitz, and others, helped to weaken or, more precisely, to relax the rigid information assumptions of the

Walrasian and A-D approaches.[27] In so doing, they introduced the concept of information asymmetry to economics, the implications of which have transformed research in the microeconomics field. Questions growing out of the recognition of information asymmetry—adverse selection, moral hazard, agency, and the like—are today considered among the most interesting in all of economics.[28] One of these questions, that referred to as the agency question, appears crucial to any satisfactory explanation of the role of the task system in the low country.

The agency question, however late-breaking in academic circles, is pervasive in economic life and has been recognized, if only casually, as far back as the eighteenth century.[29] In formal terms the question arises in situations involving two individuals, wherein the action or actions of one, designated the agent, affect not only his well-being, interest, or both, but that of another, designated the principal. In agency situations the principal, speaking formally again, possesses the power to prescribe the reward structure or compensation system to which the agent will be subject. The trick from the principal's perspective is to design a structure or system that will induce the agent to act in the principal's interest. The problem, again from the principal's viewpoint, is that in many real-world situations the principal lacks knowledge or, in other words, possesses imperfect information about what action the agent should undertake or has undertaken. The problem becomes more complicated—and more interesting—in agency situations characterized by pronounced information asymmetry between principal and agent, particularly when the latter possesses vital technical or specialized knowledge not available to the former.[30]

These problems of incomplete and asymmetrical information are embodied in principal-agent situations referred to in the literature as hidden action or moral hazard cases and as hidden information or adverse selection cases. In the former, some action on the part of the agent—typically effort—is of concern to the principal, who, for one reason or another, cannot completely monitor it. The principal's problem in this situation is to design a compensation system that will motivate an incompletely monitored agent to act in the principal's behalf. The principal's problem, alas, is exacerbated by the fact that even in cases when the agent's actions can be completely monitored, the final outcome or output may not be attributable to those actions alone, but to those actions in conjunction with some unobservable random variable or variables.[31]

In hidden information or adverse selection situations, other problems come to the fore. In such situations the principal lacks information important to his well-being or interest, and the principal knows the agent has it. The principal's problem here is somehow to motivate the agent to use such information in the principal's behalf, even though both the principal and agent know that the former is unable completely to judge whether the latter's actions, presumably based on such information, were appropriate.[32]

Now, what does all of this have to do with the task system of slave-labor organization in the low country? Everything, I submit, for the insights and implications of the theoretical concerns outlined above—and, perhaps, only these insights and implications—can square the circle, as it were, and allow us to reconcile explanations of the task system emphasizing climate and disease, staple-crop requirements, African knowledge, and European managerial expertise.[33] That we hereinafter focus on agency—agency as explanatory theory rather than *cri de coeur,* expiatory ideology, or ex post rationalization—is an irony that, given the times, cannot be allowed to pass.[34]

In any case, in simple, stylized form, an agency interpretation of the role of the task system in the low country would go something like this: the key to the low-country economy, from the early eighteenth century on, was rice, and the central problem for the rice planters (the principals from this perspective) was to devise compensation systems (positive or negative incentives, or both) that would motivate individuals (bondmen and later freedmen) possessed with what economists call private information (about rice planting) to act in the principals' behalf.[35] This problem was rendered more difficult than might first appear not only because the planters often lacked specific, detailed knowledge about the "mysteries of the art" of rice planting but also because the unhealthy situation of the rice swamps and the pleasures of Charleston and, later, Savannah meant that their supervisory and opportunity costs were extremely high.

Over time planters found in the task system an integrated solution to this complex and multilayered problem. Whatever the prototype for tasked labor in the low country—Carney makes a good case, for example, that similar regimes existed in rice zones of West Africa during the early modern period—the system took hold or rather was allowed to take hold in the area because it seemed to economically rational planters to offer the best available solution to the difficulties arising from information asymmetry and high supervisory and opportunity costs.[36] That is to say, the employment of a compensation system with positive incentives in the form of self-regulation and free time and negative incentives in the form of the lash was in their view both necessary and sufficient to induce slave laborers in the low country to share their private information about rice planting and, while working, largely to monitor themselves.[37]

We can at once develop and historicize this argument by thinking a bit more about the process of technological transfer. Because transferring technology is generally a difficult and halting affair, it is likely that the hidden information (adverse selection) dimensions of the agency problem in the low country proved more acute in the eighteenth century than in the nineteenth century. It seems clear, that is to say, that for at least a good portion of the eighteenth century African and African American laborers possessed private information about risiculture unavailable or only partially available to Europeans and Euro-Americans. Once such information was transferred to or appropriated by the latter groups, the agency problems posed by adverse selection considerations probably proved less compelling.

Agency problems resulting from hidden action or moral hazard situations, however, would not necessarily diminish in severity over time. Indeed, it is possible to argue that the supervisory and opportunity costs of monitoring slaves' behavior in the rice swamps rose as time passed, with the advent of tidal cultivation and, perhaps equally important, the elaboration and consolidation of cultural life in Charleston and Savannah.

To be sure, the task system, once in place, developed in ways not altogether to the liking of those responsible for its emplacement. Custom, as John Stuart Mill pointed out long ago, is the protector of the weak against the strong in agriculture, and over time customary practices sometimes were transformed through bargaining and negotiation into what might be called de facto or quasi rights.[38] As a result, moreover, the system gradually was carried over into other activities such as the production of long-staple cotton, where the economic rationale for tasking, at least in the low country, was less compelling.[39] In the last analysis, however, the prominence of the task system in the area was due, first and foremost, to the planters of rice.

According to some, of course, the agency approach by its very nature tends to privilege principals. In this case, though, I believe that such priority is justifiable on both theoretical and empirical grounds. Let us examine the theoretical case first.

Here, too, we must begin by reiterating the point that in recent years the economics profession has moved away from the assumption of perfectly competitive markets. As a result, few economists at this late date still subscribe to the Wicksellian notion, predicated on this assumption, that the employer-employee relationship could just as easily be described as one in which labor "hires" capital as vice versa.[40] Indeed, one of Marx's enduring contributions to economics was to call attention early on to the social embeddedness of exchange, that is to say, to the way in which exchange, "a relation between two wills," was structured by power.[41] This insight is extremely useful when studying labor exchanges between masters and slaves, for in such exchanges the priority—and power—of the former was formally encoded in law. Master-slave exchanges, in fact, would seem to be extreme forms of the "contested exchanges" analyzed recently by Samuel Bowles and Herbert Gintis.[42] In contested exchanges the parties involved have unequal access to what Bowles and Gintis call exogenous claim enforcement—comprehensive third-party (usually state) regulation of contracts—and the parties are perforce subject to "endogenous claim enforcement" mechanisms designed and controlled by the strongest party. Bowles and Gintis go on to apply their theory of endogenous claim enforcement to agency situations similar in many ways to that discussed here.[43] In such cases it seems clear that principals are, well, principal.

On the empirical level, too, there is strong support for an agency approach to the task system. Indeed, as suggested earlier, this approach can at once accommodate the findings of the other interpretations and plausibly answer questions left unanswered by scholars espousing alternative points of view. For example, although interpretations emphasizing alleged "technical requirements" of rice production are insightful—rice, *ceteris paribus,* is probably more conducive to tasking than, let us say, sugar—such interpretations fail to consider the vast differences in rice production techniques around the world, their varying levels of labor intensity, and the differential monitoring costs involved with each.[44] More to the point, they do not explain the failure of the task system of slave-labor organization to take hold in the commercial rice industry that grew up along the lower Mississippi in the antebellum period.[45] Could it be that the alleged "requirements" of rice production kicked in only in the presence of other factors specific, at least for a certain period of time, to the low country?

Moreover, although climate and disease are obviously important considerations in the history of the low country, the gang system rather than the task system was the dominant form of slave-labor organization in other parts of the Americas with equally arduous climates and disease environments. Perhaps the task system was not predicated solely on climate and disease, as some would have us believe. Still other interpretive problems remain. Approaches emphasizing African traditions or African American labor bargaining, or both, fail to appreciate the implications of the fact that white planters held a near monopoly on state-sanctioned violence in the low country and were thus unlikely to respect any traditions inimical to their interests or to be consistently outwitted or outbargained by an outgunned and apparently divided slave labor force.[46]

None of this is to suggest, however, that the task system should be attributed to white managerial prowess alone. Despite some concern for organization and method, and occasionally even for time and motion, it would be a stretch to imply, as some do, that planters preternaturally introduced Taylorism to the ricefields.[47] What planters did do was to appropriate some knowledge, to which they added insights of their own, in establishing and legitimating a compensation system that allowed them to produce great quantities of rice with slave labor in a sickly climate, while minimizing their own supervisory and opportunity costs. They did as principals do, in other words.

The principal role of planters and, indeed, the planters' role as principals are suggested, finally, by the word *task* itself. According to the *Oxford English Dictionary,* the word derives from the Latin infinitive *taxare*—to rate, estimate, or value—and in medieval Latin the word came to mean to impose or exact a tax. Imposition and exaction have been associated with the word ever since, though over time the connotation has shifted from fiscal assessments to labor requirements, particularly requirements of a heavy or burdensome nature. "Alas poore Duke," Shakespeare writes in *Richard II,* "the taske he undertakes is numbring sands, and drinking Oceans drie." Three-quarters of a century later, Milton's Samson "grind[s] in brazen fetters under task," and in the mid-eighteenth century Samuel Johnson defined *task* tersely as "something to be done imposed by another."[48]

From early on, the *OED* states, *task-work* denoted "forced labour; hence oppressive or burdensome work": Matthew Arnold captures this sense of burden well in his 1852 poem "A Summer Night":

> For most men in a brazen prison live,
> Where, in the sun's hot eye,
> With head bent o'er their toil, they languidly
> Their lives to some unmeaning taskwork give,
> Dreaming of naught beyond their prison-wall.[49]

With these images in mind, it is perhaps not surprising that a *taskmaster,* perforce, is "one who allots a duty, or imposes a heavy burden or labour." In the age of cultural studies, alas, it is probably de rigueur at this point to make a nod in that direction, too. Thus it should be noted in closing that Kevin Sullivan, who was one of the meanest and cruelest actors-grapplers in Ted Turner's World Championship Wrestling (WCW) stable, competed under the name "Taskmaster."[50] According to knowledgeable industry sources, he has also been the principal scriptwriter and choreographer for WCW bouts, further evidence, perhaps, that a task is a burden imposed.

The South Carolinian taskmaster William Elliott carried on an extensive correspondence throughout his adult life. Many of his letters are still extant, mainly in the Elliott-Gonzales Papers in the Southern Historical Collection at the University of North Carolina, Chapel Hill. In reading through this correspondence, one is struck by the many tensions in Elliott's life: between business and pleasure, between friends and family, and between travel and his beloved low country.

Such tensions are apparent in his career as a planter, too. He was avidly interested in and knowledgeable about rice and cotton cultivation but often complained that he lacked sufficient information to act decisively while his crops were in the ground. He claims to have loved the planting life but conceded that he lacked "the patience . . . to deal with mules & their partners the niggers" and was convinced that it was "unsafe to breathe the malarious air of a rice plantation in July." He distrusted his slaves but knew he needed their expertise, and tried "to stimulate them by rewards."[51]

However well such stimulation may have succeeded in the rice and cotton fields, it seems to have bred little more than contingent loyalty. In August 1862, after the collapse of Confederate power in the Beaufort District, all of the prime hands on Elliott's Oak Lawn plantation "up and left," absconding en masse to the Yankees. Although they were ultimately caught and forced to return to Oak Lawn, it seems clear that what they were doing in a sense—a narrow economistic sense, to be sure—was attempting to reject one principal and one compensation package for others yet unknown.[52]

4

Antebellum Southern Urbanization

DAVID L. CARLTON

The following was originally written as an encyclopedia article. Since it was necessary for the article to be, well, encyclopedic, it touches on numerous topics not strictly germane to this collection. Nonetheless, the core organizing principle of the piece is in keeping with our central themes, and we include it here because it illuminates some important features of our argument. The original included no notes, but it did include a bibliography, which is retained here. An important additional work, John Majewski's *A House Dividing: Economic Development in Pennsylvania and Virginia before the Civil War* (New York: Cambridge University Press, 2000), has appeared since the original publication of this article; Majewski's argument shows gratifying similarities to that presented here, but offers important new evidence and insights.

The role of cities in the antebellum and Confederate South exhibited a paradox. On the one hand, the cities of the future Confederacy were crucial to the existence of the plantation economy, linking it to the international markets that had created it and the flow of capital and supplies that sustained its growth. In the Confederacy, cities became even more vital as administrative centers, supply depots, and manufacturing points. Yet at the same time cities were marginal to the antebellum South, seriously constricted in their range of functions and in their vitality. In an age when American cities outside the region were developing integrated networks of cities and towns and launching on a process of self-sustaining and mutually reinforcing growth, the urban centers of the future Confederacy remained largely tethered to their hinterlands, on the one hand, and to the great centers of international commerce and credit, on the other. Their inadequacies, like those of other components of southern society, would be glaringly revealed in the harsh light of war.

Urbanization in the Antebellum South

That the process of urbanization in the future Confederate states lagged behind that of the future Union states is apparent from the summary statistics. As table 4.1 shows, in 1790 less than 2 percent of southerners lived in incorporated places of at least 2,500 people, the current census definition of an "urban place." To be sure, the difference from the North was not striking; the young Republic north of the Potomac was at that time only 7 percent urban. By the time of secession, however, nearly a quarter of the Union's population counted as city people; less than 7 percent of the Confederacy's population did. Of the 102 American cities of over ten thousand people in 1860, the Confederacy, with 29 percent of the old Union's total population, contained only eleven. If a more sophisticated measure, the index of relative urbanization (table 4.2), is used to trace southern urbanization over time, it reveals that the region, while generally less than half as urban as the nation as a whole, urbanized at a slightly faster rate than the larger nation until 1840 and then dramatically lost ground in the late antebellum period.

The summary statistics mask enormous variation, for there was no single kind of "southern city," nor was there a coherent urban hierarchy in the region before secession. Looming large in the summary statistics was New Orleans (table 4.3). Entering the Union through the Louisiana Purchase in 1803, it was immediately the fifth largest American city, maintaining that rank throughout the antebellum period. The development of the western river steamer after the War of 1812 allowed the city to burgeon as the great entrepôt (intermediary center of trade and transshipment) of the

Table 4.1. Percentage of urban population, future Confederate States of America and non-CSA, 1790–1860

Year	Future CSA[a]	Virginia	non-CSA
1790	1.97	1.78	6.99
1800	2.36	2.62	8.15
1810	3.18	3.63	9.38
1820	3.34	3.78	9.12
1830	3.87	4.82	11.21
1840	5.05	6.92	13.45
1850	5.86	7.97	19.33
1860	6.89	9.50	24.72

Source: Computed from figures in *U.S. Census of Population: 1970* (Washington, D.C., 1970), vol. 1, pt. 1, sec. 1, tables 8 and 18.

[a]Includes the eleven states of the future Confederate States of America; West Virginia is excluded from the future CSA and Virginia totals. Future CSA totals for 1790 include the states of Virginia, North Carolina, South Carolina, Georgia, and Tennessee; later additions are Alabama and Mississippi (1800), Louisiana and Arkansas (1810), Florida (1830), and Texas (1850).

Table 4.2. Relative urbanization indexes, 1790–1860

Year	Future CSA[a]	Virginia	CSA without Virginia, Louisiana[b]
1790	0.384	0.346	0.419
1800	0.389	0.431	0.359
1810	0.439	0.5	0.27
1820	0.465	0.525	0.293
1830	0.442	0.551	0.262
1840	0.468	0.64	0.22
1850	0.383	0.522	0.227
1860	0.349	0.481	0.224

Source: Computed from figures in *U.S. Census of Population: 1970* (Washington, D.C., 1970), vol. 1, pt. 1, sec. 1, tables 8 and 18.

[a]"Future CSA" is defined as in table 4.1. The "relative index of urbanization" is calculated by dividing the relevant subunit's share of U.S. urban population by its share of total population.

[b]This column is designed to illustrate urbanization in the future Confederacy when the anomalous cases of Virginia and New Orleans (Louisiana) are excluded. Because New Orleans's hinterland was considerably larger than Louisiana alone, excluding Louisiana understates the extent of antebellum southern urbanization. However, because New Orleans's hinterland included extensive non-southern territory as well, and because the Crescent City's role as interregional entrepôt made it unique among southern cities, including it in southern urbanization statistics is equally distorting in the other direction.

Table 4.3. Principal cities of the future Confederacy, populations and ranks

	1800		1820		1840		1860	
City	Pop.	Rank	Pop.	Rank	Pop.	Rank	Pop.	Rank
New Orleans			27,176	1	105,400[a]	1	179,598[b]	1
Richmond	5,737	3	12,067	3	20,153	3	40,703[c]	2
Charleston	18,924	1	24,780	2	29,261	2	40,522	3
Mobile					12,672	5	29,258	4
Norfolk[d]	6,926	2	8,478	4	17,397	4	24,116	5
Memphis							22,623	6
Savannah	5,166	4	7,523	6	11,214	6	22,292	7
Petersburg	3,521	6	6,690	7	11,136	7	18,266	8
Nashville					6,929	9	16,988	9
Alexandria	4,971	5	8,218	5	8,459	8	12,654	10
Augusta					6,403	10	12,493	11

Source: *U.S. Census of Population* (Washington, D.C., 1800–1860).

[a]Includes Lafayette.

[b]Includes Algiers and Jefferson.

[c]Includes Manchester.

[d]Includes Portsmouth in 1840 and 1860.

Mississippi valley as well as the leading cotton and sugar port, so that by 1840 it contained nearly 40 percent of the total urban population of the future Confederacy. Its growth slowed dramatically after 1840, though, as the canals and railroads of the later transportation revolution increasingly directed the trade of the Old Northwest toward the Northeast.

Another anomalous case was the state of Virginia. Relatively nonurban in 1790, the Old Dominion (here not including the future West Virginia) by 1840 was, after Louisiana, the South's most urban state, containing eight of the region's twenty-three cities, including the third largest, Richmond, and over a quarter of its urban population. A complex of factors contributed to Virginia's relatively rapid urbanization. The agricultural shift from tobacco to wheat encouraged a vigorous grain trade, increasingly supplemented by the manufacture and export of flour. Changes in tobacco marketing concentrated the trade in Richmond, Petersburg, and Lynchburg and fed their burgeoning tobacco factories. Norfolk and Portsmouth became entrepôts for both Virginia and nearby North Carolina, while Richmond and Petersburg became the South's only true manufacturing cities. After 1840, though, as the pace of urbanization picked up in the North, Virginia lost relative ground, and in 1860 it was less than half as urban as the nation as a whole; except for Richmond, its cities grew slowly, and only one new center, the Shenandoah Valley town of Staunton, appeared in the late antebellum period.

With minor exceptions, notably the western outfitting and provisioning center of Nashville, virtually every other significant southern city was at least in part the product of the cotton trade, and cotton largely defined the southern urban character. Dominating the lower South as far north as Tennessee and North Carolina were the cotton ports, which in addition to New Orleans included Charleston, Savannah, Mobile, and Memphis. These cities performed variably during the years before 1860. Charleston, the major city of the South in 1790, stagnated but remained the second city in 1860. As the cotton belt pushed westward, Mobile and, later, Memphis arose, first as outfitting centers for settlers and then as outlets for their staple production. To the interior of these centers there developed a string of much smaller towns, usually on rivers at or near the fall line. In late antebellum times interior points proliferated; the number of incorporated towns in the region tripled between 1840 and 1860 (table 4.4). Generally, though, cotton belt urbanization lagged badly; outside of Virginia and Louisiana only 4.4 percent of the region's people lived in cities.

Behind these and other indicators of antebellum urban underdevelopment lay the failure of most southern cities to transcend their original roles as entrepôts for the plantation staple economies of their hinterlands. All U.S. cities originated as colonial outposts, funneling settlers and supplies to expanding frontiers and exporting primary products abroad. In the nineteenth century, however, cities outside the future Confederacy launched on a path of self-sustaining and mutually reinforcing growth while at the same time drawing strength from relatively densely populated hinterlands generating strong and diverse demand. Southern cities, though, traded little with each other and engaged in little innovative growth; dealing chiefly in one major staple, cotton, these centers did not have much to offer each other. Accordingly, no southern *system* of cities developed; major centers with their hinterlands developed independently of each other, maintaining their principal trading links with the rising metropolises of western Europe and the American Northeast. Like their colonial forebears they served the undemanding needs of the plantations and the narrowly focused desires of a distant metropolitan core, with profound and deleterious consequences for their development.

The most striking structural feature of southern urban systems, especially in the cotton belt, was their *primate* character—that is, relative to the North, local centers in the hinterlands of cotton ports were few and underdeveloped, so that the central city largely monopolized both population and urban services. Charleston comprised 83 percent of South Carolina's urban population in 1860, and Mobile 60 percent of Alabama's; New Orleans (with its suburbs) and Memphis together contained 87 percent of the urban dwellers in Louisiana, Mississippi, Arkansas, and western Tennessee. Because cotton and other plantations oriented their production toward outside markets, and because modern means of transportation and communication were slow to develop in the region, planters needed to move their crops to a seaport or one of the larger river towns. Lacking adequate marketing information, they needed the services of agents in those few points enjoying adequate contact with the outside world. Accordingly, the staple trade, and the factors, buyers, and bankers who controlled it,

Table 4.4. Number of urban places, 1790–1860

Year	Future CSA[a]	Virginia	Outside Virginia	U.S.[b]
1790	2	1	1	24
1800	6	4	2	33
1810	7	4	3	46
1820	7	4	3	61
1830	16	6	10	90
1840	22	8	14	131
1850	33	8	25	236
1860	52	9	43	392

Sources: Urban places in future Confederacy compiled from *U.S. Census of Population* (Washington, D.C., 1790–1870). U.S. figures from Allan Pred, *Urban Growth and City-Systems in the United States, 1840–1860* (Cambridge, Mass., 1980), 23.

[a]Includes all incorporated places, excluding suburbs (Lafayette, Louisiana, in 1840 and 1850; Algiers and Jefferson, Louisiana, in 1860; Manchester, Virginia, in 1860).

[b]Figures include the future Confederacy.

concentrated at very few points, chiefly on the edge of the region, where shipping facilities could be located and where fast, reliable information was most readily available.

The central figures in antebellum southern urban commerce were commission merchants called *factors*. Specializing in a specific staple, factors served planters as sales agents, offering their strategic locations and specialized knowledge to interior producers seeking advantageous prices. The same advantages encouraged factors to become all-purpose commercial intermediaries for their clients, purchasing and shipping supplies, providing short- and long-term loans, and vouching for credit. Primarily serving the needs of factors, southern banks were few in number, relatively large in scale, and highly concentrated in location; in 1860 nine of the eighteen banks in South Carolina were located in Charleston. Buyers similarly clustered around factorage centers, as did merchants catering to the planting trade. Because of the slow pace of these urban outposts, and because factors' businesses relied heavily on personal relationships with their clients, the tone of business life was unhurried and social; Charleston, in particular, had a reputation for being almost as much a resort as a business center. Factors typically forged close alliances with their planter clients, and probably a majority were native southerners. There was a significant nonsouthern presence in the trade, however, especially among buyers and agents for northeastern or English houses; Scotch-Irish merchants became powerful in early nineteenth-century Charleston, and in the newer southwestern ports New Yorkers and Englishmen, often part-time residents, played major commercial roles.

Whatever the origins of urban merchants, they worked within a system that left them dependent for markets, capital, and services on cities outside the region. Although southern banks became increasingly prominent in late antebellum times, many financial services were obtained from the banks, insurance companies, merchants, and shippers of England and the great northeastern ports. Of the latter, New York became increasingly dominant, in large part because of its success in organizing the international cotton trade. Most shipping was controlled by outside interests; moreover, the pattern of shipping that developed enhanced dependence. Southern ports were typically heavy exporters but light importers; accordingly, to minimize backhaul unit costs on the westbound Atlantic voyage, New York shippers established a triangular trade, carrying cotton directly to England, manufactured goods and immigrants to New York, and manufactured goods south. Although southern urban spokesmen complained loudly of the tribute they thus had to pay the northerners, no southern city save New Orleans could sustain direct European trade on its own, and attempts, notably through the commercial convention movement, to foster a cooperative effort at establishing direct southern ties to Europe ran chronically afoul of urban rivalries within the region.

The low level of imports through southern cities was, in turn, primarily a product of the low density of demand in their outlying areas. The very lack of a significant urban population with its characteristic abandonment of rural habits of domestic production was part of the problem, as was the large proportion of poor, thinly populated mountain and pine barren land in the region. The most critical inhibitor of demand for goods, though, was the plantation system itself. Its large units helped reduce population density in the southern countryside relative to that in the North. More important, the economic logic of the slave plantation system led it to minimize outside consumption. Slaves were underutilized in staple crop production, but as "fixed capital" they were available year-round to perform a variety of provisioning and domestic manufacturing operations at little marginal cost. Because they were slaves, it was to the interest of their masters to keep their consumption, especially of high-value goods, to a minimum. Since planters served as purchasing agents for their slaves and dealt chiefly with factors in the nearest major city, plantations provided little stimulus to the development of smaller commercial centers, reinforcing the primate character of the urban system. To be sure, between two-thirds and three-quarters of the white southern rural population lived in nonslave-holding households, but the plain folk lived plainly. Fearing the risks of commercial agriculture, they involved themselves little in staple production and either produced for themselves or obtained what they needed through local trade. In any case, they lived disproportionately in up-country regions well away from the predominantly coastal major centers, regions made accessible only near the very end of the antebellum period. Whether planter, slave, or yeoman, then, rural southerners were generally poor customers for urban importers.

Likewise, they were poor customers for urban manufacturers. Although American cities generally were mercantile in character as late as 1840, manufacturing became increasingly associated with cities over the next twenty years—but not in the South. In 1860, the eleven future Confederate cities with populations of over ten thousand employed proportionately less than half as many workers in manufacturing as did their non-southern counterparts. Of the 102 American cities for which the statistics were reported, Charleston and Mobile had the lowest proportions, 2.1 percent and 2.3 percent, of the nonsuburban incorporated places; with Norfolk, Savannah, and New Orleans, they composed half of the bottom ten, and Memphis followed three ranks further down.

A yet greater deficiency for the long term was the structure of southern urban manufacturing. Most southern industry was designed to process raw materials for shipment (tobacco, lumber), supply commercial services (printing and publishing), or provide cheap slave cloth (cotton textiles). On the other hand, in contrast to the factories and shops of cities in the contemporary West, southern cities developed few of the varied consumers' and producers' goods industries that would lay the groundwork for the subsequent rise of smokestack America. Not only was consumer demand inhibited, but the crude techniques of plantation agriculture and the ability of planters to extend their operations simply by adding more slaves (contrasting with the limited labor available to family farmers in the free states) smothered the development of a large-scale agricultural implement industry. With thin demand in the countryside and poorly developed trading links between cities within the region, few southern cities could reach the threshold of demand required to sustain urban industrial production.

Finally, southern cities were handicapped by a dearth of cheap energy sources; usually neither fossil fuel nor water power was available in the coastal zones where southern cities arose. Petersburg and Richmond, the major exceptions to this rule among cities of over ten thousand in 1860, were likewise the only ones specializing in manufacturing, 17 percent and 19.7 percent of their populations being so employed. The two Virginia cities were at or near tidewater, but were endowed with ample water power by virtue of their location on the fall line and had access to nearby deposits of coal. The two cities became leading centers of tobacco manufacture; Petersburg developed extensive cotton mills, and Richmond milled flour and tapped supplies of pig iron that had been floated down the James River and Kanawha Canal from the Great Valley to develop a sizable ironworking industry, epitomized by the famous Tredegar Iron Works. Other manufacturing developed at smaller interior points, chiefly along the fall line; the cities of Fayetteville, North Carolina, and Augusta and Columbus, Georgia, became important textile centers, and Lynchburg, up the James River from Richmond, flourished as a tobacco center. Generally, though, the urban manufacturing sector was poorly developed and poorly balanced, and moreover operated under severe handicaps; Tredegar, the flagship iron maker, suffered from high costs, inadequate supplies of pig iron, and poor markets, depending heavily (and, for the Confederacy, fortunately) on federal ordnance contracts for much of its prewar sustenance.

Southern cities, then, even in relatively favored Virginia, were handicapped in their development by a host of structural disabilities, most of them imposed by the constricted role assigned them by the plantation slave economy. Although the dynamic impulse in antebellum southern urbanization was weak by comparison with that further north, it was by no means absent. Cities were almost always dominated by a commercial-civic elite, a core of merchants and their commercial allies that commanded not only the central economic institutions of the city but also its press and its government. As with booster elites elsewhere in the country, southern urban leaders identified their own aspirations with those of the town, and vice versa. To facilitate their common business they organized banks and insurance companies and developed port facilities. Through franchised private companies and municipally owned enterprises they worked to extend city services such as water, gas, paved streets, police and fire protection, and public amenities such as markets and parks; undertaken to enhance the city's attractions as a business location and improve the quality of life for the elite, these services were unevenly distributed, being concentrated in the business district and the better residential neighborhoods.

Most important, southern urban boosters sought to extend and consolidate their trade through transportation projects. Economic and geographic expansion in the nineteenth century sparked increasing rivalry among American cities generally, and southern cities were no exception, ardently seeking ways to exploit new opportunities and protect themselves from their competitors. A brief canal boom in the 1820s brought few lasting benefits outside Virginia, but new opportunities appeared with the advent of the railroad. Worried about the constriction of its hinterland by its rival Savannah, Charleston capitalists completed the South Carolina Railroad to Hamburg, opposite Augusta, in 1833; 136 miles in length, it was at the time the longest railroad in the world. In later years other major cities, notably those of Virginia and Georgia, took up the challenge. But southern railroads suffered from the same lack of hinterland demand and unbalanced traffic flows afflicting their terminal cities, and expansion was slow until the 1850s, when a major building boom tripled southern mileage.

Financed by combinations of private, municipal, state, and outside investment, southern railroads were planned and operated in accordance with what one historian has termed a developmental strategy; each city's system served to define and extend its hinterland, encourage market production, and channel shipments down the line to the primate city. Accordingly, railroad systems long remained isolated from each other, maintaining separate terminals, refusing connections, and using different gauges. Even as late as 1860, interconnections between city systems were rare and roundabout; with numerous unfilled gaps and dead ends, the southern rail network was far less articulated than its northern counterpart (no model of organization itself). Designed to serve the restricted needs of a staple-producing periphery, southern railroads were thus poorly equipped to support the Confederacy in its struggle for existence.

Some moves toward articulation, though, began to appear late in the antebellum period. Several major cities nursed regional, and even interregional, aspirations; though none successfully met the competition of northeastern ports for the western trade, these larger ambitions began to create embryonic long-haul systems by the 1850s, drawing overland shipments from the Deep South and Southwest into South Atlantic ports. Of major future consequence for southern urbanization was the resulting rise of a new kind of urban place, the interior railroad city. Most of them were still small in 1860; Atlanta, the future regional rail hub, had fewer than ten thousand inhabitants, despite mushroom-like growth since its incorporation in 1843. But the appearance on the scene of cities such as Atlanta and Chattanooga, and the rail-induced expansion of older centers such as Nashville, portended a revolution in the character and spatial distribution of southern cities. Improved transportation and telegraphic communication not only encouraged interior economic development but undercut the economic monopoly of the factorage system, on which rested the primacy of the cotton ports, and created new centers with vested interests in breaking free of coastal domination. Interior merchants had long sought to dispense with the factor's expensive services, and direct, ready access to the centers of international markets and finance offered opportunities they were eager to exploit. As a result, the southern urban landscape would look quite different in 1900 than it did in 1860.

Demographics

However commercial they were, southern cities were hardly mere nodes of merchants, and the great bulk of their inhabitants were of far humbler status than the commercial-civic elites. Inevitably in a slave society, a large number of city dwellers were slaves; the proportion ranged widely, though only rarely exceeding 50 percent. Some slaves were in town as personal servants of their owners; most worked in the commercial economy, chiefly in unskilled work but in numerous skilled trades as well. Slaves provided the principal work force for the tobacco factories, flour mills, and ironworks of Virginia. In contrast to the countryside, slave hiring was common in the cities, especially in manufacturing centers, where the majority were hired. Despite legal restrictions, many of these hired slaves managed their own employment, paying their owners for the privilege. A minority, again larger in manufacturing centers and again despite legal prohibitions, were allowed to live apart from either owner or user. As this evidence suggests, slavery could be easily adapted to the needs of an urban society, and city growth does not appear to have been inhibited by the institution's inflexibility. Nonetheless, slavery was less important in cities, where there were alternative sources of labor, than it was on the plantation, where the advantages of forced labor were much clearer. Accordingly, urban slave populations tended to drop proportionately over time and in the cotton boom of the 1850s frequently dropped absolutely. Because it encouraged planters to use their chattels in relatively lucrative rural pursuits, plantation slavery thus imparted a structural antiurban bias to the population distribution of the Old South.

Free blacks constituted a small group in southern cities (usually less than 10 percent of the population), but they were far more urban in their residence than either native whites or slaves; in the upper South one-third of free blacks, and in the lower South a majority, were urbanites, disproportionately concentrated in larger cities. In Virginia, where they constituted 10 percent of all blacks, urban free blacks engaged largely in unskilled pursuits; farther south, where they were fewer in number, they were more likely to be skilled. Typically, skilled workers tended to be of mixed blood and to be heavily concentrated in personal-service occupations catering to whites, such as barbering. The most successful of these artisans were able to establish themselves as a "colored aristocracy." Other free blacks engaged in petty retailing and other services to fellow blacks, free and slave, and over the course of the antebellum period developed institutions, notably the black church, that would lay the foundation for racial consciousness and solidarity after emancipation.

A majority of residents in most cities, as in the region generally, were white, but white urbanites differed in striking respects from whites in the countryside. A great many propertyless white poor congregated in the cities, producing greater extremes of wealth and poverty than existed even in the plantation districts; in particular, single or widowed females sought employment in the factories of cities such as Petersburg. Native white males tended to concentrate in white-collar occupations and in skilled pursuits such as printing. The most unusual characteristic of the southern white urban population, though, was its large foreign-born component. Although few antebellum immigrants chose to settle in the South, most who did moved to the larger cities; sizable minorities of city populations were foreign-born, and nonnatives not uncommonly dominated the white male working class. Many of these immigrants, the Irish in particular, were relegated to unskilled work, often substituting for slaves; many more, though, especially among the Germans, provided a number of essential skills and developed vigorous petty entrepreneurial communities. With immigrant people came immigrant culture; Judaism and (outside Louisiana) Roman Catholicism established their principal beachheads in the major cities, ethnic social and mutual-aid institutions became important to urban life and commerce, and the Irish in places like New Orleans left an enduring imprint on local accents. Finally, it was in cities that class consciousness and class conflict were most likely to arise. These took the usual forms (labor unions and strikes) appearing in other American cities, but the presence of slave and free black workers, along with an official ideology of white supremacy, added peculiar twists and complexities to class relationships among whites, leading in particular to increased pressure on vulnerable free black communities in the 1850s.

In contrast to the countryside, cities were crowded, and social relations were characterized by relative anonymity and fluidity, enhancing the concerns of the elite over their ability to control social turmoil. As was underscored by the abortive slave uprising planned by Denmark Vesey and others in Charleston, urban black populations could not be constrained as easily as rural ones. Accordingly, municipalities assumed much of the task of domination, handled on plantations by the individual slave owner, and inevitably in the name of the white race rather than the slaveholding class. Thus many of the institutions associated with postwar segregation appeared in antebellum times, although racial separation was explicitly harsher on both slaves and free blacks. The white working class could not be treated so bluntly; nonetheless, the influx of immigrants, in particular, heightened elite concerns over social control, and the visibility of the white urban poor stirred consciences among an elite wedded both to white supremacy and to Whiggish notions of moral stewardship. Cities thus became centers of social benevolence, creating orphanages, hospitals, public and private relief agencies, and, toward the end of the antebellum period, the first genuine public schools in the South. In many of these endeavors the lead was taken by societies of middle-class women assuming roles as "civic housekeepers," in the process beginning a redefinition of their constricted sphere that would prove of long-term significance.

Cities during Secession and the Confederacy

As the antebellum period progressed, especially into the 1850s, the sectional conflict increasingly brought a variety of pressures on cities, and they in turn played a significant role of their own in the events leading up to secession. Engaged as they were in commerce, the southern commercial-civic elites valued stability and maintained close business and personal ties with their northeastern correspondents. Moreover, their desires for commercial and industrial development, frequently with government aid, had traditionally clashed with the free-trade proclivities of rural southerners. They had traditionally been inclined to Whiggery, regretted the rise of radicalism in both North and South, and thus in the 1860 election tended to support Constitutional Union Party candidate John Bell. Moreover, immigrant workers, in particular, were questionable loyalists to the cause of southern rights; in 1860, in large part because of their vote, Democrat Stephen A. Douglas, otherwise scarcely a factor in the South, scored heavily in cities such as Memphis, Mobile, and New Orleans.

On the other hand, southern cities were intellectual centers for the ideology of southern rights; the leading fire-eaters tended to be young, ambitious urbanites of the sort that generally take the lead in developing nationalist movements, and cities such as Charleston became hotbeds of secessionist sentiment. Moreover, the close ties binding southern cities to the northeastern metropolises generated frustration over their continued dependency and fears that a federal government in the hands of the North would distribute internal improvement aid inequitably. Industrialists such as Tredegar's Joseph R. Anderson dreamed that an independent South would provide them a huge protected market. Finally, white southern urbanites were, above all, white southerners; when the stark choice was posed between secession and "submission" to a "tyrannical" federal government, secession won easily.

For many cities the Confederate period was brief, as their strategic importance made them early targets of Union advances. Alexandria, Virginia, nominally the tenth largest Confederate city, was under federal control from the beginning; within little more than a year after the firing on Fort Sumter, Memphis, Nashville, Norfolk, Portsmouth, and the major urban prize of New Orleans had passed behind enemy lines, spending the remainder of the war chafing under hostile occupation but prospering from the military supply trade and from illicit commerce between the two sides.

For the remaining cities, however, war brought unprecedented importance. Although the expanding Union blockade effectively shut down some ports, notably Savannah, others, such as Charleston (until the summer of 1863), Wilmington, and to a lesser extent Mobile, became major centers of blockade running, thanks not only to their harbors but to their financial and entrepreneurial communities. Richmond, the Confederate capital, swelled to 128,000, over three times its prewar size, with the burgeoning of the Confederate wartime bureaucracy. Manufacturing and supply operations doubled the populations of cities in interior Georgia. Industrial demands brought a flood of new entrepreneurs into manufacturing, along with the Confederate government itself, which established important facilities at, among other locations, Augusta, Georgia, and Selma, Alabama. Military authorities developed urban infrastructure, such as sewers, in the interest of preserving the health of their troops; the Confederate government filled in critical gaps in the rail network, notably between Greensboro, North Carolina, and Danville, Virginia, an action that would have a major impact on future southern urban patterns.

In the end, though, the war lent little enduring impetus to urbanization. The operations of critical manufacturing firms such as Tredegar were hampered by supply bottlenecks, and the monopolization of scarce industrial capacity by military production left little opportunity for city building; indeed, the southern infrastructure deteriorated in the course of the conflict. War-induced growth was hothouse growth, and enterprises begun to satisfy a single tolerant customer were ill equipped to satisfy many demanding ones. Indeed, all told, the war's significance to Confederate cities lay less in its benefits than in the intense strains it placed on them. Cities became bloated with workers and refugees. The deurbanization of slavery was reversed, as numbers of slaves were impressed for military work, brought to town by refugee owners, or simply abandoned by hard-pressed masters and mistresses. Municipal efforts to counter increased slave independence were largely dead letters, and the institution showed clear signs of decay well before formal emancipation. The swelling numbers of propertyless employees, especially women whose men were in military service, were peculiarly vulnerable to the rampant inflation tearing through the Confederate economic fabric; it has been estimated that real wages dropped by 60 percent in the course of the war. Blockade-running ports such as Charleston and Wilmington enjoyed a diseased prosperity, as runners and merchants profited from trade in military supplies and luxuries that clogged supply lines and sent the cost of living soaring. Despite efforts at expanding poor relief, inflation, impressment, and the inadequacies of the Confederate distribution system left poorer urbanites in an increasingly serious plight and generated enormous social tensions, usually directed against speculators. These tensions culminated in a number of bread riots, frequently led by women, the greatest number of which occurred in the spring of 1863.

Confederate cities generally managed to withstand social tensions, but the powerful Union offensives beginning in the summer of 1864 began to tear the urban system apart. Cities, notably Richmond, had long been important Union objectives; by the end of the summer the capital and nearby Petersburg were under siege, and in early 1865 the last major ports east of Texas, Mobile and Wilmington, were sealed by the Union navy. Moreover, beginning in 1864 the deliberate destruction of cities and the transportation links tying them together became integral to a policy of crippling the Confederate war-making capacity. After capitulating in the summer, Atlanta was burned by Gen. William Tecumseh Sherman in November as he embarked on his

March to the Sea and the capture of Savannah; in February 1865 Columbia shared Atlanta's fate, although Sherman's culpability in the burning of the South Carolina capital remains in dispute. Gen. James H. Wilson's cavalry, on its sweep through the Deep South in the spring of 1865, destroyed the war-industry centers of Selma and Columbus, aided in the looting of the Georgia city by slaves and women workers. Other cities, such as Charleston, Richmond, and Petersburg, suffered severe damage incidental to military action in the course of the war.

Above all, the end of the war brought the end of the system of plantation slavery that had shaped the character of southern cities. To be sure, its legacy would continue to influence southern urban development in profound ways, some still discernible today. Nonetheless, the destruction of the slave regime would fundamentally alter the course of urbanization in the region. From the ashes of the Confederacy would arise a different and more dynamic southern urban order.

Bibliography

Amos, Harriet E. *Cotton City: Urban Development in Antebellum Mobile.* University, Ala., 1985.

Coclanis, Peter A. *The Shadow of a Dream: Economic Life and Death in the South Carolina Low Country, 1670-1920.* New York, 1989.

DeCredico, Mary A. *Patriotism for Profit: Georgia's Urban Entrepreneurs and the Confederate War Effort.* Chapel Hill, N.C., 1990.

Goldfield, David R. *Cotton Fields and Skyscrapers: Southern City and Region, 1607-1980.* Baton Rouge, La., 1982.

———. *Urban Growth in the Age of Sectionalism: Virginia, 1847-1861.* Baton Rouge, La., 1977.

Goldfield, David R., and Blaine A. Brownell, eds. *The City in Southern History: The Growth of Urban Civilization in the South.* Port Washington, N.Y., 1977.

Goldin, Claudia Dale. *Urban Slavery in the American South, 1820-1860.* Chicago, 1976.

Gutman, Herbert G., and Ira Berlin. "Natives and Immigrants, Free Men and Slaves: Urban Workingmen in the Antebellum American South." *American Historical Review* 88 (1983): 1175–1200.

Meyer, David R. "The Industrial Retardation of Southern Cities, 1860–1880." *Explorations in Economic History* 25 (1988): 366–86.

Wade, Richard C. *Slavery in the Cities: The South, 1820-1860.* New York, 1964.

Woodman, Harold D. *King Cotton and His Retainers: Financing and Marketing the Cotton Crop of the South, 1800-1925.* Lexington, Ky., 1968.

5

Distant Thunder

The Creation of a World Market in Rice and the Transformations It Wrought

PETER A. COCLANIS

This essay, which originally appeared in the *American Historical Review* in 1993, represents an attempt to embed southern economic developments in a global context. Using the southern rice industry as a case study, the essay demonstrates that the historical trajectory of this industry—and, by implication at least, other southern industries—looks quite different when placed in a transnational frame. Since the essay was first published, global approaches have become more popular with historians, and similar studies of other foods and commodities have begun to appear.

Come listen, all you darkies, come listen to my song,
It am about ole Massa, who use me bery wrong:
In de cole, frosty mornin', it an't so bery nice,
Wid de water to de middle to hoe among de rice.
from a slave song, South Carolina low country

Planting rice is never fun;
Bent from morn till set of sun;
Cannot stand and cannot sit;
Cannot rest for a little bit.
Oh, my back is like to break,
Oh, my bones with dampness ache,
And my legs are numb and set
From the soaking in the wet.
from an old Filipino song[1]

Rice *(Oryza sativa)* has shaped the lives of relatively few westerners over time. It has dominated the lives of fewer still. While the cereal has been known in the West since antiquity, its production and consumption for the most part have been of only minor importance, occurring at the margin of Western foodways. That we speak of breadwinners rather than ricewinners and pray for our daily bread rather than our daily rice tells us something about the hold of bread—primarily wheat bread—on the Western world. In the East, where the rice plant originated, things are far different; with all due respect to James Henry Hammond, in that part of the world, rice is indeed king. That the Indian word for rice, *dhanya,* means "sustainer of the human race," that the name of the Buddha's father, Suddhodana, the sixth-century-B.C. king of Nepal, literally means "pure rice," and that the idiomatic expression "Have you eaten your rice today? was a polite way of saying hello in traditional Chinese society only begins to convey the place of rice in the East.[2]

Why bother to study rice from the vantage point of the West? For two interrelated reasons. First, because the evolution of the market for rice in the West offers insight into the expansion and elaboration of capitalism, the most important economic development in the last five hundred years. To be sure, the rice market in the West was tiny in comparison to the market for small grains. Even in the early twentieth century, after centuries of market development, rice accounted for but a small fraction of the total trade in cereals, under 10 percent. Moreover, since small grains and rice are basically similar in caloric content-rice contains between about 354 and 362 kilocalories per hundred grams, and most small grains contain between about 320 and 365—rice, measured in terms of trade volume or caloric importance, was at best a minor component of the Western grain trade.[3]

But importance is not reducible to and cannot be deduced from numbers alone. Indeed, the case of rice is instructive and illuminating not so much because of its scale but because of its increasingly global scope. This brings me to the second reason: because a study of the rice market in the West requires that we look east, such a study provides an argument for the utility of a truly international approach to history. Regional or national approaches to the subject, self-contained and self-absorbed as they often are, will not do in this case.

Before we can begin to understand the market for rice in the West, we must know something of the uses to which the cereal was put. It is difficult to generalize about demand for any commodity or product but particularly so in the case of demand for rice in the West. Because of rice's relative insignificance in comparison to small grains and maize and its many inconspicuous or intermediate usages, historical patterns of rice consumption in the West remain somewhat murky even today. We know, for example, that rice served certain ceremonial functions, while a variety of sources point to its pharmaceutical uses. Still other sources suggest that at certain times and in certain places, rice was considered a luxury item, the demand for which varied directly rather than indirectly with price.[4] Neither ceremony nor pharmacy nor luxury, however, will go very far toward explaining the West's demand for rice. Its true importance derives from its transformation in the early modern period into an everyday commodity with numerous alimentary and industrial uses.

Rice and its by-products found employment in the starch and paper industries, for example, and were used extensively for animal feed. In the eighteenth century, liqueurs such as brandies and arrack often included rice among their ingredients, and in the second half of the nineteenth century rice gained widespread acceptance in the brewing industry. To the middle class, whose incomes allowed for dietary concerns that transcended mere subsistence, rice became a ready nutritional complement or supplement. In all likelihood, however, its greatest food use in the eighteenth and nineteenth centuries was as a versatile and relatively cheap dietary staple, especially useful for feeding commoners and *lumpen* groups—orphans, soldiers, sailors, inmates, the poor—in the absence of, or instead of, other cereals. Authorities ranging from Nicolas Baudeau in the eighteenth century to the writers of the *Encyclopaedia Britannica* in the early nineteenth century to Fernand Braudel in the late twentieth century agree on these basic points.[5]

This said, one must be careful about focusing too much attention on any single source of demand. Some scholars, cognizant of the fact that rice—until recently at least—has been considered highly income-inelastic, have focused, it is true, solely on this last, lumpen source of demand.[6] However, rice demand was general rather than class-specific during periods of crop failure and shortfalls in the West, and it played an intermediary role in a number of foods and industrial products of greater income elasticity. Further complexities arise from the fact that much of the "lumpen" demand for rice actually emanated from other social groups. From this perspective, a new or at least enhanced social preference for provisioning the putative dregs of society—sometimes with rice—can itself be viewed as a kind of income-elastic "commodity."[7]

Clearly, then, caution is still called for when speaking of rice demand. That rice prices throughout the West generally varied directly with the prices of wheat and other small grains in the eighteenth and nineteenth centuries can readily be established; precisely why this was so remains more conjectural.[8]

If consumer preferences and the availability of numerous substitutes rendered rice less than indispensable in the West, its price and versatility generally rendered it vendible throughout the Western world. In the eighteenth and nineteenth centuries—the period of primary concern here—rice was traded over a vast area from Peru and Argentina to the shores of the Black Sea. During this entire period, demand emanating from northern Europe proved central to the workings of the Western rice trade. To be sure, substantial demand existed in other areas—North America, southern Europe, the West Indies, and Brazil especially—but it is within the context of northern Europe's massive grain market that the rice trade can best be construed.

Unfortunately, it is impossible to chart precisely the labyrinthine course of commodity flows within this market in the eighteenth and nineteenth centuries. Extant data, scattered widely in customs records, toll registers, and commercial manuals and journals, indicate, however, that Germany was the center of consumption in northern Europe, with large quantities of rice entering the various German states from such ports as Amsterdam, Rotterdam, Hamburg, Bremen, and Danzig. Significant amounts of rice were consumed elsewhere in the North: with regularity in France, Belgium, and the Netherlands, for example, and, as the Sound tolls reveal, at least intermittently in Scandinavia and the eastern Baltic as well. Internal consumption in Great Britain, which traditionally had been quite limited, increased in the nineteenth century for a variety of reasons. Some shipments of rice, having worked their way down the Danube, made it to the ports of Ibraila and Galatz on the Black Sea, but shipments to that region did not compare to shipments to the west and north. We still need to ask whence and how the West's demand for rice was met and how supply changed over time.[9]

It is clear that rice was traded in the West well before its commodification, indeed, well before it was even produced in that part of the world. Mentioned in the Talmud but, interestingly enough, not in the Bible, rice was imported from Syria, Persia, and India by both the Greeks and the Romans. While some believe that rice was produced in Sicily in ancient times, most authorities believe that European cultivation began in earnest only with the Moors' incursion into Spain in the eighth century and the concomitant Turkish thrust into southeastern Europe and the Balkans.[10] Rice cultivation spread to other parts of Mediterranean Europe from these points of entry, and Europeans continued, intermittently, to import rice from the East—the Saracens were particularly important in the trade—throughout the medieval period. It was not until cultivation began in northern Italy in the fifteenth century, however, that the European rice industry attained more than local significance in economic terms.[11] European production has centered in the rich alluvial valleys of the upper Po, that is, in Piedmont and Lombardy, ever since. In good harvest years during the sixteenth and seventeenth centuries, northern Italian rice was shipped both to other parts of the peninsula and to other parts of Europe, much of it being distributed by Rhineland traders as well as by the German Hanse.[12] Such trade notwithstanding, rice was of limited importance in the West as the early modern period began. Europe's outward thrust during that period transformed the economic geography of rice supply in a variety of ways. As implied earlier, the economic dynamism that at once underpinned and reinforced this thrust eventually helped transform demand for rice in the West.

The reasons for the economic dynamism in parts of Europe during the early modern period lie well beyond the scope of this article. Suffice it to say that, as a result of a multiplicity of factors ranging from increased agricultural productivity to a secular decline in transactions costs, these areas began to achieve relatively sustained and fairly robust rates of growth in output and income per capita. Over time, the positions and structures of both supply and demand in these areas shifted in ways that encouraged and facilitated expanded economic contacts with other parts of the world. The commercial aspects of what we today refer to as the Age of Discovery, particularly in its less feverish phase during the seventeenth and eighteenth centuries, can for our purposes be viewed as a rational response to perceived economic opportunities.

This led in the East to the establishment of European trading factories and the rerouting to some degree of intra-Asian trade; in the West, to direct European involvement in, or at least supervision of, production itself.[13] It led, too, to the beginnings of factor and product markets of global scope. Such markets were at first highly imperfect. Long-distance, intercontinental trade predated the era of the English East India Company and the V.O.C. (Vereenigde Oost-indische Compagnie) by a millennium or two. And prior to the seventeenth and eighteenth centuries, such trade, generally speaking, was quantitatively insignificant, often entailing the intermittent or periodic exchange of preciosities of relatively limited market purview.

In the last half of the early modern era, the value and quality of such trade changed dramatically, as Europeans generally and European merchant capital specifically responded to economic change at home. Economic growth in parts of Europe, most notably in the northwest, created conditions necessary and sufficient to allow for both the global reallocation of European labor and capital and the emergence of a loosely integrated international trading system organized and dominated by Europeans and their legatees. While this system ultimately affected world trade in innumerable ways, it is enough to note here that European merchant capital, supported when necessary by state power, succeeded during this period in regularizing and routinizing such trade and in shifting its emphasis from high-value preciosities to bulk commodities, of which rice was one.

As Europeans cast about the globe for profitable economic opportunities, an amazing array of inorganic and organic substances were put to the test. Various minerals ultimately achieved commercial importance, as did such cultigens as sugar, tobacco, indigo, cotton, and rice. The last of these, rice—a plant that can be grown virtually anywhere—was tried in such unlikely and seemingly unrelated places as the central Andes, the western part of Ruthenia, and the tidewater of Virginia. But probably by the middle of the eighteenth century, the British colony of South Carolina had become the West's leading rice exporter. This colony, along with neighboring Georgia, which soon became a major exporter as well, possessed a number of advantages that help to explain why rice proved successful there at that time.[14]

First of all, the physical environment of the lower coastal plain of both South Carolina and Georgia was highly conducive to rice production. Given the region's humid subtropical climate, abundant precipitation, seemingly inexhaustible surface water resources, and loamy Ultisols (red-yellow podzols), it would have been surprising, other things being equal, if rice had not emerged as an important export commodity. This seems particularly understandable in light of the region's human and nonhuman capital resources and its market position by the mid-eighteenth century. An ample, cost-efficient, disciplined, and technologically skilled African and creole labor force was available by that time, at least some members of which had cultivated rice (whether *O. sativa* or a related species, *O. glaberrima*) in West Africa. A powerful class of planters and merchants, eager for profits, had shown itself capable of organizing production with method and rigor, and European and American merchant capital had done likewise, greatly facilitating long-distance trade. Finally, and perhaps most important, transport costs, market information, and the degree of integration of what was still a rudimentary world economy favored this region over several other rice-producing areas.[15]

Things would change, however. During the first half of the nineteenth century, the South Carolina–Georgia rice region, despite producing more rice than ever before, saw itself surpassed as a supply source for the principal Western markets. The region's relative decline in international competitiveness was due in part to internal supply constraints. The amount of land suitable for rice cultivation—cultivation increasingly dependent on tidal irrigation technology—was limited by geography, and, by the second quarter of the nineteenth century, some of the best land in the tidal zone was losing fertility. Furthermore, the simultaneous expansion westward of the southern cotton industry not only forced coastal rice planters to compete for outside capital with a more dynamic industry but actually siphoned a good part of indigenous capital and entrepreneurship from the rice area itself.

It would nonetheless be a mistake to focus solely on internal constraints in explaining the relative decline of the South Carolina–Georgia rice region, for the economic geography of international rice supply was being drastically transformed at the same time. Obviously, markets are never completely static, and the South Carolina–Georgia region faced competitive challenges even during its heyday in the eighteenth century. The region had lost the Portuguese market to Brazil in the 1790s, and Italian rice claimed segments of the European market. The stagnation and ultimate demise of the South Atlantic rice industry was not chiefly a result of competition from these areas, however, but from distant lands, namely, Bengal, Java, and, later, Lower Burma, Siam, and Indochina. As global market integration proceeded, these Southeast Asian rice-producing areas were increasingly incorporated into the West's economic orbit, setting into motion forces from which the South Carolina–Georgia rice economy failed to recover.[16]

Asian rice had long been arriving in Europe, both via the Levant and transoceanic routes, but shipments increased dramatically once British economic and political control of Bengal intensified in the late eighteenth century. The story of Britain's gradual but seemingly inexorable incorporation of Bengal into the world market after Robert Clive's famous victory at Plassey in 1757 is already well known. While Clive's subsequent procurement in 1765 of the *diwani*—the right of revenue collection in Bengal, Bihar, and Orissa—may have been more important than the actual events of 1757, a key theme of the entire post-Plassey period is the heightened flow of both capital and raw materials from eastern India to Great Britain. Included in the category of raw materials were a variety of spices, saltpeter, and agricultural commodities such as indigo, sugar, cotton, flax, hemp, and, of course, rice. For our purposes, it is important to note that the process of market incorporation proceeded relatively rapidly in the case of rice: even before the 1820s, rice produced by Bengali peasants was cutting significantly into South Carolina's and Georgia's markets in northern Europe.[17] The degree to which such rice penetrated the British market in the first half of the nineteenth century is illustrated in tables 5.1 and 5.2. It is also important to note—as David MacPherson did in 1795—that rice was the first "necessary" sent to the West from India, all previous trade consisting of articles and products "rather of ornament and luxury than of use."[18] To what, primarily, was Bengal's rapid incorporation into Western rice markets due? In part, certainly, to aggressive entrepreneurship by British (English and Scottish) merchant capital and to aggressive action on the part of the British state. The British meant business in Bengal. No one saw this more clearly

Table 5.1. Rice imports into England, Wales, and Great Britain, 1696–1808

A. Imports into England and Wales, 1696–1780

Period	Total (cwts)
1696–1700	30,653
1701–1710	60,172
1711–1720	259,022
1721–1730	850,892
1731–1740	1,617,931
1741–1750	1,495,092
1751–1760	1,758,950
1761–1770	3,037,039
1771–1780	2,434,400

Imports by region (percent of total)

	1696–1700	1701–1710	1711–1720	1721–1730	1731–1740	1741–1750	1751–1760	1761–1770	1771–1780
The "Thirteen Colonies"	13.95	89.19	94.79	99.06	99.79	99.35	99.30	99.13	98.57
Other North America	0.01	0	0.01	0	0	0	0	0.01	0.47
West Indies and Central America	0.16	1.14	4.14	0.75	0.19	0.2	0.66	0.57	0.64
South America	0	0	0	0	0	0	0	0	0
Southern Europe and Atlantic islands	83.23	8.88	0.72	0.12	0	0.37	0	0.17	0.10
Northern Europe	1.32	0.08	0.11	0	0	0.02	0.03	0.01	0.18
Africa	0.00	0	0.06	0.01	0	0	0	0.1	0.02
Asia	1.32	0.71	0.17	0.05	0.01	0.07	0	0	0.02
	99.99	100.00	100.00	99.99	99.99	100.01	99.99	99.99	100.00

Table 5.1 *continued*

B. Imports into Great Britain, 1772–1808

Period	Total (cwts)
1772–1780	2,004,769
1781–1790	1,344,608
1791–1800	1,983,633
1801–1808	1,281,533

Imports by region (percent of total)

	1772–1780	1781–1790	1791–1800	1801–1808
The "Thirteen Colonies"	98.31	98.4	89.31	67.02
Other North America	0.51	0.01	0.32	0.07
West Indies and Central America	0.8	0.72	0.05	0.12
South America	0	0	0	1.47
Southern Europe and Atlantic islands	0.12	0.4	0.26	0.12
Northern Europe	0.22	0.04	1.04	0.24
Africa	0.02	0.04	0.26	0.1
Asia	0.02	0.38	8.76	30.85
	100.00	99.99	100.00	99.99

Sources: Customs 3/1–82, Customs Office Records, Public Record Office, London, England; Customs 17/1–30, Customs Office Records, Public Record Office. Note that data for 1705 and 1712 no longer survive. Given the purposes of this exercise, I have made no adjustments or estimates for these years. Also note that I have excluded rice taken on "prize vessels" during periods of war. On Customs 3 and Customs 17 as sources, see John J. McCusker, "The Current Value of English Exports, 1697 to 1800," *William and Mary Quarterly*, 3d ser., 28 (October 1971): 607–28.

Table 5.2. British rice imports by area, 1831–1850 (clean rice equivalents)

	1831-40	1841-50
Total imports (cwts)	3,723,027	8,312,825
Percentage of total:		
Northern Europe	0.12	0.18
Southern Europe	0.12	0.62
North America	20.52	14.26
West Indies and Central America	0	0.09
South America	0.19	0.85
Africa	0.69	0.23
Asia	78.36	83.77
Total	100.00	100.00

Sources: [Great Britain) *House of Lords, Sessional Papers, Session 1842*, vol. 10, 312–13; *House of Lords, Sessional Papers, Session 1854-1855*, vol. 10, 97–99. Note that in converting to clean rice equivalents, I assumed that a bushel of rice "in the husk" weighed 45 to 50 pounds and that a quarter of rice "in the husk" weighed 400 pounds. In addition, I employed a conservative assumption that 100 pounds of rice "in the husk," after milling, would make 60 pounds of clean rice.

than Karl Marx, whose piercing observation—"They speak of God. They mean Cotton"—cuts right to the core.

But there were other reasons as well. Without the collaboration of Indian merchant capital, for example, the British never would have succeeded in redirecting a portion of Bengal's agricultural production to Europe. Without significant changes in Western supply and demand, they might not even have tried. An unusual conjuncture of short-run and long-term factors was needed to create the context for such success.

Supply disruptions arising, first, from the American Revolution and, shortly thereafter, from the Napoleonic wars, interrupted, impeded, and at times completely shut off the flow of American rice to Europe. At roughly the same time, regional harvest failures and shortfalls in Europe—the shortfalls of 1795 and 1800 in England are cases in point—as well as broader forces related to industrialization, urbanization, commercialization, and population growth interacted to effect, if not institutionalize, a great increase in European demand for foodstuffs and industrial crops, including rice. Taken together, these forces help to explain such diverse developments as the termination in 1813 of the East India Company's trade monopoly and the gradual demise in the first half of the nineteenth century of the English Corn Laws. More directly, they help to explain the growing European interest in Bengali foodstuffs and raw materials and a similar interest in a second East Indian supply source, the Dutch-controlled island of Java.[19]

This island, the pearl of the Malay archipelago, had been trading directly with the West since it fell under Portuguese control in the sixteenth century, but its effective integration into the Western economy did not come about for several centuries thereafter. Once again, the British were involved in promoting this integration, whether through the Anglo-Dutch settlement after the American Revolution, which ended the V.O.C. trade monopoly in the Dutch East Indies, or through the economic and social reforms instituted by Sir Thomas Raffles between 1811 and 1816 when Java was under British rule. The establishment by the Dutch themselves of the so-called Preanger System in the eighteenth century and, more important, the *Cultuurstelsel* or Culture System in 1830, however, contributed even more to such integration. With the establishment of these systems, which essentially forced the indigenous population to produce cash crops, first for the V.O.C. and then for the state, tropical commodities from the island such as coffee, sugar, and indigo began streaming into Amsterdam and, later, Rotterdam, thence to be distributed throughout Europe.[20]

Rice originally was not included in either system—it was added under the *Cultuurstelsel* in 1843. But the general intensification of production and Western control both reflected and represented by these systems—and the creation of the N.H.M. (Nederlandsche Handel Maatschappij) or Dutch Trading Company in 1824—led to massive exports of this commodity to Europe as well, as illustrated in table 5.3. Beginning in the late 1830s, so far as we can tell, Java rice alone rivaled, and often surpassed, U.S. rice in the main northern European entrepôts.[21]

Table 5.3. Rice exports from Java and Madura to the West, 1826–1856 (pounds of clean rice equivalents)

Year	Netherlands	Other European countries	America	Total
1825		189,312		189,312
1826		9,792		9,792
1827	3,503,469	172,992		3,676,461
1828	9,602,470	2,211,360		11,813,830
1829	8,639,808	716,448	561,408	9,917,664
1830	3,120,493	4,896		3,125,389
1831	3,250,944	473,280		3,724,224
1832	2,265,216	2,975,136		5,240,352
1833	6,033,939	4,547,514		10,581,453
1834	2,701,178	1,431,264	695,232	4,827,674
1835	1,418,208	2,870,688	71,808	4,360,704
1836	11,450,330*	4,981,408		16,431,738
1837	9,681,024	10,696,128	538,560	20,915,712
1838	7,388,445†	17,634,521	3,945,197	28,968,163
1839	19,650,912	30,733,410	4,264,307	54,648,629
1840	9,987,143	8,874,348	1,365,440	20,226,931
1841	6,414,588‡	5,704,493‡	1,946,867	14,065,948
1842	13,860,358	7,033,702	2,446,368	23,340,428
1843	27,614,310	15,389,893	326,400	43,330,603
1844	17,446,141	8,961,421‡	850,054	27,257,616
1845	9,564,087	2,123,885		11,687,972
1846	17,301,811‡	7,371,526	108,800	24,782,137
1847	27,115,136	9,217,318	293,760	36,626,214
1848	30,956,428	14,133,450		45,089,878
1849	25,891,244	12,647,347		38,538,591
1850	23,977,888	7,132,493	48,960	31,159,341
1851	34,611,376	7,548,544	1,464,992	43,624,912
1852	26,710,722	4,252,448	104,448	31,067,618
1853	12,424,633	7,752,870	1,931,115	22,108,618
1854	21,069,306	4,520,999	1,088,000	26,678,305
1855	33,581,948	15,382,470	228,480	49,192,898
1856	66,758,807	17,917,583	3,052,602	87,728,992

Source: G. F. de Bruijn Kops, *Statistiek van Den Handel en de Scheepvaart op Java en Madura Sedert 1825*, 2 vols. (Batavia, 1857–59), 2:176–78. Note that in converting Javanese measurement units into Western equivalents, I assumed that 1 koyang was equal to 30 piculs (except for 1828, when internal evidence suggested that koyangs of 28 piculs were being employed) and that 1 Batavian picul was equal to 136 pounds. Moreover, since the rice shipped from Java to the West during this period was (partially milled) cargo rice for the most part, I used a multiplier of 0.8 to transform cargo rice into clean rice equivalents. That is to say, I assumed that 1 pound of cargo rice was equal to 0.8 pounds of clean rice. On the weight of Batavian piculs during this period, see *Hunt's Merchants' Magazine* 15 (September 1846): 328–29. On cargo rice and the derivation of the multiplier employed above, see Cheng Siok-Hwa, *The Rice Industry of Burma 1852-1940* (Singapore, 1968), 9–10 n. 24.

Almost all of the rice included in the "Other European countries" category above went to northern Europe. Between 1826 and 1856, only 4,990 piculs (542,912 pounds of clean rice equivalents) were exported from Java and Madura to southern Europe. Finally, the heading "America" above refers to the entire Western Hemisphere.

Notes:

*includes 1,534 koyangs of paddy, which would make about 3,755,232 pounds of clean rice (assuming that 1 pound of paddy was equal to 0.6 pounds of clean rice)

†includes 60 piculs of paddy (4,896 pounds of clean rice)

‡excluding minute amounts of paddy

For a variety of internal reasons—increasing demographic pressure on the island, the concomitant threat of food shortages, and the particular configuration of Javanese rural social structure—Java proved inconsistent in its role as an exporter of rice to the West.[22] By the 1850s, however, nearby Lower Burma was being transformed by the British from a closed, underpopulated "natural" economy into what would soon become the greatest rice exporter in the world.[23]

Burma had exported some rice prior to that time, particularly from Akyab in Arakan Province, but it was only after the Irrawaddy-Sittang Delta came under British rule in 1852 that Lower Burma's revolutionary economic transformation began. The development of the Irrawaddy-Sittang Delta along with that of the Transbassac provinces of the Upper Mekong Delta in Cochinchina a few years later constitute two of the greatest episodes of rapid agricultural expansion in modern history. In the former case, Asian—primarily Indian Chettyar—and European capital collaborated with pioneering peasant cultivators to create a vast rice-exporting complex in a remarkably brief period of time. This economic transformation affected other parts of Lower Burma as well. In Arakan, for example, which had come under British control in 1826, rice exports boomed after 1852: between 1854–1855 and 1860–1861, an average of 107,252 tons of rice were exported to Europe annually from this province alone. This rice in all likelihood was partially milled "cargo rice" rather than clean rice, so the above figure must be reduced by about 20 percent to get an estimate of clean rice equivalents. Nonetheless, it is important to point out that the adjusted figure for Arakan alone—85,802 tons (171.6 million pounds)—far exceeded the average for *total* U.S. rice exports over the same seven-year period.[24]

What was it about Bengal, Java, and Lower Burma in particular and about the Western economy as a whole that led both to the rise of the East Indies as a supply source and—as tables 5.4 and 5.5 demonstrate—to the tepid growth and later stagnation of U.S. rice exports in the period between 1790 and the Civil War?

Table 5.4. U.S. rice output, exports, and export/output ratios, 1819–1860 (pounds)

Year	Output (clean rice)	Exports (clean rice)	Export/output ratio (percent)
1819	53,292,000	42,997,800	80.68
1820	69,354,600	52,932,600	76.32
1821	60,544,200	52,253,400	86.31
1822	61,951,200	60,819,000	98.17
1823	75,463,800	67,937,400	90.03
1824	66,133,200	58,209,000	88.02
1825	70,348,800	66,637,800	94.72
1826	79,686,600	80,110,800	100.53
1827	87,406,800	105,011,400	120.14
1828	92,355,600	102,981,600	111.51
1829	87,565,800	78,418,200	89.55
1830	81,351,600	69,910,200	85.94
1831	91,155,000	72,196,200	79.20
1832	106,953,000	86,497,800	80.87
1833	87,222,600	73,131,600	83.84
1834	90,600,000	66,510,600	73.41
1835	101,310,600	127,789,800	126.14
1836	90,574,800	63,650,400	70.27
1837	71,604,600	42,628,800	59.53
1838	81,949,800	55,992,000	68.32
1839	80,841,422	60,996,000	75.45
1840	84,252,600	60,970,200	72.37
1841	88,952,968	68,770,200	77.31
1842	94,007,484	64,059,600	68.14
1843	89,879,145	80,829,000	89.93
1844	111,759,000	71,172,600	63.68
1845	89,765,000	74,404,200	82.89
1846	97,741,500	86,656,200	88.66
1847	103,040,500	60,241,800	58.46
1848	119,199,500	77,316,600	64.86
1849	143,614,102	76,241,400	53.09
1850	102,775,800	63,354,000	61.64
1851	105,733,800	71,839,800	67.94
1852	102,467,400	40,624,200	39.65
1853	101,430,600	63,072,600	62.18
1854	70,872,000	39,421,600	55.62
1855	103,606,200	67,616,000	65.26
1856	99,564,600	68,322,800	68.62

Table 5.4 *continued*

Year	Output (clean rice)	Exports (clean rice)	Export/output ratio (percent)
1857	108,243,600	58,122,200	53.70
1858	116,293,200	77,070,400	66.27
1859	187,167,032	81,632,600	43.61
1860	105,279,200	43,512,400	41.33

Source: U.S. Department of Agriculture, Bureau of Statistics, *Rice Crop of the United States 1712-1911*, by George K. Holmes, Circular No. 34 (Washington, D.C., 1912), 7–9. The figure above for output in 1849 differs from the figure given in the *Seventh Census of the United States, 1850* because the figure given for clean rice in the census is actually for rough rice. See J.D.B. De Bow, *Statistical View of the United States . . . Being a Compendium of the Seventh Census* (Washington, D.C., 1854), 170, 173–74. I would like to thank Robert E. Gallman for bringing this to my attention. In estimating clean rice production for 1849, I assumed that 45 pounds of rough rice were equal to 30 pounds of clean rice.

Table 5.5. U.S. rice exports by destination, 1730–1739, 1790–1799, 1830–1839, and 1850–1859

	1730–39	1790–99	1830–39	1850–59
Total exports (tons)	104,696	324,115	368,195	311,975
Destination (% of total)				
Northern Europe	77.4	64.2	53.8	48.6
Southern Europe	17.6	8.2	2.1	0.9
North America		0.7	1.8	1.9
West Indies and Central America	5.0	25.6	40.8	36.3
South America	0	0	1.1	11.3
Africa	0	0.9	0.2	0.5
Asia	0	0.1	0.1	0.4
Uncertain	0	0.3	0	0
Total	100	100	99.9	99.9

Source: U.S. Department of Commerce, Bureau of the Census, *Historical Statistics of the United States: Colonial Times to 1970*, 2 vols. (Washington, D.C., 1975), 2:1192; James Glen, *A Description of South Carolina . . .* (London, 1761), 93; Converse D. Clowse, *Measuring Charleston's Overseas Commerce, 1717-1767: Statistics from the Port's Naval List* (Washington, D.C., 1981), 59–64; *American State Papers . . . , Class IV: Commerce and Navigation*, vol. 7 (Washington, D.C., 1832), 32, 122, 235, 284, 308, 339, 359, 381, 414, 428; *U.S. House of Representatives Executive Documents, Second Session, 21st Congress, no. 209, vol. 4; U.S. House of Representatives Executive Documents, First Session, 22d Congress, no. 220, vol. 5; U.S. House of Representatives Executive Documents, Second Session, 22d Congress, no. 234, vol. 2; U.S. House of Representatives Executive Documents, First Session, 23d Congress, no. 258, vol. 5; U.S. House of Representatives Executive Documents, Second Session, 23d Congress, no. 275, vol. 5; U.S. House of Representatives Executive Documents, First Session, 24th Congress, no. 291, vol. 6; U.S. House of Representatives Executive Documents, Second Session, 24th Congress, no. 304, vol. 4; U.S. House of Representatives Executive Documents, Second Session, 25th Congress, no. 330, vol. 10; U.S. House of Representatives Executive Documents, Third Session, 25th Congress, no. 349, vol. 6; U.S. House of Representatives Executive Documents, First Session, 26th Congress, no. 369, vol. 7; U.S. House of Representatives Executive Documents, Second Session, 31st Congress, no. 604, vol. 8; U.S. Senate Executive Documents, First Session,*

Table 5.5 *continued*

32d Congress, no. 628, vol. 16; U.S. Senate Executive Documents, Second Session, 32d Congress, no. 662, vol. 5; U.S. Senate Executive Documents, First Session, 33d Congress, no. 703, vol. 12, Part 2; U.S. Senate Executive Documents, Second Session, 33d Congress, no. 865, vol. 16; U.S. Senate Executive Documents, Second Session, 33d Congress, no. 750, vol. 5; U.S. House of Representatives Executive Documents, First Session, 34th Congress, no. 865, vol. 16; U.S. Senate Executive Documents, Third Session, 34th Congress, no. 886, vol. 13; U.S. Senate Executive Documents, First Session, 35th Congress, no. 931, vol. 14; U.S. Senate Executive Documents, Second Session, 35th Congress, no. 989, vol. 15; U.S. Senate Executive Documents, First Session, 36th Congress, no. 1034, vol. 2.

Note that the broad geographic units listed in the table should be considered final rather than intermediate destinations for the most part. The figures for the 1730s required some manipulation. According to Glen, 6 percent of total rice exports was consumed in Great Britain, Ireland, and the British Plantations. Data in Clowse and Coclanis indicate that very little was consumed in Great Britain or Ireland during this period. Thus I estimated that 5 percent of total exports went to the British Plantations and 1 percent to Great Britain and Ireland. See Clowse, *Measuring Charleston's Overseas Commerce, 1717–1767*, 59–64; Peter A. Coclanis, "Bitter Harvest: The South Carolina Low Country in Historical Perspective," *Journal of Economic History* 45 (June 1985): 251–59, esp. 254. Also note that in converting antebellum data into tons, I assumed that 1 tierce was equal to 600 pounds.

On one level, the answer is simple: Southeast Asia rose to prominence as a supply source for the West because it could outcompete other rice-producing areas. But why? This question is impossible to answer categorically, but I can offer some suggestive possibilities. As Marx pointed out long ago, "windfalls" often resulted from the effective linkage of precapitalist, noncapitalist, or "natural" economies to that of the West, and such a linkage did in fact occur in Bengal, Java, and Lower Burma in the nineteenth century. Land and labor in these areas were amazingly cheap by Western standards; indeed, as in other cases of "articulation" between peasant and commercial economies, family labor in producing households was often completely unremunerated.[25]

In agro-climatic terms, this area was almost perfectly suited for rice production, and the fertility of Southeast Asian rice paddies has long been marveled at. Although the reasons for such fertility are still incompletely understood, most researchers today believe that the nitrogen-fixing effects of symbiosis between certain life forms present in the area—ferns of the genus *Azolla* and the blue-green alga *Anabaena azollae*—are crucial.[26]

Given these considerations, it is understandable that Westerners looked favorably on Southeast Asia as a source of supply. Such favor seems even more understandable in light of other factors: first, because the indigenous populations already were experienced and relatively efficient rice producers. Unlike the cases of cotton and tobacco, two other crops grown in both temperate and tropical countries, rice production in Southeast Asia was not necessarily marked by low relative productivity. As John Komlos and I have shown elsewhere, for example, the total factor productivity of Burmese peasant producers, measured in standard Cobb-Douglas form, was roughly on a par with that of slave laborers on South Carolina and Georgia rice plantations.[27] Even under stringent neoclassical assumptions, then, Burmese rice producers were competitive with U.S. producers in the nineteenth century. W. Arthur

Lewis was probably correct in citing low productivity as the main reason for the inability of tropical producers to compete with the United States in cotton and tobacco. The stunning success of Southeast Asia in world rice markets—as Lewis himself noted—may well have been the exception that proves the rule.[28]

Another factor—power—also came into play, which could only enhance both the relative competitiveness and the attractiveness of Southeast Asia vis-à-vis other potential supply sources, particularly in more developed parts of the world. In the nineteenth century, extra-economic suasion, that is to say, European political and military power, could be and often was projected forcefully in Southeast Asia, shoring up and in some cases shaping economic choices being made along the muddy banks of the Irrawaddy and on the terraces of Kedjawèn. The administrative, fiscal, and tariff innovations introduced into Southeast Asia by the European powers—innovations described at length in the rich work of James C. Scott—offer cases in point.[29]

Other factors were at work as well. Technological and organizational improvements in transoceanic shipping along with the *Pax Britannica* lowered the cost of carriage and insurance, and the coincident development of Australia and California—development spurred by the discovery of gold in both areas between 1849 and 1851—assured that numerous vessels returning to Europe from the Pacific would be interested in a bulky backhaul like rice. The customs preferences accorded colonial produce added further encouragement, if any was needed, but with or without such preferences East Indian rice could undersell higher-quality Western rice anywhere in Europe. Given the foregoing considerations, the prevailing uses made of rice at this time, and the groups for whom the cereal generally was intended, it is in no way surprising that the European market responded less to North American quality than to East Indian price.[30]

So intense was this pressure from the East that as early as the 1830s rice from this area was being sold in Western producing regions such as Italy and even South Carolina for less than homegrown rice. In the 1830s and 1840s, some Western producers—Portugal and the United States, for example—raised tariffs on imported rice, in the case of Portugal by roughly 1,000 percent. Although the United States was able to stave off East Indian competition for a time, the penetration of East Indian rice into Europe was not turned back. Rather, it accelerated sharply as time passed. As a result of both the dislocations in the U.S. industry occasioned by the Civil War and, perhaps more important, the decline in transportation costs occasioned by the rise of steam shipping and the opening of the Suez Canal, East Indian rice poured into Europe in the late nineteenth century, as illustrated by the figures in tables 5.6 and 5.7. Exports to Europe from Lower Burma alone, for instance, averaged 682,000 tons of clean rice equivalents annually between 1881 and 1890, which figure exceeded total rice production in the United States for the entire decade of the 1880s, or the decade of the 1850s, for that matter. Other transportation and communications improvements—steelhull shipping, compound and triple-expansion steam engines, and the laying of submarine telegraph cable between Europe and Southeast Asia—the rise of other

Table 5.6. Exports of rice from Bengal to the West, 1861–1862 to 1872–1873 (tons)

Year	Exports to the West	Total foreign exports	Exports to West as percentage of total
1861–62	129,655	341,198	38.00
1862–63	72,139	407,793	17.69
1863–64	53,345	388,814	13.72
1864–65	26,344	403,432	6.53
1865–66	32,559	255,167	12.76
1866–67*	24,054	160,357	15.40
1867–68	110,810	268,892	41.21
1868–69	57,485	254,244	22.61
1869–70	40,433	190,093	21.27
1870–71	65,588	244,916	26.78
1871–72	77,158	252,812	30.52
1872–73	89,687	355,054	25.26
	779,257	3,522,772	22.12

*eleven months

Disaggregated exports to the West as percent of total exports

Year	United Kingdom	France	Germany	North and South America	West Indies	Western Total
1861–62	24.09	4.56	2.04	5.46	1.85	38.00
1862–63	11.39	1.19	1.21	2.62	1.28	17.69
1863–64	9.39	0.70	0.35	2.12	1.16	13.72
1864–65	2.46	0.26	0.12	1.85	1.84	6.53
1865–66	8.40	0.15		0.47	3.74	12.76
1866–67*	7.89	0.30			7.21	15.40
1867–68	32.59	0.80	0.90	0.03	6.89	41.21
1868–69	16.57	0.56		0.73	4.75	22.61
1869–70	10.68	1.39		1.73	7.47	21.27
1870–71	18.43	0.65	0.18		7.52	26.78
1871–72	21.15	0.47	0.17	0.53	8.20	30.52
1872–73	15.61	0.02		1.49	8.14	25.26

*eleven months

Source: H.J.S. Cotton, "The Rice Trade of the World," *Calcutta Review* 58 (1874): 267–302, esp. 274–75. For detailed figures on Indian rice exports to the West between 1877 and 1915, see Sir William Wilson Hunter, *The Indian Empire: Its Peoples, History, and Products*, 3d ed. (London, 1893), 686; Imperial Institute, Indian Trade Enquiry, *Reports on Rice* (London, 1920), 8, 36–38.

Table 5.7. Mean yearly rice exports from Burma, Siam, and Cochinchina, 1872–1881 to 1902–1911 (thousands of metric tons)

	Burma		Siam		
	Asia	Other	Asia	Other	
1872–1881	204	703	161	37	
1882–1891	281	814	268	61	
1892–1901	783	862	519	53	
1902–1911	1,277	1,134	855	99	
	Cochinchina		Totals		
	Asia	Other	Asia	Other	Total
1872–1881	292	23	657	763	1,420
1882–1891	459	37	1,008	912	1,920
1892–1901	482	164	1,784	1,079	2,863
1902–1911	572	221	2,704	1,454	4,158

Source: Randolph Barker, et al., *The Rice Economy of Asia*, 2 vols. (Washington, D.C., 1985), 1:187. In order to correct for a minor computational error, I have adjusted Barker's total export figure for 1892–1901. The data above are based on material collected in Norman G. Owen, "The Rice Industry of Mainland Southeast Asia, 1850–1914," *Journal of the Siam Society* 59 (July 1971): 75–143, especially table II-A.

exporters such as Siam and Cochinchina, and the establishment of a rice futures market in Rangoon contributed further to the onslaught as the century drew to a close.[31]

Nor was Europe the only area swamped by East Indian rice in the late nineteenth century, a period in which commodity markets were being rapidly integrated throughout the world. Thus the United States, once the West's great rice exporter, became a major importer in this period and remained so until well into the twentieth century, as table 5.8 demonstrates. This occurred despite increased duties imposed on imported rice. In other parts of the world, a similar pattern of rising imports from the East prevailed as well. One should note, too, that the rice trade within Asia itself grew substantially in the period, partly as a result, ironically, of the need to feed laborers working mines and plantations established by Western interests in places such as Sumatra, Java, Malaya, and Ceylon.[32]

The economic effects of integration did not end once Asian rice passed through Western customs gates. In the United States, the reality of international competition underpinned and reinforced a geographic shift—see table 5.9—in domestic rice production from the South Atlantic region to the Old Southwest, to Louisiana, Arkansas, and Texas specifically. Rice cultivation in South Carolina and Georgia was intensive in nature, and numerous problems militated against the successful continuation of

Table 5.8. Rice imports to and exports from the United States, 1872–1911 (millions of pounds)

	Imports		Exports	
Year (ending June 30)	Rice	Rice flour, rice meal, and broken rice[a]	Rice	Rice bran, meal, and polish[b]
1872	74.6	—	0.4	—
1873	83.8	—	0.3	—
1874	73.3	—	0.6	—
1875	59.4	—	0.3	—
1876	71.6	—	0.4	—
1877	64.0	—	1.3	—
1878	47.5	—	0.6	—
1879	75.8	—	0.7	—
1880	57.0	—	0.2	—
1881	68.7	—	0.2	—
1882	79.4	—	0.1	—
1883	96.7	—	0.1	—
1884	106.6	—	0.2	—
1885	81.1	38.0	0.2	—
1886	60.1	37.5	0.3	—
1887	56.0	47.9	0.6	—
1888	100.8	54.8	0.4	—
1889	132.2	54.1	0.4	—
1890	68.4	55.7	0.4	—
1891	133.1	81.3	0.3	—
1892	85.1	63.0	—[c]	10.3
1893	81.1	66.5	0.8	13.0
1894	86.8	55.4	0.8	10.0
1895	141.3	78.3	0.1	1.5
1896	78.2	68.5	1.3[d]	13.7
1897	133.9	63.9	0.4	3.5
1898	129.8	60.5	0.6	5.6
1899	153.8	50.3	0.9	14.5
1900	93.6	23.0	12.9	28.1
1901	74.6	42.6	1.1	24.4
1902	75.7	82.0	0.6	29.0
1903	78.3	91.3	0.5	19.2
1904	75.3	78.9	2.4	26.7

Table 5.8 *continued*

Year (ending June 30)	Imports: Rice	Imports: Rice flour, rice meal, and broken rice[a]	Exports: Rice	Exports: Rice bran, meal, and polish[b]
1905	43.4	63.1	74.9	38.4
1906	58.5	108.1	4.0	34.2
1907	71.3	138.3	2.4	27.7
1908	87.6	125.2	2.2	26.2
1909	88.8	134.1	1.6	18.9
1910	82.7	142.7	7.0	19.7
1911	76.7	132.1	15.6	14.5

Source: U.S. Department of the Treasury, *Statistical Abstract of the United States, 1881, Fourth Number* (New York, 1964), 74–75, 97; U.S. Department of the Treasury, *Statistical Abstract of the United States, 1891, Fourteenth Number* (New York, 1964), 131, 136, 158; U.S. Department of the Treasury, *Statistical Abstract of the United States, 1901, Twenty-Fourth Number* (Washington, D.C., 1902), 192, 220; U.S. Department of Commerce, *Statistical Abstract of the United States, 1911, Thirty-Fourth Number* (Washington, D.C., 1912), 421, 455. Note that after June 30, 1900, commerce with Puerto Rico and Hawaii is not included in the foreign commerce of the United States. George K. Holmes, however, includes these areas in his calculations of U.S. rice imports and exports between 1901 and 1911. See U.S. Department of Agriculture, Bureau of Statistics, *Rice Crop of the United States, 1712–1911*, by George K. Holmes, Circular 34 (Washington, D.C., 1912). Note, too, that the United States first becomes a net importer in 1861.

Notes: [a]first stated 1885; [b]first stated 1892; [c]included in "Rice Bran, Meal, and Polish"; [d]896,000 pounds damaged.

Table 5.9. Rice production in the United States, 1839–1919 (millions of pounds of clean rice)

	1839	1849	1859	1869	1879	1889	1899	1909	1919
Total production	80.8	143.6	187.2	73.6	110.1	128.6	250.3	658.4	1065.2
Primary production states									
South Carolina	75.0	74.3	63.6	43.9	47.3	23.6	18.9	2.5	0.4
Georgia	15.3	18.1	28.0	30.2	23.0	11.3	4.5	0.7	0.2
North Carolina	3.5	2.5	4.1	2.8	5.1	4.6	3.2	0.0	0.0
Louisiana	4.5	2.0	3.4	21.5	21.1	58.8	69.0	49.6	45.3
Texas	0	0	0	0.1	0.1	0.1	2.9	41.2	15.0
Arkansas	0	0	0	0.1	0	0	0.0	5.9	19.2
California	0	0	0	0	0	0	0.0	0.0	19.6

Source: Peter A. Coclanis, "Economy and Society in the Early Modern South: Charleston and the Evolution of the South Carolina Low Country" (Ph.D. diss., Columbia University, 1984), 387–97. The above figure for clean rice in 1849 differs from the figure given in the *Seventh Census of the United States, 1850* because the figure given for clean rice in the census is actually for rough rice. See J.D.B. De Bow, *Statistical View of the United States . . . Being a Compendium of the Seventh Census* (Washington, D.C., 1854), 170, 173–74. For an explanation of the figure for 1849, see table 5.4 sources.

this type of cultivation in the postbellum period. Given such problems—a list of which would include damage done to production facilities during the war, the reduction in the labor participation rate after Appomattox and the concomitant breakdown in labor discipline, the severe shortage of capital in the area, and the long-term declines in both soil fertility and total factor productivity along the coastal plain—it is apparent why production shifted in relative terms toward the southwestern states, where many of these problems were less serious.[33]

Not only was cheap, fertile, readily irrigable land available in Louisiana, Arkansas, and Texas, but, after the so-called rice revolution of the mid-1880s, more rational, extensive cultivation techniques were successfully implemented in this region. Such techniques, which were based on the employment of midwestern small-grain technology, rationalized production and allowed for the achievement (once again) of economies of scale in the U.S. rice industry. At the same time, the relative importance of scarce, unruly labor in the production process was reduced. Even though these techniques proved unworkable in South Carolina and Georgia, they clearly enabled producers in the Southwest—and later in California—to persevere, at times even to thrive in the (rapidly expanding) domestic market despite competition from the Far East.[34] In essence, then, what occurred with the migration of the industry to the Old Southwest was a shift in U.S. rice supply, the main determinants of which were greater international competition, rising labor costs, and technological change.

One cannot stress too strongly that it is misleading to attribute the decline of the South Atlantic rice industry solely, or even primarily, to dislocations occasioned by the Civil War. For generations, American scholars have sought to explain the changing configuration of the domestic rice industry solely in such terms. By broadening the geographical and analytical context within which we view the industry, we can at once avoid the *post hoc* fallacy and lessen the parochialism and myopia that, with a few notable exceptions, has characterized scholarship in the field. If the freedman's cry "no more mud work" explains certain things about the evolution—and migration—of the U.S. rice industry in the nineteenth century, it does not explain everything.[35] U.S. rice exports had been stagnant since the 1790s, domestic producers were being edged out of the most important foreign markets by the 1830s, considerable quantities of rice were being shipped to the U.S. from Java by 1855, and U.S. interests had established the first steampowered rice mill in Siam by 1858.[36] In other words, market expansion, elaboration, and integration, and not just Lincoln, swamp angels, and Sherman's General Order No. 15 shaped the U.S. rice industry in the nineteenth century. We already have looked at the expansion and elaboration of world rice markets. Let us now turn to the problem of integration.

Perhaps the best test of market integration is the degree of price uniformity existing over a particular area at a given time. It is difficult, however, to speak with complete confidence about historical commodity prices anywhere in the world. International comparisons of such prices are more difficult still for a variety of reasons, including differential grading practices, fluctuating exchange rates, tiered pricing schemes, and complex and often bewildering tariff policies. Moreover, in the case of rice, we are not even altogether clear about the bases on which prices historically were determined, for we often lack systematic data on such matters as the local prices of other relevant commodities and the supply of shipping available at any given time in the major rice ports. This said, it seems reasonable to suggest from extant data that the basic tendency over time was toward uniformity in world rice prices and thus toward the creation of one integrated market. This tendency was uneven and incomplete even on the eve of World War I; but over the course of the one hundred-year period after the so-called long eighteenth century ended in 1815, the basic pattern is unmistakable.[37]

This point is illustrated in figure 5.1, which plots export prices, converted into pounds sterling, for U.S., Burmese, and Bengali rice. Correlation analysis demonstrates the trend toward integration as well: a correlation relating U.S. export prices and Burmese export prices (for cargoes to arrive in London) reveals that the association between these prices, as measured by the Pearson correlation coefficient, is both positive and statistically significant for the 1868–1910 period. To be sure, an r of 0.5 is only moderately strong, but the results are highly significant. Other interesting results emerge from analysis of the subperiod data. In only one subperiod, encompassing the years between 1882 and 1895, was there a strong and statistically significant association between the two series. This was precisely the period in which the U.S. rice industry was being transformed by the "rice revolution" in southwestern Louisiana. Furthermore, while it appears at first glance that the correlation results are weak and insignificant for the 1896–1910 subperiod, such results may have more to do with currency fluctuations in the United States than with anything else. This is suggested in figure 5.2, which plots real rice prices—nominal prices deflated by indexed wholesale prices—over time. In real terms, the trend in U.S. prices during the last subperiod seems consistent with the overall trend established in figure 5.1.

What about the relationship, noted earlier, between rice and wheat? For much of the eighteenth and nineteenth centuries, rice prices in the West seemed to move in rough tandem with prices for wheat and other small grains. This pattern continued in the late nineteenth century; but rice, which had often been more expensive than rye, barley, oats, and even wheat in northern European markets, generally became cheaper than these small grains, thanks largely to innovations in transportation and distribution and to the relative rise of shipments from the East.[38]

One final point about price behavior in this increasingly integrated market for agricultural commodities: whereas some other agricultural commodities—cotton and sugar, for example—exhibited extreme price volatility in the West during this period, rice prices generally remained low and displayed less volatility. This was probably due not only to the fact that rice had numerous substitutes in many areas but

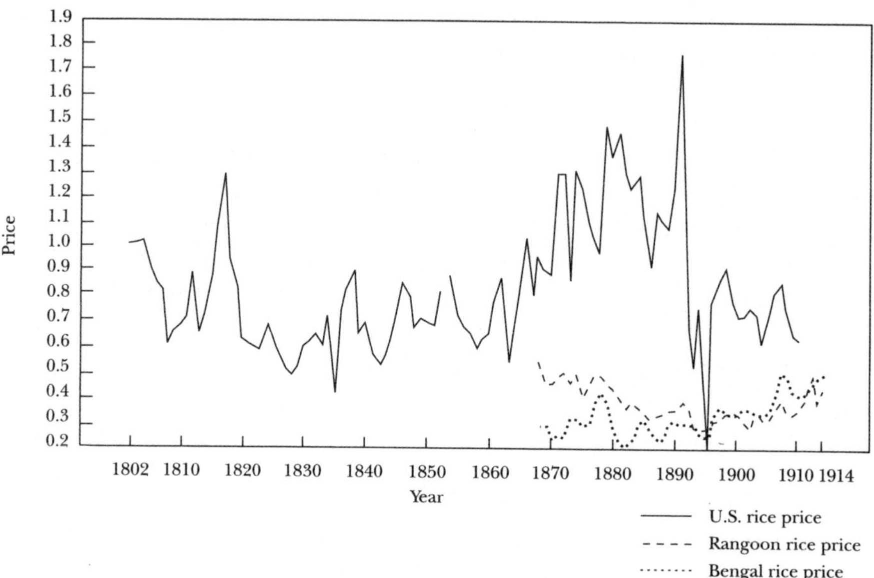

Figure 5.1: Rice Prices in Pounds Sterling (per cwt.). Sources: U.S. Department of Agriculture, Bureau of Statistics, *Rice Crop of the United States, 1712-1911,* Circular 34, by George K. Holmes (Washington, D.C., 1912), 7–10; A. J. H. Latham and Larry Neal, "The International Market in Rice and Wheat, 1868–1914," *Economic History Review,* 2d ser., 36 (May 1983): 260–80, esp. 276–77. In converting prices from dollars to sterling, I relied on series constructed by Lawrence H. Officer. See Officer, "Dollar-Sterling Mint Parity and Exchange Rates, 1791–1834," *Journal of Economic History* 43 (September 1983): 579–616; Officer, "Integration in the American Foreign-Exchange Market, 1791–1900," *Journal of Economic History* 45 (September 1985): 557–85. Note that in converting greenback prices to gold prices for the period between 1862 and 1878, I relied on Wesley C. Mitchell, *Gold, Prices and Wages under the Greenback Standard* (Berkeley, Calif., 1908), 4, table 1.

to the fact that the supply of rice from Southeast Asia was sufficiently elastic to dampen the possible effects of any changes in demand.[39]

The geographic shift of the U.S. rice industry, then, can be attributed in large part to the expansion, elaboration, and integration of the world rice market. But the evolution of this market had other effects as well, some of which we are still unable to appreciate in full. On the demand side, for example, rice helped at once to ensure and enrich the lives of Western consumers, as we have already seen. Whether one focuses on its role as a source of complex carbohydrates for the poor or of cellulose for industrial applications, the importance of rice is apparent.[40]

As for supply, we find that increased market integration produced a strange and somewhat ironic variant of Gunnar Myrdal's "backwash effect." Just as such integration had crushed the Indian (handicraft) textile industry, it wreaked havoc on the South Atlantic rice industry, an industry that had made that region extremely wealthy

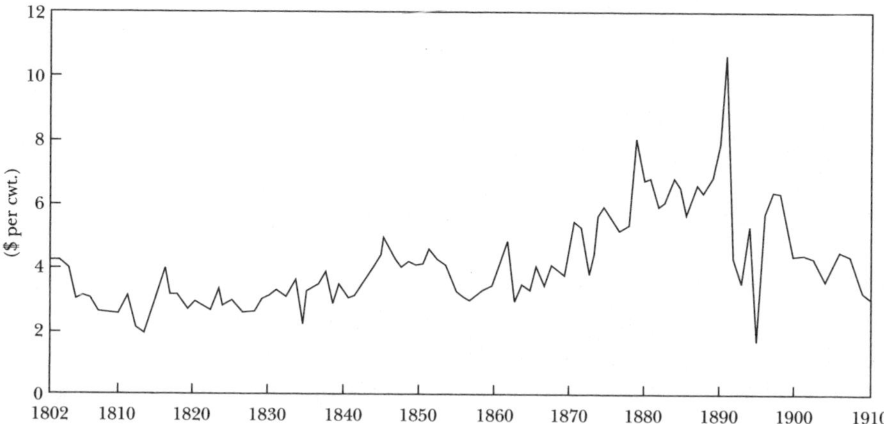

Figure 5.2: The Real Price of U.S. Rice, 1802–1910 (1910–1914 Dollars). Sources: U.S. Department of Agriculture, Bureau of Statistics, *Rice Crop of the United States, 1712-1911,* Circular 34, by George K. Holmes (Washington, D.C., 1912), 7–10; U.S. Department of Commerce, Bureau of the Census, *Historical Statistics of the United States: Colonial Times to 1970,* 2 vols. (Washington, D.C., 1975), 1:200–202. Note that in employing the Warren-Pearson and BLS wholesale price indexes, I re-indexed the latter to the same base as the former: 1910–1914 = 100).

when world markets had been less integrated in the eighteenth and early nineteenth centuries. Thus this region, suited for little else but rice, experienced relative decline in the antebellum period and absolute economic decline at least between 1860 and 1880 and probably even longer. By 1910 the region's rice industry had collapsed, and the South Carolina–Georgia low country had become one of the poorest parts of the poorest census region in the United States. It has remained uncommonly poor by the standards of the developed world for most of the twentieth century.[41]

Elsewhere in the West, the Italian rice industry, bolstered by unification and other institutional changes, not only survived the challenge of integration but grew substantially between 1861 and World War I. Recent work suggests that northern Italy's agricultural sector as a whole performed fairly well during this period, especially after 1896, contributing to the area's industrialization. By this time, however, rice exports from Italy and from other Western producing areas such as Spain were tiny in comparison to those from the East.[42] Let us therefore turn to the main centers of exportation.

Here the record is mixed and more complicated than either neoclassical or neo-Marxist models can readily accommodate. Even in light of the recent spate of revisionist works on South and Southeast Asia, few would argue that the position of peasant producers in Bengal or Java improved dramatically in the short run with the integration of world rice markets. Limited data suggest, however, that per capita income in these areas did rise somewhat after integration, and this rise can plausibly be explained in terms of either vent-for-surplus models or the standard theory of comparative advantage.[43] It seems likely, moreover, that the British-inspired transformation of the Burmese delta from a frontier into the greatest rice-exporting area in the world also raised the incomes of Burmese cultivators, at least between roughly 1855 and 1900. After that time, things began to change, and by the 1920s most of the income gains had been taken back. But that is another story, because, by that time, the closing of this frontier, problems relating to tenancy and agricultural credit, and Western developments in mechanization and genetic plant-breeding had begun to affect comparative advantage in new and profound ways.[44] The Burmese scenario seems to hold true, more or less, for Siam and Indochina as well, even though in Siam tenancy problems were never as severe as they became in Burma, and in Indochina peasants exported not only rice but also considerable quantities of copra and maize.[45]

As should be obvious by now, historians still lack information vital for a complete understanding of the effects of market integration on Southeast Asia. The effects resulting from the intersection in the late nineteenth century of gold-based Western economies and silver-based Eastern economies, for example, have not yet been adequately explored. Few have followed up Jonathan Levin's important point about the distribution of income gains derived from the export sectors of Southeast Asian economies: how many of these gains went to what he calls "foreign factors" and "luxury importers" rather than to the peasant cultivators themselves? Indeed, we are not even sure about the mechanisms by which peasants entered into market relations. Did they willingly embrace them, or were they unwittingly ensnared? The still unresolved Scott-Popkin controversy on peasant attitudes comes readily to mind in this regard. Clearly, there is much more to learn about the origins and early effects of integration. I hope at least to have initiated an instructive discussion.[46]

How, then, do we end an introduction to the international history of the Western rice trade? We could, for example, close with a vignette intended to underscore the importance of the Arabs' early transfer of *O. sativa* to the West. Or with one about the so-called seed from Madagascar—sent by the treasurer of the English East India Company—that allegedly begat the North American rice industry. Or even with one about *japonica* rices and their significance in the Old Southwest in the twentieth century. Each of these alternatives would illustrate the interrelationship between East and West, as in a vague but powerful way do the epigraphs with which I began.[47]

As a student of the South Atlantic rice industry primarily, I prefer, however, to end by alluding to war, for as every schoolchild knows, nothing hurt the competitive position of South Carolina and Georgia rice planters in the mid-nineteenth century as much as war and the aftermath of war. I will conclude, then, with a passing reference to the Second Anglo-Burmese War (1852), which in opening up the Burma Delta to the West changed the course of southern history.[48] As every schoolchild knows.

6

The Revolution from Above

The National Market and the Beginnings of Industrialization in North Carolina

DAVID L. CARLTON

The following essay was originally published in September 1990, and grew out of an old quarrel with what is sometimes termed the "Prussian Road" school of interpreting postbellum southern society. While the major figures of this school diverged in numerous particulars, they were united in seeing the region continuing to be ruled by what they described as a persistent "planter elite," whose interests and power defined southern economic development—either by condemning the region to persistent underdevelopment, or treating it to a sort of forced-march industrialization, a "revolution from above" similar to that which has often been found in Wilhelmine Germany or Meiji Japan. Carlton's own earlier studies of South Carolina industrialists left him deeply dissatisfied with this view; his people looked far more like George Babbitt than John Sartoris. Yet the "Prussian Road" historians pointed to features of the industrial South that needed to be understood. The following is an effort to construct a different framework for understanding the peculiarities of southern industrialization as a response of very *American* businessmen to a set of peculiar environmental constraints.

Over a century after Henry W. Grady proclaimed the advent of a "New South," it is now safe to term the region "industrialized." Few southerners today live on farms or work in agriculture; indeed, in certain southern states workers rely far more heavily on factory jobs than do their counterparts elsewhere in the Union. Thanks largely to this shift, regional economic welfare has improved significantly; from a level of per capita income roughly half that of the nation as late as the 1930s, the states of the old Confederacy reached about 85 percent of parity by 1973. In many cases—notably in the high-tech complexes of Texas, Florida, Atlanta, and North Carolina's

Research Triangle—southern industrial and technological attainments have been truly impressive. The temptation is strong to herald the elimination of yet another unhappy source of southern distinctiveness, widespread poverty in a land of plenty.

Despite the unmistakable signs of industrial progress, the region's economic problems are far from vanquished. Since 1973 the advance toward national levels of per capita income in the southeast has effectively halted. While pockets such as Atlanta thrive, much of the region is beset with sick industries, and the economies of such states as Mississippi have actually lost relative ground.[1]

The heritage of a staple-producing plantation slave society, disrupted by war and social upheaval and stranded by the shifting currents of world demand for its products, has had much to do with this. However, many of the South's modern troubles stem from the very nature of the region's industrial order. Southern industrial society, after all, has never really matched the prevailing image of an industrial society. Its manufacturing has never built great cities; its factories have relied heavily on low-wage labor; its workers have been the least unionized in the nation; and its state governments have been the most laggard in regulating industry, in providing social welfare services, and in developing the region's human capital.[2]

The paradoxes ingrained in southern industrial society have recently attracted renewed attention from social scientists of several stripes. While reaching divergent conclusions, many of those scholars begin from the same proposition, that the enduring distinctiveness of the region stems from a fundamental continuity in its social structure. They regard the features of the present-day southern industrial order as the fruits of a "revolution from above." Underpinning their larger argument are two closely linked contentions. First, they argue that an antebellum elite rooted in the social relations of the slave plantation continued its rule into the postbellum period; second, they regard the modern South as the more or less purposeful creation of that elite. Southern industry is decentralized, then, because a ruling class of agrarian background has been fearful of the destabilizing effects of cities. Southern workers are paid low wages because southern employers have not wanted to pay high wages, and because they have deliberately kept high-wage industry out of the region. Unions have failed to make headway because they have been ruthlessly repressed by reactionary regimes and private goon squads. Southern state governments have been niggardly and probusiness because they have been dominated by narrowly based oligarchies.[3]

The "continuitarian" approach (C. Vann Woodward's term) has had a salutary impact on our historical understanding, because it has forced us to rethink the distinctions between Old South and New, and to recognize the sometimes surprising ways in which the past has shaped modern southern life. Its seeming simplicity and comprehensiveness, however, mask fundamental weaknesses in its two basic propositions. With regard to the first, it assumes that continuity in personnel from the Old South to the New signifies continuity in class identity. But even if one grants the persistence of an antebellum elite, that elite operated in sometimes strikingly new ways that reflected important alterations in the foundations of its power. As Gavin Wright and others have argued, the loss of capital and of control over labor entailed by emancipation, the spread of commercial agriculture to the upcountry, and the expansion of interior trade directed entrepreneurial energies away from the extension of the plantation and toward more intensive forms of economic development. As enterprising southerners increasingly congregated in towns, they turned to industrialization as the most efficacious and stable means of expanding the local economy on which they relied. The appearance on the scene of these town-based entrepreneurs, particularly in the Carolina Piedmont, was a major new development in southern history, generating factories, a modern infrastructure, and an increasingly complex web of social and economic institutions.[4]

In this structural sense, then, it can be said that a "new class," if not "new men," gained power in the years after Appomattox and began to lead the South in a new direction. But while the social and personal characteristics of the new southern "bourgeoisie" were important in shaping the new industrial order, that order can hardly be understood, as the second proposition would have it, primarily as the product of class purposes. Emergent southern capitalists pursued their goals in a context that constrained and channeled their pursuits in important ways.

If southern industrialists failed to inherit the mentalité of their planter predecessors, they nonetheless had to grapple with the structural disabilities bequeathed the region by its plantation past. With an economy highly specialized in export agriculture and extractive industry, dependent primarily on routinized, forced labor, the antebellum South developed thin and poorly articulated internal markets for manufactured goods. As a result, it not only suffered from a "deplorable scarcity" of manufacturing but failed to develop the urban communities of skilled workers and entrepreneurs appearing in the contemporary Midwest. Thus the region entered the postbellum era not only impoverished but also lacking the basic human capital stock it needed to develop a diverse, dynamic manufacturing sector.[5]

Members of the "new class" of townspeople were handicapped not only by their heritage but also by their limited ability to shape the larger market system in which they were enmeshed. Recent scholarship has explored the first handicap, but it has given less attention to the latter crucial limitation. As a class of businessmen, and small businessmen at that, southern industrialists operated within a vast network of relationships stretching far beyond their localities, a network that critically constrained their opportunities to pursue development.[6] This point is especially important because the post–Civil War period saw a major alteration in those relationships, an alteration so profound as to render the postbellum industrialization of the region fundamentally different from the limited antebellum industrialization. The late-nineteenth-century industrial surge in the South was an aspect of a much larger development, the increasing integration of localities into an emerging national market. Within a generation the still-fragmented transportation system of 1860 was knit into a cohesive network, the flow of goods around the country lubricated by interchanging boxcars, uniform bills of lading, and a simultaneously arising commmunications system. The new network allowed local industrialists to market their products nationally. Moreover, by facilitating mass production for mass markets, it encouraged the concentration of economic activity, and thus of population, in the burgeoning cities of the Northeast and Midwest, creating readily accessible urban markets that further reduced the barriers between producers and their customers.[7]

The new national markets offered local manufacturers major new opportunities, but they also presented them with important new problems. Here the theory of "unbalanced growth," as formulated by Gunnar Myrdal and Albert O. Hirschman in the 1950s, becomes relevant. Originating as a critique of the neoclassical argument that unencumbered market activity will "balance out" disparities between rich and poor regions, ultimately "developing" the entire world, the "unbalanced growth" approach contends that under certain circumstances the free play of market forces can actually *reinforce* disparities among regions and nations. The early development of a "core" region endows it with capital, skills, and markets that attract yet more growth (an effect Hirschman calls "polarization") and enables the core's more efficient producers to conquer the markets of less favored regions, sweeping aside local competitors (an effect Myrdal calls "backwash"). While the balancing-out effects of free markets have their place in the theory, as "spread" (Myrdal), or "trickle- down" (Hirschman), effects, those effects are often weak and hampered by the difficulties that producers in the poorer region face in competing with those in the core. Moreover, because polarization forecloses certain business opportunities, those opened by trickle-down effects may be limited in such a way that they stimulate an internally unbalanced process of development.[8]

Such, I wish to argue, were the effects of economic nationalization on the American South. The development of national markets introduced to southern consumers relatively cheap goods from more efficient firms in the North, sweeping away many local producers previously insulated from outside competition. More important, even those producers in a position to benefit from the ready physical access to customers provided by the new railroads and urban population centers found profitable exploitation of the new markets hardly assured. They had to open channels of distribution; they had to obtain information not simply about current prices but also about long-term trends and customer preferences. Dealing on the national stage required southern manufacturers to adapt their enterprises to the market in ways unfamiliar even to the old hands among them. Thus, even though many postbellum southern industrialists may have inherited skills, capital, or elements of their social outlook from the old regime, they found themselves having to operate in a fundamentally new world. Post–Civil War southern industrialists thus faced a challenge common to "backward" regions, of pursuing development in a context defined from the outside. The product of the new environment was not so much "economic colonialism" in the sense of "outside control" as a process in which local businessmen, responding to the market signals of their time and place, launched their region on a path that proved in many ways deleterious to sound development.[9]

The best way to understand the interaction of the national market with the behavior of southern industrialists is to explore business decision making in the realm of "merchandising," as the word is used in the field of marketing: the continuing process by which product and demand are fitted to each other, involving not only sales and promotion but product planning and adjustment as well. By implication, merchandising shapes both the firm's external relations and its internal arrangements, even influencing the entrepreneurs' basic decisions about what products to make and how to go about making them.[10]

The merchandising strategies used by southern industrial entrepreneurs can thus tell us a great deal about them, and about the world in which they lived and the society they helped shape. In some cases, notably among tobacco manufacturers, the demands of merchandising in a new environment led them to develop innovative forms of enterprise, leading to successes that contributed materially to the economic progress of the region. More commonly, though, southerners' lack of appropriate skills, and the availability of well-developed merchandising institutions elsewhere, led them to pursue business trails already blazed by others, most notably by adopting the cotton textile industry. By so doing they succeeded in industrializing the South, but in the process they imposed an unbalanced industrial structure that has been inadequate to develop the region and has encouraged a dependence that continues even today to plague the South.

The effects of integration into the national market on late nineteenth-century industrialization in the South can be illustrated by looking at the evolution of manufacturing in what became the most industrial of southeastern states, North Carolina, in the last forty years of the nineteenth century. The period began inauspiciously. In 1860 Tarheels could boast value added by manufacturing (VAM) per capita of only $6.10, only a quarter of the national figure and below overall southern levels of the time.[11]

More significant for our purposes, most industry in North Carolina was of chiefly local importance. Only two of its antebellum manufacturing sectors, chemicals and tobacco, produced significantly more than domestic (in-state) markets could absorb. The state's premier export industry, constituting virtually all of the "chemical" group in tables 6.1 and 6.2, was the manufacture of tar and turpentine, which not only supplied its residents with an enduring nickname but generated over a third of its VAM on the eve of secession. Operating "orchards" and scattered distilleries throughout the vast longleaf pine forest of the coastal plain, naval stores producers were engaged in an essentially extractive industry. Ever in search of fresh trees, they drifted southward from the Albemarle region to the lower Cape Fear valley during antebellum times, shipping their product by coasting schooner to factors in New York City. Table 6.2 suggests that in 1860, 90 percent of the product left the state.[12]

The manufacture of tobacco products, almost exclusively in the form of plug and twist, was antebellum North Carolina's other heavily export-dependent industry,

Table 6.1. Percentage value added by manufacture, twenty Standard Industrial Classification (SIC) Industry Groups, United States and North Carolina, 1860 and 1900

	All industries				excluding chemicals			
	N.C.		U.S.		N.C.		U.S.	
SIC Industry	1860	1900	1860	1900	1860	1900	1860	1900
22 Textiles (includes cotton goods)	9.5	28.9	14.3	8.5	14.8	29.5	14.7	8.8
21 Tobacco	7.5	23.6	1.9	3.6	11.7	24.1	2.0	3.7
24 Lumber, wood products	13.7	20.6	9.7	7.0	21.4	21.0	10.0	7.3
20 Food	10.6	7.9	12.1	14.9	16.5	8.1	12.4	15.5
37 Transportation equipment	7.9	3.0	5.1	5.0	12.2	3.1	5.2	5.2
25 Furniture	0.8	2.2	2.4	2.1	1.3	2.2	2.5	2.2
28 Chemicals (includes tar and turpentine)	35.1	2.1	2.7	3.6				
32 Stone, clay, and glass	1.3	2.1	3.7	5.9	2.1	2.2	3.8	6.1
23 Apparel	0.2	1.9	7.8	9.3	0.3	2.0	8.0	9.6
27 Printing and publishing	1.1	1.9	2.9	5.8	1.7	2.0	3.0	6.0
35 Nonelectrical machinery	1.4	1.8	6.4	8.9	2.1	1.8	6.6	9.2
31 Leather products	5.4	1.5	11.4	4.2	8.4	1.5	11.7	4.4
33 Primary metals	1.7	1.1	7.5	7.5	2.6	1.1	7.7	7.8
34 Fabricated metals	1.6	0.5	4.7	4.7	2.5	0.6	4.8	4.9
29 Coal and petroleum products	0.1	0.4	1.5	1.8	0.1	0.4	1.5	1.9
39 Miscellaneous	0.1	0.3	3.7	3.8	0.2	0.3	3.8	3.9
26 Paper	1.8		1.5	2.0	2.9		1.5	2.1
30 Rubber products			0.4	0.8			0.4	0.8
36 Electrical machinery								
38 Instruments			0.4	0.6			0.4	0.6

Source: Computed from Albert W. Niemi, Jr., *State and Regional Patterns in American Manufacturing, 1860–1900* (Westport, Conn., 1974), 7, 117, 123. Industries are grouped into numbered categories according to the Standard Industrial Classification system; the industry numbers appear in the left hand column. The categories are coarse; tar and turpentine manufacturing is aggregated into the chemicals group, and cotton goods into the textiles group. The aggregation compensates for the comparability problems posed by shifting census categories. See ibid., ix–x, 105–11.

Table 6.2. Export orientation of North Carolina industry, 1860 and 1900

SIC	Industry	1860 Percent of product exported	1860 Percent of estimated in-state market	1900 Percent of product exported	1900 Percent of estimated in-state market
21	Tobacco	67.6	309.1	84.1	628.1
22	Textiles (includes cotton goods)		52.1	69.0	322.9
24	Lumber and wood products	10.8	112.1	64.3	280.0
25	Furniture		27.2		98.3
37	Transportation equipment	18.7	123.0		57.8
28	Chemicals (includes tar and turpentine)	90.0	997.2		56.4
20	Food		69.5		50.7
32	Stone, clay, and glass		28.8		34.1
31	Leather		44.1		33.5
27	Printing and publishing		29.8		32.0
23	Apparel		1.9		19.7
29	Coal and petroleum products		38.3		19.4
35	Nonelectrical machinery		17.1		19.3
33	Primary metals		18.2		14.1
34	Fabricated metals		26.6		11.2
39	Miscellaneous		2.5		7.0
38	Instruments				2.7
26	Paper		98.7		1.7
30	Rubber products				
36	Electrical machinery				

Source: See Appendix

generating an estimated 68 percent more of its product than could be absorbed locally. (See table 6.2) Tobacco was not yet of major importance to the Tarheel economy, though. It ranked sixth among the state's industries, contributing only 7.5 percent to total VAM. Nationally, it contributed only 3 percent of the industry's VAM and was dwarfed by the Virginia industry; the total North Carolina product in 1860 was worth less than that of the city of Lynchburg, Virginia, and worth less than a quarter of Richmond's output. While the Old Dominion had by 1860 developed a city-based tobacco manufacturing complex closely tied to northeastern commission merchants, North Carolinians, most of them remote from good transportation, continued to operate small, largely rural factories, frequently as adjuncts to plantations or country stores. If they did not dispose of their product in-state, they (or their agents) set forth to the south and west to peddle from wagons or, at best, established regional relationships with jobbers and commission merchants. John H. Dalton of Iredell County hawked his wares in the Carolinas and Georgia in the 1840s; such men as R. J. Reynolds and Washington Duke commenced their careers in the same fashion.[13]

No other important industry in the North Carolina of 1860 was as unambiguously export-oriented as the naval stores and tobacco industries. A fraction of lumber production was shipped from the coast, and there may have been significant interstate trade in paper and transportation equipment, chiefly carriages and wagons. Two of the state's larger industries, food and leather and leather products, on the other hand, scarcely exported their products.[14]

Most strikingly, given the enormous attention it has received, North Carolina's antebellum textile industry seems to have been chiefly of local importance. While antebellum publicists lauded every shipment of cotton yarn or cloth to the North, and such prominent millmen as Edwin Michael Holt did some business with Philadelphia and New York, the industry as a whole hardly created a significant surplus for sale beyond the state's boundaries. Not only was North Carolina a cotton textile pygmy alongside virtually every state of the Northeast, but it was outclassed as well by such southern states as Virginia and Georgia.[15]

The primarily local character of the industry was expressed not only in its size but in the nature of its products and its modes of marketing. Much of its output consisted of coarse yarns, sold from the mill door, from wagons, or through country stores to local farmwives. Cloth was added in the course of the antebellum period, but it too was sold chiefly locally or at most regionally. Of particular importance in the domestic trade were colored goods, especially plaids, "sturdy cloth that people could use on farms and for working," which were introduced by Holt in 1853. While Holt's "Alamance Plaids" found their way into northern and western markets as well as southern ones, their chief outlet was through the South's country stores, wholesale grocers, and itinerant peddlers. Despite evidence of business relations with northern commission houses before secession, mass markets seem to have been marginal to an industry whose destiny was closely tied to the needs of southern countryfolk.[16] On the eve of the transformations of the late nineteenth century, then, North Carolinians manufactured largely for themselves, exporting chiefly the extractive products of their forests and a portion of their tobacco.

Tarheels' autarkic ways were largely the consequence of a transportation system that sealed off local markets from outside penetration and posed grave problems for anyone wishing to exploit demand in the wider nation. The bulk of the state lay behind the fall line and was thus bereft of good navigable waterways; efforts to develop plank roads in the 1850s had but a minor impact. While the beginnings of a railroad system appeared on the coastal plain by 1840, no line extended west of Raleigh until 1855–1856, when the North Carolina Railroad (NCRR) was completed from Raleigh via Greensboro to Charlotte. Although the NCRR was supplemented with a line from Salisbury to Morganton, and several smaller lines commenced construction in the late 1850s, the Piedmont's rail network was still embryonic when the Civil War broke out.[17]

The poor articulation of both the southern and the national rail networks further limited the integrative impact of the new system. Varying track gauges, and the common failure of lines to connect with each other, not only limited southern manufacturers' access to non-southern markets (and vice versa) but also inhibited the development of a true national market of any sort. In part this was deliberate, in keeping with the "territorial" strategy common to southern—and non-southern—railroads of that time. As Maury Klein has noted, antebellum railroads generally were controlled by the commercial-civic elites of their major terminal cities, who saw rail lines as means of defining and extending their own cities' hinterlands while shutting competitors out. In North Carolina, political drives supplemented private motives. Beginning in the late 1840s, Whiggish interests in "creating and improving markets within [the state's] own limits" and bargaining between westerners eager for transportation outlets and easterners eager to supply them, led to the creation of the government-controlled NCRR, which, with its tributary lines, was to provide the state with its own self-contained transportation system, funneling North Carolina produce through North Carolina ports. While the system failed to fulfill that promise (in the end most traffic on the lines flowed to Virginia ports), eastern port interests persistently played dog in the manger when efforts were made to improve rail ties to neighboring states. The intrastate roads used the "standard" (4' 8½") track gauge, even though most neighboring lines used a 5' gauge. More important, eastern interests successfully blocked the closing of a critical gap between Greensboro, on the NCRR, and Danville, Virginia, the southern terminus of the Richmond and Danville Railroad (R&D), justly fearing that the connection would permanently annex the North Carolina Piedmont to the ambitions of Richmond. Thus 1860 found North Carolina manufacturers still largely isolated, their few routes to the outside plagued by breaks and bottlenecks.[18]

Over the next generation a complex of forces fundamentally altered the economic environment of North Carolina manufacturers. During the war military necessity overcame state isolationism to build the Piedmont Railroad, which closed the Danville-Greensboro gap and brought the Richmond and Danville Railroad into the state. More important, the postwar years brought the hitherto self-contained state system under enormous pressure to abandon its east-west orientation and cultivate north-south through traffic. Checkmated by the R&D's control over its principal feeder lines, the NCRR submitted to a lease in 1871; over the next twenty years the other major lines followed suit, tying into the emerging Atlantic Coast Line and Seaboard Air Line systems. The new giants extended and rationalized their networks in the 1880s. Meanwhile, local interests threw down alternate routes in an effort to avoid becoming pawns in a manipulator's game. Greensboro merchants and bankers completed the Cape Fear and Yadkin Valley Railroad in 1884 in part to provide competition for the R&D; similarly, Durhamites built connectors to competing lines, laying one track by night across R&D right-of-way and protecting it with an armed guard. Such freelance local lines usually found their way into the systems eventually, but they contributed to the unprecedented railroad expansion in the Old North State, as elsewhere in the South; track mileage in the state more than doubled during the 1880s. With consolidation and the increased pressure for through traffic came rationalization and articulation, notably through interconnections, car interchange agreements, the nationwide standard gauge, and the through or uniform bill of lading, which permitted shipments over several different lines with a minimum of paperwork; these innovations welded North Carolina's and the nation's rails into a unified national system.[19]

As integration proceeded, striking changes were occurring in North Carolina's industrial structure, which by the turn of the century diverged markedly from the national pattern. The pattern is obscured, however, by developments in the highly extractive forest products industries. Lumbering retained roughly the same share of the state's manufacturing economy throughout the century, although by 1900 it was unambiguously export-oriented, generating nearly two-thirds of its product in excess of estimated local needs. More impressive, and misleading, was the shriveling of the chemical industry, chiefly naval stores, which shrank by over half in the 1860s and contributed only 2 percent to the state's VAM by 1900. The decline had nothing to do with market integration; the state's turpentine producers had nearly bled its forests dry by the Civil War and afterward largely abandoned it for virgin territory further south. The fate of naval stores thus had little to do with the deeper changes afoot.[20]

If the variant case of chemicals is excluded from the analysis, the resulting picture of change becomes clearer. While all other industrial groups expanded their output, many suffered relative decline or stagnation. Food producers lost over half of the relative importance they had enjoyed in 1860. Among manufacturers of more sophisticated products, transportation equipment lost significant ground, as did the metals and metal-working industries. The tobacco and textile (chiefly cotton textile) industries posted enormous gains, becoming, along with lumber, the major export industries of the state. With their rise came increased industrial specialization; whereas in 1860 the three largest nonchemical industries accounted for 52.7 percent of nonchemical VAM, by 1900 they produced 74.6 percent. These alterations are especially striking when compared to contemporary changes in the industrial structure of the whole United States, which was shifting toward metals, machinery, and transportation equipment and away from textiles and forest products. As a result, in the late nineteenth century North Carolina's industrial structure diverged significantly from the nation's.[21]

In short, as North Carolina entered the New South it displayed many of the classic signs of unbalanced growth. Why? To some extent it was the result of backwash; market integration brought new and sometimes ruinous competition into previously sheltered areas. Several industries (apart from tar and turpentine) showed absolute declines at some point; the real value added by the manufacture of boots and shoes, for instance, dropped 20 percent in the 1880s and stood only 17 percent above 1860 levels at the turn of the century.[22] More often, industries experiencing new competition grew, but only sluggishly; such was the case with flour and grist milling, the chief component of the food group, and with carriage and wagon building, whose relative decline does most to account for the plunging fortunes of the transportation equipment group. Generally the principal sufferers from backwash were not the sizable firms included in the census, but the many petty artisans scattered through the countryside and the small towns.[23]

While market integration brought a tide of mass-produced goods that eroded traditional small-scale local enterprise, the heightened role of those distantly produced manufactures in the lives of ordinary North Carolinians enhanced the position of the local merchant and the influence of towns in postbellum southern society. In North Carolina, as in the remainder of the South, trading centers proliferated in the late nineteenth century. The number of towns for which census returns were made jumped from 37 in 1860 to 345 in 1900, and the number with populations greater than five hundred rose from 23 to 129, the greatest increase coming in the 1870s. The most impressive gains were made by the Piedmont, a region whose share of the state's population, nearly half, had traditionally not been matched by its share of commerce or town development. Between 1860 and 1880 its proportion of the state's towns with populations greater than five hundred rose from just over one-third to over one-half.[24]

The locus of opportunity in the state thus shifted decisively from the countryside toward the town, toward commerce, and toward the Piedmont. Not only did old merchants find their positions enhanced, but they were joined by members of rural elites and even artisans who perceived a more prosperous future in selling their wares than in making them. And with the rising importance of town-based commerce came a quickening interest in economic development. Boosterism put in its appearance, as townsmen, competitive but united by a common desire to expand their business and raise local land values, began to pursue economic development schemes.[25]

Interest in new forms of production likewise quickened among an older commercial elite. In pre-railroad times local commerce in the Piedmont had tended to congregate around waterpower sites; those farsighted enough to gain control of any of the numerous local waterfalls or shoals could, by using the energy to drive gristmills, sawmills, or gins, place themselves at the heart of the economic life of the surrounding countryside. The early nineteenth-century yarn mills of the backcountry were themselves the creations of such rural "bourgeois." The famous Holt family is a case in point. Michael Holt's considerable local position rested on his control of Alamance County waterpower, which he used to drive a complex of small mills and shops producing a variety of goods and services; his son Edwin Michael simply extended that control, and the family's mastery of waterpower technology, to a new field. Millers were prominent among the principal founders of Randolph County's antebellum cotton mills. With the increased commercialization of the postbellum countryside, farmer-millers such as the Carpenters of Catawba County and the Bynums of Chatham County, like their compatriots in the towns, began to see new opportunities to exploit the potential of their holdings of natural resources and technical expertise.[26]

Men of this sort became the prime movers in the industrialization of the North Carolina Piedmont in the late nineteenth century; as with their counterparts elsewhere in the South, industrial entrepreneurship had strong commercial roots.[27] In pursuing their quest they were endowed with numerous advantages: they were motivated, had access to important raw materials such as cotton and tobacco, and could tap an abundant supply of cheap labor.

In propounding development strategies, however, they suffered from serious weaknesses as well. Raising capital, whether long-term or short-term, posed significant problems. Perhaps more important, the new business climate of the late nineteenth century posed enormous institutional and entrepreneurial obstacles to overcome. Integration into a national market placed North Carolinians in direct competition with one of the most dynamic and sophisticated industrial regions on earth, the manufacturing belt of the American Northeast and (increasingly) Midwest. On the other hand, their distance from the burgeoning industrial and population centers of the nation left them at a disadvantage in exploiting the vast new markets being created there. The dynamics of late-nineteenth-century industrialization had a centripetal effect on the geographic distribution of industrial enterprise; the availability of markets, large pools of skilled labor, and services, along with access to information about customer needs and new economic techniques, turned Gilded Age cities into great economic magnets. These agglomeration, or polarization, effects gave enterprises within the emerging core critical advantages over those in peripheral areas like North Carolina.[28]

Compounding the awkward geographic position of North Carolina's aspiring industrialists was their entrepreneurial weakness. To be sure, they brought some critical skills to their new enterprises. A long-standing tradition of small-scale manufacture provided the region with individuals knowledgeable about industrial technology and the handling qualities of indigenous resources. Such antebellum manufacturers as the Holts, the Frieses, and numerous tobacco plug and twist makers played important roles in postbellum development, enough to lend credence to the oft-made claim that industrial North Carolina was the fruit of a continuous tradition.[29] In addition, the influx of merchants into manufacturing brought men skilled at negotiating the intricacies of markets, keeping accounts, organizing corporations, and especially buying and selling critical raw materials. In one crucial respect, however, even the experienced manufacturers among them were ill equipped for the new departure that industrialization represented. The new importance of national markets for industrial success created an unfamiliar marketing environment. Distant customers were far different from local ones; their tastes and requirements were more varied, and frequently more exacting, than those of the farmers and farmwives who had purchased at the shop or mill door or from the peddler's wagon. Moreover, the broadening of choice made possible by market extension and the flood of new products made possible by American inventiveness engendered a sophistication and volatility in customers' desires new to producers used to having protected, even captive, outlets for their goods. Even in antebellum times a newspaper editor could complain that "in the Northern Cities and Western States . . . people make a more careful examination as to the capacity for service [of a product] than is usually made in the South." The problems would increase as the century wore on; as late as the 1890s, the grandson of a pioneer Gastonia industrialist recalled, local yarn mills were limited to local markets for most of their produce "because it did not compete with the requirements of the national markets."[30]

The barriers imposed by distance from customers and lack of marketing experience had their greatest effect on high-growth, cutting-edge industries. According to the theory of the "product life cycle," new products are most easily developed in close proximity to their markets and to suppliers of essential support services, notably skills and technology. The rapid pace of innovation and the complexities involved in fitting product to customer desires require a constant and rapid adjustment best accomplished where customers can be serviced without delay and machine shops and other service firms stand at the ready. Such industries in North Carolina, situated in an overwhelmingly rural environment, with customers scattered and support services few, would have scant opportunity to achieve more than local, or at best regional, importance.[31]

A good case study in the problems distance from customers and support services could pose to merchandising in the sense used here and to industrial development is offered by the Charlotte machinery firm of Liddell and Company. Walter James Forbes Liddell, a Pennsylvania-born engineer, was unusually well equipped to succeed. Liddell came to Charlotte in 1875 to help manage a branch of an Erie, Pennsylvania, foundry; thus, unlike most prospective North Carolina industrialists, he was an immigrant bringing to the state both critical technical skills and close fraternal ties to his fellow tradesmen in the industrial core. Within three years he had set up a partnership with a local businessman to build steam engines. In the years following, Liddell and his sons built up an extensive southern business in steam engines, sawmills, and cotton compresses, establishing branch operations in Montgomery, Alabama, and Dallas, Texas, and creating one of the leading enterprises of Charlotte and one of the largest of its type in the state.[32]

In the end, though, the Liddells' success was severely limited by their inability to extend their business to far more lucrative northern markets. The elder Liddell was an inventor as well as an entrepreneur, holding several patents on boilers and steam engines, but his location, and chronic capital problems as well, left him in a poor position to exploit them. He enjoyed, to be sure, strong personal ties to Pennsylvania iron fabricators and attempted to market his innovations through licensing agreements, notably with his old employer, the Erie City Iron Works, to which he consigned all markets north of North Carolina. Surviving evidence suggests that these arrangements were chronically unsatisfactory. In effect Liddell surrendered control over northern production and marketing of his inventions for a royalty whose rate and collection were fruitful sources of irritation. Not only was he unable to promote his product to his satisfaction but he was also unable to maintain the intimate customer relations essential to working the "bugs" out.

A controversy between Liddell and Erie City in 1886 suggests some of the resulting problems. In April Liddell, disturbed about falling northern sales of his "New Era boiler," wrote a letter of complaint to George Selden, the head of Erie City. Selden's reply suggests that Liddell suspected Erie City of promoting a boiler of its own design in preference to Liddell's, a charge Selden went to some lengths to refute. Selden insisted that while "as you are aware we have given the boiler a great deal of attention, have advertised it fully and succeeded in working up a large trade . . . it does not seem to be a long-lived boiler." Accordingly, he was willing to surrender his exclusive rights to the northern territory. Who was correct is difficult to tell a century later, but an uncorrected design defect and the licensee's lack of interest in the product may well have been interrelated. In this case, Liddell's inability to perform a full range of entrepreneurial functions seriously inhibited his freedom of action; such limitations worked to stunt the growth of an infant North Carolina machinery industry.[33]

If the developing national markets proved difficult for many North Carolina entrepreneurs to penetrate, some achieved success by cultivating a simultaneously arising market within the South itself. The same processes that were binding southerners economically more closely to the rest of the nation were integrating the southern states into a sizable market with unique characteristics and barriers to outside entry. Dixie's integration into the national market was far from complete; despite the railroads (or, thanks to backwash, because of them) it remained rural and agricultural, with its own peculiar crops, and suffered from chronic shortages of capital. It received few immigrants from the North or from Europe, and before World War I it sent few migrants elsewhere; thus its population remained isolated from the larger nation, cultivating peculiar regional tastes frequently of little interest to producers in other parts of the country. Above all, southerners remained impoverished, with incomes, on the average, roughly half those of all Americans in the seventy-five years following Appomattox.

The continuing distinctiveness of the southern market proved advantageous for many southern producers. Although they failed to establish a national presence, the Liddells were able to extend their business in such southern specialty items as cotton compresses, which compacted cotton bales for shipment, throughout the region. The most cohesive and protected segment of the new southern market, though, was for consumer goods, durable and nondurable. The plug and twist tobacco manufacturers who converged on Winston in the 1870s built on their heritage as part-time peddlers to cultivate the cotton belt market; thus, contends their historian, "they reached many small markets disdained by the larger manufacturers of Virginia and in so doing set the standards of chewing in a large area where money was not plentiful but chewers were numerous." In 1880 J. D. Cameron reported that Winston manufacturers still sold chiefly to the South, and to a lesser extent to the West, making only occasional mention of the antebellum marketing center, Baltimore. Thus Winston maintained its independence. As railroads laced the Deep South, the old-time Winston peddler became transformed into the drummer, and the manufacturer-peddler began to employ a sales force. Giving his operation the embryonic form of a modern multifunction enterprise, the Winston entrepreneur used his protected market to equip himself to take on the world.[34]

A somewhat different strategy led to the rise of another major North Carolina industry, furniture. As outside products penetrated the southern backcountry in the postwar years, local cabinetmakers abandoned their trade, sometimes to become undertakers or furniture dealers. The traditional cultures of up-country whites and emancipated blacks, and widespread poverty in both groups, created a market for low-grade manufactured furniture that established northern producers disdained but that manufacturers in the hardwood regions of the upper South found inviting. While tobacco products could be carried to local dealers for their inspection, the bulkiness of furniture required dealers themselves to travel to factory, showroom, or exhibit hall to examine the wares. Because furniture factories tended to be small and to specialize in a single line of goods (for example, chairs, tables, mantels, or bedsteads), the desires of dealers to minimize their travel encouraged manufacturers to concentrate their plants at a single location convenient to the emerging regional market. Proximity to hardwoods, convenient rail connections to the South, an established woodworking industry, and an unusual entrepreneurial community combined by the turn of the century to make High Point, North Carolina, the furniture capital of the South. By 1902 High Point could boast a complex of twenty-six small factories making fifteen different classes of furniture; fourteen more had sprung up in nearby Thomasville and Lexington. Town boosters attributed High Point's preeminence in furniture to its position as the center of the southern regional market; not only did it offer "one-stop shopping" to furniture dealers but the variety of local production also allowed them to assemble rail carloads from small lots, saving on freight charges. Best of all, High Point's position allowed it not only to exploit the regional market but to define it as well. High Point producers could effectively create and perpetuate a southern regional taste in furniture, becoming what James E. Vance, Jr., has called an "arbiter market."[35]

The rise of a regional market was, however, a mixed blessing. Demand for producers' goods, which was fueling the industrial expansion of the Midwest, was too thin to sustain southern heavy industry. Even the market for consumer goods was limited by regional poverty, and the very success of some late-nineteenth-century North Carolina entrepreneurs in catering to the regional market complicated their efforts to expand beyond it. Specialization in the cheap goods largely in demand from southerners gave High Point manufacturers the unenviable and lingering reputation of "selling lumber and not furniture." Moreover, southern regional tastes, running to veneered, highly decorated styles, were regarded as gaudy and flimsy by purchasers in other parts of the country and as late as 1938 were described as the major limiting factor in the growth of the North Carolina industry.[36] Given the inadequacies of local and regional markets, the attention of North Carolina's town builders came to focus on those industries that could best tap the lucrative national market. As the grandson of Gastonia's George Washington Ragan put it, "the country's wealth was concentrated in the North and he early recognized the importance of getting along with and selling to Northern markets in order to have part of that wealth circulated in the South."[37] For most parts of the state, the choice lay among three industries: lumber, tobacco, and textiles.

Lumbering contributed little to the state's development. In the late nineteenth century it was essentially an extractive industry, pursued by wandering entrepreneurs who turned to the South in the late nineteenth century after depleting the forests of the upper Midwest. Lumbering became extremely important in the sparsely populated piney woods of the coastal plain and in Appalachia, especially after railroads opened those regions in the 1880s. Although some operations were huge, their long-term effects on development were evanescent and even deleterious, as it was in the interest of most operators to "cut out and get out." The extent of local timber supplies limited the industry's ability to contribute to a town's growth. Lumbering could produce a "boom," but it could not lead to the long-term prosperity most boosters desired.[38]

Except in specialized pockets like High Point and its neighboring towns, then, businessmen seeking growth for their localities had to look to tobacco and textiles, especially cotton textiles, for fulfillment of their dreams of greatness. By the turn of the century each industry was heavily oriented toward national markets, but each linked its component firms to customers in drastically different ways, with important consequences for the process of southern industrialization. Each in its own way illustrates the opportunities and constraints faced by southerners seeking to foster development.

The role of the tobacco industry in North Carolina's development was shaped by the proximity of its principal raw material and the nature of its market. Since the manufacture of chewing tobacco had traditionally been located close to the fields where it was produced, the bright-leaf belt of North Carolina entered the late nineteenth century with a well-developed corps of entrepreneurs, thoroughly acquainted with the purchasing of leaf and other raw materials and of manufacture. More important for the future of the industry were its marketing characteristics and the changes that overtook them by 1900. Bright-leaf tobacco products, especially those intended for smoking, presented a unique marketing opportunity. Originating late in the antebellum period, bright-leaf tobacco was essentially a new product, with distinctive qualities that made it attractive to a growing number of consumers after the war. Thus the classic backwash problem of competing with more efficient producers in the manufacturing belt was no great concern to North Carolina manufacturers, who gained a measure of natural protection in their opening efforts. Tobacco products were also consumer goods readily differentiated by taste and by use of brand names, a practice that had developed by the 1850s.[39] The ability of manufacturers to assure a market by controlling consumer taste engendered an interest in controlling their own marketing. Tarheel plug makers were in an especially good position to control marketing, for their backwater status before the Civil War had led them to rely less on commission merchants, and more on peddling, than had the older and larger manufacturers to their north.

The postwar years, accordingly, found North Carolina tobacco producers already well endowed with the skills needed to exploit the new business environment of the age. The most striking successes were scored by the smoking tobacco manufacturers of Durham. The legend dating the rise of the Durham tobacco industry from the arrival of Gen. William T. Sherman's army to accept Joseph E. Johnston's surrender in April 1865 has tied its beginning to the national market and its appeal to national tastes. More important, the new markets were exploited by men who were as much salesmen as manufacturers and who thoroughly exploited the possibilities of the new transportation and communications networks. The first great firm, W. T. Blackwell and Company (maker of Bull Durham), was controlled by two former tobacco jobbers and peddlers, who shortly took in as a partner Julian S. Carr, the son of a Chapel Hill merchant with a talent for advertising. The Bull's crosstown rivals, W. Duke, Sons, and Company, began in similar fashion; however, the peddling of Washington Duke and his son James Buchanan Duke quickly took the more modern form of drumming, as salesmen left their merchandise at home and concentrated on sales. The Dukes used the railroad and the telegraph to extend their reach over much of the country, establishing direct relations with wholesalers and ultimately creating a sales force with branch offices. Both firms enhanced their marketing capabilities by incorporating northern wholesalers into their firms.[40]

Above all, both firms placed their faith in advertising. Carr not only made Bull Durham world famous but etched the Bull into American folklore. Buck Duke responded in kind, spending the bulk of his profits on "add[ing] to the value of our property" through promotion; by 1889, when the firm had largely moved into cigarettes, he boasted that he could easily monopolize the industry by putting $1 million a year into publicity "because no other factory could approach what we were able to do in advertisement." The successes of the two leading firms allowed other Durham manufacturers to follow suit in reaching the American masses; Cameron's 1881 survey showed virtually all of them selling nationwide or to areas outside the South. Although their compatriots, the plug makers of Winston, still relied heavily on regional markets, one of their number, R. J. Reynolds, was beginning to invade the North and later became perhaps the leading innovator of his community in technology, product development, and marketing.[41]

Because North Carolina tobacco products were in effect new products, at an early stage in their life cycle, their producers developed a rip-roaring entrepreneurial culture characterized by Jule Carr's motto, "Let buffalo gore buffalo, and the pasture go to the strongest." The merchandising problems of fitting product to customer demand and the rapidly increasing scale of operations placed a premium on innovation. The demand for Bull Durham could not be satisfied with the traditional, primitive methods originally used to make it. Carr expanded his production first by appropriating Virginia machinery, then by encouraging innovation among his associates and subordinates. By the turn of the century cutting, packing, stamping, and labeling operations had all been mechanized, largely to serve the needs of the Bull. Under Carr's sponsorship bag-making machinery had also been developed, creating a new auxiliary industry. More spectacular innovations occurred in the cigarette industry, when Duke, who had entered the business in 1881, installed the Bonsack cigarette machine in his Durham factory. The massive numbers of cheap cigarettes it produced forced even more intensive cultivation of the national market, along with the development of a purchasing organization in the bright-leaf belt, and fueled a violent escalation of competition that led to the creation of the American Tobacco Company in 1890.[42]

In the so-called Tobacco Trust, North Carolina entrepreneurs had created one of the first truly modern "big businesses," a signal achievement. However, the very success of the combination increasingly pointed out a major shortcoming of tobacco manufacture as an engine of local development. The opportunities opened up by the national market, by spurring innovation and permitting ever larger scales of operations, led in the 1890s to a massive shake-out in the industry. In plug manufacture, mechanization and important product innovations, such as the introduction of saccharin as a sweetener, accompanied by an increasing use of salesmen and advertising, concentrated business in the hands of a few strong competitors, such as

R. J. Reynolds of Winston, even before the trust declared the "Plug War" and began its quest to monopolize the industry. By the early twentieth century Duke in Durham and his agent Reynolds in Winston had a lock on the industry, leaving in ashes not only the careers of small competitors but also the hopes of such towns as High Point, which in the 1880s had staked its future on tobacco.[43]

The industry nonetheless had profound developmental consequences for the Tarheel State. The postwar entrepreneurs established a major export industry, largely under their own control. The trust and successor firms such as R. J. Reynolds used their organizations to create worldwide markets for North Carolina goods and to draw vast quantities of capital into the state.[44] The trust's buyouts of such major figures as Carr and P. H. Hanes freed capital and entrepreneurial energies for other enterprises. The Dukes themselves invested heavily in Piedmont industry and, more important, created a superb system of hydroelectric power generation and transmission. Tobacco prosperity underwrote new financial institutions, notably the Wachovia Bank and Trust Company. Finally, with the Duke Endowment and other foundations, tobacco money created a philanthropic establishment that has contributed to (ironically) public health and education and now forms a major prop for the state's emerging high-technology complex.[45]

In the long run the tobacco industry would do much to lay the institutional and technological groundwork for long-term growth, but that was cold comfort to small-town elites seeking development for their communities. To them, the great effect of the tobacco monopoly was to constrict development opportunities and to force local boosters to take other paths. Even the glory days of tobacco entrepreneurship had been limited in their geographical impact. The Old Bright Belt, a cluster of roughly ten counties in the northern Piedmont where bright-leaf tobacco originated, had priority in development; moreover, agglomeration effects quickly asserted themselves as manufacturers clustered around the auction warehouses of Winston, Durham, and a few other places. Economies of scale arising from mechanization led the trust to concentrate production yet further.[46] Finally, a young and rapidly growing industry placed heavy demands on entrepreneurial skills, skills that were not widely distributed beyond the Old Bright Belt. Most development-hungry Tarheels had to seek an easier path to prosperity than that afforded by tobacco.

The favored path was manufacture of textiles, particularly cotton textiles. By 1899 cotton goods constituted the leading industry of the state in VAM, its contribution of 26.2 percent edging out tobacco's 22.8 percent. Moreover, it far outdistanced tobacco in those characteristics most important to local development. It employed over 30,000 wage earners, 42.9 percent of the state's total; the average firm employed 171 workers, compared to 80 in tobacco. Finally, cotton mills were more widely distributed than tobacco factories. According to the state bureau of labor statistics, in 1898, before the shakedown in tobacco was far advanced, 173 chewing and smoking tobacco factories were located in 27 of the state's 97 counties at 70 post office addresses; of these, 18 percent were in Winston. By comparison, 191 cotton textile establishments were reported in 43 counties, at 107 post office addresses. There were 13 counties with at least 5 mills, and 5 could boast at least 10 mills.[47]

The phenomenal expansion of cotton textiles in North Carolina and the South generally in the late nineteenth century has provided economic historians a favorite case study in location and economic development theory. They have generally concluded that the decisive advantage of the South in cotton textile production lay in its abundant supply of cheap labor. They thus explain the industry's southward shift as a product of factor flows, especially of capital, directed by economically rational actors seeking maximum advantage. In the long run, they argue, such flows lead to a balancing out of regional economic disparities. Certainly North Carolina's textile industrialists regarded labor costs as their major weapon in the competitive struggle. Respondents to an 1886 questionnaire prepared by the prominent North Carolina educator Calvin H. Wiley on the state's role in internal U.S. commerce universally cited low wages, long hours, and the tractability of the help as important contributors to their success.[48]

The great attraction of the textile industry for the state's economic developers, though, lay in far more than its labor-intensive factor proportions. In the latter half of the nineteenth century it was, in product-cycle terms, a mature industry. Whereas before the Civil War textile production relied heavily on skills (labor, technology, and entrepreneurship) from outside the industry, by the late nineteenth century the industry had largely embodied those skills in its technology and structure. Textile machinery was designed to minimize the demand for worker skills and was standardized in design and production to minimize the need for custom adaptation.

More important for present purposes, the industry had embodied a broad range of entrepreneurial skills in its marketing structure. The textile "industry" was divided into subindustries distinguished by product and function; most textile producers made "intermediate goods," for sale not to the ultimate consumer but to processors at a more advanced stage. To coordinate the complex transactions this system required, the industry developed an elaborate marketing establishment, deploying a large corps of expert commission agents, brokers, and other specialists to bring goods and customers together.[49]

Prospective North Carolina industrialists came to rely on this vast store of accumulated and institutionalized expertise in their efforts to tap the national market. Bess Beatty has documented the technological dependence of North Carolina textile manufacturers on northern machinery makers; their reliance on outside marketing skills was in some ways even more telling. To be sure, the transition was far from abrupt; surviving antebellum factories tended to rely on their old connections until well after the war. In the mid-1870s the Woodlawn factory of Gaston County disposed of its sheeting, shirting, and yarn through Charlotte wholesalers and merchants in the surrounding counties of North and South Carolina, one member of the firm making frequent sales trips. In the mid-1880s the old-line Salem firm of F. and H. Fries continued to market the bulk of its goods in the Carolinas and Virginia. Producers of traditional home-market goods such as plaids persisted in their traditional selling methods; the greatest of them, the Holts of Alamance County, had built up a network of outlets among jobbers throughout the South and continued to rely heavily upon it well into the 1890s. Such enterprises were on the trailing edge, however. The market for cotton plaids, in particular, grew slowly, if at all, in the late nineteenth century, and by the late 1880s it suffered from recurrent depression. While the Holts remained prosperous, their importance in the North Carolina industry began to erode sharply in the 1890s and the first decades of the twentieth century, as newer mills and methods increasingly became dominant. The shift away from local markets was much sharper with yarn manufacturers, who reported to Wiley in 1886 that virtually all their production was sent out of state.[50]

With the rise of the national market came the ascendancy of the selling agent or commission house, a specialized agency that handled the marketing of a mill's goods, charging a commission for the service. The trends are displayed in table 6.3. Whereas fewer than half of all North Carolina mills reported using an agent or agents in the 1880s, by the turn of the century over two-thirds did so.[51] Of the twenty-eight mills that used no selling agent in 1900, nineteen were yarn mills, many of which sold to other mills (in and out of state), or producers of cordage and braided goods; of the nine cloth mills, only two ran more than five thousand spindles, and they collectively accounted for less than 5 percent of the state's total spindleage.

The cloth market was dominated by Worth Street in New York, which in the late nineteenth century became the marketing center for the American dry goods industry. There the "gray goods" generally produced by southern mills were passed to the converters who oversaw their dyeing, finishing, and further marketing; there, too,

Table 6.3. North Carolina cotton mills using various modes of distribution, 1882–1905

Mode of distribution	1882 N	1882 Pct.	1884 N	1884 Pct.	1886 N	1886 Pct.	1891 N	1891 Pct.	1894 N	1894 Pct.	1900 N	1900 Pct.
Direct only					1	1.3	21	18.0	15	11.6	28	12.9
Unnamed agents							1	0.8	3	2.3	20	9.2
Named agents	27	42.2	32	43.8	33	43.4	61	52.1	80	62.0	133	61.3
More than one	3		4		5		11		12		25	
Agents and direct							2		5		12	
No data	37	57.8	41	56.2	42	55.3	34	29.1	31	24.0	36	16.6
Total	64	100.0	73	100.0	76	100.0	117	100.0	129	100.0	217	100.0
Total number of agents named in directories	9		14		15		30		27		38	

Sources: *Dockham's Directory*, 1882, 1884, 1886, 1891–1892; *Davison's Textile Blue Book*, 1894–1895, 1900–1901. "Direct" refers to direct dealings with customers, "agents" to the use of an intermediary. Separate figures are given for mills with identifiable commission houses and those listed in the directories as served by unnamed "agents." Indented categories are subgroups of the category "Named Agents."

colored goods were sold to the mass marketers. Yarn mills sold chiefly to Philadelphia. The Quaker City was the great center for specialty textile products; as a traditional wholesale center well endowed with highly skilled labor, it was home to many small weave sheds and hosiery mills producing a wide range of goods, notably hosiery, carpets, and upholstery. They constituted the principal yarn market in the country, accounting in the late nineteenth century for 45 percent of total sales. Driven both by demand and by price competition, yarn houses in Philadelphia and elsewhere increasingly sought outside supplies; as they learned that North Carolina could produce at relatively low cost, they began aggressively to solicit business in the Tarheel State, luring many new entrepreneurs into the industry.[52]

A long-standing tradition of yarn spinning in the state facilitated entry into this form of manufacturing. However, even the most expert "practical mill man" found that he needed the mediation of the selling agent to develop what was in many ways a new product. The experience of Mark Morgan, a yarn manufacturer of Richmond County, was a case in point. Morgan seems at first blush a classic exemplar of North Carolina's continuing entrepreneurial tradition. Born in 1837, Morgan had served an apprenticeship with the Rockfish Manufacturing Company near Fayetteville, North Carolina's largest antebellum mill, and had superintended Thomas M. Holt's Granite Mill. In 1872 he took a position at the Richmond Cotton Mill of Laurel Hill, owned by a local planter, becoming his partner the following year.[53]

In the 1870s and 1880s Morgan continued to sell yarn to wholesale merchants in Wilmington and local storekeepers in southeastern North Carolina; by the 1880s, however, well over 90 percent of his production was being handled by Philadelphia commission houses. The locally sold yarn was coarse, spun with a hard twist and ranging in count from eight to ten. (The "count" of yarn is measured by the number of "hanks," of 840 yards each, to a pound; the fewer the hanks, the coarser the yarn.) His customers were undiscriminating except as to price, one Anson County merchant remarking that "I have to compete with mills in [the] Western part of [the] State and they sell very close." For the most part the yarn sold to Pennsylvania was little different; the primary demand was for carpet yarns generally of two ply with counts of twelve and fourteen. However, even on such standard goods the weavers of Philadelphia were more exacting than the farmwives and crossroads merchants of the sandhills. Complaints flowed back from Philadelphia about inaccurate yarn counts, excessively hard twists, and poor packaging. More important was the constant stream of advice about what to produce and how to produce it. Unlike local markets, the Philadelphia market was highly changeable and seasonal, and the agents constantly pressed Morgan to broaden his capabilities by adding warping equipment, by changing counts, and by experimenting with new styles of yarns. In effect, Morgan and others like him relied on the mature marketing structure of their industry to make many of their most critical entrepreneurial decisions. Morgan was keenly sensitive both to his need for advice and the danger of dependence it posed; by the 1890s he made a point of dealing with several firms at once, constantly playing them off against each other in his correspondence. Even so, he was critically aware that his success depended greatly on his agents' skill and experience in anticipating the twists and turns of demand.[54]

In matching products to volatile national markets, cloth manufacturers faced perhaps even more complex problems than yarn manufacturers. William A. Erwin, touring New England in the interest of his large mill at Durham, reported to his principal backer that "as I expected the biggest thing to decide is, what is best for us to manufacture, and when we come here, in New England and find the big mills changing their products all the time, or every few months, it is not strange that it is a hard question with us."[55]

Relying on the savvy of the selling agent made it easier; as a result, in cloth mills as in yarn mills, commission houses influenced, even dictated, many entrepreneurial decisions. For old-line producers, they eased the transition into national markets. The Cone Export and Commission Company, for example, helped organize the colored goods branch of the industry. Faced with stagnating demand for their traditional product, North Carolina plaid mills had made several fruitless efforts at combination in the late 1880s. In 1890 they made a fresh attempt, using as their vehicle a selling house capitalized with the credit of the participating mills and run by two former Baltimore dry goods merchants, Moses and Caesar Cone. Charged with developing new domestic and foreign markets for plaids, checks, and stripes, the house was granted broad authority over basic production decisions, including volume and product specifications. By 1894 Cone controlled seventeen of North Carolina's twenty-eight plaid mills, along with four mills producing other goods.[56]

While established as a sort of "cotton plaid trust," the Cone Company had only limited success in that line; of its original plaid mills, one-third had made other arrangements by 1900. Its more important achievement was to bring the product mix of its client mills in line with national and international demand. Textiles being usually intermediate goods, the industry's big marketing problem was not, as with tobacco, to introduce new products to the consumer but to fit its production to demand shaped by others, a task the Cones were well suited to undertake. In succeeding years their firm switched mills away from plaids, checks, and stripes and into such goods as chambrays, cheviots (a kind of twill), denims, flannels, and especially ginghams; by 1905 as many (seven) of its mills were producing ginghams as plaids.[57]

Cone was not the only commission house involved so deeply in the affairs of producing firms. Joshua L. Baily and Company, the selling agent for the Durham Cotton Manufacturing Company of Durham, designed cheviot styles for the mill, on at least one occasion forcing it to make major alterations in its equipment in order to "replace a lot of the dead patterns with bright new ones." Not only did selling houses wield control over continuing production decisions, but they often dictated the shape a new enterprise would take. Since the equipment and layout of a cotton mill was intimately related to the kind of goods it was to make, a commission house's marketing choices involved it in so many other decisions that a local entrepreneur might be left with few functions of his own to fill. When in 1908 the Erwin Cotton Mills Company of Durham, the state's largest firm, decided to build a new mill, W. A. Erwin, its secretary-treasurer and a man of enormous practical experience, largely stood aside, being content to transmit advice from his selling house to his engineering firm. In neighboring South Carolina, F. W. Poe, a merchant and neophyte industrialist, handed over most of the decision making about the equipment and organization of his new mill to his engineering firm and his commission house, the latter not only determining output but also the "organization of the goods you would start the mill on."[58]

With time, of course, North Carolina textile men gained marketing savvy of their own. Yarn spinners began to establish direct ties to northern customers; in the 1920s Caldwell Ragan of Gastonia, a spinner of fine combed yarns, developed close relations with Philadelphia mercerizers, New York thread makers, and fancy goods manufacturers all over the Northeast. Shortly after the turn of the century one North Carolina manufacturer, J. W. Cannon, established his own selling house in New York, and other efforts at integration of marketing and production occurred in later years.[59]

Nonetheless, the initial entrepreneurial weakness of North Carolina's developers had long-lasting consequences. Their own and their workers' lack of skills led them to embrace an industry that, because it required relatively few skills of worker or owner, did relatively little to develop skills. Because auxiliary industries, such as textile machinery, were so well developed outside the state and region before the mills began to rise, there was little incentive to create them. Indeed, southern textile producers remain heavily dependent on outside (now foreign) suppliers of equipment, especially the most technologically advanced equipment.[60]

More significant, the concentration on textiles proved symptomatic of a problem that has plagued the industrial South right up to the present. Deficiently endowed with entrepreneurial expertise and labor skills, the region has chronically sought to compensate by developing or attracting industries at advanced stages in the product cycle, industries in which skills have been largely "built in" to their basic technology and structure. Thus there is a linear connection between the surge into textiles in the late nineteenth century and the more recent southern enthusiasm for "smokestack chasing." The attraction "footloose industries" and branch plants have held for southern communities has usually been attributed to the communities' need for outside capital; such solutions might better be regarded as ways to obtain prepackaged entrepreneurial expertise and skills. Indeed, state industrial development policies in the postwar South have generally been aimed at fostering development in stagnating rural areas most in need of such infusions. The apparel, plastics, and electrical equipment industries that swarmed to the region after World War II embodied labor skill in their machinery; their managers and parent companies embodied entrepreneurial skills in their preexisting organizations and business ties.[61]

Unfortunately for the South, these characteristics also rendered the new plants largely independent of the communities in which they settled and the people they employed. Like textile mills, they have been able to cow workers and local governments by threatening mass firings or shutdowns, threats that have become ever more credible with the globalization of the economy. While such areas of North Carolina as the Research Triangle may develop as nodes of self-sustaining economic growth, the bulk of the state, even in high-technology industries, depends heavily on branch plants and routinized production processes, many of which find "off-shore" operations increasingly attractive. The friendly New South critic Edward Atkinson may not have been far off the mark when, criticizing the southern cotton mill mania of his day, he argued that the great strength of northern industrial society was not its great factories, but its numerous small shops, the development of which would "require heads as well as hands, and . . . represent diversity and not concentration of employment."[62]

Insofar as North Carolina's integration into the national economy inhibited such diversity and encouraged the unbalanced process of development that did occur, its fruits remain problematic and ambiguous. It is clear, however, that the consequences of that integration were profound and need to be taken into account when we set out to explain the origins of the modern South. Discussions of the New South in recent years have tended to view its social characteristics, from "paternalism" to low wages to worker powerlessness, as internally generated, the creations of a persistent ruling class. The argument presented here suggests that class persistence may explain much less than meets the eye. North Carolina's developers had in mind the creation of an industrial society modeled on the one they knew best, that of the North. That they created something different was due not so much to deliberate choice as to the business constraints under which they operated. A "revolution from above" in fact occurred, but it was not a "revolution" sponsored by southern Junkers so much as imposed upon them. Like the social upheaval of emancipation and subjugation, the nationalization of North Carolina, and southern, economic life left the business environment of its "ruling class" (in large part a business class) fundamentally altered for better *and* for worse. Accordingly, as Gavin Wright has suggested, the study of that environment and of the business strategies employed in response to it can do much to clarify our understanding of the basis of modern southern society. At the very least it may remind us that, while "men make their own history, . . . they do not make it just as they please."[63]

Appendix

Data comes from *State and Regional Patterns in American Manufacturing;* the method of analysis is adapted from the same sources.[64] These estimates compare the proportion of a national industry's VAM generated within North Carolina to the proportion of the national market for all manufactured goods attributable to North Carolina, measured by an estimate (see below) of the state's percentage of national personal income received. Thus, for instance, if North Carolinians received 0.88 percent of the nation's income and produced 0.88 percent (by VAM) of the nation's paper, the total amount of paper produced would exactly satisfy local demand with no surplus left for out-of-state sale. Two columns appear for each census year. The first indicates, for industries with an estimated surplus, the percentage of their product that was presumably for export; the second gives the percentage of the estimated in-state market that could be supplied by in-state producers.

Unfortunately, no state-level estimates of personal income exist for 1860. After experimenting with several alternative methods of estimation, I decided to use the proportion of national personal income received by North Carolinians in 1880 (1.03 percent) as a proxy.[65] While not accurate, this figure is a plausible approximation; more important, it is probably an *underestimate.* One alternative proxy, adopted by Albert W. Niemi, Jr., uses state shares of United States population to measure the in-state market; his method yields an implausibly high estimate (3.16 percent), which fails to take into account the low per capita personal income (PCI) of North Carolinians.[66] A modified approach, equating North Carolina's share of the population of the South Atlantic census region with its share of regional personal income, yields a figure of 1.79 percent.[67] This estimate is probably still too high, because North Carolina benefitted less economically from slavery than did the rest of the census region and thus almost certainly had a lower PCI; in 1880, the first year for which state estimates are available, the state's PCI stood at only 70.79 percent of South Atlantic levels. My preferred estimate, on the other hand, is probably too low; it implies that state PCI stood at only 57.5 percent of the South Atlantic level in 1860 and that the state escaped the adverse economic impact of the Civil War and emancipation, thus raising its relative standing by 1880. In this context, however, the lowest estimate is the least misleading of the three because its use exaggerates the export production of North Carolina's industrial groups in 1860 and thus biases the 1860 figures in table 6.2 *against* my argument. Fortunately, state personal income estimates are available for 1900, indicating that in that year North Carolina received 0.88 percent of all national personal incomes.[68]

These estimates must be used with great caution. As Niemi notes, they assume no international trade and no regional or state variations in consumer tastes and income distribution.[69] Moreover, the broad categories used wash out important variations among industries *within* groups. Finally, they assume that goods will not leave the region (state) before local demand is satisfied, an assumption that is problematic on numerous counts. When used in conjunction with other evidence, though, I find these figures suggestive.

7

Capital Mobilization and Southern Industry, 1880–1905

The Case of the Carolina Piedmont

DAVID L. CARLTON AND PETER A. COCLANIS

This piece, published in 1989, was an early effort to come to terms with one peculiar aspect of the environment within which southern industrial entrepreneurs had to operate: the lack within the region of a well-developed set of institutions to mobilize capital for industrial enterprise. The resulting difficulty in financing new firms, we argue, had a decided impact on the risk tolerance of southern entrepreneurs, which in turn shaped the structure of southern industry in a decidedly risk-averse manner. Not much work has been done since on the relationship of the South to capital-mobilizing institutions. However, recent unpublished work on the Midwest by the economist Margaret Levenstein has shown that the manufacturing belt could boast a number of local and regional stock exchanges well into the twentieth century; by comparison, the only such exchange in operation in the southeast was in Richmond, although commodity exchanges in important cotton centers may have dealt in industrial stocks as a sideline. This suggests that the gap in sophistication between southern and manufacturing belt business institutions may be even greater than we suspected at the time of this writing.

If there is a "central theme" to southern economic historiography, especially of the period since the Civil War, it has been the South's economic exceptionalism. How, the question goes, could one of the wealthiest and most sophisticated of the world's societies, the United States of America, harbor under its roof a region characterized by such chronic poverty and underdevelopment? For all the fierce differences of opinion among scholars of varying persuasions over the details, there is general agreement on the fundamental problem posed by the region's economic record.

Among the more prominent items in the traditional catalogue of southern economic ills has been the difficulty experienced by the region in its efforts to industrialize.[1] As is well known, in antebellum times the states that became the Confederacy suffered from a "deplorable scarcity" of manufacturing; while the reasons for this dearth remain in dispute, most recent treatments of the subject emphasize structural impediments imposed by the prevailing system of plantation slave agriculture.[2] With the end of slavery, a completely different structure of opportunity took hold in the region, permitting a serious movement toward industrialization to develop in certain sections.[3] As a result, since 1880 the growth of the South's manufacturing employment and value added by manufacture has outpaced that of the nation. Nonetheless, for nearly three-quarters of a century after the Civil War manufacturing did little to extricate the region from the mire of underdevelopment. The dead weight of an impoverished and backward countryside, characterized by massive rural underemployment, had much to do with this.[4] So the question remains: could the South have industrialized faster than it did? Were there conditions preventing southern industrialization from achieving its full potential?

Along with some other observers, we believe the answer to be yes. In this article, we present evidence from the Carolina Piedmont—the industrial "heartland" of the South—to suggest one such condition. We argue that at the outset of the South's modern industrialization in the late nineteenth century the region's possibilities were particularly limited by the lack of well-developed institutional means of amassing long-term capital for manufacturing purposes, either on the regional or national level. This meant that the South, already impoverished by the events of the 1860s, found itself ill equipped to move its capital to those areas and industries offering the greatest opportunities; moreover, this left the region isolated from outside sources of manufacturing investment, a condition analogous to the isolated southern labor market recently posited by Gavin Wright.[5] Prospective industrialists were thus forced to rely heavily on local sources, notably on numerous small savers from the immediate vicinity. These "widows and orphans," in turn, often enforced their own distinctly conservative financial goals on the enterprises they aided, contributing to the undynamic, even stodgy nature of much southern industry. In this fashion the business environment of the postbellum South materially shaped the character of southern entrepreneurship itself.

In order to understand the difficulties faced by southern entrepreneurs in financing their enterprises, it is necessary first to discuss the options available in late-nineteenth-century America generally. By and large, those options were few. To begin with, one has to remember that virtually all U.S. manufacturing in the nineteenth century was carried on in relatively small-scale, single-plant enterprises.[6] Because of this, and because of their reputation for financial instability, manufacturers tended to be isolated from major sources of capital. Most of the financial intermediaries and markets available to industrialists today were either not yet in existence or, if they did exist, were wary of industrial investments. Banks and insurance companies, the major intermediaries of the age, preferred either short-term loans or more traditional long-term outlets such as real estate.[7] Outside of New England, few manufacturing securities traded on major stock exchanges before the 1890s, and even then only a few of the very largest firms, mainly the rising national industrial corporations of the Northeast and Midwest, had access to such capital sources.[8] Once an enterprise was off the ground, of course, it could rely on retained earnings for expansion, but this option obviously was unavailable to beginning enterprises. Lacking central marketing institutions for industrial securities or retained earnings, aspiring entrepreneurs were thrown back on their own resources, or on the ad hoc personal networks they were able to construct as men of business.[9]

In this localistic and highly personal financial environment, prospective southern industrialists found themselves saddled with several disadvantages. First, whether judged in terms of wealth or income, the postbellum South was by far the poorest region of the nation. The destruction and dislocation wrought by the Civil War, and the legal abolition of its principal form of capital, slave property, left the region with a severely depleted store of wealth. At the same time, per capita income levels plummeted to roughly half the national average, there to remain for half a century.[10] This left many, if not all, southerners with little ability to save, or to invest. To take two measures, southerners deposited only one-fifth as much money per capita into regional banks as did Americans generally, and their per capita investments in life insurance fell far below national levels.[11] These measures are admittedly imperfect; there were wealthy southerners, and southern savers had other outlets available, both within and without the region. However, when considered in conjunction with the institutional impediments treated below, they do suggest something about the local resources available to prospective industrialists.

Relative poverty, to be sure, would not have been too great a handicap in and of itself, if regional or national markets had channeled capital to enterprises in the South as efficiently as they did elsewhere. While, as we have seen, American industrial capital markets in the late nineteenth century were generally poorly integrated, they nonetheless worked reasonably well in the emerging manufacturing belt. There, for instance, prior commercial and industrial development provided northeastern and midwestern entrepreneurs not only with sizeable sums of capital but also with intricate networks of personal business relationships, which eased their access to available funds. These proved especially useful in handling interregional transfers of industrial capital, which appear to have been associated with population flows. The lines of business migration, like population migration, generally ran from east to west; as a result the Midwest received capital both through the physical movement of capitalists and through the business connections they enjoyed back east.[12]

Herein the South was doubly handicapped. First, the density of southern business relationships historically had been lower than those elsewhere; because of this, the

South's internal mechanisms for mobilizing capital developed even more slowly than those outside the region.[13] Compounding the internal inadequacies of southern business networks was their relative isolation from non-southern capital sources. Certainly the persistent regional differentials in interest rates found by Lance Davis suggest that serious impediments obstructed the entry of outside capital into the region. Major financial intermediaries did not pursue southern opportunities; one recent study of the investments of major insurance companies in the late nineteenth century indicates that little of the pittance they allocated to industrial securities at that time found its way south of the Mason-Dixon Line.[14] Nor were more personal forms of interregional capital transfer of great benefit to the South; unlike contemporary midwestern manufacturers, most Piedmont industrialists, at least, were of local origin.[15] Although exceptional southern enterprises were able to tap emerging money markets or to draw upon wealthy outside business associates, most prospective entrepreneurs were forced by their lack of national or regional connections to rely on the relatively meager resources of themselves and their local allies.

Poverty, and the high information and transaction costs associated with poorly integrated capital markets, thus imposed serious restraints on the ability of would-

Table 7.1. Capitalization and character of organization: cotton goods industry, 1900

Region or state	Capital investment ($$)	Capital per firm (in $$ thousands)	Number of firms	Number of corporations	Percent incorporated
New England	272,668,914	821	332	274	83
Massachusetts	155,761,193	956	163	138	85
Mid-Atlantic	59,078,820	263	225	70	31
Pennsylvania	22,386,121	145	154	30	19
South	124,532,864	311	400	352	88
Virginia	4,403,206[a]	629	7	7	100
North Carolina	33,011,516	187	177	149	84
South Carolina	39,258,946	491	80	75	94
Georgia	24,158,159	361	67	59	88
Alabama	11,638,757	375	31	31	100
West	4,562,174	285	16	12	75
Non-South	336,309,908	587	573	356	62
United States	460,842,772	474	973	708	73

Source: U.S. Census Office, *Twelfth Census of the United States, 1900: Manufactures*, Part 3, 60.

[a] The bulk of this total can apparently be attributed to a single firm, the Riverside Cotton Mills of Danville, Virginia. Robert S. Smith, *Mill on the Dan: A History of Dan River Mills, 1882–1950* (Durham, N.C., 1960), 550, reports that in 1899 the firm's equity and surplus totaled $2,372,000.

be southern industrialists to raise sufficient funds to grasp opportunities even when perceived. The low levels of capitalization among late-nineteenth-century southern manufacturing firms suggest some of these constraints. In 1900 the typical southern firm was capitalized at $11,000, compared to the non-southern average of $21,000.[16] Tables 7.1 and 7.2 reveal similar disparities in leading individual industries common to South and non-South. Southern cotton mills averaged $311,000 in capitalization, considerably less than the non-southern average of $587,000, and far less than the New England average of $821,000; for the Carolinas, the average was $281,000. Similarly, in furniture, an industry of future importance beginning to develop in North Carolina, the typical southern firm weighed in at $35,000, relative to a national figure of $60,000. While the typical firm in the leading furniture-producing region, the Midwest, used $80,000 in capital, the typical North Carolina furniture maker capitalized at $23,000.[17]

Although southern industrial enterprises had to rely on local capital raised from a population with limited means at its disposal, they could partially compensate by assuming a corporate form of organization and pooling small investments. Even before the Civil War the corporate form for manufacturing firms was well established throughout most of the South; in the late nineteenth century this form strengthened its position, with South Carolina, a laggard state, passing its general incorporation law in 1886. Limited liability of stockholders was a virtually universal feature of corporate charters in the Carolinas by the 1880s.[18]

The corporate form was, to be sure, hardly unknown in the industrial North; in fact, in 1900, when the Census of Manufactures first recorded data on "character of

Table 7.2. Capitalization and character of organization, furniture factories, 1900

Region or state	Capital investment ($$)	Capital per firm (in $$ thousands)	Number of firms	Number of corporations	Percent incorporated
New England	4,096,032	21	194	43	22
Mid-Atlantic	35,738,663	58	614	124	20
South	5,805,784	35	164	79	48
North Carolina	1,023,374	23	44	28	64
Midwest	51,533,435	80	644	347	54
Trans-Mississippi West	7,250,847	37	198	76	38
Non-South	98,678,610	60	1,650	590	36
United States	104,484,394	58	1,814	669	37

Source: U.S. Census Office, *Twelfth Census of the United States, 1900: Manufactures,* Part 1, 222, 538.

organization," there was no discernible difference between South and non-South in its use, only 8 percent of firms in each "region" being incorporated.[19] As tables 7.1 and 7.2 show, however, cross-regional comparisons involving selected leading industries tell a more complex story. In cotton goods, the numerous smaller mills of the South incorporated at a slightly higher rate than the much larger mills of New England, 88 percent compared to 83 percent. North Carolina industrialists, whose firms averaged little larger than those of the "proprietary capitalists" of Pennsylvania, nonetheless incorporated their cotton textile enterprises at a rate of 84 percent, compared to 19 percent for the Keystone State.[20] Furniture factories tended to be much smaller than cotton mills, and thus relied less on incorporation as a means of finance. Despite an average capitalization below even the industry average, southern furniture makers relied more heavily on incorporation than non-southerners; 48 percent of southern firms were chartered, compared to only 36 percent outside the region. In North Carolina, 64 percent of firms incorporated, a much higher rate than obtained in the relatively highly capitalized furniture industry of the Midwest.[21]

Adjusted for firm size, then, southern industries used the corporate form more heavily than did their counterparts elsewhere. While the distinction between the South and the non-South in this regard is hardly dramatic, the use of incorporation for such small firms does suggest a greater need in the South to pool the savings of many small investors in order to raise equity capital. This dependence on the small investor, we will argue, imposed certain restraints on entrepreneurial flexibility in the region. Small savers, with their traditionally strong preferences for safety and regularity of income, insisted on steady dividends, often at the expense of internally financed expansion; the resulting intricate links between enterprise and community had like results. Moreover, the concern of "widows and orphans" for safe investments led to the channeling of investment funds into a relatively small range of technologically stagnant and thus relatively "safe" industries, thereby biasing the southern industrial economy against the pursuit of a broadly based and innovative development.

How important was the small saver to southern manufacturing? In order to assess the distribution of stockholding in southern firms, we need a comparative framework, which, given the state of our understanding of the history of U.S. small business, will of necessity be of patchwork construction.[22] For purposes of illustration, let us begin with the late nineteenth century, when southerners were commencing the modern industrialization of their region, and with the launching of a reasonably representative manufacturing firm of the North. The Buckeye Malleable Iron and Coupler Company, an iron and steel products company located in Columbus, Ohio, displays both the financing difficulties confronted by most manufacturing concerns in the late nineteenth century and the advantages that northern firms derived from their location. Buckeye's predecessor firm began operations in 1881, but suffered through thirteen years of chronic financial difficulties before finally gaining stability with a reorganization in 1894. Although Buckeye emerged with a capitalization of $500,000, much larger than contemporary southern firms, its creators made no public stock offerings, but relied heavily on their own resources and those of personal friends and business acquaintances for their long-term capital needs. Given their locale, the founders' personal connections were by this time relatively numerous and well heeled. Many of the shareholders were prominent Ohio bankers, railroad men, and steelmakers; most notable among them was John D. Rockefeller's brother Frank, who became one of Buckeye's largest stockholders. Through Frank Rockefeller, moreover, Buckeye gained access to the resources of Rockefeller-controlled concerns such as Colorado Iron and Steel, which made the firm a sizable loan in 1904. Networks such as these enabled the company to achieve long-term success.

Not every new manufacturing enterprise in the North, of course, could call on an angel named Rockefeller, and small industrial concerns, especially in capital-intensive industries such as Buckeye's, could expect to face difficulties in raising long-term funds. Those in the North, however, benefitted from their location in an expanding industrial economy generating large pools of capital, potentially available for financing new ventures.[23] Similar advantages were available in a time and place perhaps more appropriate to the southern situation, antebellum New England. It is well known that the rise of the early textile industry there was heavily financed by accumulated mercantile capital from Boston. The great "Massachusetts-type" mills of the Boston Associates were financed almost entirely by capitalists of considerable means, bound together by business, cultural, and affective ties into a powerful network. Lance Davis reports that investments of $2,500 or more made up 95 percent of the original capitalization of nine major cotton manufacturing firms.[24] The Associates' capital spilled over into related enterprises as well. For example, individual investments in the Lowell Manufacturing Company, a pioneer in the mass production of carpeting, ranged from $15,000 to $30,000; indeed, as with the other Boston Associates' enterprises, small investors were effectively shut out by a par price per share of $1,000. Personal connections, through state government and Harvard College, drew the Associates into the textile, metal-working, and machinery industries of Taunton, Massachusetts, as well, prompting their historian to observe that "the willingness of capitalists to assume the risk of investing in new technologies accounted as much for the progress of the industrial revolution as did the ingenuity of inventors."[25]

From early on, then, the evidence suggests that there were large blocks of investment capital in the Northeast, and later by extension the Midwest, that were available to entrepreneurs whose business and social ties gave them access to the individuals controlling them. The relative lack of such individuals in the Carolina Piedmont was a significant handicap, as can be seen in the case of the Trenton Cotton Mills, getting underway in Gastonia, North Carolina, at about the same time that Buckeye was scrambling to its feet. Trenton was a much smaller firm than the Ohio enterprise, its initial capitalization amounting to $62,400. Its promoters, a Gastonia merchant and a "practical mill man," found assembling even this sum difficult; according to the merchant's son, they "went all around to anyone that they knew who had a thousand or two dollars":

> Over in Mecklenburg County, just across the river, they heard of an old gentleman over there, a Mr. Stowe that had several thousand dollars. They rode over to see him on horseback and they talked all morning and Mr. Stowe said, "Well, gentlemen, it is getting about time for [dinner] and I want you gentlemen to have dinner with me." When they got to the table, Mr. Stowe was telling Mrs. Stowe, "These gentlemen are organizing a mill in Gastonia and they feel like the prospects are good for making money and paying dividends." Mrs. Stowe said, "I'll tell you one thing, I don't believe that I would have anything to do with a cotton mill." Of course, that sort of cooled things off for a while, but my father and Mr. Gray persisted and stayed on for several hours and finally when they left, Mr. Stowe agreed to take two or three thousand dollars worth of stock and Mrs. Stowe apparently agreed to it.

Mr. Stowe, needless to say, could not play Rockefeller to Trenton's Buckeye; nor could any of the other original stockholders. The eight incorporators, all local men, included two merchants, a banker, a physician, a hotel keeper, the "mill man," and a farmer (not Mr. Stowe, by the way) whose share was the mill site. Their contributions ranged from one to five thousand dollars apiece. Thus one of the earliest of the Gas-

Table 7.3. Proportion of shares held by small shareholders, six Piedmont cotton mills

Name of firm	Year	Percent of shareholdings equal to or less than				
		$1,000	$2,000	$2,500	$4,000	$5,000
Bloomfield Manufacturing Co., Statesville, N.C.	1903	22.1	28.6	36.2	36.2	46.2
Mooresville Cotton Mills, Mooresville, N.C.	1896	40.2	46.3	69.9	77.6	77.6
Newberry Cotton Mill, Newberry, S.C.	1883	23.8	32.3	33.8	45.2	56.6
Piedmont Manufacturing Co., Piedmont, S.C.	1874	38.8	45.5	48.0	50.9	65.3
Shelby Cotton Mills, Shelby, N.C.	1902	16.6	29.4	32.3	40.7	52.6
Spartan Mills, Spartanburg, S.C.	1890	18.3	30.3	36.6	45.9	48.2

Source: See nn. 27, 28, and 30.

tonia mills was launched, successfully as it turned out; but if its initiators were not exactly beggars, it could nonetheless be said to have begun on nickels and dimes.[26]

Not all textile enterprises launched in the late-nineteenth-century Piedmont displayed precisely the same pattern as Trenton. Nonetheless, examination of the available stockholders' lists suggests that the mobilization of small-scale capital was important even to those enterprises with stronger outside connections (see table 7.3). The case of Spartan Mills of Spartanburg, South Carolina, formed in 1890, is particularly instructive. Spartan Mills was initially capitalized at nearly half a million dollars, comparable to Buckeye, and received considerable aid from important New England textile interests. However, while Buckeye had forty-seven stockholders, Spartan had 197. The median Spartan shareholder contributed only $1,000 to the capital stock, while those investing $2,500 or less (the dividing line used by Davis to distinguish large from small investors) controlled over one-third (36.6 percent) of the stock.[27] In North Carolina, the much smaller Mooresville Cotton Mills, organized in 1893 and capitalized at about $50,000, obtained over two-thirds of its capital stock from subscribers holding twenty-five shares (valued at $100 each) or less. One of the pioneer mills of the South, the Piedmont Manufacturing Company of Piedmont, South Carolina, drew on small investors for nearly 48 percent of its initial stake. The Newberry Cotton Mill in South Carolina, which began business in 1883 with $175,000 in capital stock, relied on small holders for one-third of total investment. A stockholders' list of the Shelby Cotton Mills submitted with a petition for amendment of charter in 1902 showed that even after the initiation of the enterprise, small stockholders supplied nearly one-third of equity.[28] Finally, a survey of twenty-one corporate charters of Gaston County mills built after 1880 indicates that the median proportion of initial capitalization contributed by small holders was 25 percent; eight received more than 40 percent from those sources, and one obtained 100 percent.[29]

Given the reliance of these enterprises on small investors, and the lack of adequate institutional means by which such investments could be mobilized, it stands to reason that many shareholders would be local residents. Available evidence suggests that this was indeed generally the case. At Newberry, two-thirds (67.8 percent) of the shares were held by individuals sharing the same post office as the mill. When the Bloomfield Manufacturing Company of Statesville, North Carolina, was organized in 1903, only six of fifty-six subscribers lived outside Iredell County, and local folk controlled nearly three-fourths (74.2 percent) of the shares. The nearby Mooresville Mills relied even more heavily on its neighborhood; of almost $50,000 subscribed, only $500 came from out of state, or even out of the vicinity. Larger firms, to be sure, were able to draw their investments from wider areas, and sometimes could even tap into regional and national money centers. Spartanburg's Pacolet Manufacturing Company, which by 1895 was capitalized at $700,000, an enormous sum by Piedmont standards, attracted extensive interest from New Yorkers (16.1 percent), New Englanders (8.3 percent), Baltimoreans (8.7 percent), and Charlestonians (12.3 percent).

Even in this case, nearly 38 percent (37.6) of its stock rested in the hands of local residents.[30]

Similar patterns seem to have characterized another significant Piedmont industry: furniture. The typical furniture firm in the region was even smaller than the typical cotton textile firm; a survey of fifty-two furniture-manufacturing corporations chartered in the two principal centers of the North Carolina industry before 1906 suggests that half of them began business with less than $10,000 capitalization, and only six were capitalized at over $18,000.[31] Of those with more than $10,000 capitalization, the median firm depended on small investors ($2,500 or less) for nearly half (47.5 percent) of its organizing capital. Needless to say, virtually all listed incorporators were residents of the same county as the firm.[32]

This is not to say that all investors were local. Commission merchants in the northeastern wholesaling centers often took stock in southern cotton mills in order to assure themselves some control over their supply, and also provided their clients with much of their short-term credit. Moreover, northern textile machinery manufacturers sometimes accepted securities in partial payment for machinery purchases, chiefly as a competitive tool in bidding for southern business. The latter practice was avoided much of the time, though, both because of the usual concerns about investment in distant manufacturing enterprises and because securities holdings could strain the working capital of the machinery makers themselves.[33]

In any case, extensive participation by neighborhood stockholders was crucial to a firm's hopes of attracting northern interest, for outside investors regarded substantial local support as essential to the soundness of the enterprise. "Capitalists want the people at home largely identified with any enterprise they put their money into," declared one industrialist in 1887; "they want this to protect it against local prejudices, adverse legislation, and that it shall have the moral support of the people living around it."[34] To be sure, one could argue from this that small, local investors served merely as bait for the enticement of external investment. However, since outside capital proved elusive quarry, the end result was essentially the same.

Clearly, then, in more ways than one, the participation of local people, particularly small investors, was vital to initiating an industrial enterprise. This is not, of course, to argue for some sort of "industrial democracy"; any individual able to subscribe for as much as $2,500—our upper limit of "small" investment—hardly qualifies as a "common man" in the Carolina upcountry of this period. However, it does suggest that, stripped of its religious overtones, Broadus Mitchell's classic emphasis on the intricate ties between industrial enterprise and the Piedmont community retains much explanatory power.[35] The Piedmont's drive to industrialize was largely a product of decisions made by local notables with an eye to developing their communities, while benefitting themselves in the process.

The numerous connections between industrial enterprise and community prosperity in the late-nineteenth-century South have been explored elsewhere.[36] Here, though, we wish to point to an aspect hitherto slighted: the utility of industrial stocks as investments. One major difficulty faced by southerners with savings in the late nineteenth century was a dearth of satisfactory investment outlets. Certain forms of securities, notably railroad stocks and bonds, were available, as were state and local bonds, bank deposits, and insurance policies. However, the most widely available outlet by far was real estate. Land, particularly rural land, had numerous disadvantages as an investment. It was difficult to liquidate, and low postbellum land values limited its usefulness as collateral.[37] Furthermore, the supervision of real estate holdings entailed close management, which was impractical at a distance and required skills lacked by many potential investors.

Given the limitations of traditional forms of investment, the advent of industrial securities on the scene in the 1880s offered an attractive new alternative. Of these, cotton mill stocks were far and away the most widespread and popular. That this was so requires some explaining, for fixed-maturity, fixed-interest obligations, ordinarily the safest forms of investment, were rarely offered by textile and other manufacturing firms of the time. Low and highly variable profit margins, along with the need to attract extensive credit for working capital, discouraged mills from encumbering their property; those few firms that sought highly leveraged solutions to their financial problems usually came to grief.[38] Southern textile manufacturers, then, relied chiefly on stock issues for their long-term capital requirements.

While less satisfactory to small investors than debt instruments, mill stocks nonetheless offered them numerous advantages over the remaining options. Unlike land, mill securities were portable and liquid, enhancing their values as collateral. Moreover, they were backed not only by a firm's physical assets but by its managerial talent as well, relieving investors of some of the burdens of caring for their wealth. Here the local character of the investment became important. In an age in which provincials regarded Wall Street securities as malodorous, the prestige of local promoters imparted a sweeter fragrance to their enterprises.

The resulting advantages of mill securities are illustrated by a story told some years later by Dave Hall, a Gaston County textile executive. At the turn of the century Hall's farmer father was prevailed upon to invest in a local mill promoted by a merchant friend. Soon afterward he died, leaving his widow with eight children to support. In need of schooling for her brood, she was forced to move to town, rendering it difficult for her to oversee her tenants and gain a return from her farm properties. Thus "practically the sole support of that family during those years was the return on that [mill] investment": "Many times emergencies arose in that family and those dividends had to be anticipated and that stock taken to the bank and there found to be good collateral. There its dividends redeemed it and it came back, but other emergencies arose . . . and the stock went back. Thus, through the long period of 30 years, it moved back and forth from the bank to that home."[39]

The basis of that original investment may well have been, as Hall maintained, his father's "faith in the integrity and the honesty and the judgment and the human nature of a man that he loved." But the enduring value of the investment lay in its stability, convertibility, and dependable return. It was these features that made securities attractive to the small savers to whom prospective industrialists needed to appeal. Mill stock, in fact, became one of the preferred "widows and orphans" investments of the New South. The portfolios of Charleston maiden aunts bulged with them; newspaper men endowed their wives with them as forms of life insurance; ministers sought from them, if not salvation, at least some earthly security.[40]

The need to accommodate such investors, however, inevitably entailed attention to their financial priorities, which did not comport well with avid risk taking. Complaining to a friend, William Watts Ball, about the passing of a dividend by a major South Carolina mill corporation in 1912, a Charleston investor remarked that "the cutting off of more than $700 per annum from income is a very serious and startling matter for me." The president of the firm concurred, responding to Ball that "nothing is more important to a corporation than the confidence of its shareholders" and privately disagreeing with the decision of his own board of directors to pass the dividend.[41]

This concern with steady dividends and the good will of numerous small, local investors exerted strong pressures toward managerial conservatism and risk aversion. For one thing, it tended to militate against the use of retained earnings, historically a major source of industrial capital, to finance expansion. When the officers of Belmont's Chronicle Mills wished to expand their operations in 1905, they were loath to enlarge their current five-thousand-spindle plant because "it would be necessary to call upon the stockholders for additional capitalization or ask them to forego the dividends they were receiving on the present operation or sell additional stock to other stockholders." They chose to expand, instead, by organizing another corporation, the Imperial Yarn Mill, and building a new plant the same size as the old just across the railroad tracks, thereby depriving themselves of possible economies of scale ostensibly for the sake of community relations. Their motives in this were probably not altogether altruistic. Six years earlier, a proposal to expand the nearby Trenton Cotton Mills through a new stock issue had sparked a shareholder revolt and a court injunction; the projectors of the Imperial Mill, furthermore, seem to have taken care to concentrate its ownership more heavily in their own hands than had been the case with Chronicle.[42]

Whatever the motive, the Imperial Mill case suggests that the influence of small stockholders had important ramifications for the southern textile industry. In particular, the relative difficulty of expanding the existing plant, and the resulting preference for building a new mill, suggests a possible reason for an oft-noted characteristic of the early southern textile industry, the presence of many units of less than optimal scale. In 1905 North Carolina mills had on average only one-fifth the spindleage of New England mills; of cloth mills reporting spindleage to *Davison's Textile Blue Book*, 60.5 percent reported fewer than ten thousand spindles, a conservative lower limit for technical efficiency. Yarn mills such as Imperial were far smaller.

In the face of such figures, Melvin Copeland worried that southern mills "sacrifice[d] the technical and administrative advantages to be gained by centralization and large scale production."[43] Such inefficiencies would have important consequences as cost pressures began to bedevil the cotton textile industry in the 1920s.[44]

Investor pressures of this sort were, to be sure, neither new to the South nor unique to it. Safety and high dividends were paramount investment concerns of the Boston Associates; as Paul McGouldrick has pointed out, after the end of their innovative phase in the 1810s and 1820s, the great Massachusetts-type mills paid out virtually all their profits in dividends.[45] One can argue, however, that similar policies would have strikingly different effects in the varied contexts of antebellum New England and the late-nineteenth-century South. The Massachusetts mills were generally amply capitalized, and thanks to decreasing capital costs could finance much of their expansion, as well as replacement of worn-out machinery, out of depreciation. Large dividends, flowing primarily into the hands of large capitalists, could be easily reinvested; indeed, McGouldrick has suggested that this was a highly efficient method of reallocating capital to new firms, even new industries.[46] On the other hand, in a capital-short region such as the South, operating in an environment of more or less stable capital costs, the pressures exerted on earnings by dividends would be more acute.[47] Furthermore, the heavy reliance on small investors meant that a much larger proportion of dividends would be diverted to consumption, making retained earnings a more important means of capital accumulation than they would be in wealthier regions.

Concerns for safety, in any case, may well have had serious consequences not simply for individual enterprises but for the industrial structure of the region as well. It is well known that between 1860 and 1900 the structure of southern manufacturing industry became remarkably unbalanced. Whereas in the mid-nineteenth century the region's manufacturing profile was similar to that of the nation as a whole, by its end a small range of processing industries dominated the statistics, at the expense of those, such as machinery, which have historically been regarded as basic to a dynamic and diverse industrial development.[48] There are many complex reasons for this troubling development, but among them must rank a peculiarly strong aversion to risk among southern investors. Textiles, again, is a prime example. By the late nineteenth century it was a structurally and technologically mature industry, endowed with a fully articulated complex of capital goods and other suppliers and a sophisticated marketing system. The panoply of services available to prospective entrepreneurs sharply reduced the risk of entering the textile industry, further adding to its attractiveness as an investment for small savers concerned with protecting their nest eggs. As textile securities developed reputations as safe and steadily remunerative havens for savings, accumulated capital increasingly flowed into mill stocks and bonds. At the same time, reliance on established northern suppliers of capital goods dampened the prospects of southern machine-makers; in this way aversion to risk became a self-fulfilling prophecy, increasing the *real* risks confronted by indigenous capital goods industries and directing investment away from them.[49]

Thus the investment climate of the late-nineteenth- and early-twentieth-century Piedmont worked to confine the entrepreneurial impulse, by and large, within limited and unimaginative channels. That this was primarily a structural problem, rather than a consequence of some peculiar southern "conservatism" inherited from the slave regime, can be seen by examining the major exception to the foregoing pattern, the case of the tobacco industry. Tobacco men came from the same cultural milieu as the textile men, but they confronted, and mastered, a strikingly different structure of opportunity. Unlike yarn and cloth, the mass production of tobacco products was in essence a new industry, riding the crest of an explosively expanding national market for consumer goods. Burgeoning demand for their wares generated huge profits for the foremost tobacco barons, permitting them to escape the capital constraints faced by their brethren in other Piedmont industries. At the same time, the growing pains experienced by this relatively youthful industry created numerous opportunities for entrepreneurial innovation.

Two important cases in point are those of Julian S. Carr and James B. Duke. Carr, the son of a Chapel Hill merchant, used a genius for marketing to make the Durham Bull possibly the best-known advertising symbol in the world by the end of the nineteenth century. As his business grew, however, a series of bottlenecks developed, particularly on the packing and shipping ends. To solve these problems, Carr bankrolled talented mechanics throughout the late nineteenth century, who developed machinery to sew bags, pack them with tobacco, and stamp and label the bags for shipment. One of his protegés, Rufus L. Patterson, went on to a brilliant career of innovation, founding the American Machine and Foundry Company.[50]

Carr's accomplishments in manufacturing smoking tobacco were far surpassed by Duke's in cigarettes. Exploiting more fully than his fellow Durhamite the potential of the emerging national market, "Buck" Duke used control of critical technology and innovative purchasing and sales organizations to build one of the first modern "big businesses" and make himself a kingly fortune in the process. Significantly, Duke's scale and control over his market allowed him to be among the first industrial entrepreneurs to tap Wall Street investment funds and to make use of such innovative financial instruments as preferred stocks.[51] The Duke innovation most beneficial to the Piedmont, though, was his underwriting of the vast Southern Power Company transmission grid, which by the 1920s was one of the most advanced regional electric power systems in the country, if not the world. Interestingly enough, the vision originated with another Piedmont entrepreneur, an engineer named William States Lee; but only Duke possessed the vast resources required to create the interlocking network of generators, lines, and users necessary to assure its success. Duke's millions made him unique among Piedmont investors. While so many of them were small, weak, and perforce timid, Duke (and to a lesser extent Carr) was able to function as a sort of venture capitalist, taking the pioneering risks that few others in his society were able to afford.[52]

Men like Duke and Carr, however, were by nature few and far between in the Piedmont; with its vast economies of scale and increasingly high barriers to entry, the tobacco industry provided opportunities for the making of only two or three great fortunes. Moreover, its high concentration and small aggregate size limited the importance of its linkages to other industries. For these reasons Carr's sponsorship of innovation failed to create a machinery industry in Durham. Much of the development work was done in Baltimore, in order to take advantage of already existing machine shops, and Patterson ultimately placed the headquarters of AMF in New York. Duke's impact on the course of Piedmont development was more enduring, but he alone could not prevent it from pursuing the unbalanced industrial path it took. Even though it was the leading industrial region of the South, the Piedmont's development lacked the broadly energizing characteristics attributed to earlier industrializing regions such as New England, the lower Delaware Valley, and the Midwest.[53]

The fragmented, localized, ad hoc capital markets of the early industrializing Piedmont, then, posed grave obstacles to the region's ability to achieve healthy economic development. The story is far from uniformly bleak, however, for the very reliance of so many firms on small investors gave impetus to the development of more modern institutions for capital mobilization. Small savers' desire for safety and concern with convertibility generated a hunger for information and created a demand for more efficient securities markets. As early as the 1880s newspapers in Charleston, the Carolinas' leading money center, were quoting a small number of "factory stocks," chiefly those issued by South Carolina mills. By 1900 such listings were more extensive and broader in geographical coverage, including mills from Virginia to Alabama; they were also beginning to appear in newspapers in interior towns. More important, by then quotations were usually identified as originating with brokers and brokerage houses that made the trading of what had come to be called "cotton mill stocks" a specialty.[54] Over time, some of the larger houses in major textile centers, such as the Furman Company of Greenville and Law and Company of Spartanburg, entered the business of underwriting new issues of mill securities.[55] Another important avenue through which small savings could be channeled into industrial enterprise was the trust company, of which the Piedmont prototype was the Wachovia Bank and Trust Company of Winston-Salem, North Carolina. Wachovia's bond department, which opened after the turn of the century, performed numerous investment banking functions.[56] The emphasis on safety and on traditional investment continued, to be sure. Even as late as 1927, a significant number of securities dealers, especially in South Carolina, identified themselves as specialists in cotton mill stocks. Wachovia stressed investments in old-line local corporations such as R. J. Reynolds, Mayo Mills, and the various Hanes enterprises.[57] Nonetheless an institutional foundation was being laid that in future years would improve in sophistication and versatility.

As these subsequent developments suggest, the early difficulties faced by Piedmont industrializers can in one sense be viewed as instances of the "tensions" and "pressures" that figure so much in Albert Hirschman's scheme of "uneven development." While "the efficient path toward economic development . . . is apt to be somewhat disorderly and . . . will be strewn with bottlenecks and shortages of skills, facilities, services, and products," argued Hirschman, the very act of facing obstacles propels the system forward.[58] Insofar as the economic evolution of the Piedmont reflects this process, it can be said to present a success story. Even today, however, that success is incomplete; recent industrial dislocations, and continuing lags in personal income and manufacturing wages, leave its overall record still decidedly mixed.[59] And, given the Piedmont's industrial preeminence within the region, the same observations can be made far more forcefully about most other parts of the South.

Accordingly, it is not amiss to pay careful attention to the limitations, as well as the successes, of the South's industrial experience. We have here suggested one such limitation. Obviously other factors have shaped southern industrial development as well. For instance, considerations of comparative advantage have played a major role in determining the choice of industries in the region; indeed, a sizable literature has grown up pointing to the cost advantages enjoyed by southern industries, textiles in particular.[60] Among the numerous other elements in play have been the South's dearth of human capital and the agglomeration advantages of the manufacturing belt.

Any well-rounded account of the southern economic struggle, however, must pay some heed to the major actors in the story, including entrepreneurs. After all, it has been the historic function of entrepreneurs to solve problems such as those outlined above. Certainly similar obstacles have been overcome in other times and places and, as the examples of Carr and Duke illustrate, even to some degree in the South itself. It is thus important not simply to cite economic forces in explaining historic patterns, but to show the ways in which those forces affect the behavior of individuals. Not only might this approach prove useful in explaining such strictly economic questions as we have treated here, but it can also aid historians, as well as economists, in better understanding the complex interrelationships between economics and broader patterns of social and cultural life.

8

The Uninventive South?

A Quantitative Look at Region and American Inventiveness

DAVID L. CARLTON AND PETER A. COCLANIS

This essay, published in 1995 in the journal *Technology and Culture*, originated as an attempt on our part to explore a relationship between the "unbalanced" structure of southern industry and what appears to have been an increasing lag in southern inventiveness compared to the rest of the country. At the behest of the journal editor, we reframed the piece as an exercise in "learning by doing," using the development of our argument to explain our use of regression analysis and show how it could not only help answer our original questions but raise new questions about the larger relationship of region to American inventiveness. Most recent work on the history of innovation in America has been associated with Naomi Lamoreaux and Kenneth Sokoloff. In their writings they have stressed the importance to the history of innovation in the United States of the rise of intermediary institutions (patent attorneys and the like) that allowed inventors to specialize in research and development, "assigning" (selling) their patents to others. Like the capital markets we treat in the previous chapter, these intermediaries were in the late nineteenth and early twentieth centuries much more highly developed in the rest of the nation than in the South.[1]

Historical economists studying the United States have typically been preoccupied with explaining the American economic success story. With their gaze firmly set on the national level, it is not surprising that they have stressed the role played by the creation of a highly integrated national economy in furthering growth. Although economists' fascination with the benefits of free trade, factor mobility, and the division of labor is justifiable, that same enthusiasm has led them to downplay an important countercurrent, that of persistent disparities in regional development. Yet, beginning with the Sunbelt-Frostbelt controversy of the late 1970s, we have seen increasing indications that, despite the prophets of "convergence," regions have continued to matter greatly in our economic life.

The major exception to this neglect of region by economic historians is the American South, whose observers have long been preoccupied with the paradox of persistent regional backwardness in a land of progress. An especially striking instance of this paradox has been the South's experience with industrialization, particularly prior to World War II.[2] Despite impressive growth in manufacturing output in the half century after 1880, the South remained far below national norms not only in income per capita but in a variety of other indexes associated with socioeconomic development. To be sure, the lack of stimulation imparted by manufacturing to southern economic growth was in part a function of its relatively small share of regional employment; however, it was also in great measure a product of the character of southern industrialization itself. Not only was southern manufacturing generally plagued by low output and value added per worker, with resulting low wages, but its industrial structure was heavily skewed toward industries, such as cotton textiles and lumber, whose wealth-producing ability was especially low.[3] Why was this the case? Were these problems merely functions of lagging development, the recapitulation of a stage passed through earlier by the manufacturing belt? Or was there something about the South—its society, culture, or values—that impeded the region's progress down the classic industrial road to modernization?

In view of the sheer obduracy of southern problems, simple economic factors have never seemed sufficient to explain them. While some observers, especially in the 1930s, have looked to constraints from without, for example, "economic colonialism," as the key to southern industrial underdevelopment, more have been drawn to broadly social and cultural explanations, popularly in images of the "lazy South" and intellectually in visions of the region as an "agrarian" alternative to the crass, industrial North. In the postwar era, these notions intersected with the vogue of "modernization" theory, which tended to attribute lags in economic development to persistent "traditional" social values, particularly hostility to unconventional thinking, lack of political flexibility, and the exaltation of "ascribed" over "achieved" social status. If, as was commonly believed, the United States as a whole was archetypically "modern" in its openness to change and innovation, the South, with its hidebound racial hierarchy and its repressive reaction to the emerging civil rights movement, seemed clearly "traditional." To many, this social and cultural backwardness explained the region's economic backwardness. The link between backward values and a backward economy was made even more powerfully by Eugene Genovese, with his introduction of Gramscian concepts of "cultural hegemony" to studies of the slave regime, concepts extended in the 1970s to the post-emancipation South.[4]

Cultural explanations for economic behavior are notoriously slippery and difficult to assess. However, one aspect of the "traditional values" argument seems open to testing: its implications for the relationship of southern culture to innovative activity. It is our purpose in this article to attempt just such a test. According to those who stress the South's cultural backwardness, both before and after the death of the slave regime, the region was peculiarly hostile to the inventive impulse. Its rigid class and racial hierarchies inhibited human capital development, including the acquisition of mechanical skills. Its conservatism discouraged the sort of independent thought that might give rise to innovation and denied innovators adequate rewards (perhaps even punished them) for their efforts at improvement.[5]

Here we have a hypothesis explicitly relating a geographic region—the South—to a relative level of innovative activity—low. But how do we know that it is valid? And how do we go about explaining it if it is? Certainly the literature of southern development provides no dearth of examples. However, such anecdotal approaches pose several major problems. First of all, the choice of anecdotes too often assumes the proposition to be proven, that case studies reflect clearly defined, homogeneous regions exhibiting plain differences from each other. But regions are more likely to be internally heterogeneous, with internal variation and overlap blurring the distinctions among them. Second, a nonsystematic approach to explanation can too easily degenerate into a descriptive "laundry list" of causative factors, all implicitly given equal and independent weight. In particular, historians too easily fall back on vaguely "cultural" explanations for economic behavior without first taking account of more straightforward factors. We do not mean to argue against multicausal explanatory schemes; as the following will indicate, our own is decidedly complex, not to say messy. Nonetheless, we believe that the best explanations are unified explanations, with relevant factors assessed for their relative weights and their relationships with one another. Moreover, when accounting for economic behavior, the most logically parsimonious approach accounts for economic factors *before* reaching for any broader "cultural" explanations. Finally, a systematic approach should be testable in a reasonably conclusive fashion; that is, it should be "falsifiable."

One analytic approach that meets the above requirements is multiple regression analysis. Multiple regression analysis, broadly speaking, is a statistical technique for estimating the underlying relationship between a "dependent" variable (normally designated Y), whose variation one wishes to explain, and two or more "independent" variables (designated $X1$, $X2$, etc.) that might help explain that variation. Regression analysis describes that relationship in the form of a standard algebraic equation, one that if plotted on a Cartesian, or XY, graph will define a plane passing as closely as possible to all the observations. The "best-fitting plane" is one that best describes graphically the relationship of observations to each other in terms of the variables; a "perfect fit" allows an observer to predict the value of *Y* exactly if the observer knows the values of the *X* variables.

The "goodness of fit" of the regression plane to the set of observations is measured by a numerical coefficient, ranging from 0 to ±1, called the coefficient of codetermination, or multiple R^2. While the evaluation of R^2s is less than straightforward, a good rule of thumb posits that one has a good fit if R^2 is 0.5 or greater, indicating that at least half the variation among the observations is accounted for by the *X* variables.[6]

A strong R^2, however, is not sufficient to confirm the relationship estimated by the regression equation. Here a problem mentioned earlier comes into play—the possibility that, because of *internal* variation among the observations, the estimated relationship is purely one of coincidence. For instance, if southern states appear to be in the aggregate less literate than non-southern states, but if there is enormous diversity among the states of each "region" and enormous overlap between the two groupings, one could well conclude that the relationship of illiteracy to "southernness" might be illusory. Therefore, each independent variable must be tested for its *statistical significance,* that is, for the likelihood that it measures a real, not a random, relationship. Normally statisticians regard a variable as "significant" if there is at least a 95 percent likelihood that the observed relationship was *not* the product of chance (technically called "significance at the 95 percent level"). The testing procedures are too complex to be discussed here; suffice it to say that below we indicate with an asterisk (*) whether or not a regression coefficient has met the criterion for significance.

How, though, might this method be used to analyze the problem we have set ourselves—the relationship between region and innovation? Our starting point here is the work of the historical economist Robert Higgs, who in several articles in the 1970s used multiple regression analysis to investigate, for the census years from 1870 to 1920, the relationship between geographic variations in inventive activity and several possible explanatory variables.[7] Higgs began with two critical decisions. First, he made the state his unit of analysis.[8] Second, he used as a proxy for inventive activity the number of patents awarded to residents of a state per 100,000 inhabitants.[9] Then he proceeded to devise, for each census year between 1870 and 1920, an estimating regression equation relating his dependent variable (*Y*) to several factors that he hoped would at once explain and predict its variation.[10] His independent variables (*Xs*) were as follows: (1) The urban proportion of each state's population (percent urban). This variable was designed to test a hypothesis, most closely identified with the urban geographer Allan Pred, that inventive creativity was enhanced by the ability of city-dwelling entrepreneurs and skilled workers to easily obtain information and exchange ideas.[11] (2) The manufacturing proportion of each state's labor force *(MF/LF)*. Here Higgs reasoned that manufacturing itself created funds of skills and experience that generated innovation in a self-generating process. (3) A so-called dummy variable—the South—designed to test whether or not there was something peculiar or unique about the region that affected its relative inventiveness vis-à-vis states in other parts of the Union. This "dummy" variable was created by assigning each southern state the value one and each non-southern state the value zero (this variable is hereafter called the "southern dummy").[12]

Higgs's results, reproduced in table 8.1, are very good. His estimating equations fit his set of observations extremely well, yielding R^2s ranging between 0.80 and 0.92 for the census years between 1870 and 1920.[13] Such strong coefficients suggest that Higgs's estimating equation explains much of the state-level variation in inventive activity in the United States in the late nineteenth and early twentieth centuries.

However, as table 8.1 also shows, the variable of chief concern to us, the "southern dummy," provides mixed, even contradictory, evidence about the independent impact of "southernness" on patent activity. In the late nineteenth century, according to Higgs, southern states performed poorly at innovation, but their deviation from national norms can adequately be explained by their relatively slight degree of urbanization and industrialization.[14] This conclusion is indicated by the low ratio between the coefficients for the "southern dummy" and their "standard errors" (in parentheses), a measure of the *internal* variation among the southern and non-southern states

Table 8.1. Ordinary least squares regression estimates: patents/100,000 vs. percentage urban, percentage of workforce in manufacturing (*MF/LF*), "South" (Higgs)

Year	Percent population in cities	*MF/LF*	Southern dummy	R^2	N
1870	0.558*	0.899*	−3.423	0.893	36
	(0.174)	(0.261)	(3.614)		
1880	0.753*	0.355	−0.251	0.921	37
	(0.125)	(0.182)	(2.639)		
1890	0.939*	0.176	−1.956	0.923	37
	(0.122)	(0.183)	(3.044)		
1900	0.756*	−0.208	−7.370*	0.885	44
	(0.102)	(0.166)	(2.304)		
1910	0.783*	−0.598*	−14.234*	0.802	45
	(0.126)	(0.214)	(3.059)		
1920	0.794*	−0.535*	−13.386*	0.816	47
	(0.118)	(0.190)	(2.814)		

Source: Robert Higgs, "American Inventiveness, 1870–1920," *Journal of Political Economy* 79 (May–June 1971): 661–67; table 1 on 665.

Note: "South" is defined as Alabama, Arkansas, Florida, Georgia, Kentucky, Louisiana, Mississippi, North Carolina, Oklahoma (after statehood in 1908), South Carolina, Tennessee, Texas, Virginia, and West Virginia. Standard errors are in parentheses.

*Significant at the 95 percent level.

and of the extensive overlapping of the two groups of states in their patent rates, controlling for industrialization and urbanization. The failure of the southern states to behave with reasonable consistency suggests that the coefficient itself is an accidental product of random variation or, in technical terms, that it is "statistically insignificant." This is not to say that southern social rigidity might not be reflected in some way in the very *lack* of urbanization and industrialization in the South; in fact, with respect to both measures, southern states cluster so tightly at the lower end of the scale as to make such an argument plausible indeed. It is to say, though, that alleged southern social rigidity does not seem to exert an *independent* effect on regional inventive behavior in the nineteenth century.

In the twentieth century, though, the "southernness" of a state begins to have a serious independent effect on its level of inventiveness. In technical terms, the coefficients of the "southern dummy" remain negative but become quite large. More important, they become statistically highly significant.[15] These results indicate that in the early twentieth century, the region not only trailed the nation in its patent activity, but trailed even further than its degree of urbanization and industrialization would have suggested. The South, in other words, seemed to have become *more* traditional—curiouser and curiouser, so to speak—over time. Higgs noted the puzzle at the time, but moved on, and his observation has not been followed up since.

Higgs's findings about the impact of "southernness" on inventive activity suggest that the southern "patent lag" can be attributed neither to any basic peculiarity of southerners' mentality nor to a simple persistence of plantation-era social rigidities; if "tradition" is at work, it appears, at least at first glance, to be itself invented. Another possibility remains, though: that a combination of enduring characteristics and historical timing produced in the twentieth century a structural disability that had not been apparent before.

But what might be the nature of that structural problem? To begin with, consider the following interrelated considerations: (1) the appearance of the southern "patent gap" coincided with the South's first industrial surge, (2) a body of economic literature suggests that capital goods industries are crucial to inventiveness and innovation, and (3) the South's capital goods sector during its early industrialization was extremely small relative to those of numerous other regions during similar stages of industrialization.[16]

As to the first, it is striking that the South's apparent failure to develop a culture of inventiveness and innovation first appeared as it began to industrialize and urbanize. The modern industrialization of the South can be said to have begun about 1880. Its first major upsurge, however, came in the 1890s, when the Carolinas, Georgia, and Alabama became important textile producers, continuing into the twentieth century with the movement of iron-producing Birmingham into steel and other metals industries, and the expansion of the oft-overlooked forest-products industries throughout the region. But, judging from Higgs's evidence, expansion of industry did *not* bring commensurately higher levels of inventiveness and innovation; the technological backwardness of the South, which did not look all that unusual when the region was virtually entirely rural and agricultural, began to look exceptional when it started to develop an "industrial" character.[17]

As to the second, many economists over the years have stressed the importance of capital goods industries during early industrialization, not least because of their key roles as incubators of inventiveness and innovation. A number of authorities can be cited here—there is, for example, a large literature on the role of the machine-tool industry in India and other less developed countries[18]—but for present purposes one will suffice: Nathan Rosenberg. Rosenberg argues that supply and demand considerations—the need for a sufficient stock of skilled labor and adequate demand for a relatively narrow range of specialized products—suggest that capital goods industries will locate disproportionately in areas with sizeable and relatively well-integrated markets, particularly cities or at least areas characterized by relatively high levels of urbanization. Once situated, such industries will at once mobilize and, over time, expand a mass of workers endowed with skills basic to industrialization; these, in turn, will use those skills to solve a stream of new problems.[19] Often, such solutions entail invention and innovation, sometimes spectacular but generally incremental, even quotidian, in nature. Over time, though, a stream of even seemingly minor innovations can have monumental results: a process of sustained growth.[20]

In contrast, a good deal of unsystematic but telling empirical evidence suggests that the South lacked a strong, vibrant capital goods sector during its early industrialization—our point number 3. Louis Ferleger has noted a special dearth of such industries in the so-called plantation South, but the larger region made only a slightly better showing.[21] In 1920, for example, the lumber industry accounted for nearly 17 percent of southern manufacturing employment, but machine tools, perhaps *the* most critical industry to technological development, was almost nonexistent in the region. In 1920 seven machine-tool firms in Kentucky, the South's machine-tool "center," reported 292 employees, one-half of 1 percent of the U.S. total, and even these apparently were chiefly clustered in the Kentucky suburbs of Cincinnati.[22]

A more revealing case, because it is suggestive of the disabilities of the South as a "latecoming" region, comes from its second leading industry in 1920, textiles. Historically, the textile industry had been "the first industry," widely credited with generating a demand for new kinds of machinery that in turn stimulated the development of mechanical skills. Such was certainly the case in New England, where machinery was developed in close cooperation with mills, and where the emerging mill and jointly owned machine shops, like the Lowell and Amoskeag shops, could turn their expertise to the production of other products such as machine tools and locomotives.[23]

By the late nineteenth century, though, textiles were a "maturing" industry; the pace of innovation did not necessarily slacken, but innovation became increasingly separated from production. A separate textile machinery industry arose, developing "off-the-shelf" technology readily packaged for delivery at a distance. Moreover, innovation itself was becoming institutionalized; as William Mass has noted, the major textile innovation of the late nineteenth century, the Northrop automatic loom, was the product of one of the largest research and development projects prior to World War I.[24]

Thanks to the separation of innovation from production, when the textile industry moved south the central sources of innovation remained in the North. The South's textile industry accounted for 21 percent of nationwide textile employment in 1920, when the region was but a decade away from becoming dominant in the U.S. industry. Yet the textile machinery industry, separated for the first time from "foundry and machine products" in the 1919 Census of Manufactures, remained a New England and mid-Atlantic industry; in that year 97.3 percent of industry employment still remained in those regions, while less than 2 percent of production occurred in the South.[25]

The above theoretical and empirical considerations suggest a modification of Higgs's approach so as better to explain the apparent increasing inventive backwardness of the region. As table 8.1 shows, the proportion of the workforce of a state engaged in manufacturing (*MF/LF*) loses its explanatory effectiveness over time, even becoming a *negative* influence in the twentieth century, suggesting that the *structure* of a state's manufacturing sector may be as significant as its proportionate size. Accordingly, we substitute for *MF/LF* a variable that better captures the importance, from state to state, of those industries most conducive to technological change. These we define as those census industries falling into two two-digit Standard Industrial Classification (SIC) groups, "fabricated metals" and "machinery" (electrical and non-electrical), following Albert W. Niemi's application of those categories to the industrial classifications of the 1900 census. These we term (admittedly roughly) "capital goods" industries, and the ratio of their employment to the total labor force of each state (*CG/LF*) becomes our substitute for *MF/LF* in Higgs's estimating equations.[26]

As table 8.2 shows, our proposed measure of industrial structure displays an explanatory power in certain respects superior to Higgs's variable. Our estimating equations explain roughly the same proportion of the observed variation as do his, as can be seen through a comparison of the R^2s in tables 8.1 and 8.2. Moreover, ours successfully explain an anomaly at which Higgs in 1971 threw up his hands: the behavior of Connecticut. Connecticut was not only the most inventive state by far; it was also the metalworking and machine-making state par excellence, the home of the proverbial Yankee mechanic, and its workforce was disproportionately concentrated in our selected industries. Therefore, leaving the Nutmeg State out of our universe

Table 8.2. Ordinary least squares regression estimates: patents/100,000 vs. percentage urban, percentage of workforce in capital goods manufacturing (*CG/LF*), "South"

Year	Percent population in cities	*CG/LF*	Southern dummy	R^2	N
1890	0.585*	6.724*	−4.613	0.930	38
	(0.100)	(0.789)	(3.327)		
1900	0.413*	3.297*	−8.155*	0.888	45
	(0.076)	(0.596)	(2.546)		
1910	0.273*	2.496*	−14.281*	0.789	46
	(0.095)	(0.598)	(3.444)		
1920[a]	0.422*	0.924*	−12.699*	0.805	48
	(0.083)	(0.374)	(2.959)		

Source: Population and urban population figures are from U.S. Department of Commerce, Bureau of the Census, *Historical Statistics of the United States: Colonial Times to 1970*, 2 vols. (Washington, D.C., 1975), 1:24–37. Labor force figures come from Harvey S. Perloff et al., *Regions, Resources, and Economic Growth* (Baltimore, 1960), 622, 632. Employment figures for specified industries come from U.S. Department of Commerce, Bureau of the Census, *U.S. Census of Manufactures Reports* (Washington, D.C., various years). Patent statistics are from U.S. Patent Office, *U.S. Commissioner of Patents Annual Reports* (Washington, D.C., various years).

[a]The patent data for 1920 have been modified to take account of an apparent typographical error in the 1919 patent figure for Connecticut. The number of patents reported for Connecticut in that year was over three times higher than in adjacent years, was identical to that given for the much larger state of Illinois, and was inconsistent with a ratio of patents to state population provided in an adjacent column. The ratio was divided into the 1910 population figure (evidently the figure used by the commissioner in 1919) to obtain an indirect estimate of Connecticut's patent activity in 1919. Use of the new patent figure does not alter the substance of our findings but makes Connecticut's behavior much more intelligible, bringing its residual (see fig. 8.4) into line with the other states of Greater New York; the regression estimates are significantly improved.

*Significant at the 95 percent level.

would actually *reduce* the power of the estimating equations.[27] Finally, our capital goods measure remains both positive and highly significant, albeit of steadily declining importance, throughout the four census years we reconstructed.

Unfortunately, though, our estimator makes no significant headway at all in explaining the behavior of the South. In fact, not only does the "southern dummy" show up as significant and negative for 1900, 1910, and 1920, but the absolute values of the coefficients are very close to those reported by Higgs. That the effect is so slight may be due to the coarseness of our "capital goods" category. In 1900 one classification, "foundry and machine shop products," accounted for 81 percent of all "machinery" employment and 55 percent of "capital goods" employment. As new industries arose, and as older ones were spun off into separate classifications, the proportion of industrial employment reported under this catch-all category declined, but as late as 1920 it accounted for nearly half of machinery employment and nearly a third of "capital goods" employment. One suspects that the 5,531 employed in the foundries and machine shops of Tennessee in 1920 were probably far less highly skilled and versatile than their 23,342 counterparts in Connecticut; but the census categories themselves are, with respect to skills, black boxes.

At this point it would appear that the region David M. Potter once called a "sphinx on the American land" remains, in this respect at least, an enigma.[28] However, if one looks at the behavior of *all* states with respect to patent activity, urbanization, and capital goods employment, it becomes apparent that the South was not the *only* region behaving peculiarly. We discovered this by calculating, for each of our census years from 1890 through 1920, a hypothetical number of patents per hundred thousand for each state based on its urban population and capital goods employment. These estimates were then compared to the actual numbers, and the differences plotted on figures 8.1–8.4. On these graphs, the *X*-axis represents the *actual* patents per capita reported for each state at each time; the *Y*-axis represents the residual after the esti-

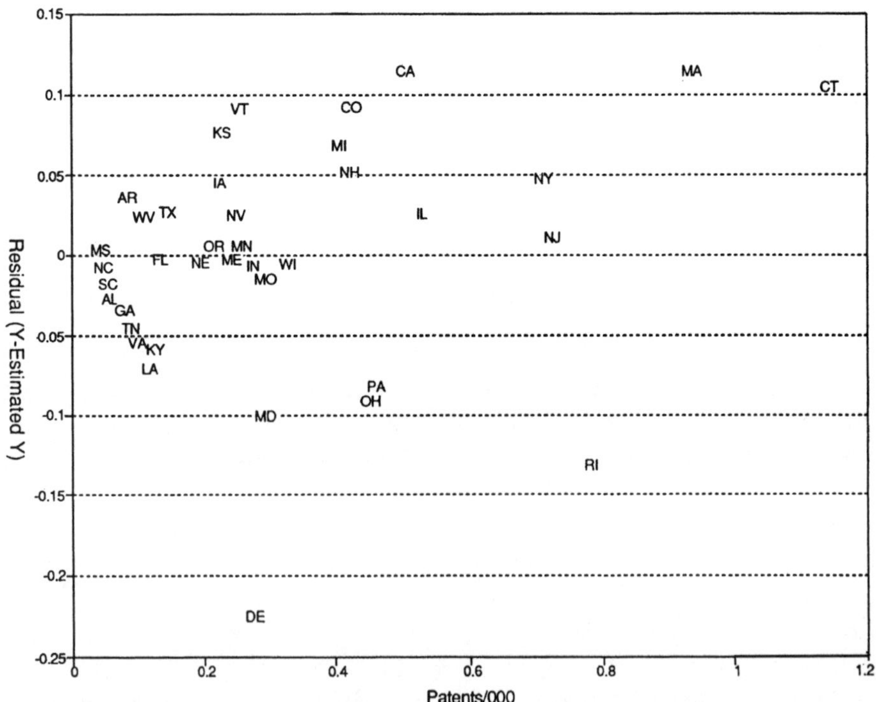

Figure 8.1: Patents/100,000 vs. Percent Urban, Percent of Labor Force in Capital Goods Manufacturing (CG/LF)—Residuals, All States, 1890. Source: see text.

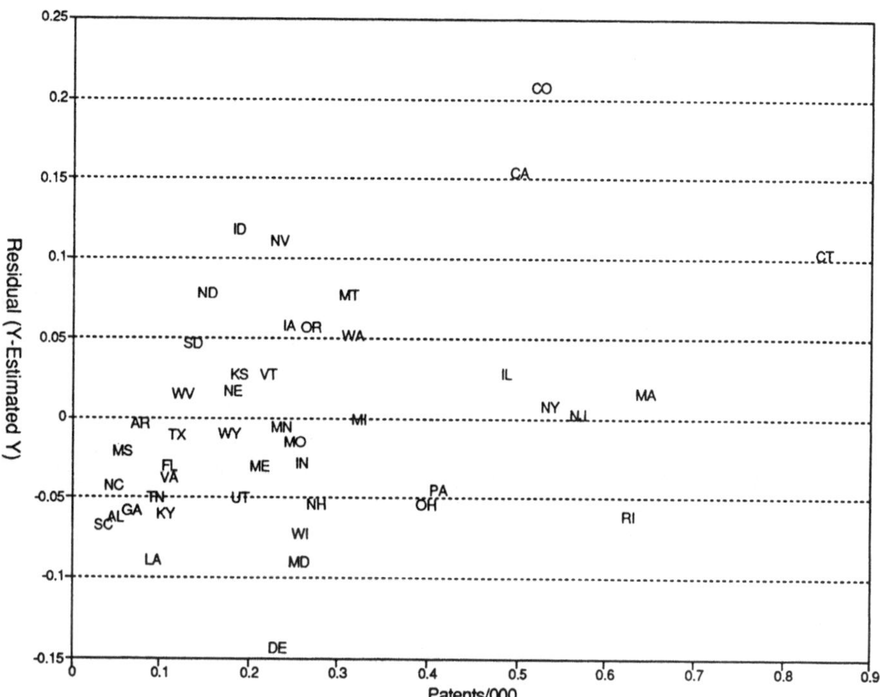

Figure 8.2: Patents/100,000 vs. Percent Urban, Percent of Labor Force in Capital Goods Manufacturing (CG/LF)—Residuals, All States, 1900. Source: see text.

mate is subtracted from the actual figure. The horizontal line labeled "0" thus represents the regression plane, and the relation of the states to the line shows the direction and extent to which their actual patent activity diverges from the activity predicted by our model, minus any provision for regional effects.[29]

The scatterplot of residuals for 1890 shows little of note, apart from a tendency of states to cluster densely around the regression plane and a curious negatively sloped linear cluster of most of the southern states. Beginning in 1900, however, the states sort themselves out along what appear to be two lines, each beginning with the southern states, but one with a higher slope than the other. Moreover, the line with the higher slope is clearly associated with a geographic region—the West. By 1920, of those twenty-two states whose patent activity exceeded our estimates, fifteen were west of the Mississippi River; of the twenty-six states with negative residuals, only three non-southern states were west of the Mississippi.

The peculiarity of the western states seems to be borne out if we add a dummy for "West," defined as the Mountain and Pacific states, to our variables. The results are

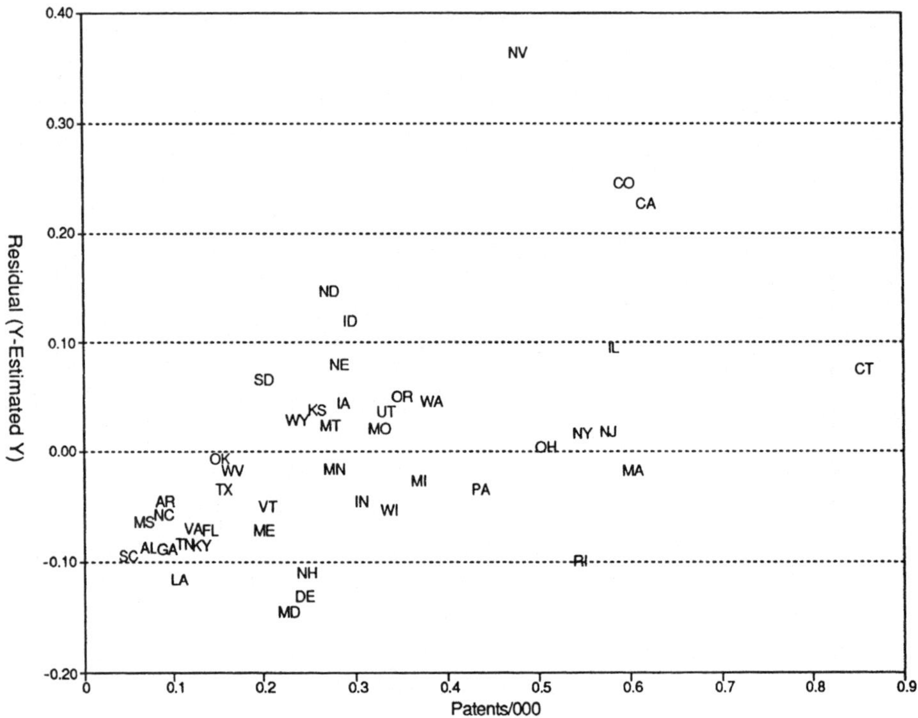

Figure 8.3: Patents/100,000 vs. Percent Urban, Percent of Labor Force in Capital Goods Manufacturing (CG/LF)—Residuals, All States, 1910. Source: see text.

reported for the years 1900, 1910, and 1920 in table 8.3. In all three cases the estimates are significantly improved; the "western dummy" is always significant, positive, and noticeably larger than its paired "southern dummy." Above all, the "southern dummy" loses significance in 1900 and 1920, retaining it only in 1910. If the Plains states of Kansas, Nebraska, and the Dakotas are included in the "West," even the 1910 "southern dummy" becomes insignificant. An alternative approach, shown in table 8.4, omits the Plains, Mountain, and Pacific states from the observations, with the same result.

To be sure, much of the western pattern may be simply a function of small populations; it took only an average of thirty-two patents to make Nevada, with its population of 77,000 and its thirteen metalworkers, our star performer in 1920. But the pattern is shared by sizeable states, such as Colorado, Washington, and especially California. Moreover, non-western states (by our current definition) with arguably "western" characteristics, such as Minnesota, Iowa, and Missouri, clearly range themselves in intermediate positions between the West and other regions.

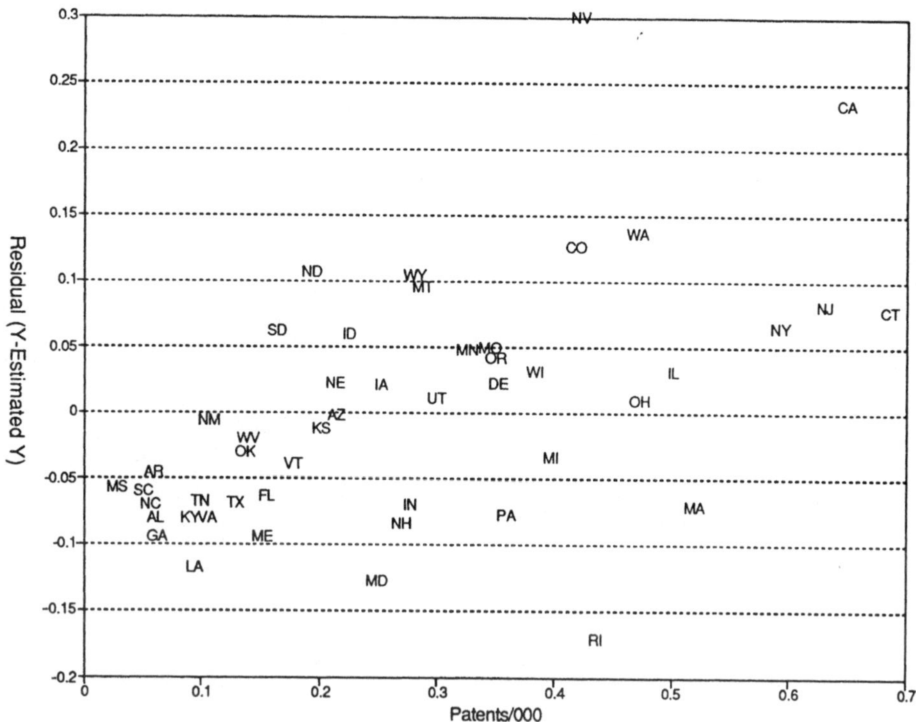

Figure 8.4: Patents/100,000 vs. Percent Urban, Percent of Labor Force in Capital Goods Manufacturing (CG/LF)—Residuals, All States, 1920. Source: see text.

Of course, the most important validation of the importance of the "western effect" would be a good explanation for it. Here we can at best be tentative, except to note that, by the most expansive definition (the non-southern trans-Mississippi West), the region begins roughly where the old manufacturing belt ends.[30] Beyond the nineteenth-century frontier of American manufacturing, innovative activity in the early twentieth century apparently proceeded at a faster rate, relative to urbanization and capital goods employment, than it did in the East. One can speculatively name a variety of factors contributing to the ferment. Early western specialties such as hard-rock mining posed problems in need of innovative solutions and brought skilled workers into the region to solve them. The need of a newly settled country to solve local problems remote from machine shops may also have been a goad to the imagination. Moreover, there is good reason to believe that the United States from the Great Plains to the Pacific Ocean operated in many ways like a separate country. In California, as Alan L. Olmstead and Paul Rhode have pointed out in a recent article on agricultural mechanization there, a peculiar local environment posed unique

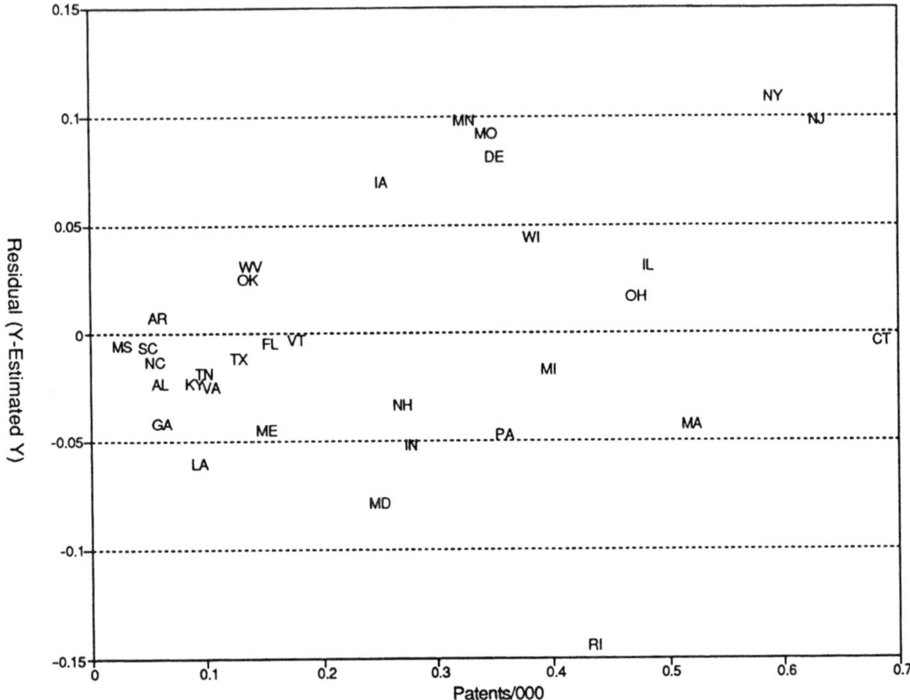

Figure 8.5: Patents/100,000 vs. Percent Urban, Percent of Labor Force in Capital Goods Manufacturing (CG/LF)—Residuals, All States Minus West and Plains, 1920. Source: see text.

problems to farmers, problems worked out in close consultation with an indigenous farm machinery industry. The distance of California from the vast implement industry of the Midwest allowed local firms a measure of protection and rendered the state an incubator for new technologies, some of which, notably grain combines and track-laying tractors, became of world importance.[31] Finally, as an "unfinished" region of the country, the West lacked the commitments to earlier approaches that may have already begun to ossify the later "rustbelt," while its boosters were willing and eager to help launch "sunrise" industries. In their recent study of the geography of American defense procurement, Ann Markusen et al. suggest that the migration of the aviation industry from its midwestern birthplace to Los Angeles and Seattle, just barely underway in our period of study, had much to do with the preference of aviation pioneers for a business climate open and hospitable to their relatively nonroutinized, innovation-intensive enterprises.[32] These suggestions are at best tentative; moreover, it is not clear how, or if, they would apply to the eastern portions of the region. Nonetheless, we believe that we have ample reasons to regard the West, as well as the

Table 8.3. Ordinary least squares regression estimates: patents/100,000 vs. percentage urban, percentage of workforce in capital goods manufacturing (*CG/LF*), "South," "West"

Year	Percent population in cities	*CG/LF*	Southern dummy	Western dummy	R^2	N
1900	0.392*	4.130*	−4.402	9.727*	0.921	45
	(0.065)	(0.546)	(2.348)	−2.37		
1910	0.250*	3.409*	−8.624*	14.522*	0.861	46
	(0.078)	(0.530)	(3.081)	−3.144		
1920	0.524*	1.426*	−3.302	12.129*	0.854	48
	(0.077)	(0.353)	(3.585)	−3.198		

Source: See table 8.2.

Note: "West" includes Arizona, California, Colorado, Idaho, Montana, Nevada, New Mexico, Oregon, Utah, Washington, and Wyoming.

*Significant at the 95 percent level.

Table 8.4. Ordinary least squares regression estimates: patents/100,000 vs. percentage urban, percentage of workforce in capital goods manufacturing (*CG/LF*), "South" (Mountain, Pacific, and Great Plains states omitted)

Year	Percent population in cities	*CG/LF*	Southern dummy	R^2	N
1900	0.418*	4.258*	−2.270	0.958	32
	(0.066)	(0.466)	(2.449)		
1910	0.406*	3.324*	−2.221	0.943	33
	(0.071)	(0.382)	(2.798)		
1920	0.448*	1.503*	−5.491	0.918	33
	(0.079)	(0.292)	(3.190)		

Source: See table 8.2.

Note: For "western" states, see table 8.3; "Great Plains" states include Kansas, Nebraska, North Dakota, and South Dakota.

*Significant at the 95 percent level.

South, as having a distinctive innovative character, one worth factoring into our estimating equations.

One alternative means of comprehending regional variations in innovative activity bears consideration, however: human capital formation, particularly with reference to formal schooling.[33] The difficulty of measuring human capital, and its problematic relationship to classroom instruction, is well known; nonetheless, the educational backwardness of the post–Civil War South is sufficiently noteworthy to suggest a possible association between propensity to innovate and access to educational resources. The best measure of such access, educational attainment measured by number of years in school, is one for which data were not gathered prior to 1940 and is of dubious relevance to an era in which modern graded school systems were largely absent outside cities.[34] We chose a measure more readily computed from available census reports, the proportion of school-age children attending school in the census year, and reestimated the regression equations reported in tables 8.2 and 8.3 with the new independent variable. The results are reported in tables 8.5 and 8.6. Looking at table 8.5, in two out of three census years the school attendance variable is significant; more important, in those equations its addition renders the southern dummy insignificant. Thus, the variables for urbanization, capital goods, and schooling alone apparently allow us to explain the South's divergence from national norms without recourse to our multiregional explanation and arguably with greater parsimony.

Why not, then, discard the multiregional argument altogether? Because we have reason to doubt the causal sequence implied by the use of school attendance as an independent variable. Here it is important to note an important limitation of multiple regression analysis. The terms "independent variable" and "dependent variable" are applied by a researcher, respectively, to the variable he or she wishes to explain and the variable(s) that might explain it. The results of the equation, though, do not definitively prove that the second "caused" the first. The independent variable may be closely related to another, unknown or unconsidered, variable that might be the true "cause"; the lines of causation might be reversed, or a process of circular and cumulative causation might link "dependent" and "independent" variables. Sometimes causation can be tested using lagged variables, but commonly regression results must be interpreted as best one can, using theoretical and empirical knowledge along with plain common sense.[35]

Why, then, do we question our schooling results? It is well known that at early stages of economic development the links between formal education and inventive activity are ambiguous in their character.[36] For instance, growth-inducing innovation may well lead to expanded educational coverage, both by providing financial support and by generating needs for a more rationalized social order.[37] Moreover, the South's education gap and its emerging twentieth-century "patent gap" are arguably two aspects of the same problem. If the South, as a technologically backward region beset by "backwash" effects, chose to industrialize by importing its technology, thus minimizing its investment in invention, the region also tended to choose technology that would minimize the need to develop the skills of its workforce. Again, the most striking examples come from the textile industry. The rise of the early southern cotton mills was conditioned in large part on their adoption of new machinery, such as the ring spindle and the Northrop loom, that reduced the skill requirements of cotton manufacturing and permitted the extensive use of raw rural hands. Able, in effect, to import inventive activity in the form of portable, durable, and dependable machines, southern leaders lacked incentives to invest all-too-scarce resources in locally available, but fragile and ornery, human beings.[38] In sharp contrast, the innovative West consistently provided its people greater access to schooling than did any other region of the country. As the southern experience suggests, however, public investment in education was probably less the cause than it was the effect of an economic culture conducive to innovation. Investigations of the rise of modern literacy, for instance, have indicated that broadly diffused commercial opportunities generate an equally broad popular desire for basic education. Similar lines of causation in the case of the West are suggested by the coefficients in table 8.6, which indi-

Table 8.5. Ordinary least squares regression estimates: patents/100,000 vs. percentage urban, percentage of workforce in capital goods manufacturing (*CG/LF*), school attendance, "South"

Year	Percent population in cities	*CG/LF*	School	Southern dummy	R^2	N
1900	0.450*	3.360*	0.532*	1.789	0.907	45
	(0.071)	(0.550)	(0.185)	(4.184)		
1910	0.299*	2.542*	0.336	−11.017*	0.795	46
	(0.098)	(0.599)	(0.318)	(4.620)		
1920	0.482*	1.018*	0.844*	−6.295	0.83	48
	(0.082)	(0.355)	(0.335)	(3.777)		

Source: For all variables except school attendance, see table 8.2. For school attendance figures, see U.S. Department of Commerce, Bureau of the Census, *Thirteenth Census of the United States, 1910: Population*, 1:1144, *Fourteenth Census of the United States, 1920: Population*, 2:1047.

Note: The school attendance variable is the proportion of school-age population reported as attending school in the appropriate census of population. The definition of school-age population varies slightly by census year; in 1900 it includes the whole population ages 5–20, while in 1910 it includes the whole population ages 7–20. Regressions run on 1910 data using both definitions indicate that our results are insensitive to the difference.

*Significant at the 95 percent level.

Table 8.6. Ordinary least squares regression estimates: patents/100,000 vs. percentage urban, percentage of workforce in capital goods manufacturing (*CG/LF*), school attendance, "South," "West"

Year	Percent population in cities	*CG/LF*	School	Southern dummy	Western dummy	R^2	N
1900	0.423*	4.100*	0.432*	3.310	8.780*	.934	45
	(0.061)	(0.508)	(0.161)	(3.607)	(2.233)		
1910	0.268*	3.424*	0.228	−6.504	14.272*	.864	46
	(0.081)	(0.532)	(0.263)	(3.939)	(3.167)		
1920	0.479*	1.397*	0.588	−3.424	9.703*	.867	48
	(0.073)	(0.337)	(0.309)	(3.488)	(2.853)		

Source: See tables 8.2, 8.3, and 8.5.
*Significant at the 95 percent level.

cate that in 1910 and 1920 the western regional effect renders schooling statistically insignificant.[39]

If we are correct in our multiregional analysis, we find ourselves with an important modification of Higgs's argument. First, the dynamic underlying the process of innovative activity varies between the "core" and the "periphery" of the early-twentieth-century nation. Second, we have in fact *two* peripheries, behaving in dramatically different fashions. What, then, about our original concern, the South? With the West factored in, the region loses most of its peculiarity; our variables seem to account for its behavior nicely. Moreover, the clustering of states at the lower end of the scale of innovative activity, as shown for 1920 in figure 5, suggests that among eastern states the relevant determinant of that cluster may be less "southernness" per se than geographic location along the southern *and northern* fringes of the manufacturing belt. The cluster includes two states, Maine and Vermont, that are burdened with none of Dixie's peculiar disabilities, but that nonetheless behave in a "southern" manner with respect to their innovative activity. Both were, like their southern contemporaries, heavily involved in wood-products industries and textiles, the latter established later than the pioneer firms of southern New England and dependent at least in part on imported technology.[40] Like the southern states, northern New England was close enough to the manufacturing belt to suffer from "backwash" effects, depriving it of the natural protection that we speculate incubated western innovation. The commonalities of these states with their old Civil War antagonists suggest, then, that with respect to innovation states might properly be sorted not according to their internal social structures, but according to the character of their relationship to the by-now established industrial core of the nation.[41]

That said, one must nonetheless acknowledge that most states in the "eastern periphery" were in fact southern and that their backwater status had much to do with their continuing internal peculiarities. Unlike the far West, the South was not a "developing" region at this time but one that had, as the saying goes, developed underdevelopment. Its technological problems were either already solved (at a low level, thanks to a huge underemployed population available at bargain wages) or could be solved by established firms in the manufacturing belt, sufficiently close at hand to provide daunting competition to local entrepreneurs. Its industrialization was conditioned as well on access to northern markets and business techniques; as one of us has previously argued, southern entrepreneurs, conservative legatees of a society deficient in business or technological skills, were perfectly willing to become, in effect, franchisees of the already developed technological community of the manufacturing belt.[42]

Moreover, to a degree that subordinate relationship persists today. Speaking of the establishment of branch plants in the region by Los Angeles–based aerospace firms, Markusen et al. remark that, apart from military-related installations in places like Huntsville, such facilities are usually described by industry executives as "slave manufacturing plants"; they are generally assembly-type operations, relying on poorly skilled (and largely female) workers. Jane Jacobs makes the same point more pungently in her book *Cities and the Wealth of Nations,* in which she presents the South as the archetypical "transplant region," parasitic on "city economies" outside the region for its means of sustenance.[43]

Nonetheless, as Gavin Wright and James C. Cobb have pointed out, the chronic dependency of the South on "outside" control of its economic life is increasingly shared by much of the rest of the nation as well.[44] If we are correct, the region's subordinate status was not unique to it even in the early twentieth century; only because of the preponderance of southern states on the "eastern periphery" have generations of observers been able to dismiss their disabilities as peculiar to that most easily dismissed of American regions. Certainly the peculiarly twisted heritage of the former home of American plantation slavery cannot be dismissed, but the picture that emerges here is one of a thoroughly *American* region, suffering ills with which other, more favored, parts of the Union are only now becoming acquainted. To be sure, the problems of established industrial regions like the Midwest are not strictly comparable to those of latecomers such as the South, but, as many a structurally unemployed auto- or steelworker can attest, the problems involved in adapting an economy to a world beyond local control are no less intractable, or less painful, than those facing the South when it first sought its place at the industrial table.

Thus comparative studies of region and innovation can tell us a good deal, not simply about the varying innovative behavior of Americans in different communities, but about how the experience of one region can illuminate that of others at differing stages of development. For such comparisons to be at all useful, however, the regions need to be treated as commensurable, not as culturally so distinctive as to make comparisons useless. The regression technique we have used here is thus an enormously useful tool for comparative analysis, for it seeks to understand the peculiarities of regions using clearly specified, broadly applicable measures rather than intellectually unproductive cultural essentialist explanations. Our method leaves plenty of room for argument, to be sure; others will suggest different variables and refinements of technique and will question the theoretical scaffolding we used to frame our approach. As the foregoing makes clear, a method is a useful support for an argument but not a substitute for one; like most historical arguments, ours has depended critically on initial choices, subjective judgments, and the occasional leap of faith. While many readers may rightly be skeptical of many of our concepts and choices, though, we believe that the approach we have taken here can prove useful to readers of a different mind. We hope they see our point.

9

Unbalanced Growth and Industrialization

The Case of South Carolina

DAVID L. CARLTON

This essay, published in 1988, is an attempt to combine an "unbalanced growth" perspective on southern development with an argument about the early-twentieth-century political culture of the South. The literature of southern politics in this period was, and still is, dominated by the magisterial work of V. O. Key and Alexander Heard. Their concerns grew directly out of the New Deal, and especially out of the era of the abortive "purge," which convinced many liberal southerners that their conservative political leaders were unresponsive to a populace whose pro–New Deal sympathies were evident. In the view of Key, Heard, and their associates, simple equity, and economic progress as well, required that this "backward" system be reformed. Here, though, we suggest that the political system they were looking at was in certain respects considerably more "modernizing," if not fully "modern," than they thought; conservative elites seized upon new technologies to *expand* state power and use it as a tool of both their own continued domination and of a decidedly conservative form of economic development. In this regard the "Prussian Road" school referred to earlier may well have been more correct about the twentieth century than about the nineteenth; parts of the South, if not the entire region, *did* experience a "revolution from above" at that time.

The efforts of historians to understand the post–Civil War economic development of the South, especially industrialization, have to a striking degree resembled the efforts of the proverbial blind men to describe the equally proverbial elephant. Some scholars, especially of the old New South school, have been impressed by the vigor of the region's manufacturing sector and by the rise of a new bourgeoisie from the wreckage of the slaveholders' hopes. Others, contrarily, argue for southern industrial failure, presenting to our gaze a region relegated to the status of a "hewer of wood and drawer of water" for the imperial Yankee, dominated by a persistent planter mentality hostile to innovation and flux and countered only by a weak and supine middle class.[1] The picture is further clouded by the persistent search for a turning point, a catastrophe killing off the Old South as thoroughly as an earlier calamity allegedly did in the dinosaurs. For years it was customary to use either the Civil War or the year 1880 as the southern manufacturing watershed; more recently the industrial takeoff has been dated from the 1920s or from World War II.[2]

All of this is terribly confusing, not least because all of the above arguments have some plausibility. The postbellum expansion of the industrial Piedmont contrasts with the stagnation of the low country and Black Belt. Aggregate figures showing strong southern industrial performance in the years since 1880 mask serious structural deficiencies and wide variations among localities and time periods.[3] Takeoffs have proliferated in the literature until the very notion seems meaningless. Nonetheless, it should be possible to construct a framework within which the complexities of southern industrialization can be contained. I wish here to propose such a framework, designed, first, to unify the seemingly disparate experiences of different southern regions, and, second, to suggest how the South has changed over time.

The key concept I wish to use is that of "unbalanced growth," especially as developed by Gunnar Myrdal and Albert Hirschman.[4] Some version of "unbalanced growth" has, of course, long been familiar to southern historians, since it is in many ways similar to the long-standing notion of the South as a "colonial economy."[5] My primary interest here, though, is with an aspect of southern development less often noted, namely, the unbalanced nature of growth *within* the region. The first half century of southern industrialization tended chiefly to benefit certain areas, to the neglect, or even detriment, of others. The process is especially striking in the case of South Carolina, where a developing industrial concentration in the Piedmont coexisted with a large, undeveloped area dependent, at best, on agriculture and unstable extractive industry. Regional disparities were, in large part, the result of a process of "polarization," whereby development bred more development; as is common in relatively less developed areas, the energizing impulse was strong enough to attract further development in the favored region but remained too weak to spread its benefits to the state at large. This process of "cumulative causation" was made possible by the post-Reconstruction political economy of South Carolina, which left most economic decision making in private hands and viewed state activity as inherently corrupt and potentially tyrannical. The result was, by 1930, an increasingly sharp division of the state into "core" and "peripheral" regions, a sectionalization which, we shall see, spilled over into politics and led to important changes in the economic direction of the state.[6]

In the year 1880, industrial development in South Carolina involved chiefly the crudest sort of raw materials processing. The leading manufacturing industry in the state, in terms of value added by manufacturing (VAM), was the production of phosphate fertilizer, followed by tar and turpentine; cotton goods were a fairly close third. No county could boast a VAM per capita greater than Charleston's $25.50, and only four generated more than $10 a head; the statewide average was $16.81, a far cry from the $106.50 added per capita in the larger United States. More important for present purposes, the weakness of manufacturing in the state was compounded by its diffusion; no clear manufacturing region existed (see figure 9.1). Charleston's residentiary industries and fertilizer plants placed it in the lead; Aiken, on the fall line, the site of the developing Horse Creek Valley textile complex, placed second, followed by Greenville with its five cotton mills. If there was any concentration at all, it led toward the coast, where phosphate rock and the long-leaf pine lay convenient to cheap water transportation; incredibly, the sawmills and turpentine stills of the desolate upper coastal region elevated Georgetown and Horry counties into the ranks of leading "manufacturers."[7]

In the succeeding half century, the industrial map of South Carolina was drastically redrawn. By 1930 the state's VAM per capita had reached $91.65, far off the

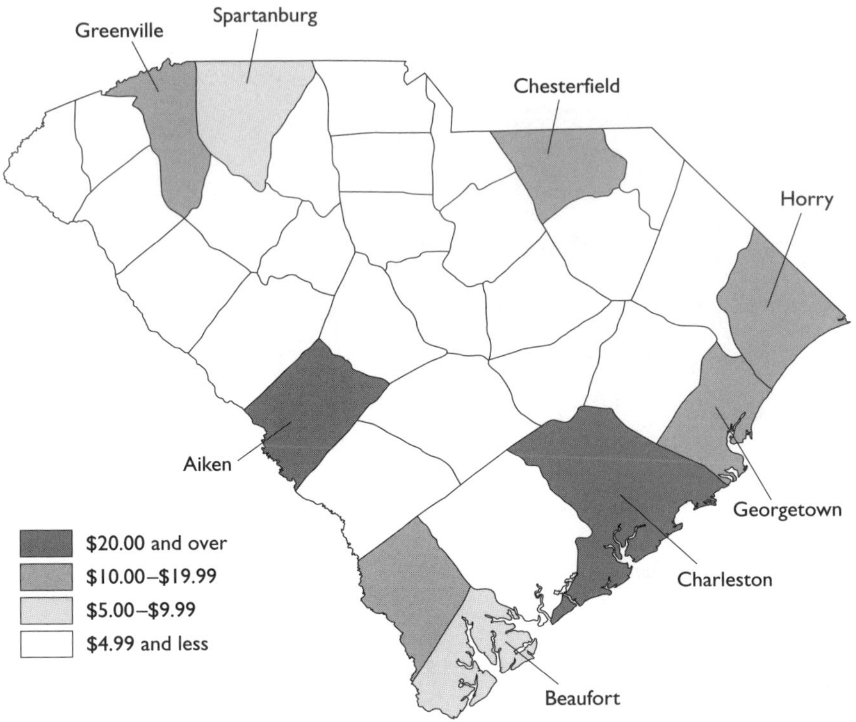

Figure 9.1: Value Added by Manufacturing Per Capita, 1880 (South Carolina, by county). Source: see note 7.

$259.75 registered by the larger nation, but a handsome proportional advance nonetheless. The most striking alteration, though, occurred *within* the state. Figure 9.2 shows that twelve counties relatively specialized in manufacturing now formed a compact cluster within the Piedmont, with industrial activity most intense in the upper Piedmont, around Greenville and Spartanburg. Of the important manufacturing counties, only Richland (Columbia) so much as straddled the fall line; 1880's leaders, Charleston and Aiken, now fell below the state average for VAM. By 1930, then, a clear manufacturing center had emerged in South Carolina, a core whose value added per capita approached three times that of the remainder of the state.[8]

What produced this sectionalization? To a large degree it was the product of long-term shifts in the structure of manufacturing. The old extractive base of the state's industry was limited by the availability of raw materials, which discouraged concentration of production. Furthermore, the low density of population in the piney woods, and the competitive pressures exerted by other areas, discouraged conservation practices, which required relatively intensive use of scarce labor and drove up costs; the logical business strategy, in forest products, was "cut out and get out." By 1930 the peak of extractive industry had clearly passed. Badly hurt by the opening of

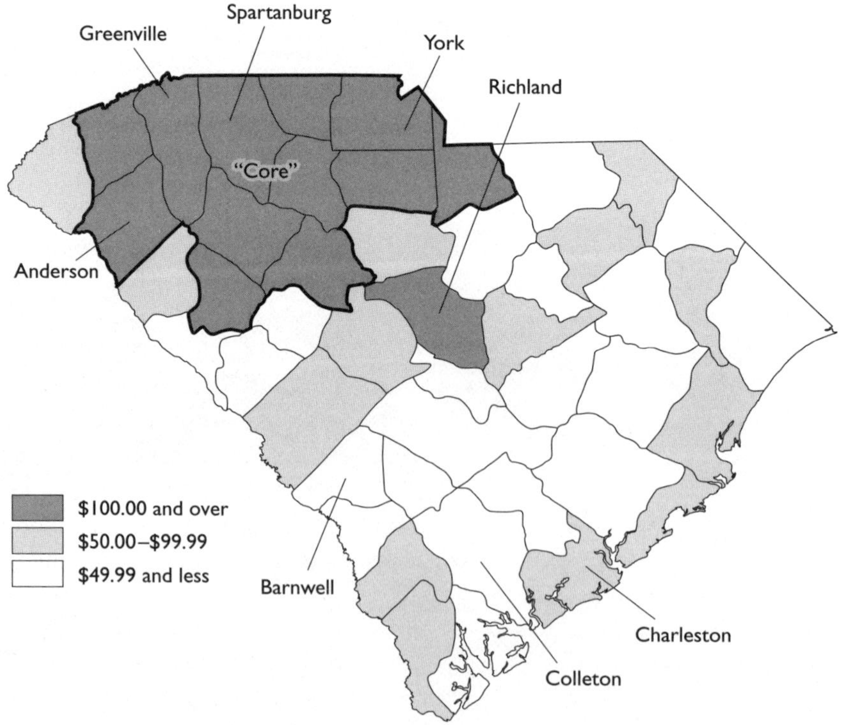

Figure 9.2: Value Added by Manufacturing Per Capita, 1930 (South Carolina, by county). Source: See notes 7 and 8.

larger and higher quality phosphate deposits in Florida and Tennessee, the fertilizer industry was by then generating only 2 percent of the state's VAM. Lumber, the mainstay of the piney woods, had wiped out much of the coastal forest, and had to deal with new competition from the Pacific Northwest; its contribution to state VAM was now only 12 percent. The turpentine distillers had long since moved across the Savannah River and out of the statistics altogether. As extractive industry shrank, the cotton textile industry burgeoned; contributing only 15.9 percent to the state's VAM in 1880, cotton mills generated 59.4 percent by 1930. Furthermore, the industry tended to cluster in the Piedmont core; of the state's spindles in place in 1930, 81.2 percent were located in these counties. The rise of the Piedmont and the expansion of cotton textiles were thus intimately bound together.[9]

Shifts in South Carolina's industrial structure, however, only begin to explain sectional patterns, for while natural resources controlled the location of the state's other industries, they had little influence on the distribution of the cotton mills. The core counties were, to be sure, relatively specialized in cotton, producing in 1880 more than twice as many bales per square mile as the periphery; they represented only 36.8 percent of state production, however, and were less specialized than such upper coastal plain counties as Marlboro and Sumter. In any case, economic historians have generally argued that the availability of cotton weighed relatively lightly in determining the location of the southern cotton mills. Since little weight was lost in processing, savings in freight on raw materials was offset by the relative distance of southern mills from the markets and distribution centers of the North.[10]

A more important resource advantage of the Piedmont stemmed from the numerous shoals along its small, swift streams. American manufacturers in the nineteenth century relied heavily on water power, and mill men early found that the Piedmont rivers could be easily put in harness. Unfortunately, a lack of adequate transportation sealed off the region from significant development before the 1880s, when direct-drive water power began to yield to more flexible motive sources, such as steam and, later, hydroelectric power. Less than one-third of the growth in cotton textile horsepower in late-nineteenth-century South Carolina came from direct-drive water power, while 56.5 percent came from steam engines, an energy source in which the upstate had no comparative advantage. Natural resources, then, seem to have counted little in the localization of cotton textiles in the core.[11]

A more wide-ranging upstate advantage lay in its relatively dense population. In 1880 the later manufacturing core had 38.8 people settled on each square mile of its territory. While comparable densities could be boasted by certain counties of the upper coastal plain and the upper Savannah Valley, figures for most "peripheral" counties ranged in the twenties, down to a low of 14.5 in isolated, piney-woods Horry; the average was 27.2. Moreover, the core counties could boast a *white* population density of 20.8 per square mile, ranging downward from a high of 30.8 in Greenville; by comparison, the lower Piedmont and coastal plain counties contained between ten and fifteen whites per square mile, with densities dropping under five in parts of the tidewater.[12] The relative plenitude of whites in the up-country, a product of its antebellum position on the periphery of the plantation economy, provided a sizable labor pool for an industry which, by the 1870s, had come to rely on a virtually all-white work force. Owing in large part to the extensive use of women and children in mills, prevailing social mores forbade integration of the factories, and efforts by management to introduce blacks into mills usually caused trouble, both with the workers and with community opinion. The result was a racial segmentation of the work force, the white pool having an increasing edge over the black pool in experience, education, and general adaptability to the factory environment. "Experiments" were undertaken with all-black cotton mills, notably at Charleston; these were generally unsuccessful, however, and in any case investors were not inclined to have their money experimented with; white labor was perceived to be far the safer reliance and was available at "reasonable" wages. Given the importance of labor costs in textile manufacturing, firms naturally sought out concentrations of "superior" but cheap workers, concentrations most easily found in the Piedmont.[13]

Population density made deeper contributions to Piedmont ascendancy as well. With the massive shift of the up-country yeomen into the cotton economy in the years following the Civil War, they began to create a large volume of commerce, which in turn sustained a fairly vigorous commercial class. Each hundred square miles of the core sustained 18.4 stores in 1880; the ratio in Greenville County, its heart, was thirty-one. Of the peripheral counties, however, only Richland and Charleston, with sizable regional commercial centers, surpassed the Piedmont average; the vast lower coastal plain managed only a little more than half the commercial density of the upstate.[14] The presence of so many merchants provided the Piedmont with a sizable pool of entrepreneurs possessing capital, business skills, and access to outside sources of funds, expertise, and technology. The influence of merchants was magnified by their propensity to settle in towns. If the anomaly of Charleston is set aside, town population in 1880, while quite small in both core and periphery, was twice as dense in the former as in the latter. Town life facilitated joint endeavors and engendered a booster ethos in its citizens that harnessed their acquisitive hungers to further the advancement of the community and quickened their faith in the new southern religion of progress. Furthermore, their strategic locations along the emerging national railroad network provided townspeople with golden opportunities to mobilize southern resources to penetrate northern markets. Accordingly, then, it was townspeople who created the state's textile industry, and their disproportionate location in the Piedmont core played a major role in influencing its concentration there.[15]

These factors go far to explain the *initial* advantage of the Piedmont core in the race for development. That advantage, however, was marginal, and would erode in time. As noted above, the attraction of water power was fading rapidly as the nineteenth century neared its close. The upstate labor supply was not inexhaustible, and the twentieth century saw manufacturers search restlessly for new sources of help, experimenting with blacks and recruiting heavily in the nearby mountains.[16] By then, however, a new factor had entered the picture, namely, polarization. As Myrdal has argued, countries at lower stages of development typically display great regional disparities, because the classical tendencies toward equilibrium—the "spread" effects, in Myrdal's terminology—tend to be quite weak. The free play of market forces, which according to classical theory should produce regional convergence, instead produce its opposite.[17]

As an agricultural state coming late to industrialization, forced to compete in a common market with the northern leviathan, the South Carolina of the late nineteenth and early twentieth centuries was almost a textbook example of such regional polarization. The industry primarily responsible for the rise of the Piedmont, cotton textiles, had by the postbellum era lost much of the power to generate broadly based development that it had displayed earlier in Old and New England. Equipment and services that older industrial regions had been forced to develop from scratch, such as machinery, textile finishing, and marketing services, were in place in the Northeast and fully competitive with any infant industry that might arise in the South.[18] Furthermore, the state almost totally lacked a major source of "spread" effects, an activist government. South Carolinians had throughout most of their independent history regarded government as dangerous; it was at best a parasite, supplying the lazy and incompetent with sinecures financed by working men, and at worst a tyrant sapping the independence of the citizenry with taxes and regulations. The state had, to be sure, sought to foster railroad and manufacturing development both in antebellum and immediate postbellum times; economic catastrophe and Reconstruction excesses, however, produced a reaction, and the conservative regime abdicated virtually all active efforts to assist in industrial development. Railroad aid, and later tax exemptions, were abandoned; services were cut, and new indebtedness was avoided for half a century. Absent any strong government involvement, the polarizing effects of private action would have their maximum effect.[19]

Two aspects of pre-1930 development, in particular, demonstrate how the relationship of private enterprise, local government, and state government affected its course. The first of these was the state highway system. By the 1920s the new technology of the internal combustion engine was clearly promising to revolutionize transportation. The flexibility and open accessibility of a transport system based on motor vehicles and paved highways liberated men and communities from the rigid schedules and traffic monopolies characteristic of rail technology. However, while the ability to reserve track for the exclusive use of their own rolling stock had made railroads attractive to private investors, access to highways had always been far more difficult to control. Historically, then, governments had built roads, and so the auto age brought an expansion of government activity that had been unneeded in the late-nineteenth-century heyday of the iron horse. For the most part, road building came to be controlled by state and federal agencies.[20] In South Carolina, however, highways, like rural roads, remained largely the responsibility of county governments, and local authorities remained jealous of their prerogatives. A state highway department was created in 1917 but served largely as an advisory body and as a conduit transferring federal funds to the counties. The passage of a gasoline tax in 1922 enlarged the state's role, but counties laid claim to half of all revenues collected within their boundaries. In 1924 the state gained full control of gasoline tax revenues, but its road-building activities were restricted to a pay-as-you-go basis. Wealthier and more activist counties, eager for development, obtained a two-cent local gas tax in 1925 and increasingly used state disbursements to underwrite bond issues. The result, by the end of 1928, was a crazy-quilt system of paved roads. As figure 9.3 shows, the relatively wealthy upper Piedmont was reasonably well equipped with roads, although numerous gaps prevented it from having a true system as yet. In the midlands, a system was developing with Columbia at its hub. In the low country, development was largely confined to the Coastal Highway, a link in the federal route to Florida; two special multicounty road districts directed its construction, which was heavily promoted by Charlestonians eager to tap the burgeoning Florida tourist trade. The system obviously left large areas of the coastal plain and the lower Piedmont out in the cold. Although road building was a government function, the continuing county control of revenues and construction, coupled with a concentration of motor vehicle use

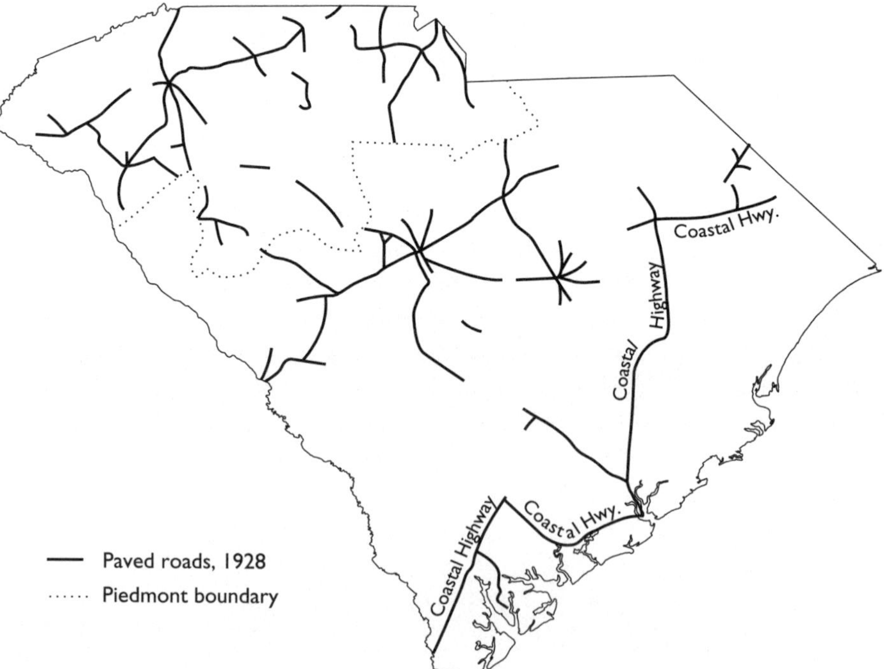

Figure 9.3: South Carolina Paved Roads, 1928. Source: South Carolina Highway Department, *Report, December 31, 1928*, map opposite p. 48.

in urban or industrial counties, fostered an unbalancing effect not dissimilar to that which Myrdal suggests is produced by excessive reliance upon private economic decision making.[21]

The implications of South Carolina's reliance on private capitalists to direct its pre-1930 economic development are strikingly displayed by the development of its electric power generating and transmitting system. The water power of the Piedmont and the fall line lent itself naturally to hydroelectric development; the Congaree River drove Columbia's factories from 1893, and high-tension lines carried energy from the Seneca River to the industrial city of Anderson beginning in 1897. The major event in the electrical history of the state, though, was the founding of the Southern Power Company in 1905 by a group headed by James Buchanan Duke. Over the next twenty years Duke created one of the first truly *regional* power systems in the nation. His brilliant chief engineer, W. S. Lee, constructed a series of dams on the Catawba River whose operations were coordinated to capture the maximum possible horsepower from its flow; the company's transmission lines interconnected with the parallel network of the Carolina Power and Light Company and with other lines elsewhere in the South.[22]

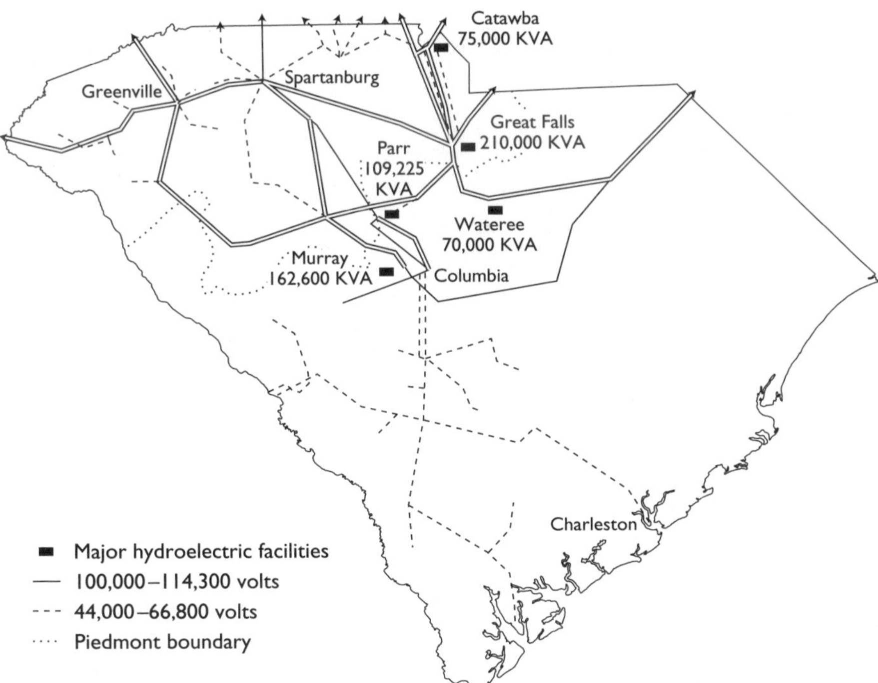

Figure 9.4: South Carolina Major Electric Power Transmission Lines, 1931. Source: South Carolina Power Rate Investigating Committee, *Report on the Electric Utility Situation in South Carolina, December 31, 1931,* plate B-1.

Duke and his associates were thus on the cutting edge of modern technology; they were also, however, private entrepreneurs concerned with making a profit. As a result, developmental aims (e.g., building ahead of demand) were less important to them than the minimization of costs and the direction of supply to customers who could bear those costs. The result was a distribution system almost exclusively serving the Piedmont. As noted, Duke relied heavily on hydroelectric power generated by a string of large stations located in the Catawba River valley. As figure 9.4 indicates, these generators were located *not* within the core but along one edge of it, near the center of the state. However, most of the transmission lines led away from the generating site into the core, either to Greenville and Spartanburg or into the North Carolina industrial belt (in 1930 South Carolina exported more than one-fifth of its power, Duke nearly one-third).[23]

The reason was, simply, demand. The key to success for a private electric utility is a high load factor, i.e., a high ratio of average to maximum power demand. This could best be provided by round-the-clock industrial customers such as cotton mills, which had already begun to concentrate in the Piedmont and whose business was specifically targeted by Duke. Furthermore, the industrial towns and cities of the Piedmont sought power for municipal lighting and for streetcars, and the service area's high population density (73.6 persons per square mile in 1930, highest in the state) and heavy industrial traffic allowed Duke to develop an interurban line, the Piedmont and Northern Railroad, to further diversify the load. As a result of all this, the company was able to sell in 1930 some 64,000 kilowatts per square mile, over twice as much as its closest competitor, the Broad River Power Company of Columbia, and over five times as much as the South Carolina Power Company, which served the southern coastal plain from Augusta to Charleston. Duke's load factor was a superb 67 percent, compared to 48.8 percent for the South Carolina Power Company and 29.7 percent for the Broad River Power Company. The path of profit, then, did not lead everywhere, but rather led into the core, which it in turn provided with new advantages.[24]

If demand drew power lines to the up-country, its lack produced frustration for the low country. Except for Carolina Power and Light lines feeding South Carolina-generated power into North Carolina, no transmission lines of greater than 100,000 volts extended east of the fall line. While lines of lower voltage reached most towns, large areas of the upper coastal counties, especially Horry, Georgetown, and Berkeley, lacked any transmission links with the remainder of the state. To be sure, efforts were made to electrify the periphery. In the 1920s an independent generating company, the Lexington Water Power Company, built what was then the largest hydroelectric facility in the South on the Saluda River near the center of the state, to the huzzahs of local developers. Unfortunately, local demand was so weak that Lake Murray's potential was not fully utilized for forty years; indeed, in order to cover its enormous fixed costs, the company was forced to sell all its power on long-term contracts to Duke and Carolina Power and Light, who, of course, exported it to the core. In 1934 a local promoter of the Lexington project complained that none of its power was used in Lexington or Richland counties, but rather chiefly served the industrial development, commercial welfare, and domestic convenience of the citizens of North Carolina."[25] If Lake Murray was a disappointment, the chronic failure of the Santee-Cooper project was even worse. In the late 1910s a Columbia steamboat operator, exploring a possible water route to Charleston, discovered that power could be generated in the otherwise unpromising coastal plain by diverting the waters of the Santee River into the Cooper River. During the 1920s a succession of private developers sought to exploit the improbable opportunity. However, the overwhelmingly rural, thinly populated lowlands could not provide the demand or the high load factor offered by Piedmont cities and factories, and in 1930 the electrification of the low county remained largely a dream.[26]

Thus, while the Piedmont core was creating a framework on which to hang a modern industrial society, a cycle of underdevelopment was afflicting the remainder of the state. The accumulated wealth of the upper Piedmont was invested in strictly local improvements, expanding that wealth still more; its development created opportunities for still more development. As a frustrated Columbia industry hunter of the 1920s put it, industrial enterprises wanted "to be where the crowd is."[27] Plainly, the traditional reliance of Carolinians on the marketplace and private enterprise to assure development was working, but only for a portion of the state. Its very success, moreover, contrasted increasingly with the stagnation of the remainder. In the 1920s agricultural depression and outmigration heightened concerns in the periphery; between 1920 and 1930, while the core population grew by 11.4 percent, that of the periphery declined by 0.9 percent.[28]

What to do? To many leading citizens of the periphery, the answer was clear; if it lacked the wealth and dynamism of the core, it had one signal advantage, that of voting strength. Outmigration notwithstanding, the peripheral counties contained over 60 percent of the state's population in 1930, with legislative representation to match; moreover, they numbered thiry-four of the state's forty-six counties among their ranks, each with a state senator.[29] If private wealth and local initiative could not bring development, it would be sought through the political arena, under the sponsorship of the state. Accordingly, the 1920s saw the rise of an important cadre of low-country leaders dedicated to remaking the state government into a tool for economic development. Although they allied with Charleston mayor Burnett R. Maybank on some issues, most were state senators from small counties of the periphery, who typically entered the upper house in the 1920s. Their principal leader was Richard Manning Jefferies, a lawyer and probate judge from the piney-woods town of Walterboro, Colleton County. Reaching the senate in 1926, he began almost immediately to push for state-sponsored development projects and proved himself a master at assembling the necessary support; indeed, his negotiating talents would ultimately make him perhaps the most powerful man in the state and render his succession to the governorship in 1942 a virtual demotion. Closely associated with him was Edgar A. Brown of Barnwell, who moved to the Senate from the speakership of the House of Representatives in 1928. Sharing Jefferies's passion for development, Brown became a close political and personal ally (Jefferies's son married Brown's daughter and became Brown's law partner), and ultimately his successor as head of what their enemies called "The Ring."[30]

Something of their approach to development problems, and the sectional divisions that resulted, can be divined from examining their policies on highways and electric power. While efforts had been made earlier to develop a genuine system of paved roads, the turning point in the history of South Carolina's highways came with the passage in 1929 of Jefferies's proposal for a $65 million state bond issue. The bill, easily the dominant matter facing the session, produced several roll call votes, the most revealing of which occurred when the House of Representatives was called upon to endorse the final Senate-House conference report on the measure. While the peripheral members favored the bonds by a vote of fifty-four to nineteen, the core was more closely divided, with twenty-six bond opponents partially offset by ten advocates, chiefly from smaller counties. Nonetheless, the Piedmont was, on balance, opposed, with the most vocal anti sentiment coming from the most highly developed counties of the upper Piedmont, Anderson, Greenville, Spartanburg, and York.[31]

Despite the bill's passage and the subsequent rejection by the courts of constitutional objections to it, the bond issue and the highway department continued to arouse indignation among Piedmonters. Not only was their self-interest at stake, but having been taught over the years to identify an active, expansive government with corruption, extravagance, and tyranny, they found the new departure profoundly suspect. The highway program's mind-boggling expenditures (after 1929 the highway department controlled more money than the rest of the state government combined), and the concentrated power it placed in the hands of the burgeoning highway bureaucracy and their legislative allies, provided an easy target for political candidates eager to warn the people of a new threat to their liberties. The foremost practitioner of this traditional form of politics was Olin D. Johnston of Spartanburg. While Johnston, a former mill worker, was a major spokesman for the state's factory hands, his broader appeal to Palmetto State voters stemmed from his long struggle against the highway department, an issue he used to shape South Carolina politics through most of the 1930s. He led the bitter-enders in the House in 1929, charging then and subsequently that the building program was rife with extravagance and corruption, and that the "highway ring" in the General Assembly was cemented together with bribery. Johnston's accusations were most effective in the core counties and gave his pattern of support in the gubernatorial races of 1930 and 1934 a decidedly sectional cast. Even though he gained the governorship in 1934, though, he quickly discovered that the will of the Piedmont electorate carried little weight in the General Assembly, whose leaders relied on small, homogeneous white constituencies and looked disdainfully on the turbulence of the manufacturing counties. Frustrated with the impotence of his office, he was finally reduced to mounting a comic-opera attempt to seize control of the department with the National Guard. His successor, Burnett R. Maybank, fared little better in his efforts to direct the flood of highway funds into other areas. The "highway crowd," rendered cohesive by patronage and common interest, repulsed all attacks on what they regarded as the most critical developmental need of South Carolina.[32]

While the highway program became the central issue organizing South Carolina politics in the 1930s, the emerging legislative oligarchy did not confine its attentions to the matter of good roads; among its other major goals was the electrification of the coastal plain. Such men as Jefferies, Brown, and George K. Laney of Chesterfield were deeply resentful of the large hydroelectric companies, which they regarded as exploiting a major natural resource without helping to develop the state. Hostility to the power companies especially flared in 1931, when a one-half-mill-per-kilowatt-hour tax on hydroelectric power was pushed through the legislature. The measure was intended to prop up state revenues reeling from the impact of the Great Depression, and was endorsed by landowners' groups eager to shift the tax burden off real property. However, advocates also harped upon the companies' monopolistic profits and complained that the rivers, "the property of the state," had been "given away" to turn the wheels of out-of-state industry. In addition to the tax, the General Assembly set up a commission to investigate the power producers.[33]

The major achievement of "peripheral" legislators in electric power, though, was the conversion of the moribund Santee-Cooper project into a state-owned enterprise. Remarkably, a scheme that in later years would have been promptly laid to rest as socialistic attracted broad support from a range of otherwise conservative South Carolinians. The movement was spearheaded by Jefferies and Maybank (a pro-development alliance of Charleston and the coastal plain), who arranged to finance the facility with funds supplied by an important new capital source, the federal government. Playing on President Roosevelt's faith in public power, the example of the Tennessee Valley Authority, and the political influence of Senator James F. Byrnes, the project's advocates countered fears that it would prove a burden on the taxpayers by incorporating it as an independent South Carolina Public Service Authority.[34] All suspicions were not defused, to be sure; the lack of demand in the coastal plain led many to suspect that the authority was a boondoggle designed to funnel public money into private hands, and skeptical engineers warned that the power produced would be prohibitively expensive. Predictably, the opposition came from the core. In the principal roll call on the measure, core representatives voted twenty-two to thirteen against, with twelve of the nays coming from Greenville and Spartanburg, while the periphery favored the Authority by fifty-one to eighteen. After the bill reached the Senate, the Duke interests, fearful that the Authority might someday seek to control all electric utilities in the state, forced its sponsors to confine its operations to the region below Columbia, in the process writing a recognition of regional divergence into law.[35]

Generally, though, the state embarked on an enterprise bearing considerable risk and second in size only to the highway program itself with remarkably little fuss. The new Authority, with Maybank as its chairman and Jefferies as its general counsel (later general manager), completed the plant by 1942. In succeeding years it had a revolutionary impact on low-country electric rates and consumption. The upper coastal plain, in particular, had suffered from poor service and rates above national norms; by 1947, however, rates there had dropped by from 45 to 60 percent, and consumption had more than tripled. The cheap power attracted wartime metallurgical plants and other energy-intensive manufacturing; other industry was attracted through the efforts of the Authority's industrial development section, which conducted research, supplied information, and assessed the "financial responsibility" of potential industrial customers.[36] The Authority's financial success recommended it as a model for other state enterprises. One of these, the South Carolina State Ports Authority, developed and managed terminal facilities at the stagnant port of Charleston in the years after World War II; aided by the expanding highway network and the postwar expansion of the state's foreign trade, it played a major role in the city's modern renaissance.[37]

Highways and electric power were only two of the agencies opening up South Carolina's periphery to development; moreover, they would have been of little value had there not been a sustained national economic boom after World War II. However, these and other state-sponsored developments laid the groundwork for the postwar extension of industry to hitherto deprived areas of the state. The new role of state government had another, more subtle, effect on the shape of modern South Carolina. Because the state's political system concentrated power in the hands of state senators, the expansion of government helped forge the old "highway crowd" into a durable oligarchy. From the mid-1920s, when Brown and Jefferies first entered the Senate, incumbency began sharply to increase (see figure 9.5); whereas prior to 1926 the rate of incumbency over four years averaged 28.5 percent, the rate reached 50 to 60 percent by 1960. Of the eighteen senators elected between 1876 and 1962 and serving more than four terms, twelve were elected after 1925. The increasing concentration of power in their hands made senators increasingly prone to see government as a life's work, not a public-spirited avocation. The postwar leader of the oligarchy, Edgar A. Brown, became, in V. O. Key's words, virtually a "prime minister." Brown and his fellows used their power actively to promote economic development, being credited by one business leader with "taking the quirks out of our laws . . . , establishing sounder tax laws, and . . . making the necessary adjustments to remove obstacles to industry." Their development strategy, stressing fiscal parsimony and hostility to labor organization, is usually, with good reason, called conservative. The word is misleading though, if

Figure 9.5: Four-Year Incumbency Ratios, by Biennium, South Carolina State Senate, 1876–1962. Source: Emily Bellinger Reynolds and Joan Reynolds Faunt, *Biographical Directory of the Senate of the State of South Carolina, 1776–1964* (Columbia, S.C., 1964).

it suggests the continuity of traditional leadership. They have sought not the defense of tradition but modernization; their conservatism has come not from the Old South, but from the New.[38]

In sum, South Carolina during the years between the two World Wars experienced an important shift in the relationship of the state government to industrial development, and consequently in the pattern of manufacturing growth. By 1980 over one quarter of the work force employed in the periphery would be engaged in manufacturing pursuits; although the core would retain its industrial primacy, with 42.2 percent of its employees so occupied, the spread effects first appearing in the 1930s would be having increasing effect.[39] While the changes outlined above have thus been significant, they have not so much represented a fundamentally new direction for the state as a new stage in a process of development which had begun much earlier. The polarized industrialization of the years prior to 1930 set in motion the forces which would lead to the spread of the impulse to other areas afterward.

Obviously, the story told above is in many ways one that is peculiar to one small and rather odd southern state. Nonetheless, a similar approach, if applied elsewhere in the South, could provide us with a way to talk about social change in the region without becoming trapped in an increasingly sterile debate pitting "continuity" against "change." The history of the New South has been convoluted and awkward, but it has never been stagnant; rather, it has been constantly having to wrestle with the consequences of social and economic change. Indeed, the conflicts that have arisen, the resentments generated by development, have themselves performed creative functions in carrying the region closer to its modern self. By taking a closer look at the interregional dynamics of southern growth, we can perhaps better understand how the many different Souths the historians have described are, in fact, one South.

10

The American South and the U.S. Defense Economy

A Historical View

DAVID L. CARLTON

This essay has not been published previously. It was originally designed for presentation at a symposium on war and urban society in the South, scheduled for April 1995, that never took place. It appears here in modestly revised form. It was designed to give conference participants a general historical overview of the relationship of the region to the history of federal defense spending, one that takes a somewhat different tack from most accounts. As noted below, most historical and journalistic treatments of the subject have treated defense spending as having played a critical, even decisive role in generating the so-called "second wave" of post–World War II southern development; in such treatments, the South as of 1940 is commonly treated as a blank slate and its subsequent development as largely state-sponsored. Our structuralist perspective, though, regards such arguments with skepticism. Here we point out that the region had a lengthy history of defense involvement prior to the 1940s; that the benefits it has derived from defense spending have not been extraordinary compared to the nation as a whole and have been far fewer than enjoyed by, say, California and New England; and that the impact of the defense economy on the region has to be understood not solely in terms of domestic politics but also in relation to the South's locational advantages and disadvantages, the economic character of the defense industry, and the needs of the American military. While most recent literature on the topic tends in a different direction, a newly published analysis by Gregory Hooks roughly fits with our view.[1]

It has long been common knowledge, even to the point of being a cliché, that the American South has had a peculiar relationship to the so-called "military-industrial complex." Several generations of American draftees endured basic training at bases such as Fort Jackson and Camp Lejeune, coming in the process to associate the region with drill sergeants and desolate artillery ranges. Politicians and journalists from outside the South have accused powerful southern congressmen such as John Stennis and Mendel Rivers of using defense spending to build up the Sunbelt at the expense of the old "smokestack America." Scholars of the Sunbelt have stressed the role of the defense industry in building up such metropolitan regions as Dallas–Fort Worth, Hampton Roads, Virginia, and Atlanta.[2] Throw in legends of Confederate military exploits, and the association of the South with the military seems almost a matter of cultural predilection. Dixie, we are often told, has had a "military tradition."

The alleged martial ardor of southerners is, as several historians have noted, a matter of debate.[3] But it is clear that the South (which I define here as the eleven states of the old Confederacy plus Kentucky and Oklahoma) has long relied heavily on defense to support its economy. For most of the period since World War II the region

Table 10.1. The South and defense spending: ratios and indexes for the postwar era, 1960–1998

	1960	1970	1980	1990	1998
Southern share of U.S. population (percent)	27.21	27.47	30.00	31.19	32.24
Southern share of U.S. income (percent)	20.68	23.22	26.82	27.70	29.51
Southern share of U.S. value added by manufacturing (VAM) (percent)	17.15	20.67	26.24	29.84	32.24
Southern proportion of total defense spending (percent)	23.41	30.91	30.47	35.82	42.33
Southern proportion of prime contracts (percent)	15.09	25.46	23.46	28.45	37.08
Indexes:					
Southern share of total spending/ share of population	0.86	1.13	1.02	1.15	1.31
Southern share of prime contracts/ share of population	0.55	0.93	0.78	0.91	1.15
Southern share of prime contracts/ share of income	0.73	1.10	0.87	1.03	1.26
Southern share of prime contracts/ share of VAM	0.88	1.23	0.89	0.95	1.21

Source: *Statistical Abstracts of the United States* for relevant years.

has received a greater proportion of its income from defense spending than has the nation as a whole (table 10.1). From 40 to 50 percent of the total defense department payroll has regularly been paid out to southern-based personnel, who currently constitute nearly half of Defense Department employees. Transfer payments to military dependents and retirees, who cluster near the numerous southern bases, further swell the aggregate of economic benefit to the region. Add in the benefits the region has received from military procurement contracts and from defense-related expenditures by other government agencies (e.g., the Department of Energy at Oak Ridge, Tennessee, and the Savannah River Site in South Carolina, and the National Aeronautics and Space Administration's investments at Cape Canaveral, Huntsville, Houston, and elsewhere), and the importance of military spending to the well-being of the region becomes even more striking.

If one looks behind the impressive facade of southern military might, however, a more modest and sobering picture presents itself. First, the mix of defense spending in the region has through most of the postwar era been decidedly disadvantageous to the region. While payroll expenditures per capita in the South are normally around 50 percent greater than in the nation as a whole, table 10.1 shows that southern states have until fairly recently received less than their share of per capita prime contracts; the West Coast has often received nearly twice as much prime contract money per capita as the South. Since procurement accounts for roughly two-thirds of defense spending, until the end of the 1980s the South's lag in this area effectively nullified the advantage it gained from its concentration of bases and personnel. Moreover, defense contracting in several leading southern states has often been dominated by single firms, which has historically imparted a boom-and-bust character to the local industry. Mississippi's defense industry has effectively amounted to the huge Ingalls shipyard in Pascagoula; for much of the postwar era, half of Georgia's was the gigantic Lockheed-Georgia plant in Marietta. Such behemoths, expanding and contracting as their large projects have ramped up and wound down, have offered the region a less than firm basis for consistent growth. Procurement has also been geographically marginal. While bases are fairly broadly distributed (though concentrated along the coastal plain from Virginia into Texas), procurement contractors have chiefly located in the least "southern" parts of the South, in heavily urban locales such as Dallas–Fort Worth, central Florida, and what some call "occupied Virginia." Finally, in its general character southern "defense industry" has not necessarily conformed to the usual image of "high-tech" glamour; in the early 1980s the largest DOD contractor in South Carolina packaged field rations. One commentator at that time described southern-based defense suppliers as making the region not the arms bazaar for the nation's military but its commissary—a purveyor not of weapons but of textiles, tobacco, and food.[4]

What accounts for these patterns? Certainly not deliberate choice. While southern state development officers and local boosters have often been accused of deliberately choosing low-wage, low-skill industry, they have in fact eagerly sought high-tech development, with its high wages, skill development, and potential for spin-offs, whenever they could reasonably get it. Nor has the pattern been a product of passive drift, for the efforts of local boosters have been critical in attracting defense dollars to southern locales. As Roger Lotchin and others have stressed, the siting of defense activities, military or industrial, must be understood not simply in terms of national security or efficiency but also as part of the processes of city building and regional development.[5] Nonetheless, developers cannot have things just as they please; their strategies must fit with their circumstances and their needs and must accommodate to larger shifts in the structure of economic opportunity. In order to understand the historical relationship of the South to defense, then, we need to look at the character of the region before the rise of the modern military-industrial complex, and examine how the region's leadership sold it to a defense establishment whose own needs have shifted frequently and dramatically in the course of this century.

We begin our story with the South in 1880, after its defeat in the Civil War, after the emancipation of its slaves, and after the tumult of the Reconstruction era had died down. By that time the South had entered the state in which it would be mired for the next sixty years, that of an underdeveloped country incongruously joined to an emergent economic superpower. Per capita income was roughly 50 percent that of the nation as a whole, a deep poverty that not only produced widespread personal deprivation but seriously hampered southerners in their ability to develop their region. Parasitic and dietary diseases were endemic; illiteracy was chronically high. The Deep South, especially, was overwhelmingly rural and largely given over to a ruinous form of one-crop staple agriculture, chiefly focused on tobacco and cotton. Cities had always been few and far between; in 1860, when a quarter of the non-southern population dwelled in cities, fewer than 7 percent of the people of the future Confederacy were urbanites, a proportion that had scarcely changed by 1880. Cities had developed so poorly because plantations required only a narrow range of urban services, chiefly involving the movement of crops abroad and the importation of goods not readily produced at home; as a result, little manufacturing was done in southern cities. The South as a whole accounted for less than 10 percent of American manufacturing in the late nineteenth century, and tended to specialize in the roughest processing industries and in those that could make the best use of the region's poor supply of skilled workers and entrepreneurship, and its ample supplies of desperately poor country folk.[6]

For all its handicaps, though, the region was hardly bereft of energy and enterprise. The so-called "New South" saw a sharp increase in industrial growth; indeed, the region's manufacturing expansion has outpaced that of the nation since 1880. Moreover, the dramatic changes resulting from emancipation and the spread of railroads into the region sparked a proliferation of small towns in the southern interior. Each was a future metropolis, in its own eyes at least; each had its class of civic boosters, prominent merchants and bankers and newspaper editors who wanted to make their towns grow by creating new enterprises or, when possible, attracting enterprises from the outside.[7]

In this regard southern townspeople were basically similar in character to the civic boosters who played such central roles in creating the vast defense complexes of the American West. However, only rarely before World War I did military facilities or spending afford opportunities in the South. The army was small and was largely deployed in the West; while concerns with frontier defense redounded to the benefit of such Texas cities as San Antonio, the limited size and stagnant growth of the army prevented it from being a strong city-builder.[8] Its industrial impact on the South was virtually nil.

The navy maintained several bases along the coast, along with a major navy yard at Norfolk (actually Portsmouth), Virginia; the latter facility was supplemented after 1901 by an installation at Charleston, South Carolina, an operation avidly sought by local boosters and moved from an inferior location down the coast through the political influence of Senator Benjamin R. ("Pitchfork Ben") Tillman. However, in the era that saw the creation of the modern American steel-bottomed "blue-water" navy, the only southern facilities in a position to garner shares of the major defense procurement expenditures of the day were the Norfolk yard and its Hampton Roads neighbor, the Newport News Shipbuilding and Dry Dock Company. Created in 1886 by railroad magnate Collis P. Huntington to service the steamship line connecting with the eastern terminus of his Chesapeake and Ohio Railroad, the shipyard was unique among southern enterprises in having massive financial backing from a tycoon willing to absorb years of losses to assure the success of an operation blessed with state-of-the-art technology but poorly situated with respect to supplies of raw materials and skilled labor. By the early twentieth century the Hampton Roads complex, along with nearby Richmond, was the only urban region in the South to find in defense production a serious tool for city-building.[9]

Such was the situation in the South when the United States entered World War I. Lacking major steel or metal-working industries, the region was in poor position to bid on contracts for ships, tanks, or aircraft. Its major asset, in fact, was its land. There was much land available in the South that was worthless for most purposes, situated on soils too poor to support anything but pine trees or worn out by years of cotton growing. That land was situated in undeveloped areas where the costs of construction, fuel, supplies, and labor were cheap, but that were well connected by rail to the major population centers of the Northeast, making them excellent sites for training camps. It scarcely hurt that at the onset of the prewar buildup the presidency and the Congress were in Democratic (and southern) hands. Local civic boosters leaped at the opportunities afforded by the decision of the army to locate the majority of its basic training camps in the South. In 1916 the city fathers of Columbia, South Carolina, offered the army the former plantation of Confederate general Wade Hampton III for use as a facility subsequently named Camp Jackson. By August 1917 over ten thousand workers were constructing a camp for twenty thousand trainees. Similar collaborations of military men and local developers cropped up throughout the region, creating both temporary facilities and such enduring southern landmarks as Fayetteville's Fort Bragg, Augusta's Fort Gordon, and Columbus's Fort Benning.[10]

In the area of procurement, existing southern industries such as tobacco, textiles, and forest products were the major southern industrial beneficiaries of the war. The chief defense industry to arise in its course was the munitions industry. The expanse of southern land afforded protected locations for militarily sensitive production, and its trees and cotton fields produced an abundance of cellulose, a critical raw material. The rivers of the South offered huge potential for hydroelectric development, critical to producing nitrates. Accordingly, munitions facilities sprouted in the central South. DuPont operated the world's largest gunpowder plant outside Nashville, employing twenty-five thousand, while the federal government began construction on two nitrogen fixation plants in Alabama, to be powered by a dam at Muscle Shoals on the Tennessee River.[11] Other industries bloomed as well; in East Tennessee a group of local and New York developers, having recently established the new town of Kingsport, lured defense-related methanol and dyestuffs producers to the Holston Valley, while United States Steel and others built a shipyard at Chickasaw, near Mobile.[12]

While World War I provided enormous short-term stimulus to the southern economy, much of it was evanescent. Most of the cantonments were closed or mothballed; demobilization, the loss of Democratic control of the federal government, and the 1923 Washington naval arms limitation treaty resulted in major cutbacks at Norfolk, Newport News, and Charleston, the last of which narrowly averted the closure of its navy yard. The DuPont plant in Nashville was shut down, as were all the war facilities in Kingsport; the federal nitrate plants and hydroelectric project at Muscle Shoals remained uncompleted.

To be sure, some wartime defense facilities could be reconverted. DuPont, for instance, reopened its Nashville plant in the 1920s, discovering that the same resources—plentiful water and abundant supplies of cellulose—that made its location advantageous for powder production also made it a good production site for one of the growth industries of the 1920s, rayon. The methanol plant in Kingsport became the nucleus for the giant Tennessee Eastman film complex—to this day (under the name Eastman Chemical) the largest manufacturing employer in Tennessee. The management of the Newport News shipyard cannily sought out other opportunities in constructing railroad rolling stock and hydroelectric generating equipment.[13]

Other reconversion efforts, though, were less successful. While Charleston received excellent port facilities from the navy, existing channels of trade continued to bypass the city through the interwar years. The Muscle Shoals project remained uncompleted through the 1920s, the issue of its disposal a major political football. As these examples show, additions to facilities hardly guaranteed their profitable use if the larger regional economy was unable to support them. Nonetheless, the facilities were available; in the 1930s Muscle Shoals became the nucleus for the greatest single federal investment in the region, the Tennessee Valley Authority. Another permanent legacy of World War I was the development of close, continuing ties among local boosters, congressional representatives, and the military. Some camps, notably Forts Benning and Bragg, remained in operation, while others, such as Camp Jackson, remained available for reactivation. The military had learned the advantages of southern locations for bases, and local boosters and politicians worked hard to cultivate military and civilian decision makers, cementing an alliance of great subsequent significance.[14]

In the meantime, the problem of southern economic underdevelopment transcended local efforts and became part of the national agenda. The plight of southern tenant farmers and mill workers was widely publicized in the 1930s through novels, photo essays, and movies; from its very beginning the New Deal made the raising of southern incomes a central concern, one articulated by Franklin D. Roosevelt in his 1938 pronouncement that "the South presents right now the Nation's No. 1 economic problem—the Nation's problem, not merely the South's."[15] Fundamental to that problem was the enormous proportion of the region's population dependent on a technologically backward and frequently exploitive agricultural sector; while many southern social commentators revered the region's rural heritage and sought to preserve it, the consensus among economists and business leaders stressed the need to move workers off the farms and into manufacturing.[16]

Despite New Deal concerns, southern per capita incomes remained in their traditionally low relative position throughout the 1930s. A new way out of the economic impasse, however, suggested itself as early as 1936, when concerns for the security of American trade led to the creation of the U.S. Maritime Commission to subsidize merchant shipbuilding. As war clouds gathered in the late 1930s, the shipbuilding program expanded. Newport News benefitted significantly from the new demand, increasing its employment in the late 1930s from 6,500 to over ten thousand. Further south, Robert Ingalls, a Birmingham steel fabricator, built a new shipyard in Pascagoula, Mississippi, to tap the new demand, financing it in part with a bond issue arranged by Pascagoula boosters under Mississippi's famous BAWI (Balance Agriculture with Industry) program. Ingalls, which had developed innovative methods of building all-welded fabricated steel products, dealt with the lack of shipbuilding traditions in Pascagoula by fabricating subassemblies in Birmingham and shipping them to the Gulf site, which was managed by a team of managers hired away from a northern shipyard.[17]

The onset of "preparedness" mobilization in 1940 offered further opportunities. To be sure, the earliest military contracts went to established companies and regions; only "smokestack America" had the facilities, the experience, and the Depression-induced excess capacity available to handle a defense buildup of unprecedented size and speed. Thus by the middle of 1941 the South was receiving only about half as much per capita from military procurement spending as was the nation as a whole;

moreover, a third of that was being spent in Hampton Roads, the region's major concentration of preexisting shipyard capacity. The disadvantageous distribution of war contracts continued throughout the war years; between June 1940 and September 1945 the thirteen-state South garnered only a third as much as its share of national population warranted, and less than 60 percent as much as its share of prewar manufacturing employment.[18]

As one economist remarked at the time, however, "the factor of major importance . . . in bringing about the industrialization of the South is, not the orders for finished goods, but the location of new productive facilities." The war era saw a major expansion of both industrial facilities and infrastructure; while the South received less than its per capita share of investment in defense facilities, it received one-third more than its prewar share of manufacturing employment would warrant.[19]

Several concerns drove this industrial redirection. As manufacturing and infrastructural capacities in the smokestack belt and the aircraft belt of the West Coast became strained, it made sense to locate new production in areas of labor surplus. Reinforcing that motive was the desire of military planners to decentralize war production to more sheltered areas. Thus the region found itself again disproportionately dotted with munitions plants.

Shipyards expanded along the Gulf coast from Panama City to New Orleans. The U.S. Steel yard at Chickasaw, near Mobile, and the Ingalls yard at Pascagoula built steel-bottomed vessels, drawing on Birmingham for both metal and expertise. In New Orleans, a midwestern-born lumberman turned shipbuilder, Andrew Jackson Higgins, gained lasting fame for mass-producing a vital amphibious landing craft whose design he adapted from one he had developed in the 1930s for navigating Louisiana bayous.[20] The southern airframe industry, which consisted of only one small factory in Nashville before the war, expanded enormously, with giant plants in Marietta, Georgia, and Dallas–Fort Worth, Texas, along with numerous smaller facilities. (Significantly, engine production, the highest-tech branch of the industry, remained heavily concentrated in the manufacturing belt and California).[21]

Moreover, while the South was industrially backward in general, it held a considerable competitive edge in certain newer industries critical to contemporary war technology. The region, notably Arkansas, contained most domestic bauxite supplies, with access to more through Gulf ports, while plants in Alcoa, Tennessee, and Badin, North Carolina, produced over half the nation's aluminum. Of even greater importance was the petroleum-petrochemical complex along the Texas-Louisiana Gulf coast, centered on Houston. On the eve of the war Houston was already the largest manufacturing city in the Old Confederacy, but the ravenous military thirst for fuels and the strategic need for synthetic rubber made the upper Texas Gulf coast the chief beneficiary of defense plant spending, gaining more investment than any southern state outside of Texas itself and over one-sixth of the southern total.[22]

Much of this expansion was financed by the federal government, moreso in the South than in the nation as a whole. In order to finance facilities of dubious peacetime value and entice firms into new and untried locations, the government built numerous facilities, letting management contracts to private corporations. How much this practice affected shifts in location is difficult to say. It was reported at the time that private firms retained enormous say in the location of new plants, since they would be the logical purchasers at the conclusion of the war. Moreover, many southern facilities, especially munitions and synthetic rubber plants, were built with the understanding that most would not survive peacetime; one judicious postwar assessment predicted that reconversion problems would largely nullify the region's relative gains. All told, it could be argued that wartime facilities simply reinforced economic patterns already set.[23]

Nonetheless, massive federal investments speeded up the process of development. Strategic concerns with supplying Houston refineries with pipe led to the construction of a steel mill on the Houston Ship Channel in 1941. The insatiable appetite of aluminum producers (and, secretly, of the enriched uranium plant at Oak Ridge) for electricity forced an enormous expansion in the generating capacity of the TVA (often over the violent objections of those flooded out by the new dams), capacity that ultimately supplied 10 percent of the nation's defense power needs and that, when made available for civilian use after the war, would prove a significant spur to expansion in the valley. In order to protect the movement of Gulf petroleum products, the government built the first transcontinental pipelines.

Most significantly, government investment established Dallas–Fort Worth as a major center for airframe construction. While nearly all major aircraft manufacturers pulled back to their traditional bases after the war, Convair (now General Dynamics) remained in Fort Worth; a new Company, the Texas Engineering and Manufacturing Company (Temco) located in a portion of the vast North American Aviation plant in Grand Prairie; and in 1948 the Department of Defense persuaded Chance Vought Corporation, a Bridgeport, Connecticut, producer cramped for space, to move its operations inland to the rest of the North American facility. The Metroplex was thus in a prime position to benefit from the subsequent history of defense procurement.[24]

Local boosters and politicians played prominent roles in the effort to attract the defense industry. Atlanta and Cobb County leaders courted the giant Bell Aircraft plant built in Marietta; Fort Worth newspaper publisher Amon Carter pressed hard for the Convair plant, while Congressman Wright Patman secured federal financing for a steel mill in northeastern Texas. A group of politicians and businessmen called the Mid-Continent Industrial Council took credit for Chance Vought's postwar move to Texas, though at least one historian believes they overstated their influence.[25]

In any case, the great bulk of opportunities available to local developers were afforded, again, by military bases. Locales such as Charleston, Norfolk, and San Antonio found their longtime cultivation of the military bearing abundant fruit, while others scrambled for a piece of an unprecedentedly huge pie. Again, a plenitude of cheap land proved to be the major inducement. In wiregrass Alabama, for instance, a vast tract of submarginal land removed from cultivation by the Resettlement Administration in the 1930s was promoted as a defense installation by a group of local notables headed by the newspaper editor and the local congressman, Henry B. Steagall; their efforts ultimately resulted in the creation of Fort Rucker. With the aid of North Carolina congressman Graham Barden, two desolate expanses on the North Carolina coast became the vast Marine bases at Camp Lejeune and Cherry Point. All told, sixty of one hundred new army camps were located in the South, and 40 percent of base construction expenditures were paid out in the southern states, a total larger than that invested in industrial facilities in the region.[26]

Demobilization after World War II, as after World War I, dramatically shrank the southern defense economy. Bases, including Forts Rucker and Jackson, were deactivated; some were mothballed, while others were turned over to local authorities for development. Disposal of redundant manufacturing plants proved to be a thorny problem, as numerous aircraft and munitions plants proved difficult to convert to peacetime use; other facilities were retained by the government for standby use. Other wartime businesses found it difficult to adjust to a world in which a single customer tolerant of costs but demanding of volume and performance gave place to many customers necessarily concerned with costs. A 1948 assessment of the southern experience with war industry concluded that "the wartime developments were not sufficient to overcome the influence of the basic economic factors that guide industrial location and expansion."[27]

In contrast to the post–World War I era, however, demobilization in the late 1940s was short-lived. The beginning of the Cold War kept up national interest in maintaining American air power, especially as a delivery system for atomic bombs; the contract for a new intercontinental bomber, the B-36, had been awarded to Convair in Fort Worth in 1944, and development continued through the late 1940s. The outbreak of the Korean War expanded military production again. Most significantly, the federal government invited Lockheed to reactivate the mothballed aircraft plant at Marietta, Georgia; Lockheed retained control following Korea. Training camps were reactivated, and the creation of the peacetime draft gave them a permanent role in processing a constant flow of raw recruits.[28]

By 1960 the Cold War pattern of southern defense dependency was largely set. By that year the region was receiving a per capita share of defense payroll disbursements 40 percent higher than the national average, a share that, through buildups and downsizings, remained strikingly constant until the end of the Cold War. The region continued at a disadvantage with respect to defense procurement, however; in 1960 it received a share of total prime contracts amounting to only around half its population share and three-quarters of its income share. With defense procurement driven by the drive to build a ballistic missile-based nuclear deterrent, traditional aerospace centers such as southern California and missile base states in the West had the advantage over the relatively low-tech South; the victory of private weapons contracting over the traditional peacetime army reliance on in-house development largely nullified the advantage the region might have gotten from the conversion of the World War II–era Redstone Arsenal at Huntsville into the nation's rocket research center.[29]

The Vietnam War saw a sharp increase in the southern share of defense contracting; by 1970 the region was receiving for the first time its full population share and more than its income share. Prosecution of the war required conventional supplies, such as clothing, that the region normally supplied to American troops; it also required aircraft and troopships. General Dynamics and LTV (Ling-Temco-Vought), created by a 1961 merger of several Texas firms, prospered in Dallas–Fort Worth; Lockheed-Georgia burgeoned into the largest single employer in the southeast, thanks chiefly to its contract to build the C-5A Galaxy transport. The California-based defense contractor Litton Industries acquired the Ingalls shipyard in Mississippi in 1961 and in the late 1960s constructed a new, state-of-the-art facility at the site with the help of $130 million in industrial revenue bonds from the state government. By the late 1970s Ingalls was producing 60 percent of all new American warships.[30]

While the southern share of procurement spending fell with the end of the war, it remained at a higher plateau than before. The linchpins of southern defense contracting—Litton, Lockheed (now Lockheed-Martin), General Dynamics, Newport News—are well connected in the Pentagon, which considers it in the national interest to maintain existing capacity and allocates contracts accordingly. While it is difficult to tell what role politicians and civic boosters have played in steering defense industry to the South—evidence indicates that their reputation in that regard has been greatly overblown—they have helped reinforce established patterns. The Strategic Defense Initiative boom around Washington in the 1980s boosted Virginia into the upper ranks of defense states, and laid the foundation for the emergence of the Virginia suburbs of Washington as a major center of the Internet economy. Defense has thus played a signal role in the Old Dominion's emergence as the first southern member of the select list of the ten wealthiest American states.[31]

Nonetheless, defense procurement remains an unsteady contributor to regional well-being, and downsizing may well threaten even the stability brought by bases. While bases have provided far more stable income flows than the boom-and-bust procurement industry, they have been of relatively little value in building infrastructure or developing readily transferable skills; in some cases they may actually have slowed economic growth by competing with possible private employers for local labor. Base towns are usually out of the way and are often poor; Jacksonville, North Carolina, near Camp Lejeune, ranks among the lowest-paying metropolitan areas in the nation.[32] While once militarily dependent cities such as Greenville and Charleston, South Carolina, have found redeveloped bases to be economic assets, such cities have tended to be places with established economic potential quite apart from their role in defense.[33]

To be sure, such locales are increasingly numerous in the South. Since World War II the region's economy has persistently converged on that of the rest of the nation; moreover, as the economic historian Gavin Wright has pointed out, the economic life of the region has become much more diverse, so much so that at one point he concluded that there is no longer a coherent economic South at all. The defense economy has played some role in this stunning development, though considerably less than some have alleged. The agricultural revolution, availability of low-cost labor, an openness to new economic approaches and innovative migrants, and a willingness on the part of local, state, and federal governments to invest heavily in new infrastructural and educational improvements have all played a role. The prosperity of the Research Triangle of North Carolina owes virtually nothing to defense; that of Atlanta, Houston, and Dallas owe relatively little.[34]

With the maturation of the southern economy, post–Cold War defense downsizing has been at worst only mildly disadvantageous to the region. Indeed, the process of downsizing has forced some fundamental changes in defense procurement that have been of significant benefit to the South. Concerned with stretching ever scarcer budget dollars, the Pentagon and its contractors has found low-cost, low-wage southern locations more attractive than they were when high performance was an obsession and expense was no object. Thus, while California and the Northeast have found their defense industries "hollowed out" since the end of the Cold War, the southeast has seen its proportion of procurement spending increase, as companies like Lockheed-Martin concentrated their production in places such as Marietta and Fort Worth.[35] As table 10.1 shows, since 1989 the South's share of procurement spending has surged from 78 to 115 percent of its share of U.S. population, and from 87 to 126 percent of its share of U.S. personal income.[36] Some traditionally militarily dependent cities, such as Charleston, have been able to turn downsizing to their advantage, as the expanding foreign trade of South Carolina buoys its port facilities.[37]

Still, much of the region remains shaped by the old patterns. Places such as Jacksonville and Fayetteville, North Carolina, Columbus, Georgia, and Dothan, Alabama, whose chief initial attraction to the armed forces lay in the very desolation of their land, may not be in position to bounce back easily from a major base closing. Even the growth of defense procurement reflects an old characteristic of southern growth, its propensity to snare larger shares of declining or slow-growth industries selling mature products sensitive to cost. For these very reasons, however, it might be well for southern policy-makers to begin to look beyond defense. Like many of its other traditional industries, such as textiles, the defense economy has had an ambiguous legacy, injecting income but, outside certain locales, doing relatively little to develop skills, institutions, or entrepreneurship capable of generating dynamic growth. As with the shrinkage of the textile industry since 1980, defense downsizing offers the South an opportunity to rethink an aging set of development policies, policies that may well have outlived their time.[38]

11

The American South and the American Manufacturing Belt

DAVID L. CARLTON

This essay appears here in print for the first time. Earlier versions were presented at the annual meeting of the Organization of American Historians in St. Louis, March 31, 2000, and the annual meeting of the St. George Tucker Society in Nashville, August 11, 2000. The author would like to thank the OAH commentators, Margaret Levenstein and Harold Woodman, the Tucker Society commentators, Louis Ferleger and David Moltke-Hansen, and the audiences at both conferences.

In his 1958 classic *The Strategy of Economic Development,* Albert O. Hirschman offered the following observations about the relationship of region to economic development:

> The progressive sectors and regions of an underdeveloped economy are easily overimpressed with their own rate of development. At the same time, they set themselves apart from the less progressive operators by creating a picture of the latter as lazy, bungling, intriguing, and generally hopeless. . . . Even though the initial success of these groups may often be due to sheer luck or to environmental factors such as resource endowment, matters will not be left there. Those who have been caught by progress will always maintain that they were the ones who did the catching; they will easily convince themselves, and attempt to convince others, that their accomplishments are primarily owed to their superior moral qualities and conduct. . . . The less developed groups and regions also make unwittingly a contribution to the process. . . . Faced with the sudden improvement in the fortunes of some of their own compatriots, they will frequently retort to the claims of moral superiority of these *nouveaux riches* by accusing them of crass materialism, sharp practices, and disregard for the country's traditional cultural and spiritual values.[1]

Hirschman was writing of the so-called less-developed world, but the irony of his lines aptly capture the ways in which those who study the American South have long imagined the region. Time after time we have been told that the American "North" and "South" have fundamentally different cultures. We have been told this by southern conservative polemicists positing an opposition between northern "industrial" and southern "agrarian" values; by marketers who find the ideal of "gracious" (and monied) "southern" living a dandy means of dressing up modern consumerism; by historians claiming either that the region deserved its historic backwardness or owes its recent relative prosperity to its use of political intrigue to suck wealth from those regions that had initially created it. The South has been hailed as a repository of spiritual, antimaterialist values, and its history described as a chastening exception to "American" expectations of unending economic progress. It has also been denigrated as a "feudal" throwback, where "traditional" attitudes and "unprogressive" elites have persistently held back both development and economic equity.[2]

Too often commentators on the relationship of "North" and South" in American economic life have neglected Hirschman's cautionary remarks. Rather than consider whether regional stereotypes might be *products* of divergent economic paths, students of the "southern" side of the relationship in particular have all too readily assigned causative significance to these stereotypes, declaring that they reflect the "values" that really make societies what they are. Thus, if the region is seen to have failed to measure up in terms of economic progress and equity, the shortfall is attributable to laziness, to fatalism, to contempt for entrepreneurial ambition, to repressive rule by an elite fearful of the disorderliness of economic change. Conversely, if the region is regarded as an agrarian Arcadia, its happy exceptionalism is credited to its leisurely sense of proportion about life, its reliance on Providence, its antimaterialism, its respect for tradition and community.[3]

But pinning down the values of a whole people, or even a whole "class," is horrendously difficult. Descriptive accounts of southern mentalitè, whether by southerners or outside observers, point in contradictory directions. For every Thomas Nelson Page, painting honey-dipped pictures of the plantation idyll, there is a Henry Grady declaring that southerners "have fallen in love with work." Moreover, even the notion of enduring southern backwardness is by no means beyond question. Southern rates of economic, industrial, and urban growth, both before and after the Civil War, have compared favorably with those of the nation as a whole, and a credible argument holds that the region's postbellum poverty is chiefly attributable to the chasm into which it fell as a result of the war and the collapse of plantation slavery. Certainly the record of the post–World War II South is difficult to square with the notion that such deep, long-term variables as "values" can explain much of the region's earlier grim economic and social record.[4]

Yet grim it was. From the earliest postbellum estimate available (1880) until the eve of World War II, southern per capita income held at more or less half the U.S. average. Agriculture dominated the economy, and staple-crop monoculture dominated agriculture. While white southerners suffered considerably, for that large minority of southerners who were black, all these ills were intensified and augmented by disfranchisement, Jim Crow, and sometimes out-and-out terror.

But agriculture was only part of the story. Many of the South's economic troubles reflected the nature of the new industrial order that began to appear in the late nineteenth century. Southern industrial society, after all, has never really matched our image of how an industrial society is supposed to look—an image set by the Manchesters and Pittsburghs of the nineteenth century and the Detroits of the early twentieth. The vast corporate complexes and dense industrial communities of smokestack America had southern imitators, but they were few and pale; manufacturing there did not spring from great cities, nor did it build them. Its workers remained poorly paid, poorly skilled, and poorly educated, and were prey to nutritional and parasitic diseases virtually unknown elsewhere in the nation. African American workers were relegated to the worst jobs when they had access to them at all. Working and living conditions in and around the factories were lightly regulated, at best, and by the late 1930s the region was gaining evil renown for its heavy-handed managers and beaten-down workers. Mill villages and coal camps were bywords for misery and oppression.

So, in the pre–World War II South, the region's real progress was obscured by its poverty, just as in the postwar era the continuing poverty of many southerners came to be increasingly overshadowed by the "Sunbelt" boom.[5] Moreover, the "progress" experienced by large areas of the postwar South has proved to be thin and easily reversed. Even now "deindustrialization" plagues much of the small-town and rural South, and even such high-tech showpieces as North Carolina's Research Triangle have yet to generate the entrepreneurial vitality of a Silicon Valley. For all its gloss, the modern South has yet to (as the cliché goes) reach the next level.[6]

Why not? In the face of this tangled picture of dynamism and stagnation, explanatory schemes that locate the region, or its "ruling class," along a continuum between "tradition" and "modernity" seem inadequate. Yet one need not have to appeal to either a "backward" society or "backward" rulers to understand regional disparity. As economic development theorists, economic geographers, and students of international trade have long been aware, the distribution of economic activity across space is by its nature "lumpy." Small initial advantages give certain locations enhanced power to attract subsequent business and labor, growing by a process of circular and cumulative causation until the disadvantages of congestion begin to outweigh the advantages of togetherness. Industries reinforce each other by developing pools of appropriately skilled labor, by creating auxiliary industries and institutions, and by informally exchanging ideas. Where they concentrate, they serendipitously develop communities that prize flexibility and "progressive" attitudes, while providing labor with extra bargaining power against employers. Lagging regions, conversely, have difficulty getting traction; lacking the initial advantages of their sister regions, they find their disadvantage reinforced over time.[7]

A lagging region, then, need not have "values" that are materially different from those of more fortunate regions—simply an initial, perhaps marginal, disadvantage that snowballs. To be sure, if its entrepreneurs are resourceful enough, they can develop techniques to neutralize its disadvantages and begin closing the gap with first-comer regions.[8] But the "separate path" chosen will be shaped by the specific context in which the region's entrepreneurs operate, and will in turn limit their future options by imposing what economists sometimes refer to as "path dependence."[9] While the path chosen may well be productive of significant growth, it may also foreclose opportunities, narrow the range of economic possibilities, and skew the distribution of economic, social, and political power.

That, in brief, is the approach this essay takes to the problem of the industrial South. More specifically, I wish to argue that the history of an economically "distinctive" South is best understood in tandem with the history not of "the North" but of a region with a more explicitly economic definition—the region that geographers call the American manufacturing belt.

First delineated in the 1920s, the manufacturing belt stretches from southern New England across the Middle Atlantic region and the Midwest to the Mississippi River; transcending national boundaries, it also extends across Lake Erie into southern Ontario. More recent observers such as the economist Harvey Perloff and the geographer David Meyer have observed of the manufacturing belt that, once it consolidated in its present form in the 1880s, its boundaries remained roughly stable well into the postwar era. Within this belt, the heartland of "smokestack America," the bulk of manufacturing was carried on, generating the greatest diversity of products and the preponderance of American innovation; in 1900 it accounted for nearly three-quarters of all American manufacturing employment and patent activity, and as late as the 1950s accounted for nearly two-thirds of manufacturing jobs. Outside the belt—with the partial exception of California—manufacturing was not only relatively unimportant but much less diverse, much more closely tied to local resources, and less innovative.[10]

The South, of course, lay outside the belt—but so did most of the trans-Mississippi West; the Upper Midwest; the Adirondacks and northern New England; and much of eastern Canada, including Quebec and the Maritime Provinces. To be sure, most of these regions were historically thinly populated; but Quebec, the Maritimes, and northern New England are long-settled districts that have not only suffered chronic disadvantage relative to their southerly neighbors but have frequently had their disabilities explained in terms not unlike those applied to the South.[11] Given that the South's historic economic disadvantage has been generally attributed to the legacy of plantation slavery, the presence to the north of other relatively disadvantaged regions lacking such a legacy suggests that they may have shared in some measure a common experience with the South—an experience shaped by their common relationship to the manufacturing belt itself. Furthermore, if the formation of the manufacturing belt is a key to understanding southern industrial history—and indeed, I would suggest, southern identity itself—the "invention of the South" itself might be closely tied to the same dynamic that created the manufacturing belt. Finally, if the industrial history of the United States over the past fifty years has featured the relative decline, and increasing fuzziness, of the manufacturing belt, the dynamics of that decline might suggest some of the reasons for the remarkable pace of southern industrialization over the past half century.

But—you object—wasn't there a South long before the 1880s? Yes; but while the manufacturing belt consolidated in its enduring form by the 1880s, its roots go much further back, to the earliest years of the Republic. On the other hand, it is arguable that before it began to form there was no reason to speak of what became the South as a place with a peculiarly "unmodern" mentalité. Jack P. Greene, for instance, has argued in *Pursuits of Happiness* that the roots of American culture, including most especially its economic culture, can be found not in New England, with its near medieval, corporatist, and theocratic mind set, but in the Chesapeake, a predominantly secular, profit-oriented place whose settlers came seeking neither God nor community but their own private "pursuits of happiness." Likewise Joyce Chaplin has found that planters and merchants of the Lower South, and their ambitious cousins in the backcountry, were innovative entrepreneurs devoted to economic progress, and Glenn Crothers has discovered the "projecting spirit" flourishing on the northern neck of Virginia.[12] Before the Revolution and for some years after, the principal wealth-producing end of British North America was its southern end. By comparison, the northern colonies appeared to be reasonably well off but rather backward peasant societies, largely dependent on transatlantic trade for their manufactured goods, and certainly not capable of generating the wealth that the captains of tobacco or rice could command. Indeed, until the Civil War demolished the social basis of the slave plantation system, the great bulk of large-scale, labor-mobilizing business enterprises in the United States were not northern factories but southern plantations.[13]

But then, beginning after the Revolution, the manufacturing belt began to develop. At first it was confined to a stretch of the Atlantic seaboard roughly between Boston and Philadelphia, and was less a "belt" than a cluster of city regions centered on Boston, Providence, Rhode Island, the Connecticut valleys, the New York–New Jersey region, and Philadelphia. But these cities, in interaction with each other and with their rural hinterlands, began to develop industrial complexes. Why here? Certainly not because these places escaped the taint of slavery. While plantations were largely absent, slaves were important sources of labor in the streets of New York and on the large farms of Rhode Island until the post-Revolutionary emancipation movement began to free them; profits from the transatlantic slave trade helped underwrite the early textile enterprises of Samuel Slater. But the relative unimportance of the plantation in the colonies/states above Mason and Dixon's line allowed those districts to become thickly peopled with free farm households. Over time these rural folk prospered from the burgeoning international grain trade of the eighteenth century. Eager to augment their production through adopting new capital-goods technology, and even more eager to enjoy the fruits of what was already becoming a consumer society, they afforded increasingly dense and deep markets, first for proto-industrial household manufacturing, then increasingly for specialized manufacturing enterprises. In the early Republic, as Diane Lindstrom and others have suggested, local entrepreneurs were drawn into industrialization in order to substitute for imports either unavailable or priced out by the trade disruptions of the early Republic. But manufacturers also prospered thanks to their access to rural Pennsylvania pig iron and southern cotton, and the availability of native-born and immigrant labor. Above all, proto-industrialization and dense settlement created clusters of diversely skilled workers and entrepreneurs (often the same people); the proverbial Yankee tinkerer was no isolated figure but could rely on broad networks of fellow innovators to help him solve problems. Because the ability to tap into such "local knowledge" was critical to success, entrepreneurs and workmen sought to congregate; as a result, industrialization began to center in core cities, where people exchanged diverse arrays of manufacturing products for the raw materials of their densely settled rural hinterlands.[14]

As yet these city regions were not consolidating into a single manufacturing complex; rather, as David Meyer has argued, the proto-manufacturing belt grew by adding new city regions to the West. As settlement moved into the continental interior, Richard Wade told us years ago, towns and cities were at the vanguard, serving as ports of entry and outfitting and marketing centers for the hinterlands; because transportation costs between the transmontane West and eastern markets were initially quite high, manufacturers were encouraged to manufacture locally the consumer and capital goods needed by farmers and other manufacturers, as well as to process agricultural produce. Thus by the mid-nineteenth century cities such as Cincinnati were becoming important manufacturing centers with diverse products and communities of skilled workmen/entrepreneurs; no mere "Porkopolis," the Queen City was already well along in developing a remarkable mechanical complex generating its own distinctively innovative products, technologies, and business organizations. Below the Cincinnatis, as the western countryside replicated the dense free-farmer societies back east, legions of promoters scattered towns across the landscape; while not all were successful, and few fully realized the extravagant dreams of their boosters, they began to fill out urban hierarchies feeding off a countryside populated with farmers eager, like their eastern predecessors, to adopt new technology and enjoy the fruits of an emergent consumer society.[15]

As these western city regions integrated themselves through the development of roads, canals, and later railroads, they also reached out to forge links to each other and to older regions in the East. After around 1840, as a result, the city regions began to reach out to each other. Increasingly industrial cities began to specialize and to exchange with each other, not simply with their hinterlands, spurring a sharp increase in urban growth rates. Moreover, as the "transportation revolution" knitted the various regions of the East and West together, the water and rail ties furthered what Allan Pred has termed the "circulation of information." Skilled workers and small-industry entrepreneurs moved throughout the belt, freely borrowing and adapting innovations in what was becoming a thousand-mile-long innovative community. In the process, the belt became a magnet for the skilled and the ambitious, both native and foreign. Immigrants, of course, forced Americans drastically to revise their understanding of their own culture, but they also made crucial contributions to the expanding stock of technological know-how and entrepreneurial experience.[16]

The emerging networks directing these flows of people, goods, capital, and knowledge, though, effectively bypassed the South. Why? As we've seen, certainly not because of entrepreneurial lassitude; the expansion of the plantation system halfway across the continent in two generations was itself a stunning entrepreneurial achievement. Slavery was never inconsistent with hard-driving, calculating economic behavior on the part of masters, nor, assertions to the contrary notwithstanding, did it necessarily devalue work. Moreover, evidence has mounted over the past generation that slavery was a far more flexible institution than had been earlier suspected, capable of accommodating itself to a variety of activities, including urban-industrial ones.[17]

That said, it was nonetheless the case that the southern plantation system, along with the system of forced labor and racial domination it fostered and depended upon, effectively stifled the development of either industrial communities or industrial institutions. First of all, plantations, unlike family farms, made poor markets; slaves were forced under-consumers, and the imperative to spread the fixed costs of slaves across a maximum of productive activities drove plantations toward a degree of self-sufficiency that was neither necessary nor desirable for northern family farmers. Because planters could expand their production simply by buying more slaves, plantations provided thin markets at best for capital goods. Finally, planters' orientation toward extra-regional markets, along with their need to tap into the expertise and connections of intermediaries situated at the few points of good communication with those markets, led them to farm out such critical functions as marketing to factors residing in a handful of coastal and river cities, thus minimizing the need for an elaborate business infrastructure in the interior. To be sure, the very simplicity of the plantation complex was one of its great strengths; it allowed the Thomas Sutpens of the Old South to move the cotton frontier rapidly west at minimal cost and with minimal need to innovate. But it also deprived the southern interior of the network of cities and small towns, tied together by canals and railroads, that were laying the groundwork for the industrialization of the antebellum era's other "peripheral" region, the Midwest.[18]

To be sure, the South, like the West, was mainly settled by free farming households, not planters or slaves. But the plantations tended to dominate those major agricultural regions that lay closest tò the coast, leaving to the "yeomanry" those upland districts where the growing season was too short for cotton. Thus small-farming communities were concentrated in places such as the Piedmont, remote from market access and less lucrative to railroad promoters than Black Belt regions closer to the port cities that in antebellum times primarily drove railroad development. Unlike their counterparts to the north, these yeoman-dominated areas, lacking the cash generated from commercial agriculture, tended toward a sort of community self-sufficiency that supported a significant number of local craftsmen; moreover, these districts nourished a significant number of small industries, such as charcoal-fired iron forges and furnaces and small yarn mills, mainly supplying interior blacksmiths and the looms of farmwives. Generally, though, the yeoman-dominated interior lacked either the integrated markets or the consumption levels sufficient to spark major town-based manufacturing; indeed, many of its existing industries survived precisely because their isolation protected them from the consequences of high-cost, technologically backward production.[19]

The combination of slave under-consumption, planter and yeoman self-reliance, and poor market integration stunted antebellum southern urbanization, especially relative to the post-1840 takeoff in the proto-manufacturing belt. Here again, as David Goldfield and others showed long ago, the problem with southern cities had little to do with backward mentalitè; even Charleston, the poster child of antebellum southern urban decadence, could boast a striving entrepreneurial elite that, among other things, constructed one of the first major U.S. railroads and elaborated it by 1860 into a network stretching as far west as Memphis.[20] But booster aspirations were limited by the larger environment defined by the plantation. The few southern cities were "primate" in character, feeding not off an elaborating urban hierarchy as in the West but off an export-staple economy in the countryside—a hinterland inherently limited in its demand for manufactured goods and its capacity for growth. While southern entrepôts such as Charleston and New Orleans developed manufacturing, only Richmond, in the half-southern, half-mid-Atlantic state of Virginia, developed a significant, diversified industrial economy; most southern cities focused instead on export-import trade. Transportation links were shaped by the strategies of port promoters, who directed rail construction to major staple areas, funneling farm produce out of the region and manufactured goods in. Lacking (until late in the day) interior cities eager to develop multiple linkages with their neighbors, and hamstrung by the unwillingness of competing cities to allow connections with the lines of their rivals, the southern railroad network was for the most part disarticulated and inflexible. Thus, except for the border cities of Louisville, St. Louis, Baltimore, and (more tenuously) Richmond, the urban South was slow to develop the dense, deep markets and diverse communities of skills needed to join the belt. With the impulse for interurban trade relatively weak, southern cities failed to participate in the process that knitted cities in the Northeast and West into a unified community of production and innovation.[21]

Despite these disabilities, the South on the eve of the Civil War was hardly a backward place by world standards; the new Confederacy instantly became one of the leading industrial powers of the world, and by comparison to other plantation slave economies of the time the American South was a showpiece of development.[22] Nor was it especially backward by comparison to the American West, whose per capita income was lower and whose industrial base was comparable to the South's both in size and in structure; both "peripheral" regions were characterized by small firms and oriented toward agricultural and resource processing. Insofar as there were differences between the "slave" and "free" peripheries, they were as yet marginal, not fundamental.

However, as Hirschman would have predicted, the process of regional differentiation became self-reinforcing, and survived even the destruction of slavery itself. Historical contingency played a role here as well. The manufacturing belt was in its final stages of consolidation between 1865 and 1880, while the former Confederacy was lurching through the traumatic collapse of the plantation slave economy and a catastrophic decline in regional income; indeed, some economists have contended that the hole the South fell into in the 1860s is alone sufficient to explain its postwar underdevelopment.[23] But the South's problems did not end with a single shock, however profound, for the very consolidation of the manufacturing belt itself began to distort the options available to southern entrepreneurs as they sought to develop their prostrate region.

To be sure, the postwar years also saw a dramatic expansion in the southern rail system, bringing to the region the sort of dense, articulated network that the belt had developed before 1860. Yet the new network served as much to reduce the South to peripheral status as to energize its growth. Antebellum southern railroads had been under the control of major port cities and states, and had been designed to help develop their territories and enrich the terminal cities. After the war, however, southern railroads could no longer wring enough revenue from their impoverished territories to remain viable; the only way to regain profitability was to attract more cost-effective through traffic from connecting lines—lines that, as we have seen, did not connect before the war. The resulting mad scramble for connections, and the huge capital flows required to finance reconstruction and expansion, led quickly to the consolidation of southern railroads under the control of systems, headquartered in New York, whose business priorities, while hardly unmindful of the welfare of the region, were not identified with it in the way that the old city- and state-controlled lines had been.[24]

Among the most important consequences of this new rail network was the opening of the southern interior to penetration by producers in the manufacturing belt. The earlier market integration of the belt had allowed its producers to benefit from increasing returns to scale. Not that firms themselves necessarily became large in scale, at least at first; for most industries firms remained small both in size and in number of functions performed. But the reduction of transportation costs allowed small specialty firms to cluster in specialized districts where skilled labor and technical and marketing services were available: machine-tool firms in Cincinnati, specialty textiles in Philadelphia, furniture makers in Grand Rapids. In other industries, characterized by large-scale bulk production and high fixed costs, the benefits of "throughput" economies led to the creation of giant, low-cost firms making steel, dressed meat, flour, and petroleum products—firms whose competitive power began to drive smaller producers to the wall.[25]

Lacking either sort of scale economy—that resulting from high throughput or production within a specialized industrial community—the development of the southern rail network hit southern manufacturers hard. Rather than encouraging diverse industrialization, as the earlier "transportation revolution" did in the West, the railroads at least initially introduced often ruinous competition from the battle-hardened entrepreneurs of the belt. A form of "deindustrialization" set in, as the many small-scale flour mills and iron works scattered through the southern interior succumbed to powerful new competition from the powerful firms of Minneapolis and Pittsburgh. In short, in the two decades or so following Appomattox the South began to suffer from what Gunnar Myrdal termed "backwash"—the swamping of local industry in a developing country by the cheap goods of a developed competitor.[26]

Deindustrialization, to be sure, reversed after 1880; indeed, from 1880 into the 1970s the South's rate of manufacturing expansion consistently outpaced that of the rest of the nation. Even the fading of the region's older industrial base had in part to do with the rise of more modern industries within the region; local flour mills retreated before Nashville as much as Minneapolis, and charcoal furnaces were driven out by the massive works of Birmingham as much as by Pittsburgh. But the South's pace of industrialization masked deeper difficulties at generating the sort of self-propelling growth that had generated the industrial cultures of the first comers; adept as the region was at adopting the mature industries of the so-called First Industrial Revolution, it faced serious obstacles to competing in the cutting-edge industries of the "Second Industrial Revolution."

The difficulties can be illustrated by looking at the southern cotton textile industry and its relationship to the older industry of the manufacturing belt. The cotton mills of New England and other parts of the Northeast developed their own distinctive entrepreneurial styles, adopting British technology but passing it through their communities of mechanics, whose "local knowledge," applied to the peculiar problems of American production and marketing, created a distinctively American textile machinery technology. At first mills worked closely with mechanics in equipping themselves; then, beginning with the Lowell mills' central machine shop, independent firms specializing in textile machinery began to arise. By the late nineteenth century textile machinery was its own separate industry, and machine makers, not the mills themselves, were primarily responsible for innovation in the industry.[27]

This development was telling, because while Piedmont entrepreneurs readily moved to build cotton mills in the late nineteenth century, they relied almost wholly on the manufacturing belt for their technology; machinery makers remained concentrated in the Northeast until World War II, long after the spinning, weaving, and knitting of fabrics in the belt had begun their precipitous decline. What came to the South, rather, were those portions of the textile complex whose production processes were most routinized, whose skill requirements were lowest, and whose forms of organization could most easily accommodate such traditional practices as the use of the household to mobilize labor. Southerners made no effort to replicate the specialty textile production of Philadelphia, with its skilled workers and flexible entrepreneurs—even though the Philadelphia style had much lower capital costs than the machine-intensive style actually adopted. The ability of southern textile men to purchase the products of skilled labor and innovation in the belt stifled opportunities for skilled workers at home and sapped the motivation of working-class southerners to obtain them. The "family labor" system, which privileged the day-to-day needs of the household above risk taking and "human capital" expenditure on children, helped ingrain in mill culture a deep cultural conservatism that inhibited both individual assertion and class mobilization. Finally, because southern textile industrialists appropriated the embodied skills and experience of manufacturing belt workers, while their employees lacked nearby allies among a skilled "labor aristocracy," they were able to wield a power over the workplace and the community that few of their northern counterparts could muster.[28]

The cotton textile industry was not the only or even the largest of the southern industries; some, such as the new manufacture of cigarettes, were themselves able to tap into the new national markets and adopt the "high-throughput" strategy of such behemoths as Swift and Pillsbury. Like them enormously profitable, they drew large amounts of capital into the region, capital that helped develop other industries and, especially, cutting-edge infrastructure such as electric power grids.[29] Apart from textiles, however, leading industries, such as tobacco, lumber, and pig iron and its products, were resource based and export oriented, developing few internal linkages and, outside of Birmingham, building no significant cities.[30] In the meantime, leading-sector industries such as machinery and machine tools scarcely appeared at all in the former Confederacy, their absence both an effect and a cause of the region's small machinery industry. While the Midwest built on its machining experience (especially the "local knowledge" of the machine shops of Detroit) to dominate the mass production of automobiles by the 1920s, early southern auto manufacturers were usually little more than glorified body shops, importing their engines and chassis and adding value primarily with coachwork; virtually all vanished with the triumph of Ford.[31] The South's lack of strong presence in the machine-making industries seriously depressed its innovative capacity. Throughout the nineteenth century, the South's patent activity, measured in patents per capita, was by far the lowest in the nation—though one study indicated that it was no lower than that of other states with similar levels of manufacturing employment and urbanization. However, in the early twentieth century, even as the South industrialized and urbanized, its measurable innovative vigor failed to keep pace—a shortfall attributable, Peter Coclanis and I have argued elsewhere, to the region's poor position in the capital-goods industries that were leading American innovation.[32]

The weakness of more sophisticated southern industry in the face of manufacturing belt competition was worsened by infrastructural disabilities, typified by regional disparities in rail freight rates and service. From the late nineteenth century southern rail freight rates were chronically higher than those in the belt, because traffic over southern lines was relatively thin and highly seasonal; furniture manufacturers in North Carolina, for instance, persistently complained of poor service from railroads set up to move cotton rather than case goods. Moreover, the great systems of the belt (or, as it was designated for rate-setting purposes, "Official Territory"), with their east-west trunk lines, found it more cost-effective to move goods for long hauls along those trunks than to supply relative short hauls to southern shipments. To be sure, established southern industries (including furniture in time) could compensate by negotiating preferential commodity rates with regional carriers eager to develop traffic; but these rates were in turn subsidized by the "class rates" that southern "infant industries" would have to incur. Thus by the early twentieth century the logic of rail operations (quite apart from "colonialist" motivations) tended to freeze existing industrial relationships in place. Indeed, when southern governors began to push for interregional rate equalization in the 1930s, among their major opponents were traditional southern bulk-commodity producers, organized in the Southern States Industrial Council, who had long since cut their private deals with the railroads and saw no reason to share the rate burdens for the sake of regional development.[33]

Thus, by the early twentieth century, the South found itself an industrial mendicant, living off the scraps of mature industries that dropped from the groaning board of the manufacturing belt. Note, however, that one need not imagine any sort of alternative southern value system to explain this development. The South's position resulted from a combination of two mutually reinforcing conditions: its uncompetitiveness in the most innovative, cutting-edge industries of the time, and the relative ease with which it was able to adopt the least risky, because the least innovative, of older forms of industry.

Yet forces were building by the early twentieth century that would lead after World War II to a fundamental alteration of the regional balance of power, transforming the South into the "Sunbelt" and the manufacturing belt into the "Rust Belt"—two journalistic tags that, like most journalistic tags, have obscured more than they reveal. First, the dense networks of skills, entrepreneurship, and exchange that led to the supremacy of the manufacturing belt developed over time in a manner that made those networks increasingly formal and detached from community. As we have already seen in the case of bulk production of cotton textiles, local knowledge became increasingly portable, and thus more readily available to entrepreneurs in lagging regions endowed with relatively ubiquitous unskilled labor. Furthermore, while the creation of a national economy initially enhanced the competitive advantages of the manufacturing belt, it also encouraged the rise of a many-pronged movement to standardize production. The drive for economies of "throughput" that created the great Chandlerian industrial corporations put a premium on sameness that reached its extreme with the black-only Model T. The rise of mass marketing had as its corollary the standardization of consumer product lines; Philip Scranton's flexible producers, with their small batches, their emphasis on style, and their quick adaptation to shifts in market demand, began to lose ground as bulk producers, many of them located in the South, began to mass produce goods formerly regarded as specialties. The locally embedded single-plant enterprise, dependent on neighborhoods or regions for services and skilled labor, increasingly gave ground to the branch plant, reliant on semi-skilled and unskilled labor and dependent less on its locality than on far-flung networks of services organized by national and, increasingly, international corporations. In effect, the role of the *community* in organizing industrial life was increasingly usurped by the *corporation*—and the corporation, operating broadly over space, made space, in the terms of the geographer Ann Markusen, "slippery."[34] The development of "markets" for patentable ideas, and the increasing importance of corporate and government research, began to nationalize the process of innovation and information exchange.[35]

Finally, some of the regional agglomeration economies that had previously benefitted the belt were becoming *diseconomies* by the 1920s. Industrial concentration raised the cost of land, labor, and services; industrial infrastructure, which in earlier times had seen unit costs decline with fuller utilization, began to encounter the legendary law of diminishing returns. Thus the railroads of "Official Territory" had derived their regional advantage from their ability to spread the fixed costs of their networks over higher and steadier volumes of long-haul traffic than had existed in the South. By the 1930s, however, the increasingly vocal southern advocates of freight rate equalization could argue (ultimately successfully) that the manufacturing belt's historical edge had become overbalanced by the higher costs and congestion of its urban terminals.[36]

As the belt's advantage in local knowledge and industrial concentration eroded, the South benefitted. While southern car-makers could not survive the advent of mass production, the new standardized techniques allowed the emergent giants, Ford and General Motors, to build assembly plants in the region from the 1920s onward. The shift of textiles out of the Northeast reached massive proportions by that decade, and was followed by the "runaway shops" of the apparel industry in the 1930s, 1940s, and 1950s, and the light assembly operations of the 1960s. The manufacturing belt remained vital into the 1960s, and indeed continued to play one of its historic roles as a great magnet of opportunity for workers. Now, however, those workers were southern—African Americans tossed off the land in what Pete Daniel has called the "southern enclosure" of the 1930s, and whites lured from the depressed fields and the mines of Appalachia.[37]

Thus the old boundaries between the South and the manufacturing belt began to blur—greatly to the disadvantage of the belt and, especially, its workers. The reputation of the South for being peculiarly anti-union and hostile to high-wage employment, a stereotype intrinsic to southern labor historiography, tends to ignore the fact that American labor relations generally have privileged employer prerogative over worker aspirations; belt employers, and the legal establishment with which they have generally been allied, have not necessarily been friendlier to labor organization than southern employers. The regional differences that developed in labor relations were due to the relative structural power held by working people in the regional economy. The historic importance of local concentration of manufacturing to the belt's industrial success had enhanced the power of workers, whose skills had been so essential a part of the local knowledge that underwrote early industrial growth. This relative advantage allowed the formation of strong unions, which in some cases could overwhelm employer resistance and in others lead employers to accommodate to unions as a means of maintaining worker morale and discipline and aiding in labor recruitment. The rise of mass production initially undercut worker power, as skilled labor was replaced with unskilled. By the 1930s, though, the complexity of such behemoths as General Motors, along with their continuing dependence on a belt increasingly dominated politically by New Deal-ish politicians, gave the CIO organizers of that time major strategic advantages. On the other hand, the ability of oligopolies to pass on the costs of unionization to their customers lowered the incentive for managers to resist unionization. From the New Deal into the post–World War II era, workers, both through their unions and through their clout in the Democratic Party, used this power to mitigate the insecurities of working-class life, creating the so-called New Deal Order.[38]

With the declining distinctiveness of the manufacturing belt, however, has come the well-known erosion in worker power, and in the will of the state to underwrite, in the broad sense, "social security," that has been one of the great, grim themes of recent American history. Some observers have blamed this erosion on conspiratorial politics, in particular an unholy alliance of southern politicians and the military-industrial complex that in the postwar years has systematically bled the old industrial core dry to finance a defense-led Sunbelt boom. This argument, I contend, is unwarranted by the actual economic record of the post–World War II years; in fact, the postwar South has not been especially dependent on defense to drive its economic growth. But it does recognize two fundamental points: that the New Deal order at its apogee was deeply rooted in the manufacturing belt, and that the decline of that order has been intimately bound to the shifting relationship between the manufacturing belt and the South.[39]

Finally—and a more positive aspect of the latter-day blurring of regional distinctiveness—the collapse in the 1960s of Jim Crow and its accompanying siege mentality has made the South a much more open society than it was in the glory days of its distinctiveness—more receptive to outside people and ideas, more amenable to the gospel of progress. The modern South is more hospitable to immigrants, more culturally tolerant, and more accommodating of modernity than ever before—in many ways replicating the cultural path taken by the manufacturing belt in the nineteenth century, but with arguably less nativist turmoil. The South, like the belt, has learned that pluralism can be economically energizing.[40]

What are we to conclude from this survey? Most importantly, that in order to understand the course of southern history, it is not enough simply to study the South, in its particularity, against a "North" that dissolves into an ideal-typical abstraction. This narrative, in particular, involves not one but *two* distinctive regions, each with its own particular regional history: the American South and the American manufacturing belt. Furthermore, their historical trajectories are intimately related to each other. Most notably, the rise of a South *perceived* to be distinctive was so constructed as a mirror image of what in fact may have been an even more distinctive region, the manufacturing belt. The history of the belt, of course, has been obscured to us, because it has generally been confounded with the history of "America" itself. As we saw at the beginning, though, historically the belt has occupied only a small portion of the North American continent, and was surrounded on most sides by peripheral regions—the South, the American West, the American far North, Quebec and the Maritimes—that shared many common characteristics and historical experiences, including economic stepchild status, resentment of the core, and sporadic attempts by historians to attribute their problems to cultural backwardness. According to the current analysis, though, these regions were in many ways shaped by the dynamics of the belt itself; even the recent successes of the South have been at least in part the product of its ability to turn the logic of capitalist development within the belt to its own advantage. Finally, much has been written over the past generation about the decline of southern distinctiveness; however, this analysis suggests that it is the belt, at least as much as the South, whose distinctiveness has eroded.[41]

Not that it has vanished, to be sure. Despite the wave of pessimism about the fate of the "Rustbelt" that overtook economic commentary in the 1970s and 1980s, the recent resurgence of the industrial Midwest indicates that local knowledge still plays a vital role in anchoring industrial production and generating industrial innovation. While corporations have internalized many functions, even the giants of the auto industry remain critically dependent on capital-goods firms and suppliers concentrated around Detroit.[42] On the other hand, the rural and small-town South continues its dependence—enhanced by the postwar collapse of agricultural employment—on branch plants and hand-me-down industries, an economic base increasingly under siege from the forces of globalization. Even the showpieces of the modern industrial South—the auto complexes of Smyrna, Spring Hill, Tuscaloosa, and Spartanburg, and the Research Triangle of North Carolina—remain essentially branch-plant economies, and have yet to develop vital, self-propelling entrepreneurial cultures of the most advanced sort. The gales of creative destruction that make Silicon Valley such an exhilarating—and ghastly—place have at best placid southern counterparts.[43]

But if the American South and the American manufacturing belt retain much of their old relationship, that relationship has gotten a lot more complicated. The two regions, which once had to come to terms primarily with each other, must now come to terms with other regions spread across the globe. The South and the manufacturing belt remain with us, endowed with many of their old disabilities and strengths—but the age when they defined themselves primarily against each other is now closed.

Notes

1. Introduction

1. Representative titles that make use of cultural heritage in explaining southern backwardness, though often with a liberal admixture of "class" analysis, include Jonathan Wiener, *Social Origins of the New South: Alabama, 1860–1885* (Baton Rouge, 1978); Dwight B. Billings, Jr., *Planters and the Making of a "New South": Class, Politics, and Development in North Carolina, 1865–1900* (Chapel Hill, N.C., 1979); and Marc Egnal, *Divergent Paths: How Culture and Institutions Have Shaped North American Growth* (New York, 1996). Such analyses frequently hearken back to Eugene D. Genovese, *The Political Economy of Slavery: Studies in the Economy and Society of the Slave South* (New York, 1965), esp. the essay "The Slave South: An Interpretation," 13–39, although Genovese has in later restatements developed more sophisticated models of the relationship of "culture" to structure. See Eugene D. Genovese and Elizabeth Fox–Genovese, "The Janus Face of Merchant Capital," in *Fruits of Merchant Capital: Slavery and Bourgeois Property in the Rise and Expansion of Capitalism* (New York, 1983), 3–25.

2. Robert William Fogel, *Without Consent or Contract: The Rise and Fall of American Slavery* (New York, 1989); Thomas L. Haskell, "Capitalism and the Origins of the Humanitarian Sensibility" *American Historical Review* 90 (April and June 1985): 339–61; 547–66; Seymour Drescher, *Econocide: British Slavery in the Era of Abolition* (Pittsburgh, 1977); Seymour Drescher, *Capitalism and Antislavery* (New York, 1986); Gavin Wright, "The Civil Rights Revolution as Economic History," *Journal of Economic History* 59 (June 1999): 267–90.

3. Albert O. Hirschman, *The Strategy of Economic Development* (New Haven, 1958), 185–87; the relevant quote appears below, 374–75.

4. C. Vann Woodward, "The Search for Southern Identity," in *The Burden of Southern History*, rev. ed. (Baton Rouge, 1968), 3–25.

5. On the regional incidence of American poverty, see the maps in Ronald C. Wimberley and Libby V. Morris, *The Southern Black Belt: A National Perspective* (Lexington, Ky., 1997).

6. Lee J. Alston and Joseph P. Ferrie, *Southern Paternalism and the American Welfare State: Economics, Politics, and Institutions in the South, 1865–1965* (New York, 1999); Gavin Wright, *Old South, New South: Revolutions in the Southern Economy since the Civil War* (New York, 1986); Gavin Wright, *The Political Economy of the Cotton South: Households, Markets, and Wealth in the Nineteenth Century* (New York, 1978).

7. A good discussion of these points appears in Jack P. Greene, *Pursuits of Happiness: The Social Development of Early Modern British Colonies and the Formation of American Culture* (Chapel Hill, N.C., 1988).

8. Greene, *Pursuits of Happiness.*

9. Edmund S. Morgan, *American Slavery, American Freedom: The Ordeal of Colonial Virginia* (New York, 1975).

10. Ira Berlin, *Many Thousands Gone: The First Two Centuries of Slavery in North America* (Cambridge, Mass., 1998); David Brion Davis, *The Problem of Slavery in Western Culture* (Ithaca, N.Y., 1966).

11. David Eltis, *The Rise of African Slavery in the Americas* (New York, 2000).

12. For discussions of these points, see Wright, *Political Economy of the Cotton South;* David F. Weiman, "Staple Crops and Slave Plantations: Alternative Perspectives on Regional Development in the Antebellum Cotton South," in *Agriculture and National Development: Views on the Nineteenth Century,* ed. Lou Ferleger (Ames, Iowa, 1990), 119–61.

13. Allan R. Pred, *Urban Growth and the Circulation of Information: The United States System of Cities, 1790–1840* (Cambridge, Mass., 1973).

14. Wright, *Political Economy of the Cotton South.*

15. Representative titles include Wright, *Old South, New South;* Roger L. Ransom and Richard Sutch, *One Kind of Freedom: The Economic Consequences of Emancipation* (New York, 1977); and Jay R. Mandle, *Not Slave, Not Free: The African American Experience since the Civil War* (Durham, N.C., 1992).

16. Hirschman, *Strategy of Economic Development;* Paul R. Krugman, *Geography and Trade,* Gaston Eyskens Lecture Series. (Leuven, Belgium, and Cambridge, Mass., 1991).

17. Alexander Gerschenkron, "Economic Backwardness in Historical Perspective," in *Economic Backwardness in Historical Perspective: A Book of Essays* (Cambridge, Mass., 1962); the term "second wave" comes from *The Second Wave: Southern Industrialization from the 1940s to the 1970s,* ed. Philip Scranton. Economy and Society in the Modern South. (Athens, Ga., 2001).

18. Representative titles dealing with this period include Scranton, *Second Wave;* James C. Cobb, *The Selling of the South: The Southern Crusade for Industrial Development, 1936–1990,* 2d ed. (Urbana, Ill., 1993); James C. Cobb, *Industrialization and Southern Society, 1877–1984,* New Perspectives on the South. (Lexington, Ky., 1984); and Bruce J. Schulman, *From Cotton Belt to Sunbelt: Federal Policy, Economic Development, and the Transformation of the South, 1938–1980* (New York, 1991).

2. The Paths before Us/U.S.

This essay originally appeared as "Tracking the Economic Divergence of the North and the South" in *Southern Cultures* 6 (winter 2000): 82–103, and is reprinted here with permission of *Southern Cultures.*

1. See Gabor S. Boritt, ed., *Why the Civil War Came* (New York, 1996); John Niven, *The Coming of the Civil War, 1837–1861* (Wheeling, Ill., 1990), 144–73. On the older historiography, see Thomas J. Pressly, *Americans Interpret Their Civil War* (Princeton, N.J., 1954). Note that in recent years many scholars have stressed issues other than slavery per se in arguing for difference. For example, nativism and interpretive differences on the meaning of the Constitution and the meaning of republicanism are often highlighted.

2. "Path dependence" can be defined as a causal sequence in which the eventual outcome is virtually predetermined by antecedent factors or events. These factors or events may be proximate or remote in temporal terms and either circumstantial or structural in nature. "Path influence" relaxes the deterministic implications of the "path dependence" approach, while still retaining the implication that numerous outcomes are excluded because of antecedent factors or events. For an excellent example of the latter approach, see Stanley L. Engerman and Kenneth L. Sokoloff, "Factor Endowments, Institutions, and Differential Paths of Growth among New

World Economies: A View from Economic Historians of the United States," in *How Latin America Fell Behind: Essays on the Economic Histories of Brazil and Mexico, 1800–1914*, ed. Stephen H. Haber (Stanford , Cal., 1997), 260–304. For alternative "cultural" approaches to explaining the economic differences between North and South, see Stephen Innes, *Creating the Commonwealth: The Economic Culture of Puritan New England* (New York, 1995); Marc Egnal, *Divergent Paths: How Culture and Institutions Have Shaped North American Growth* (New York, 1996).

With apologies to Stanford economic historian Paul David, who has famously explained the persistence of the inefficient QWERTY keyboard arrangement (the first six letters in the top row of standard keyboards) for typewriters and personal computers by invoking path dependence, what we see in the South are lock-in mechanisms associated not with Q-W-E-R-T-Y, but with S-L-A-V-E-R-Y. See Paul A. David, "Clio and the Economics of QWERTY," *American Economic Review* 75 (May 1985): 332–37; Paul A. David, "Understanding the Economics of QWERTY: The Necessity of History," in *Economic History and the Modern Economist*, ed. William N. Parker (Oxford, 1986), 30–49. Note that David's "QWERTY" argument has not gone unchallenged. See in particular S. J. Liebowitz and Stephen E. Margolis, "The Fable of the Keys," *Journal of Law and Economics* 33 (April 1990): 1–25. For a recent review of the debate, see the *Economist* 351 (April 3, 1999): 67, 351; (May 8, 1999): 6.

3. See, for example, Jack P. Greene, *Pursuits of Happiness: The Social Development of Early Modern British Colonies and the Formation of American Culture* (Chapel Hill, N.C., 1988), 81–100, 141–501; John J. McCusker and Russell R. Menard, *The Economy of British America, 1607–1789* (Chapel Hill, N.C., 1991), 117–43, 169–88.

4. See Peter A. Coclanis, *The Shadow of a Dream: Economic Life and Death in the South Carolina Low Country, 1670–1920* (New York, 1989).

5. McCusker and Menard, *The Economy of British America*, 117–43, 169–88; Coclanis, *The Shadow of a Dream*, 48–110; Philip D. Morgan, *Slave Counterpoint: Black Culture in the Eighteenth-Century Chesapeake and Lowcountry* (Chapel Hill, N.C., 1998), 58–101.

6. Coclanis, *The Shadow of a Dream*, 54–56, 142–54.

7. Greene, *Pursuits of Happiness*, 55–100, 124–51; McCusker and Menard, *The Economy of British America*, 91–116, 189–208.

8. For the original formulation of the opposite approach, the so-called big push strategy, see P. N. Rosenstein-Rodan, "Problems of Industrialization of Eastern and South-Eastern Europe," *Economic Journal* 53 (June–Sept. 1943): 202–11; Alice Hanson Jones, *Wealth of a Nation to Be: The American Colonies on the Eve of the Revolution* (New York, 1980), 53–58.

9. Karen O. Kupperman, *Providence Island, 1630–1641: The Other Puritan Colony* (New York, 1993).

10. See James T. Lemon, *The Best Poor Man's Country: A Geographical Study of Early Southeastern Pennsylvania* (Baltimore, 1972); Thomas M. Doerflinger, *A Vigorous Spirit of Enterprise: Merchants and Economic Development in Revolutionary Philadelphia* (Chapel Hill, N.C., 1986); Diane Lindstrom, *Economic Development in the Philadelphia Region, 1810–1850* (New York, 1978).

11. On "linkages," see, for example, Albert O. Hirschman, *The Strategy of Economic Development* (New Haven, 1958); Hirschman, "A Generalized Linkage Approach to Development, with Special Reference to Staples," *Economic Development and Cultural Change* (supplement) 25 (1977): 67–98.

12. See, for example, Alfred D. Chandler, Jr., *The Visible Hand: The Managerial Revolution in American Business* (Cambridge, Mass., 1977); Thomas C. Cochran, *Frontiers of Change: Early Industrialism in America* (New York, 1981); Philip Scranton, *Proprietary Capitalism: The Textile Manufacture at Philadelphia, 1800–1885* (New York, 1983); David L. Carlton, "How American is

the American South?" in *The South as an American Problem,* ed. Larry J. Griffin and Don H. Doyle (Athens, Ga., 1995), 33–56; Walter Licht, *Industrializing America: The Nineteenth Century* (Baltimore, 1995), 21–45, 102–32.

13. The quote is from Paul Goldberger, "A Helluva Towne: Finding the Future in Old New York," *New Yorker* 74 (Nov. 30, 1998): 120. The economist Paul Krugman, perhaps more than anyone else, is associated with the so-called new economic geography, the principal interests of which to date have been "cluster" economies and regional economic disparities.

14. See, for example, David R. Meyer, "Emergence of the American Manufacturing Belt: An Interpretation," *Journal of Historical Geography* 9 (April 1983): 145–74; David R. Meyer, "Midwestern Industrialization and the American Manufacturing Belt in the Nineteenth Century," *Journal of Economic History* 49 (Dec. 1989): 921–37; William Parker, "The Industrial Civilization of the Midwest," in William N. Parker, *Europe, America, and the Wider World,* 2 vols. (New York, 1991), 2:215–57; Brian Page and Richard Walker, "From Settlement to Fordism: The Agro-Industrial Revolution in the American Midwest," *Economic Geography* 67 (Oct. 1991): 281–315; Peter A. Coclanis, "The Business of Chicago," in *The Encyclopedia of Chicago History* (Chicago, forthcoming).

15. David F. Weiman, "Staple Crops and Slave Plantations: Alternative Perspectives on Regional Development in the Antebellum Cotton South," in *Agriculture and National Development: Views on the Nineteenth Century,* ed. Lou Ferleger (Ames, Iowa, 1990), 132–37.

16. Coclanis, *The Shadow of a Dream,* 137–40; David L. Carlton and Peter A. Coclanis, "Capital Mobilization and Southern Industry, 1880–1905: The Case of the Carolina Piedmont," chap. 7 in this volume; David L. Carlton and Peter A. Coclanis, "The Uninventive South? A Quantitative Look at Region and American Inventiveness," chap. 8 in this volume; James M. McPherson, "Antebellum Southern Exceptionalism: A New Look at an Old Question," *Civil War History* 29 (Sept. 1983): 230–44.

17. David Ward, *Cities and Immigrants: A Geography of Change in Nineteenth-Century America* (New York, 1971), 7.

18. Robert William Fogel and Stanley L. Engerman, *Time on the Cross: The Economics of American Negro Slavery,* 2 vols. (Boston, 1974), 1:247–57.

19. Fogel and Engerman, *Time on the Cross,* 1:256; Fred Bateman and Thomas Weiss, *A Deplorable Scarcity: The Failure of Industrialization in the Slave Economy* (Chapel Hill, N.C., 1980), 14–20.

20. See, for example, Eugene D. Genovese, *The Political Economy of Slavery: Studies in the Economy and Society of the Slave South* (New York, 1965), 13–39, 157–239; Elizabeth Fox-Genovese and Eugene D. Genovese, "The Slave Economies in Political Perspective," *Journal of American History* 66 (June 1979): 7–23; Coclanis, *The Shadow of a Dream,* 142–54.

21. Gavin Wright goes even further, suggesting that the South and North may have been more distinct economically in the 1920s and 1930s than they were in 1860. See Wright, *Old South, New South: Revolutions in the Southern Economy since the Civil War* (New York, 1986), 8–10; Licht, *Industrializing America,* 102–32.

22. *Twelfth Census of the United States, 1900,* vol. 1, *Population, Pt. 1* (United States Census Office, 1901), cxii; Ward, *Cities and Immigrants,* 7, 39–46; Harvey S. Perloff et al., *Regions, Resources, and Economic Growth* (Baltimore, 1960), 170–84; Roger L. Ransom and Richard Sutch, *One Kind of Freedom: The Economic Consequences of Emancipation* (New York, 1977); Wright, *Old South, New South,* 17–123; Jay R. Mandle, *Not Slave, Not Free: The African American Economic Experience since the Civil War* (Durham, N.C., 1992), 5–67.

3. How the Low Country Was Taken to Task

How the Low Country Was Taken to Task: Slave-Labor Organization in Coastal South Carolina and Georgia" originally appeared in *Slavery, Secession, and Southern History,* ed. Robert L. Paquette and Louis Ferleger (Charlottesville: University Press of Virginia, 2000), 59–78, and appears here with permission of the University of Virginia Press.

Earlier versions of this chapter were presented in 1997 at the Triangle Economic History Workshop, National Humanities Center, Research Triangle Park, N.C.; the Johns Hopkins University, Baltimore; and the St. George Tucker Society, Atlanta. I would like to thank those in attendance at each of these talks for their helpful criticism. In particular, I wish to acknowledge the suggestions offered by Robert E. Gallman, Lee Craig, Dean Lueck, Philip D. Curtin, Louis Galambos, Douglas Ambrose, David Moltke-Hansen, William K. Scarborough, and Mark Smith. I would also like to thank Robert L. Paquette and Louis Ferleger for their editorial assistance.

1. William Elliott, *Carolina Sports by Land and Water,* introduction by Theodore Rosengarten (1846; Columbia, S.C., 1994), 152. On Cheeha, see Suzanne Cameron Linder, *Historical Atlas of the ACE River Basin, 1860* (Columbia, S.C., 1995), 111–22. Note that Elliott's holdings at Cheeha during the antebellum period actually consisted of four individual plantations—Bluff, Middle Place, Smilies, and Social Hall—each with a distinct land history.

2. Elliott, *Carolina Sports,* x. See also Linder, *Historical Atlas,* 112–17.

3. Elliott, *Carolina Sports.* Note that Elliott used the pseudonym "Agricola" for essays on agriculture as well as for essays on politics. For an example of the former, see Agricola [William Elliott], "Observations on the Present Condition of the Southern States," *Southern Agriculturist* 7 (June 1834): 287–93; for an example of the latter, see Agricola [William Elliott], *Southern Standard* (Charleston), July 12, 1851.

4. Elliott, *Carolina Sports,* 173–91 (quotation on 174). Note that this chapter originally was published as a sketch in the *Southern Literary Journal,* n.s., 3 (May 1838): 354–63.

5. Elliott, *Carolina Sports,* 176.

6. Ibid., 175.

7. Ibid., 178. Postcolonial literary scholars have recently called attention to some of the problems arising when subaltern groups are viewed through "imperial eyes." See, for example, Mary Louise Pratt, *Imperial Eyes: Travel Writing and Transculturation* (London, 1992). One can see some of these problems in *Carolina Sports.* In this work Elliott calls plantations "deserted" whenever he is absent from them; moreover, the slaves present on his hunting and fishing trips are largely invisible in his accounts of such trips.

8. Elliott, *Carolina Sports,* 175–81 (quotation on 175–76).

9. On Elliott as a planter, see ibid., ix–xliii; Lewis P. Jones, "Carolinians and Cubans: The Elliotts and Gonzales, Their Work and Their Writings" (Ph.D. diss., University of North Carolina, 1952), 16–29; Jones, "William Elliott, South Carolina Nonconformist," *Journal of Southern History* 17 (Aug. 1951): 361–81; Linder, *Historical Atlas,* 112–17. Note that according to the 1850 census Elliott "produced" over 200,000 pounds of (rough) rice on two of his Cheeha plantations alone in 1849 (MS returns, Seventh Census of the United States, 1850, Agriculture, Colleton District, St. Bartholomew's Parish, returns for William Elliott, Cheeha, SCDAH). In personal communications David Moltke-Hansen has suggested to me that in *Carolina Sports* Elliott may, in fact, have been engaging primarily in social commentary and criticism.

10. That there was widespread absenteeism among low-country rice planters, particularly those practicing tidal cultivation, is well known. See, for example, Frederick Dalcho, *An Historical Account of the Protestant Episcopal Church in South Carolina* (Charleston, S.C., 1820), vi; Basil

Hall, *Travels in North America in the Years 1827 and 1828,* 3 vols. (Edinburgh, 1829), 3:188. For a broader view, see Lawrence Fay Brewster, *Summer Migrations and Resorts of South Carolina Low-Country Planters,* Historical Papers of the Trinity College Historical Society, ser. 26 (Durham, N.C., 1947), esp. 3–9, 109–22. For a recent demonstration and discussion of planter absenteeism in South Carolina and Georgia, see William Dusinberre, *Them Dark Days: Slavery in the American Rice Swamps* (New York, 1996), 78, 150 n. 90, 204, 215, 310–12. On Elliott's absenteeism, see *Carolina Sports,* xxi–vi; Beverly Scafidel, "The Letters of William Elliott." Ph.D. diss., University of South Carolina, 1978.

11. Philip D. Morgan, "Work and Culture: The Task System and the World of Lowcountry Blacks, 1700–1880" *William and Mary Quarterly,* 3d ser., 39 (Oct. 1982): 563–99 (quotation on 564).

12. On the basic contours of the task system, see, for example, Lewis C. Gray, *History of Agriculture in the Southern United States to 1860,* 2 vols. (1933; rept. Gloucester, Mass., 1958), 1:550–56; Kenneth M. Stampp, *The Peculiar Institution: Slavery in the Ante-bellum South* (New York, 1956), 54–56; Morgan, "Work and Culture"; Philip D. Morgan, "Task System," in *Dictionary of Afro-American Slavery,* ed. Randall M. Miller and John David Smith (Westport, Conn., 1988), 715–16. Note that some scholars, most notably Michael Mullin, believe that the degree of "independence" achieved by low-country slaves may be overstated. See Mullin, *Africa in America: Slave Acculturation and Resistance in the American South and the British Caribbean, 1736–1831* (Urbana, Ill., 1992), 126–58.

13. Gray, *History of Agriculture* 1:550–56; Philip D. Morgan, "Task and Gang Systems: The Organization of Labor on New World Plantations," in *Work and Labor in Early America,* ed. Stephen Innes (Chapel Hill, N.C., 1988), 189–220, esp. 190–202.

14. Morgan, "Work and Culture," 568–69; Morgan, "Task and Gang Systems," 190–211. See also B. W. Higman, *Slave Population and Economy in Jamaica, 1807–1834* (London, 1976), 21–25; B. W. Higman, *Slave Populations of the British Caribbean, 1807–1834* (Baltimore, 1984), 164–68, 179–88; Robert B. Outland III, "Slavery, Work, and the Geography of the North Carolina Naval Stores Industry, 1835–1860," *Journal of Southern History* 62 (Feb. 1996): 27–56.

15. See Charles B. Dew, *Bond of Iron: Master and Slave at Buffalo Forge* (New York, 1994), 108–21; Gray, *History of Agriculture* 1:551–52, 554; Elisha Cain to Mary Telfair, Nov. 20, 1836, Telfair Family Papers, Georgia Historical Society, Savannah. On the use of the task system in the cultivation of such crops as corn, groundnuts, and oats in the low country, see Walter Peyre Plantation Journal, 1812–1851, 332, South Carolina Historical Society, Charleston.

16. See Mullin, *Africa in America,* 126–58; Peter A. Coclanis, "Slavery, African-American Agency, and the World We Have Lost," *Georgia Historical Quarterly* 79 (winter 1995): 873–84.

17. Higman, *Slave Populations of the British Caribbean,* 179; J. R. Ward, *British West Indian Slavery, 1750–1834: The Process of Amelioration* (Oxford, 1988), 8, 14–18, 61–118; Morgan, "Task and Gang Systems," 190–211; Emilia Viotti da Costa, *Crowns of Glory, Tears of Blood: The Demerara Slave Rebellion of 1823* (New York, 1994), 61–63, 79–80; Dale Tomich, "Une Petite Guinée: Provision Ground and Plantation in Martinique, 1830–1848," in *The Slaves' Economy: Independent Production by Slaves in the Americas,* ed. Ira Berlin and Philip D. Morgan (London, 1991), 68–91. By the early nineteenth century, aspects of the task system apparently had emerged in the sugar industry of northeast Brazil as well. See Stuart B. Schwartz, *Slaves, Peasants, and Rebels: Reconsidering Brazilian Slavery* (Urbana, Ill., 1992), 39–59. As for cotton, note that John Hebron Moore argues that in Mississippi, beginning in the 1840s, mechanization of some aspects of cotton cultivation led to use of a modified form of the task system in that crop, too. See Moore, *The Emergence of the Cotton Kingdom in the Old Southwest: Mississippi, 1770–1860* (Baton Rouge, 1988), 95–98.

18. On the gang system, see Gray, *History of Agriculture* 1:550–57; Stampp, *Peculiar Institution,* 54–56; Charles P. Roland, "Gang System," in Miller and Smith, *Dictionary of Afro-American Slavery,* 283–84.

19. Ulrich B. Phillips, "The Slave Labor Problem in the Charleston District," *Political Science Quarterly* 22 (Sept. 1907): 416–39, esp. 417–18. For a modern restatement of this position, see Julia Floyd Smith, *Slavery and Rice Culture in Low Country Georgia, 1750–1860* (Knoxville, Tenn., 1985), 50. On the relationship among climate, disease, and African American slavery in the low country, see, for example, Elliott, *Carolina Sports,* xxv; James Habersham et al. to Benjamin Franklin, May 19, 1768, to the Earl of Hillsborough, April 24, 1772, in *The Letters of Hon. James Habersham, 1756–1775,* Collections of the Georgia Historical Society, vol. 6 (Savannah, 1904), 71–74, esp. 71–72, 173; Roswell King, Jr., to Thomas Butler, Feb. 19, 1831, Butler Family Papers, Historical Society of Pennsylvania.

20. Morgan, "Work and Culture," esp. 568–69; Morgan, "Task and Gang Systems," 202–6.

21. On "bargaining" by slaves and the evolution of the task system, see ibid. See also Ira Berlin and Philip D. Morgan, "Introduction," in Berlin and Morgan, *The Slaves' Economy,* 1–27; Betty Wood, *Women's Work, Men's Work: The Informal Slave Economies of Lowcountry Georgia* (Athens, Ga., 1995), esp. 1–30. On the African role in the creation of the task system, see Ira Berlin, "Time, Space, and the Evolution of Afro-American Society on British Mainland North America," *American Historical Review* 85 (Feb. 1980): 44–78, esp. 59, 64–67; Judith A. Carney, "From Hands to Tutors: African Expertise in the South Carolina Rice Economy," *Agricultural History* 67 (summer 1993): 1–30, esp. 26–28. On the broader African role in the shaping of low-country rice technology, see Peter H. Wood, *Black Majority: Negroes in Colonial South Carolina from 1670 through the Stono Rebellion* (New York, 1974), 55–62; Peter H. Wood, "'It Was a Negro Taught Them': A New Look at African Labor in Early South Carolina," *Journal of Asian and African Studies* 9 (July–Oct. 1974): 160–79; Daniel C. Littlefield, *Rice and Slaves: Ethnicity and the Slave Trade in Colonial South Carolina* (Baton Rouge, 1981), 74–114; Daniel C. Littlefield, *Rice and the Making of South Carolina: An Introductory Essay* (Columbia, S.C., 1995); Charles Joyner, *Down by the Riverside: A South Carolina Slave Community* (Urbana, Ill., 1984), 41–89; John Solomon Otto, *The Southern Frontiers, 1607–1860: The Agricultural Evolution of the Colonial and Antebellum South* (Westport, Conn., 1989), 34–37; William S. Pollitzer, "The Relationship of the Gullah-Speaking People of Coastal South Carolina and Georgia to Their African Ancestors," *Historical Methods* 25 (spring 1993): 53–67; Amelia Wallace Vernon, *African Americans at Mars Bluff, South Carolina* (Baton Rouge, 1993), 119–23; Joyce E. Chaplin, *An Anxious Pursuit: Agricultural Innovation and Modernity in the Lower South, 1730–1815* (Chapel Hill, N.C., 1993), 227–76; Judith A. Carney and Richard Porcher, "Geographies of the Past: Rice, Slaves, and Technological Transfer in South Carolina," *Southeastern Geographer* 33 (Nov. 1993): 127–47; Judith A. Carney, "Landscapes of Technology Transfer: Rice Cultivation and African Continuities," *Technology and Culture* 37 (Jan. 1996): 5–35.

22. Carney, "From Hands to Tutors," 26–28 (quotation on 26).

23. Jacob Metzer, "Rational Management, Modern Business Practices, and Economies of Scale in the Ante-Bellum Southern Plantations," *Explorations in Economic History,* 2d ser., 12 (April 1975): 123–50, esp. 139–43. See also R. Keith Aufhauser, "Slavery and Scientific Management," *Journal of Economic History* 33 (Dec. 1973): 811–24.

24. See Léon Walras, *Elements of Pure Economics,* trans. William Jaffe (2 pts., 1874, 1877; Homewood, Ill., 1954). For an introduction to the Walrasian approach, see Donald A. Walker, "Léon Walras," in *The New Palgrave: A Dictionary of Economics,* 4 vols., ed. John Eatwell, Murray Milgate, and Peter Newman (London, 1987), 4:852–63; Walker, *Walras's Market Models* (Cambridge, 1996).

25. Irving Fisher, "Translator's Note to Léon Walras, 'Geometrical Theory of the Determination of Prices,'" *Annals of the American Academy of Political and Social Science* 3 (July 1892): 45–47. For other problems with the Walrasian approach, see, for example, Walker, "Léon Walras," esp. 854–62; Henry William Spiegel, *The Growth of Economic Thought,* rev. ed. (Durham, N.C., 1983), esp. 552–55.

26. Kenneth Arrow and Gerard Debreu, "Existence of an Equilibrium for a Competitive Economy," *Econometrica* 22 (July 1954): 265–90. See also John Eatwell, Murray Milgate, and Peter Newman, "Preface," in *The New Palgrave: Allocation, Information, and Markets,* ed. John Eatwell, Murray Milgate, and Peter Newman (New York, 1989), xi–xii.

27. See Kenneth Arrow, "Uncertainty and the Welfare Economics of Medical Care," *American Economic Review* 53 (Dec. 1963): 941–73; Arrow, "The Organization of Economic Activity: Issues Pertinent to the Choice of Market versus Nonmarket Allocation," in Joint Economic Committee, U.S. Congress, *The Analysis and Evaluation of Public Expenditures: The PPB System,* vol. 1 (Washington, D.C., 1969), 47–64; George A. Akerlof, "The Market for 'Lemons': Quality Uncertainty and the Market Mechanism," *Quarterly Journal of Economics* 84 (Aug. 1970): 488–500; James Mirrlees, "Notes on Welfare Economics, Information, and Uncertainty," in *Essays in Economic Behavior under Uncertainty,* ed. M. S. Balch, D. L. McFadden, and S. Y. Wu (Amsterdam, 1974), 243–58; James Mirrlees, "The Optimal Structure of Incentives and Authority within an Organization," *Bell Journal of Economics* 7 (spring 1976): 105–31; Stephen A. Ross, "The Economic Theory of Agency: The Principal's Problem," *American Economic Review* 63 (May 1973): 134–39; Joseph E. Stiglitz, "Incentives and Risk Sharing in Sharecropping," *Review of Economic Studies* 41 (April 1974): 219–55; Joseph E. Stiglitz, "Incentives, Risk, and Information: Notes towards a Theory of Hierarchy," *Bell Journal of Economics* 6 (autumn 1975): 552–79.

Alternatively (or additionally), one can trace the genealogy of the principal-agent approach to Ronald Coase, Oliver Williamson, Harold Demsetz, and others emphasizing the importance of institutions and transaction costs in economic life. The rich work of Douglass North comes immediately to mind in this regard. See North, *Structure and Change in Economic History* (New York, 1981); North, *Institutions, Institutional Change, and Economic Performance* (New York, 1990).

28. See, for example, Eatwell, Milgate, and Newman, *The New Palgrave: Allocation, Information, and Markets;* Jack Hirschleifer and John G. Riley, *The Analytics of Uncertainty and Information,* Cambridge Surveys of Economic Literature (Cambridge, 1992); Donald E. Campbell, *Incentives: Motivation and the Economics of Information* (Cambridge, 1995).

29. See Adam Smith's statement of the basic agency problem in *An Inquiry into the Nature and Causes of the Wealth of Nations,* ed. Edwin Carman (1776; New York, 1937), book 5, chap. 1, pt. 3, 699–700.

30. See Ross, "The Economic Theory of Agency"; Kenneth J. Arrow, "The Economics of Agency," in *Principals and Agents: The Structure of Business,* ed. John W. Pratt and Richard J. Zeckhauser (Boston, 1985), 37–51; Joseph E. Stiglitz, "Principal and Agent," in Eatwell, Milgate, and Newman, *The New Palgrave* 3:966–72.

31. See, for example, Arrow, "The Economics of Agency," 38–45; Yehuda Kotowitz, "Moral Hazard," in Eatwell, Milgate, and Newman, *The New Palgrave* 3:549–51; Campbell, *Incentives,* 78–136.

32. Arrow, "Economics of Agency"; Charles Wilson, "Adverse Selection," in Eatwell, Milgate, and Newman, *The New Palgrave: Allocation, Information, and Markets,* 31–34; Campbell, *Incentives,* 137–207.

33. For somewhat similar approaches, which is to say, approaches employing transaction-costs models in analyzing American slavery, see Stefano Fenoaltea, "Slavery and Supervision in Comparative Perspective: A Model," *Journal of Economic History* 44 (Sept. 1984): 635–68; Yoram Barzel,

Economic Analysis of Property Rights (New York, 1989), 76–84; Charles Kahn, "An Agency Approach to Slave Punishments and Rewards," in *Without Consent or Contract: The Rise and Fall of American Slavery, Technical Papers*, ed. Robert William Fogel and Stanley L. Engerman, 3 vols. (New York, 1992), 2:551–65.

34. On the overuse of the concept of agency by historians of American slavery and emancipation, see Coclanis, "Slavery, African-American Agency, and the World We Have Lost."

35. In reality, of course, there are several layers of principal-agent problems here, involving field workers, drivers, overseers, and planters and their relationships to one another. For simplicity's sake I have reduced a much more complex set of principal-agent problems to one involving only two parties: planters and enslaved field workers. One should also note that the principal-agent approach assumes—correctly, in my view—that all parties involved are seeking to optimize, subject to their respective constraints.

On the low country's economic history and the place of rice and slaves therein, see, for example, Peter A. Coclanis, *The Shadow of a Dream: Economic Life and Death in the South Carolina Low Country, 1670–1920* (New York, 1989); Smith, *Slavery and Rice Culture;* Mart A. Stewart, "Rice, Water, and Power: Landscapes of Domination and Resistance in the Lowcountry, 1790–1880," *Environmental History Review* 15 (fall 1991): 47–64; Stewart, *"What Nature Suffers to Groe": Life, Labor, and Landscape on the Georgia Coast, 1680–1920* (Athens, Ga., 1996).

36. Carney, "From Hands to Tutors," 26–27.

37. Note that the principal-agency approach employed here is not necessarily inconsistent, much less incompatible, with interpretations emphasizing paternalism, ameliorationism, or hegemony.

38. John Stuart Mill, *Principles of Political Economy*, 4th ed., 2 vols. (London, 1857), 1:292–99. On the task system, customary practices, and de facto rights in the low country, see Morgan, "Work and Culture." Olmsted, one should note, was a bit ambiguous on the role of custom in the low-country task system. In *A Journey in the Seaboard Slave States . . .* (New York, 1856), 435–36, he wrote: "In nearly all ordinary work, custom has settled the extent of the task, and it is difficult to increase it." Later in the same passage, however, he added: "Notwithstanding this, I have heard a man assert, boastingly, that he made his negroes habitually perform double the customary tasks. Thus we get a glimpse again of the black side. If he is allowed the power to do this, what may not a man do?" For the record, I personally do not believe that the task system was ever as "fixed" as some scholars—Philip Morgan most notably—believe. For evidence of the open and contingent nature of the task system even in the antebellum period, see, for example, Alexander Telfair, "Rules & Directions for my Thorn Island Plantation . . .," June 11, 1832, Rule 5, Telfair Family Papers, Georgia Historical Society; A Practical Farmer, "Observations on the Management of Negroes," *Southern Agriculturist* 5 (April 1832): 181–84; entry, May 28, 1841, Plantation Journal, 1838–1842, Davison McDowell Papers, South Caroliniana Library; Francis S. Holmes, *The Southern Farmer and Market Gardener* (Charleston, S.C., 1842), 230–32; William Elliott to Ann Elliott, [spring 1849], Elliott-Gonzales Papers, Southern Historical Collection; S. D. Wragg, "Overseeing," *Farmer and Planter* 5 (June 1854): 141–42 and (Sept. 1854): 229–30; A.M.H., Jr., "Rice Culture," *Southern Cultivator* 24 (Dec. 1866): 278–79; interview with Uncle Ben Horry, Aug. 1937, in George P. Rawick, ed., *The American Slave: A Composite Autobiography*, 19 vols. (Westport, Conn., 1972), vol. 2, pt. 2, 302; interview with Uncle Gabe Lance, n.d., vol. 3, pt. 3, 92; interview with Prince Smith, n.d., pt. 4, 117; interview with Sam Polite, n.d., pt. 3, 271–72. For more on the variability of tasking, see Peter Coclanis, "Thickening Description: William Washington's Queries on Rice," *Agricultural History* 64 (summer 1990): 9–16.

39. Morgan, "Work and Culture." On "tasking" in the cultivation of Sea Island cotton in particular, see, for example, T. J. Woofter Jr., *Black Yeomanry: Life on St. Helena Island* (New York,

1930), 30; John Solomon Otto, *Cannon's Point Plantation, 1794–1860: Living Conditions and Status Patterns in the Old South* (Orlando, Fla., 1984), 34–37.

40. In terms of "purity," Wicksell's conception of economic relationships was similar to that of Walras. See Spiegel, *Economic Thought,* esp. 590–92. On the formulation mentioned in the text, see Stiglitz, "Principal and Agent," 967. For Paul A. Samuelson's acceptance of this formulation in the mid-1950s, see Samuelson, "Wages and Interest: A Modern Dissection of Marxian Economic Models," *American Economic Review* 47 (Dec. 1957): 884–912, esp. 894.

41. The quote in the text is from Karl Marx, *Capital,* ed. Frederick Engels, trans. Samuel Moore and Edward Aveling, 3 vols. (1867–94; New York, 1967), 1:94. To Marx, obviously, a given "relation between two wills" need not be equal.

42. Samuel Bowles and Herbert Gintis, "Contested Exchange: New Microfoundations for the Political Economy of Capitalism," *Politics and Society* 18 (June 1990): 165–222.

43. Ibid., 166–67 and passim.

44. The calibrated, gridlike layout of most rice fields in the low country and the relatively discrete nature of cultivation activities—activities punctuated by three or four flows of water over the fields—probably rendered labor there easier to grade than was the case for labor in the sugarcane fields of Jamaica, Cuba, or Louisiana. This does not mean that the costs for whites of monitoring labor in the rice fields were low; indeed, the disease environment in the low country rendered such costs quite high.

Note, too, that it is dangerous to speak categorically, as some do, about the "technical requirements" of rice or any other crop. Rice can be grown in many different ways. In more labor-intensive cultivation systems—systems employing nurseries and transplanting, for example —labor-monitoring costs would likely be greater than in systems such as that in the low country of South Carolina and Georgia. See, for example, Clifford Geertz, *Agricultural Involution: The Processes of Ecological Change in Indonesia* (Berkeley, Calif., 1963), esp. 28–37; Lucien M. Hanks, *Rice and Man: Agricultural Ecology in Southeast Asia* (Arlington Heights, Ill., 1972),16–68; Francesca Bray, *The Rice Economies: Technology and Development in Asian Societies* (Oxford, 1986). See also Raymond E. Crist, "Rice Culture in Spain," *Scientific Monthly* 84 (Feb. 1957): 66–74, and the works by Carney cited in note 21 above.

45. See James Pitot, *Observations on the Colony of Louisiana from 1796 to 1802,* trans. Henry C. Pitot (Baton Rouge, 1979), 68–69, 77; Timothy Flint, *A Condensed Geography and History of the Western States, or the Mississippi Valley,* 2 vols. (Cincinnati, 1828), 1:522–23; R. A. Wilkinson, "Production of Rice in Louisiana," *De Bow's Review* 6 (July 1848): 53–57; "Rice Culture in Louisiana," *De Bow's Review,* 3d ser., 21 (Sept. 1856): 290–92; entries, July 15, 1862, Aug. 1, 1862, Isaac Erwin Diary, Hill Memorial Library, Louisiana State University, Baton Rouge; "Rice Culture in Louisiana," *Southern Cultivator* 32 (Oct. 1874): 395–96; Armando A. Calleja, "Agronomic Practices and Their Influence on the Development of the Louisiana Rice Industry" (master's thesis, Louisiana State University, 1938), 15–28; Mildred Kelly Ginn, "A History of Rice Production in Louisiana to 1896," *Louisiana Historical Quarterly* 23 (April 1940): 544–88, esp. 549–54; Gray, *History of Agriculture* 1:65–66, 2:722–23; Chan Lee, "A Culture History of Rice with Special Reference to Louisiana" (Ph.D. diss., Louisiana State University, 1960), 89–150; Joe Gray Taylor, *Negro Slavery in Louisiana* (Baton Rouge, 1963), 78; Henry C. Dethloff, *A History of the American Rice Industry, 1685–1985* (College Station, Tex., 1988), 60–62. On the problems of one would-be rice planter in southern Louisiana, see J. Blodget Britton to Mother [Julia Ann Allen Britton], June 1, 1854, Dec. 7, 1856, Britton and Moore Family Papers, Southern Historical Collection. On the role of Africans in the early history of the rice industry in Louisiana, see Daniel H. Usner, Jr., "From African Captivity to American Slavery: The Introduction of Black Laborers to Colonial Louisiana," *Louisiana History* 20 (winter 1979): 25–48; Gwendolyn Midlo Hall, *Africans in Colonial Loui-*

siana: The Development of Afro-Creole Culture in the Eighteenth Century (Baton Rouge, 1992), 121–24. The gang system of slave-labor organization seems to have predominated in all agricultural activities in southeastern Louisiana. On its prevalence in sugar cultivation there, see Frederick Law Olmsted, *The Cotton Kingdom . . .*, ed. Arthur M. Schlesinger (1861; New York, 1953), 254–55; Roderick A. McDonald, "Independent Economic Production by Slaves on Antebellum Louisiana Sugar Plantations," in Berlin and Morgan, *The Slaves' Economy*, 182–208, esp. 184–85.

46. On divisions within the slave communities of the low country, see Dusinberre, *Them Dark Days*, 190–206, 342–49; Larry E. Hudson, Jr., *To Have and to Hold: Slave Work and Family Life in Antebellum South Carolina* (Athens, Ga., 1997), 181; Lawrence T. McDonnell, "Slave against Slave: Dynamics of Violence within the American Slave Community" (paper presented at the annual meeting of the American Historical Association, San Francisco, Dec. 1983).

47. See Metzer, "Rational Management." Some planters did call for "clock-work" discipline, uniformity, and system, of course. See, for example, Anon., "On the Management of Slaves," *Southern Agriculturist* 6 (June 1833): 281–86, esp. 283–84, 286; Strait Edge, "Plantation Regulations," *Soil of the South* 1 (Feb. 1851): 20–21 and (May 1851): 68; St. Geo Cocke, "Plantation Management-Police," *De Bow's Review* 14 (Feb. 1853): 177–78. See also Mark M. Smith, "Time, Slavery, and Plantation Capitalism in the Ante-Bellum American South," *Past and Present*, no. 150 (Feb. 1996): 142–68. Note that R. Keith Aufhauser makes the most explicit and forceful case for Taylorism as a useful concept for analyzing labor-management relations in American slavery. See Aufhauser, "Slavery and Scientific Management."

48. William Shakespeare, *Richard II* (1593) 2.2.145; John Milton, *Samson Agonistes* (1671), line 35; Samuel Johnson, *A Dictionary of the English Language*, 2 vols. (1755).

49. Matthew Arnold, "A Summer Night" (1852), lines 37–41.

50. On Kevin Sullivan, see, for example, George Napolitano, *The New Pictorial History of Wrestling* (New York, 1990), 118–19.

51. See, for example, William Elliott to Ann Elliott, Nov. 4, 1847, Nov. 15, 1851; to Phoebe Elliott, Oct. 11, 1852, Aug. 16, Nov. 9, 1854; to Emily Elliott, Aug. 7, 1858, Elliott-Gonzales Papers, Southern Historical Collection. The quoted passages are from William Elliott to Ann Elliott, Nov. 24, 1829, Aug. 10, 1856, and n.d. [spring, c. 1850–53].

52. William Elliott to William Elliott, Jr., Aug. 26, 1862; to General [Johnson Hagood]; n.d. [late Aug. 1862], Elliott-Gonzales Papers, Southern Historical Collection.

4. Antebellum Southern Urbanization

"Antebellum Southern Urbanization" was originally published as "Urbanization," in Richard N. Current, ed., *Encyclopedia of the Confederacy*, 4 vols. (New York: Simon and Schuster, 1993), 4:1641–1648. Reprinted by Permission of the Gale Group.

5. Distant Thunder

"Distant Thunder: The Creation of a World Market in Rice and the Transformations It Wrought" first appeared in *American Historical Review* 98 (Oct. 1993): 1050–78, and appears here with permission of the American Historical Association, publisher of the *AHR*.

Earlier versions of this article were presented at the annual meeting of the Organization of American Historians (March 1990), the New England Seminar in American History (Nov. 1990), the Harvard Economic History Workshop (March 1991), the Charles Warren Center Seminar (April 1991), and the Triangle Economic History Workshop (Nov. 1991). I would like to thank the OAH commentators, John J. McCusker and Robert M. Weir, and the participants in the other seminars for their helpful criticisms. I would also like to thank Jan de Vries, James C. Riley, Stefano Fenoaltea, Robert E. Gallman, Lance Davis, Sugata Bose, Stuart Leibiger, Deanna Pagnini, Bryant Simon, and several anonymous referees for their help. Note that the title of the article was inspired by the title of a 1973 film by the great Bengali director Satyajit Ray: *Asani Sanket* ("Distant Thunder"). This film, in its own way, suggests some of the themes expressed here.

1. The slave song can be found in Edmund Kirke [James Roberts Gilmore], *Among the Pines; or, South in Secession-Time* (New York, 1862), 22. The Filipino song is from Edith Fowke and Joe Glazer, eds., *Songs of Work and Protest* (New York, 1973), 102–3.

2. See D. H. Grist, *Rice,* 5th ed. (London, 1975), 3–10; Lucien M. Hanks, *Rice and Man: Agricultural Ecology in Southeast Asia* (Arlington Heights, Ill., 1972), 16–22; E. J. Kahn, Jr., *The Staffs of Life* (Boston, 1985), 210, 212, 219.

3. Figures on the world grain trade are inexact, but available data do convey the order of magnitude of the rice trade in the West. Between 1902 and 1911, for example, rice shipments from Southeast Asia to the West averaged about 1.454 million metric tons annually. Available data suggest that this figure should be raised by another 4 percent or so to account for rice exports from Bengal and other Eastern supply sources during this period. The West's six largest wheat exporters shipped about 14.8 million metric tons of wheat annually between 1909 and 1913. There were other wheat exporters and, of course, other small grains besides wheat. See Randolph Barker et al., *The Rice Economy of Asia,* 2 vols. (Washington, D.C., 1985), 1:187; Frank M. Surface, *The Grain Trade during the World War* (New York, 1928), 22; Imperial Institute, Indian Trade Enquiry, *Reports on Rice* (London, 1920), 8, 35–62. On the caloric values for rice and other cereals, see Arnold E. Bender, *Dictionary of Nutrition and Food Technology,* 6th ed. (London, 1990), 245, 302–3; Daniel N. Lapedes, ed., *McGraw-Hill Encyclopedia of Food, Agriculture, and Nutrition* (New York, 1977), 697, 699, 704, 705.

4. See William Shakespeare, *The Winter's Tale* (c. 1610–11), 4.3.39–44; Thomas Elyot, *The Castel of Helth, Corrected and in some places augmented by the fyrste authour therof* (London, 1541), fyrste boke, 15; Francis Bacon, *Sylva Sylvarum; or, A Naturall Historie, in Ten Centuries* (London, 1627), century 1.49, 16; John Arbuthnot, *Practical Rules of Diet in the Various Constitutions and Diseases of Human Bodies* (London, 1736), 256, 301–2; Alexis Soyer, *The Pantropheon; or, History of Food . . .* (London, 1853), 43; Jost Amman and Hans Sachs, *Eygentliche Beschreibung aller Stande auff Erden* (Frankfurt am Main, 1568), entry "Der Koch"; V. D. Wickizer and M. K. Bennett, *The Rice Economy of Monsoon Asia* (Stanford, Calif., 1941), 15.

5. On the uses of rice in Europe and the Americas in the eighteenth and nineteenth centuries, see James Glen, *A Description of South Carolina . . .* (London, 1761), 91; Nicolas Baudeau,. . . *Commerce . . . ,* 3 vols. (Paris, 1783–84), 3: 588–89; Court of Directors to Governor General and Council at Fort William, April 5, 1793, in *Indian Records Series: Fort William-India House Correspondence . . .* (Public Series), 21 vols. (Delhi, 1949–85), 12:1793–95, 55; *Encyclopaedia Britannica,* 3d ed., 20 vols. (Edinburgh, 1797–1801), supp. 2 (vol. 20), 462; [Great Britain] *House of Commons Sessional Papers of the Eighteenth Century, Reports & Papers,* vol. 131: *George III, Food Supply, Fisheries 1799–1800 and 1800,* ed. Sheila Lambert (Wilmington, Del., 1975), 65–68, 353–58, 367–73, 445–65, 519–22; *The (London) Times,* Nov. 9, 1811; Fernand Braudel, *Civilization and Capitalism 15th-18th Century,* 3 vols., trans. Siân Reynolds (New York, 1981–84), 1:109–14, 145–58.

6. On the income inelasticity of rice, see, for example, Theodore W. Schultz, *The Economic Organization of Agriculture* (New York, 1953), 71–73.

7. See Peter A. Coclanis, *The Shadow of a Dream: Economic Life and Death in the South Carolina Low Country, 1670–1920* (New York, 1989), 53–54, 239. That rice commonly was consumed in hospitals for the poor and aged and in orphanages in early modern Europe is apparent from

data available in standard works on European prices. See, for example, William Beveridge, *Prices and Wages in England from the Twelfth to the Nineteenth Century* (London, 1939), 255, 292, 540; N. W. Posthumus, *Inquiry into the History of Prices in Holland,* 2 vols. (Leiden, 1946–64), 2:459–66, 773, 781, 785, 788, 790, 792, 794, 795. On rice consumption in British prisons in the nineteenth century, see Valerie Johnston, "The Diets of the Local Prisons 1835 to 1878," in *Diet and Health in Modern Britain,* ed. Derek J. Oddy and Derek S. Miller (London, 1985), 207–30.

8. See Arthur H. Cole, *Wholesale Commodity Prices in the United States, 1700–1861,* 2 vols. (Cambridge, Mass., 1938), 2:15–69; Posthumus, *Inquiry into the History of Prices in Holland,* 1:2–8; Vitorino Magalhaes Godinho, "Precos e conjuntura do século XV ao XIX," in *Dicionário de història de Portugal,* 4 vols. (Lisbon, [1971?]), 4:488–516, esp. 506, 508–9; Godinho, *Prix et monnaies au Portugal 1750–1850* (Paris, 1955), 72–78, figures following 371; Henri Hauser, *Recherches et documents sur l'histoire des prix en France de 1500 à 1800* (1936; Geneva, 1985), 97–135; Beveridge, *Prices and Wages in England,* 734–35; Braudel, *Civilization and Capitalism,* 1:109–14; Luigi Faccini, *L'economia risicola lombarda dagli inizi del XVIII secolo all'Unità* (Milan, 1976), 23–26; A. J. H. Latham and Larry Neal, "The International Market in Rice and Wheat, 1868–1914," *Economic History Review,* 2d ser., 36 (May 1983): 160–80; U.S. Department of Agriculture, Bureau of Agricultural Economics, *Gross Farm Income and Indices of Farm Production and Prices in the United States, 1869–1937,* by Frederick Strauss and Louis H. Bean, Technical Bulletin No. 703 (Washington, D.C., 1940), 36–40, 69–71.

9. See Glen, *Description of South Carolina,* 90–93; (Charleston) *South Carolina Gazette,* Jan. 10, 1761; Marie Scholz-Babisch, *Quellen zur Geschichte des Klevischen Rheinzollwesens vom 11. bis 18. Jahrhundert,* 2 vols. (Wiesbaden, 1971), 2:870, 912, 997, 999; Nina E. Bang and Knud Korst, *Tabeller over skibsfart og varetransport gennem Øresund, 1661–1783, og gennem Storebaelt 1701–1748,* 4 vols. (Copenhagen, 1930), 2, part 2; Ralph Izard to Thomas Jefferson, June 10, 1785, in Julian P. Boyd, et al., eds., *The Papers of Thomas Jefferson,* 25 vols. (Princeton, N.J., 1950–), 8:195–204; H. P. H. Nusteling, *De Rijnvaart in het tijdperk van stoom en steenkool 1831–1914* (Amsterdam, 1974), 123–79, esp. 132, 153–55, 464; *Hunt's Merchants' Magazine,* 21 (July 1849): 104; *De Bow's Review* 25 (Sept. 1858): 350–51; Peter Buss to Robert Pringle, Feb. 14, 1784, Pringle Family Papers, South Carolina Historical Society, Charleston; *Hunt's Merchants' Magazine,* 11 (Aug. 1844): 179–80; 16 (Feb. 1847): 138–51, esp. 148–49; 23 (Aug. 1850): 177–88; 31 (Nov. 1854): 558–65; 13 (Aug. 1845): 193–96; 18 (April 1848): 413–15; 43 (July 1860): 91–94; Lewis C. Gray, *History of Agriculture in the Southern United States to 1860,* 2 vols. (Gloucester, Mass., 1958), 1:286; *Hunt's Merchants' Magazine* 27 (Sept. 1852): 289–309; 28 (Jan. 1853): 81–86.

Most of the rice imported into Great Britain during the eighteenth century was re-exported to the continent. On the reasons for the rise of domestic rice demand in Great Britain in the nineteenth century, see below.

10. Grist, *Rice,* 5–6; E. H. Warmington, *The Commerce between the Roman Empire and India,* 2d ed. (New York, 1974), 40, 218–19; Norman J. G. Pounds, *An Historical Geography of Europe 450 B.C.–A.D. 1330* (Cambridge, 1973), 69. Also see David MacPherson, *Annals of Commerce, Manufactures, Fisheries and Navigation,* 4 vols. (London, 1805), 1:162.

11. Grist, *Rice,* 6; "Rico," in *Enciclopedia italiana di scienze, lettere ed arti,* 36 vols. plus appendixes and index (Rome, 1929–52), 29 (1936): 424–31; Faccini, *L'economia risicola lombarda;* Peiraldo Bullio, "Problemi e geografia della risicoltura in Piemonte nei secoli XVII e XVIII," *Annali della Fondazione Luigi Einaudi,* 3 (1969): 37–93; Ira A. Glazier, *Il commercio estero del regno Lombardo-Veneto dal 1815 al 1865* (Rome, 1966), 30–45 and passim.

12. See the works cited in note 11. Also see Philippe Dollinger, *The German Hansa,* trans. and ed. D. S. Ault and S. H. Steinberg (Stanford, Calif., 1970), 212–13, esp. 223.

13. See Immanuel Wallerstein, *The Modern World System,* 3 vols. (New York, 1974–); M. A. P.

Meilink-Roelofsz, *Asian Trade and European Influence in the Indonesian Archipelago between 1500 and about 1630* (The Hague, 1962); K. M. Panikkar, *Asia and Western Dominance* (London, 1959), 13–174; Holden Furber, *Rival Empires of Trade in the Orient, 1600–1800* (Minneapolis, 1976); Anthony Reid, *Southeast Asia in the Age of Commerce 1450–1680*, vol. 1: *The Lands below the Winds* (New Haven, 1988), 1–119.

14. On the global reallocation of European labor and capital, see Wallerstein, *Modern World-System.* On the dissemination of rice by Europeans, see, for example, Wickizer and Bennett, *Rice Economy of Monsoon Asia,* 13–16; Grist, *Rice,* 5–8; Kahn, *Staffs of Life,* 220–24. Note that rice exports from northern Italy in the eighteenth century varied considerably from year to year but were sometimes impressive. Quantitative data from the period are extremely sketchy, however. See Faccini, *L'economia risicola lombarda,* 23–26.

15. Coclanis, *Shadow of a Dream,* 27–38, 48–110.

16. See Coclanis, *Shadow of a Dream,* 111–58. On the Brazilian rice industry, see Paul L. Mandell, "The Rise of the Modern Brazilian Rice Industry: Demand Expansion in a Dynamic Economy," *Stanford Food Research Institute Studies* 10 (1971): 161–219. Note that data on rice exports from northern Italy for the period between 1800 and 1861 are also very sketchy. See Tom P. Barbiero, "A Reassessment of Agricultural Production in Italy, 1861–1914: The Case of Lombardy," *Journal of European Economic History* 17 (spring 1988): 103–16; Gianni Toniolo, *An Economic History of Liberal Italy 1850–1918,* trans. Maria Rees (London, 1990), 39–40. Also note, however, that Lombardy and Venetia apparently were net importers of rice at times during the 1815–1865 period. See Glazier, *Il commercio estero del regno Lombardo-Veneto,* 30–45.

17. On the British penetration of Bengal, see Narendra Krishna Sinha, *The Economic History of Bengal: From Plassey to the Permanent Settlement,* 2 vols. (Calcutta, 1961–62); Amales Tripathi, *Trade and Finance in the Bengal Presidency 1793–1833,* rev. ed. (Calcutta, 1979); C. A. Bayly, *Indian Society and the Making of the British Empire* (Cambridge, 1988). On rice exports from Bengal to Europe in the early nineteenth century, see John Phipps, *A Guide to the Commerce of Bengal* (Calcutta, 1823), 211, 223–24; [Great Britain] *House of Commons Parliamentary Papers 1828,* vol. 18:379–86.

18. MacPherson, *Annals of Commerce,* 4:362.

19. See, for example, C. Northcote Parkinson, *Trade in the Eastern Seas 1793–1813* (Cambridge, 1937), 86; Holden Furber, *John Company at Work: A Study of European Expansion in India in the Late Eighteenth Century* (Cambridge, Mass., 1948); P. J. Marshall, *East Indian Fortunes: The British in Bengal in the Eighteenth Century* (Oxford, 1976), 29–50. On the supply disruptions occasioned by the American Revolution and the Napoleonic wars, see Customs 17/4–30, Customs Office Records, Public Record Office, London. The revolution wreaked havoc on the Lower South, bringing considerable damage and dislocation to the South Carolina–Georgia rice industry. See Jerome J. Nadelhaft, *The Disorders of War: The Revolution in South Carolina* (Orono, Maine, 1981), 45–104; Benjamin Quarles, *The Negro in the American Revolution* (Chapel Hill, N.C., 1961), 158–81; Rachel N. Klein, *Unification of a Slave State: The Rise of the Planter Class in the South Carolina Backcountry 1760–1808* (Chapel Hill, 1990), 114–15.

On the British harvest failures of 1795 and 1800, see W. Freeman Galpin, *The Grain Supply of England during the Napoleonic Period* (New York, 1925), 14, 20–21; Walter M. Stern, "The Bread Crisis in Britain, 1795–96," *Economica,* n.s., 31 (May 1964): 168–87; Richard Perren, "Markets and Marketing," in *The Agrarian History of England and Wales,* vol. 6: *1750–1850,* ed. G. E. Mingay (Cambridge, 1989), 191–274, esp. 202. Note that England was a net importer of grain throughout the late eighteenth century. See Perren, "Markets and Marketing," 205. On the shortage of provisions in Great Britain and Europe in 1795 and 1800, the demand for Indian rice, and the competitive advantage Indian rice enjoyed over Carolina rice, see Draft of letter from the Secret Committee to the Government of Bengal, July 7, 1795, in *Indian Records Series: Fort William–India*

House Correspondence . . . vol. 17: *1792–1795*, 137–39; David Scott to the Marquis of Wellesley, Sept. 30, 1800, and David Scott to William Pitt, Dec. 24, 1800, in *The Correspondence of David Scott, Director and Chairman of the East India Company . . . 1787–1805*, ed. C. H. Philips, 2 vols. (London, 1951), 2:287–88, 294–95; MacPherson, *Annals of Commerce*, 4:362–63. One should note that very large quantities of East Indian rice were imported by Great Britain in 1796 and in 1802. See Customs 17/18, 24, Customs Office Records, Public Record Office.

20. On the Preanger System and the Culture System, see, for example, J. S. Furnivall, *Netherlands India: A Study of Plural Economy* (Cambridge, 1939), 115–47; J. J. van Klaveren, *The Dutch Colonial System in the East Indies* (The Hague, 1953), 59–64, 115–31; Clifford Geertz, *Agricultural Involution: The Process of Ecological Change in Indonesia* (Berkeley, Calif., 1963), 47–82; C. Fasseur, "The Cultivation System and Its Impact on the Dutch Colonial Economy and the Indigenous Society in Nineteenth-Century Java," in *Two Colonial Empires: Comparative Essays on the History of India and Indonesia in the Nineteenth Century*, ed. C. A. Bayly and D. H. A. Kolff (Dordrecht, 1986), 137–54.

21. On the N.H.M., see van Klaveren, *Dutch Colonial System in the East Indies*, 108–14. Data compiled by G. F. de Bruijn Kops reveal that Javanese rice exports to northern Europe averaged 293,442 piculs annually between 1837 and 1839. Upon conversion to Western measures, this means that Java exported, on average, over 39.9 million pounds of (partially milled cargo) rice annually to this area between 1837 and 1839. The United States, on the other hand, exported, on average, about 25.7 million pounds of clean rice equivalents to northern Europe in 1837 and 1838, with another 1 million pounds annually going to southern Europe. Under the conservative assumption that 1 pound of cargo rice at the time equaled 0.8 pounds of U.S. clean rice, we find that Java was already exporting more rice to northern Europe than the United States was sending to Europe as a whole. Moreover, Javanese exports to northern Europe increased in the 1840s and 1850s. See G. F. de Bruijn Kops, *Statistiek van Den Handel en de Scheepvaart op Java en Madura Sedert 1825*, 2 vols. (Batavia, 1857–59), 2:176–80; *U.S. Senate Executive Documents, 2d Session, 25th Congress, 1837–1838, No. 318; U.S. Senate Executive Documents, 3d Session, 25th Congress, 1838–1839, No. 342.*

Indian rice also continued to make inroads into Great Britain's rice trade during this period. See table 5.2.

22. See Furnivall, *Netherlands India*, 137–38; W. R. Hugenholtz, "Famine and Food Supply in Java 1830–1914," in Bayly and Kolff, *Two Colonial Empires*, 155–88. Note that in the late nineteenth century, the orientation of the export trade of the Dutch East Indies shifted from Europe back to Asia. See A. J. H. Latham, *The International Economy and the Undeveloped World 1865–1914* (London, 1978), 92–93.

23. See, for example, Cheng Siok-Hwa, *The Rice Industry of Burma 1852–1940* (Singapore, 1968), 1–15; Michael Adas, *The Burma Delta: Economic Development and Social Change on an Asian Rice Frontier, 1852–1941* (Madison, Wis., 1974), 15–57.

24. See the works mentioned in note 23 above. Also see U Tun Wai, *Economic Development of Burma from 1800 till 1940* (Rangoon, 1961); Norman G. Owen, "The Rice Industry of Mainland Southeast Asia 1850–1914," *Journal of the Siam Society* 59 (July 1971): 75–143. Note that prior to about 1880, the Chettyars' role in agricultural finance in Burma was largely indirect. After that date, however, the Chettyars increasingly moved into direct lending to Burmese cultivators themselves. See Michael Adas, "Immigrant Asians and the Economic Impact of European Imperialism: The Role of the South Indian Chettiars in British Burma," *Journal of Asian Studies* 33 (May 1974): 385–401. The figures on Arakan's rice exports to Europe between 1854–1855 and 1860–1861 are from [H. R. Spearman], *British Burma Gazetteer*, 2 vols. (Rangoon, 1880), 1:462.

25. See Karl Marx, *Capital*, ed. Frederick Engels, trans. Samuel Moore, and Edward Aveling, 3 vols. (New York, 1967), 1:750–74. On the "cheapness" of land and labor in Southeast Asia, see, for example, C. Edwards Lester, *The Glory and the Shame of England*, 2 vols. in 1 (New York, 1850),

2:27–52; (London) *Times*, Feb. 6, 1874; U.S. Congress, House of Representatives, Ways and Means Committee, *Statements to the Committee of Ways and Means on the Morrison Tariff Bill* . . . (Washington, D.C., 1886), 205–32, esp. 215; *U.S. House of Representatives Miscellaneous Documents, First Session, 51st Congress, 1889–90, No. 2774, vol. 15, Tariff Hearings*, 927–37. On the specific advantages gained from the use of unremunerated labor in Southeast Asia, see *U.S. House of Representatives Documents, 142, Second Session, 60th Congress, 1908–1909, No. 5552*, 3666; *U.S. House of Representatives Documents, 129, Third Session, 62d Congress, 1912–13, No. 6495*, 2704. The theoretical problem of "articulation" between competing modes of production has been studied most closely by Pierre Philippe Rey and Giovanni Arrighi. For an empirical demonstration, see Joseph C. Miller, "A Marginal Institution on the Margin of the Atlantic System: The Portuguese Southern Atlantic Slave Trade in the Eighteenth Century," in Barbara L. Solow, ed., *Slavery and the Rise of the Atlantic System* (New York, 1991), 120–50.

26. See, for example, M. Y. Nuttonson, *Rice Culture and Rice-Climate Relationships* . . . (Washington, D.C., 1965). On the nitrogen-fixing effects of symbiosis, see Mary J. F. Gregor, "Associations with Fungi and Other Lower Plants," in *Manual of Pteridology*, ed. Frans Verdoon (The Hague, 1938), 141–58; A. W. Moore, "*Azolla:* Biology and Agronomic Significance," *Botanical Review* 35 (Jan.–March 1969): 17–34; D. J. Hill, "The Role of *Anabaena* in the *Azolla-Anabaena* Symbiosis," *New Phytologist* 78 (May 1977): 611–16; A. F. Dyer, ed., *The Experimental Biology of Ferns* (London, 1979), 575–76; M. S. Swaminathan, "Rice," *Scientific American* 250 (Jan. 1984): 80–85, 90–93.

27. See Peter Coclanis and John Komlos, "Time in the Paddies: A Comparison of Rice Production in the Southeastern United States and Lower Burma in the Nineteenth Century," *Social Science History* 11 (fall 1987): 343–54.

28. W. Arthur Lewis, *Growth and Fluctuations 1870–1913* (London, 1978), esp. 201–2.

29. On the projection of Western power in Southeast Asia generally during this period, see, for example, D. G. E. Hall, *A History of South-East Asia*, 4th ed. (London, 1981), part 3, 497–742. On the coercive effects of Western administrative, fiscal, and tariff innovations in Southeast Asia, see James C. Scott, *The Moral Economy of the Peasant: Rebellion and Subsistence in Southeast Asia* (New Haven, 1976).

30. On technological and organizational changes in transoceanic shipping, see Douglass C. North, "Ocean Freight Rates and Economic Development 1750–1913," *Journal of Economic History* 18 (Dec. 1958): 537–55; Douglass C. North, "Sources of Productivity Change in Ocean Shipping, 1600–1850," *Journal of Political Economy* 76 (Sept.–Oct. 1968): 953–70. On the importance of the development of Australia and California for the Southeast Asian rice trade, see *Hunt's Merchants' Magazine* 41 (Oct. 1859): 445–48; 42 (Jan. 1860): 62–66. On British tariff preferences in favor of imperial rice, for example, see the schedules reprinted in *Southern Agriculturalist* 1 (Oct. 1828): 459–61; *Hunt's Merchants' Magazine* 7 (Oct. 1842): 367–88, esp. 379; *Hunt's Merchants' Magazine* 16 (April 1847): 405–8.

U.S. rice generally was considered by Westerners to be of higher quality than East Indian rice. See H. J. S. Cotton, "The Rice Trade of the World," *Calcutta Review* 58 (1874): 267–302; Gray, *History of Agriculture*, 2:725. On the price differentials between "Carolina" rice and East Indian rice in the first half of the nineteenth century, see the collection of "Prices Current" from Liverpool and Rotterdam in the Enoch Silsby Collection, Southern Historical Collection, University of North Carolina, Chapel Hill, N.C.

31. *Southern Agriculturalist* 11 (March 1838): 127–29; Armando Castro, "Orizicultura," in *Dicionário de História de Portugal*, ed. Joel Serrao, 3:243–45; U.S. Bureau of Statistics, *Report of the Chief of the Bureau of Statistics on Customs-Tariff Legislation, Appendix A* . . . , prepared by A. W. Angerer (Washington, D.C., 1872), 72–73, 76–77, 82–83. Note, too, that in Italy duties on imported rice rose substantially in the late nineteenth century. See Elda Gentili Zappi, *If Eight*

Hours Seem Too Few: Mobilization of Women Workers in the Italian Rice Fields (Albany, N.Y., 1991), 6–7. On the decline in transport costs associated with steam shipping, allied technological improvements, and the opening of the Suez Canal, see Latham, *International Economy and the Undeveloped World,* 17–39; A. J. H. Latham, "From Competition to Constraint: The International Rice Trade in the Nineteenth and Twentieth Centuries," *Business and Economic History,* 2d ser., 17 (1988): 91–102; Daniel R. Headrick, *The Tentacles of Progress: Technology Transfer in the Age of Imperialism, 1850–1940* (New York, 1988), 25–31. The data for Burma and the United States are from Cheng, *Rice Industry of Burma, 1852–1940,* 9–15, 237–39, 257–59; Coclanis, *The Shadow of a Dream,* 133–42; U.S. Department of Agriculture, Bureau of Statistics, *Rice Crop of the United States, 1712–1911,* by George K. Holmes, Circular No. 34 (Washington, D.C., 1912), 3–11.

On Germany's massive rice imports from Asia in the second half of the nineteenth century and in the early twentieth century, see Paul Arndt, *Die Handelsbeziehungen Deutschlands zu England und den Englischen Kolonien* (Berlin, 1899); Edwin J. Clapp, *The Navigable Rhine* (Boston, 1911), 33–37, 71–92; Ludwig Wendemuth and Walter Boucher, *The Port of Hamburg . . .,* trans. Wilhelm Eggers (Hamburg, 1927), 222, 224, 226; Dieter Glade, *Bremen und der Ferne Osten* (Bremen, 1966), 35–39, 90–99; Hermann Kellenbenz, "German Trade Relations with the Indian Ocean from the End of the Eighteenth Century to 1870," *Journal of Southeast Asian Studies* 13 (March 1982): 133–52; Kellenbenz, "Shipping and Trade between Hamburg-Bremen and the Indian Ocean, 1870–1914," *Journal of Southeast Asian Studies* 13 (Sept. 1982): 349–86.

32. See Coclanis, *Shadow of a Dream,* 136–38, 282–84; Latham and Neal, "International Market in Rice and Wheat"; Loren Brandt, *Commercialization and Agricultural Development: Central and Eastern China 1870–1937* (New York, 1989), 14–38. On U.S. rice duties in the late nineteenth century, see *Tariff Acts Passed by the Congress of the United States from 1789 to 1895 . . .,* compiled and indexed by William H. Michael and Pitman Pulsifer (Washington, D.C., 1896), 187, 215, 290, 342, 343, 426. Note that while U.S. duties on rice in the late nineteenth century were higher even in nominal terms than they had been prior to the Civil War, their real burden was even greater because of the deflationary monetary conditions prevalent in the United States over much of the late nineteenth century. See Robert A. McGuire, "Deflation-Induced Increases in Post–Civil War U.S. Tariffs," *Economic History Review,* 2d ser., 43 (Nov. 1990): 633–45. On the demand for rice for Western-controlled mines and plantations in Asia, see Latham, *International Economy and the Undeveloped World,* 75–94.

33. Coclanis, *Shadow of a Dream,* 136–42, 280–87.

34. See Coclanis, *Shadow of a Dream,* 136–42, 280–87; Arthur H. Cole, "The American Rice-Growing Industry: A Study of Comparative Advantage," *Quarterly Journal of Economics* 41 (Aug. 1927): 595–643; Pete Daniel, *Breaking the Land: The Transformation of Cotton, Tobacco, and Rice Cultures since 1880* (Urbana, Ill., 1985), 39–61, 215–36; Henry C. Dethloff, *A History of the American Rice Industry 1685–1985* (College Station, Tex., 1988), 63–194.

35. See John Scott Strickland, "'No More Mud Work': The Struggle for the Control of Labor and Production in Low Country South Carolina, 1863–1880," in *The Southern Enigma: Essays on Race, Class, and Folk Culture,* ed. Walter J. Fraser, Jr., and Winfred B. Moore, Jr. (Westport, Conn., 1983), 43–62. At this point, it is important to recall how severely the South Carolina–Georgia rice industry was damaged during the American Revolution. Not only were markets disrupted but lands were laid waste, and many slave laborers were lost. The market context was such at the time, however, that the industry had a chance to recover and to reclaim its position. See note 19.

36. On shipments of rice from Java to the United States in 1855, see Prices Current Collection, Box 4, Folder "Java," Special Collections, Baker Library, Harvard University Graduate School of Business Administration, Boston, Mass. Note that considerable quantities of rice apparently were shipped from Manila to California during the 1850s as well, although such shipments do

not appear in official U.S. records. See *Singapore Free Press,* March 5, 1857; Feb. 18, 1858. On the steam-powered rice mill set up by U.S. interests in Siam, see James C. Ingram, *Economic Change in Thailand 1850–1970* (Stanford, Calif., 1971), 70.

37. See the price data assembled in Cole, *Wholesale Commodity Prices,* vol. 2; Strauss and Bean, *Gross Farm Income,* 69–71; Latham and Neal, "International Market in Rice and Wheat," 276–77.

38. See the works mentioned in note 8, especially Latham and Neal, "International Market in Rice and Wheat."

39. See the works cited in note 37 above. Also see Gray, *History of Agriculture,* 2:1027–34; U.S. Department of Commerce, Bureau of the Census, *Historical Statistics of the United States: Colonial Times to 1970,* 2 vols. (Washington, D.C., 1975), 1:516–17. On prices for cotton and sugar, see, for example, Strauss and Bean, *Gross Farm Income,* 63–65; Noel Deerr, *The History of Sugar,* 2 vols. (London, 1949–50), 2:530–31.

40. On the roles and uses of rice, see above.

41. On "backwash effects," see Gunnar Myrdal, *Rich Lands and Poor: The Road to World Prosperity* (New York, 1957), 23–28. On the legacy of the rice regime in the South Carolina Low Country, see Coclanis, *Shadow of a Dream,* 141–60, 286–302.

42. See Barbiero, "Reassessment of Agricultural Production in Italy." For statistics on Italian rice production and exports between 1861 and 1920, see Istituto Centrale di Statistica [ISTAT], *Sommario di Statistiche Storiche dell'Italia 1861–1975* (Rome, 1976), 76, 118. On unification and other institutional changes, see Toniolo, *Economic History of Liberal Italy 1850–1918,* 48–59.

43. For a relatively balanced assessment of the impact of market integration on Bengal, see Tripathi, *Trade and Finance in the Bengal Presidency 1793–1833.* Note that C. Fasseur—to cite but one of the Culture System revisionists—argues that market integration had certain positive effects on Java. See Fasseur, "Cultivation System." For a rough attempt to estimate per capita income in Southeast Asia between 1860 and 1913, see L. J. Zimmerman, "The Distribution of World Income 1860–1960," in *Essays on Unbalanced Growth: A Century of Disparity and Convergence,* ed. Egbert de Vries (The Hague, 1962), 28–55. According to Zimmerman, per capita income in this area (using 1953 dollars) grew from about $48 in 1860 to about $65 by 1913; see page 53. Also see Angus Maddison, *Dynamic Forces in Capitalist Development: A Long-Run Comparative View* (New York, 1991), 24–25; Ann Booth, "The Economic Development of Southeast Asia: 1870–1985," *Australian Economic History Review* 31 (March 1991): 20–52. For a discussion of the rice trade's effects on Singapore, Southeast Asia's regional entrepôt for the trade, see W. G. Huff, "Bookkeeping Barter, Money, Credit, and Singapore's International Rice Trade, 1870–1939," *Explorations in Economic History,* 2d ser., 26 (April 1989): 161–89.

44. On Burma, see Cheng, *Rice Industry of Burma, 1852–1940.* On shifting comparative advantage in rice and the advent of the modern rice industry, see Cole, "American Rice-Growing Industry."

45. See Owen, "Rice Industry of Mainland Southeast Asia"; Ingram, *Economic Change in Thailand 1850–1970;* James C. Ingram, "Thailand's Rice Trade and the Allocation of Resources," in C. D. Cowan, ed., *The Economic Development of South East Asia: Studies in Economic History and Political Economy* (London, 1964), 102–26; David B. Johnston, "Rice Cultivation in Thailand: The Development of an Export Economy by Indigenous Capital and Labor," *Modern Asian Studies* 15 (Feb. 1981): 107–26; Latham, *International Economy and the Undeveloped World,* 155–56.

46. See Latham, *International Economy and the Undeveloped World,* 41–64, 65–101; Jonathan V. Levin, *The Export Economies: Their Pattern of Development in Historical Perspective* (Cambridge, Mass., 1960). Among the few scholars who have worked on income distribution (in Lower Burma) during the rice boom are Aye Hlaing and Michael Adas. See Aye Hlaing, "Trends of Economic Growth and Income Distribution in Burma, 1870–1940," *Journal of the Burma Research Society* 47 (June 1964): 89–148; Adas, *Burma Delta,* 69–82, 141–53. The Scott-Popkin controversy

has blazed in several of the social sciences for over a decade now. For the original positions, see Scott, *Moral Economy of the Peasant;* Samuel L. Popkin, *The Rational Peasant: The Political Economy of Rural Society in Vietnam* (Berkeley, Calif., 1979).

47. Andrew M. Watson, *Agricultural Innovation in the Early Islamic World: The Diffusion of Crops and Farming Techniques, 700–1100* (Cambridge, 1983), 15–19; William Foster, *The East India House: Its History and Associations* (London, 1924), 113–24; Grist, *Rice,* 7, 94–97; Dethloff, *History of the American Rice Industry,* 78, 91.

48. On this war and its background, see Hall, *History of South-East Asia,* 625–58.

6. The Revolution from Above

"The Revolution from Above: The National Market and the Beginnings of Industrialization in North Carolina" first appeared in the *Journal of American History* 77 (Sept. 1990): 445–75, and is reprinted here by permission of the Organization of American Historians, publisher of the *JAH.*

The author would like to thank the following people for their assistance and advice: David Thelen, Susan Armeny, and Emilye Crosby, along with Jonathan M. Wiener, William H. Phillips, and the other readers for the *Journal of American History* and the *Journal of Southern History;* Joyce E. Chaplin, Don H. Doyle, Marshall C. Eakin, James A. Epstein, and Donald L. Winters of Vanderbilt; Peter A. Coclanis and Linda Sellars of the University of North Carolina at Chapel Hill; Lacy K. Ford; and the staffs of the Southern Historical and North Carolina Collections at the University of North Carolina and the Manuscripts Division of the Perkins Library at Duke University.

1. For per capita income from 1929 to 1970, see U.S. Department of Commerce, Bureau of the Census, *Historical Statistics of the United States: Colonial Times to 1970* (2 vols., Washington, D.C., 1975), 1:243–45; data since 1970 appear annually in U.S. Department of Commerce, *Survey of Current Business.* On occupational structure, see U.S. Department of Commerce, Bureau of the Census, *1980 Census of Population,* vol. 1: *Characteristics of the Population,* chap. C: *General Social and Economic Characteristics,* pt. 1: *United States Summary* (Washington, D.C., 1983), 47, 329–31. On the economic weaknesses of the recent South, see William W. Falk and Thomas A. Lyson, *High Tech, Low Tech, No Tech: Recent Industrial and Occupational Change in the South* (Albany, N.Y., 1988); and Thomas A. Lyson, *Two Sides to the Sunbelt: The Growing Divergence between the Rural and Urban South* (New York, 1989).

2. On southern industrial society, see James C. Cobb, *Industrialization and Southern Society, 1877–1984* (Lexington, Ky., 1984).

3. Jonathan M. Wiener, *Social Origins of the New South: Alabama, 1860–1885* (Baton Rouge, 1978); Philip J. Wood, *Southern Capitalism: The Political Economy of North Carolina, 1880–1980* (Durham, N.C., 1986); Dwight B. Billings, Jr., *Planters and the Making of a "New South": Class, Politics, and Development in North Carolina, 1865–1900* (Chapel Hill, N.C., 1979). On the continuity of industrial leadership in North Carolina, see Billings, *Planters and the Making of a "New South,"* 42–95; Paul D. Escott, *Many Excellent People: Power and Privilege in North Carolina, 1850–1900* (Chapel Hill, N.C., 1986), 196–219; and John J. Beck, "Building the New South: A Revolution from Above in a Piedmont County," *Journal of Southern History* 53 (Aug. 1987): 441–70. This stress is traditional among North Carolina historians; see J. Carlyle Sitterson, "Business Leaders in Post–Civil War North Carolina, 1865–1900"; in *Studies in Southern History in Memory of Albert Ray Newsome, 1894–1951,* ed. J. Carlyle Sitterson (Chapel Hill, N.C., 1957), 111–21; and Richard W. Griffin, "North Carolina: The Origin and Rise of the Cotton Textile Industry, 1830–1880" (Ph.D. diss., Ohio State University, 1954).

4. The term *continuitarian* is borrowed from C. Vann Woodward, *Thinking Back: The Perils*

of Writing History (Baton Rouge, 1986), 70. Such "continuitarians" as Jonathan M. Wiener, Dwight B. Billings, Jr., and Philip Wood draw on the interpretation advanced in Eugene D. Genovese, *The Political Economy of Slavery: Studies in the Economy and Society of the Slave South* (New York, 1965). Their equation of continuity of personnel with class continuity, however, diverges sharply from Genovese's concept of class as grounded in relations of production, which changed dramatically with the demise of slavery; see Barbara Jeanne Fields, "The Nineteenth-Century American South: History and Theory," *Plantation Society in the Americas* 2 (April 1983): 7–27, esp. 21–22; Harold D. Woodman, "Sequel to Slavery: The New History Views the Postbellum South" *Journal of Southern History* 43 (Nov. 1977): 523–54. Wiener grants that his postbellum planters faced "new social relations of production," but nonetheless argues that "the social roots of the postwar planters help explain why the South took the Prussian rather than the classical capitalist road after the Civil War." See Jonathan M. Wiener, "Class Structure and Economic Development in the American South," *American Historical Review* 84 (Oct. 1979): 970–92, esp. 986. For a critique of the distinction between "planter" and "bourgeois" outlooks, see James C. Cobb, "Beyond Planters and Industrialists: A New Perspective on the New South," *Journal of Southern History* 54 (Feb. 1988), 45–68. Gavin Wright, *Old South, New South: Revolutions in the Southern Economy since the Civil War* (New York, 1986), esp. 17–50; David L. Carlton, *Mill and Town in South Carolina, 1880–1920* (Baton Rouge, 1982), 13–81; Lacy K. Ford, "Rednecks and Merchants: Economic Development and Social Tensions in the South Carolina Upcountry, 1865–1900," *Journal of American History* 71 (Sept. 1984): 294–318.

5. The literature on the long-term disabilities generated by a plantation economy is voluminous and growing. On southern manufacturing, see Fred Bateman and Thomas Weiss, *A Deplorable Scarcity: The Failure of Industrialization in the Slave Economy* (Chapel Hill, N.C., 1981); Gavin Wright, *The Political Economy of the Cotton South: Households, Markets, and Wealth in the Nineteenth Century* (New York, 1978), 107–20; Heywood Fleisig, "Slavery, the Supply of Agricultural Labor, and the Industrialization of the South," *Journal of Economic History* 36 (Sept. 1976), 572–97. On the long-term impact of plantation agriculture, see Peter A. Coclanis, *The Shadow of a Dream: Economic Life and Death in the South Carolina Low Country, 1670–1920* (New York, 1989). For a new interpretation of the development of the American manufacturing belt that emphasizes the antebellum formation across the Northeast and Midwest of local industrial centers, see David R. Meyer, "Emergence of the American Manufacturing Belt: An Interpretation," *Journal of Historical Geography* 9 (April 1983), 145–74; and David R. Meyer, "The Industrial Retardation of Southern Cities, 1860–1880," *Explorations in Economic History* 25 (Oct. 1988): 366–86.

6. On the constraints on southern planters as a result of their political subordination within a larger national polity, see Lawrence N. Powell, "The Prussians Are Coming," *Georgia Historical Quarterly* 71 (winter 1987): 638–67, esp. 662–67; and Steven Hahn, "Class and State in Postemancipation Societies: Southern Planters in Comparative Perspective," *American Historical Review* 95 (Feb. 1990): 75–98. See also Cobb, "Beyond Planters and Industrialists," 46, 54–55, 66–68.

7. Alfred D. Chandler, Jr., *The Visible Hand: The Managerial Revolution in American Business* (Cambridge, Mass., 1977), 79–205.

8. Gunnar Myrdal, *Rich Lands and Poor: The Road to World Prosperity* (New York, 1957); Albert O. Hirschman, *The Strategy of Economic Development* (New Haven, 1958). Myrdal's thinking was stimulated by his research on blacks in the American South; see Gunnar Myrdal, *An American Dilemma: The Negro Problem and Modern Democracy* (2 vols., New York, 1944); and Myrdal, *Rich Lands and Poor*, 14–22.

9. Readers with an interest in the American South may note a similarity here to the old "colonial economy" argument about southern development. I prefer to avoid that terminology, in part

because of connotations of "Yankee exploitation" that I find overwrought, but mainly to allow me to explore the ways in which that "context defined from the outside" has sometimes worked to the advantage of southern industrialists. On the "colonial economy" thesis, see C. Vann Woodward, *Origins of the New South, 1877–1913* (Baton Rouge, 1951), 291–320; Clarence Danhof, "Four Decades of Thought on the South's Economic Problems," in *Essays in Southern Economic Development*, ed. Melvin L. Greenhut and W. Tate Whitman (Chapel Hill, N.C. 1964), 7–68; and Wright, *Old South, New South*, 156–75.

10. On merchandising, see William J. Stanton, *Fundamentals of Marketing* (New York, 1981), 163.

11. Albert W. Niemi, Jr., *State and Regional Patterns in American Manufacturing, 1860–1900* (Westport, Conn., 1974), 90–91, 183–88.

12. On the contribution of tar and turpentine manufacture to North Carolina value added by manufacture (VAM), see ibid., 114–18; Percival Perry, "The Naval Stores Industry in the Antebellum South, 1789–1861" (Ph.D. diss., Duke University, 1947), 123–58.

13. U.S. Department of the Interior, Census Office, *Eighth Census, 1860*, vol. 3: *Manufactures of the United States in 1860: Compiled from the Original Returns of the Eighth Census* (Washington, D.C., 1865), 438; Joseph Clarke Robert, *The Tobacco Kingdom: Plantation, Market, and Factory in Virginia and North Carolina, 1800–1860* (Durham, N.C., 1938), 165–76, 186, 190, 222–26; Nannie May Tilley, *The Bright-Tobacco Industry, 1860–1929* (Chapel Hill, N.C., 1948), 536–38; Mary C. Dalton to John H. Dalton, July 1, 1845, Oct. 17, 1847; P. H. Dalton to John H. Dalton, Sept. 11, 1848, Mary H. Kennedy Papers, Southern Historical Collection, Wilson Library, University of North Carolina, Chapel Hill.

14. The rural and isolated nature of North Carolina complicates attempts to measure export orientation. Much food production (for instance, the butchering and curing of meat) was carried on in households or in small establishments beneath the notice of the census takers. Much textile production was carried on at the domestic spinning wheel and handloom. These problems, though, only reinforce the argument made here; not only was North Carolina industry largely isolated from the national economy in 1860 but in addition its internal economy was poorly integrated.

15. Census Office, *Eighth Census, 1860*, vol. 3: xxi. Even in cotton goods, Tarheel manufacturers accounted for only 0.73% of United States VAM, or 71% of the most conservatively estimated local market.

16. Broadus Mitchell, *The Rise of Cotton Mills in the South* (Baltimore, 1921), 18–21; Holland Thompson, *From the Cotton Field to the Cotton Mill: A Study of the Industrial Transition in North Carolina* (New York, 1906), 45–51; Andrew Warren Pierpont, "Development of the Textile Industry in Alamance County" (master's thesis, University of North Carolina, Chapel Hill, N.C., 1953), 35–37, 53, 103–4; Richard W. Griffin and Diffee W. Standard, "The Cotton Textile Industry in Antebellum North Carolina. Part II: An Era of Boom and Consolidation, 1830–1860," *North Carolina Historical Review* 34 (April 1957): 131–64; Mary Josephine Oates, "The Role of the Cotton Textile Industry in the Economic Development of the American Southeast" (Ph.D. diss., Yale University, 1969), 106. On "sturdy cloth," see Caldwell Ragan interview by Robert Allison Ragan, April 3, 1976, transcript, p. 6, folder H-285, Southern Oral History Program Collection, Southern Historical Collection. On the Holt family's selling methods, see Edwin Michael Holt to James W. White, Oct. 29, 1873, James Wilson White Papers, Southern Historical Collection. For accounts of use of northern markets and commission merchants that tend to exaggerate their importance for the antebellum period, see Griffin and Standard, "Cotton Textile Industry in Ante-bellum North Carolina"; Bess Beatty, "The Edwin Holt Family: Nineteenth-Century Capitalists in North Carolina," *North Carolina Historical Review* 63 (Oct. 1986): 511–35; and Bess Beatty, "Lowells of the

South: Northern Influences on the Nineteenth-Century Southern Textile Industry," *Journal of Southern History* 53 (Feb. 1987): 44–45.

17. Hugh Talmage Lefler and Albert Ray Newsome, *North Carolina: The History of a Southern State* (Chapel Hill, N.C., 1973), 379–84; Cecil Kenneth Brown, *A State Movement in Railroad Development: The Story of North Carolina's First Effort to Establish an East and West Trunk Line Railroad* (Chapel Hill, N.C., 1928), 1–14, 36, 82–83, 145–46.

18. On the regional and national network, see George Rogers Taylor and Irene D. Neu, *The American Railroad Network, 1861–1890* (Cambridge, Mass., 1956), 15–48. On "territorial" strategy, see Maury Klein, "The Strategy of Southern Railroads," *American Historical Review* 73 (April 1968): 1052–68, esp. 1054–55. On the politics and strategy of North Carolina railroads and on "whiggish interests," see Brown, *State Movement in Railroad Development,* 15–30, 63–77, 93–94, esp. 18; and C. K. Brown, "A History of the Piedmont Railroad Company," *North Carolina Historical Review* 3 (April 1926): 198–222.

19. Brown, *State Movement in Railroad Development,* 148–73; Maury Klein, *The Great Richmond Terminal: A Study in Businessmen and Business Strategy* (Charlottesville, Va., 1970), 55–65; Peter McGuire, "The Seaboard Air Line," *North Carolina Historical Review* 11 (April 1934): 94–115; Lefler and Newsome, *North Carolina,* 517–18; Taylor and Neu, *American Railroad Network,* 49–83. Track mileage figures come from Henry V. Poor, *Manual of the Railroads of the United States,* 1881 (373–82) and 1891. On the efforts of North Carolina towns to develop alternatives to the emerging interstate systems, see Roland B. Eustler, "The Cape Fear and Yadkin Valley Railroad," *North Carolina Historical Review* 2 (Oct. 1925): 427–41; Samuel M. Kipp III, "Urban Growth and Social Change in the South, 1870–1920: Greensboro, North Carolina as a Case Study" (Ph.D. diss., Princeton University, 1974), 77, 81–87; and Tilley, *Bright-Tobacco Industry,* 565–68.

20. Perry, "Naval Stores Industry in the Ante-bellum South," 276–84.

21. Divergence is measured by subtracting the percentages of total state VAM accounted for by North Carolina industrial groups (minus chemicals) from their equivalents for the U.S. (from table 6.1), then taking the standard deviations, which are as follows: 1860 = 4.91; and 1900 = 8.60. If chemicals are included in the calculations, the standard deviations are: 1860 = 8.34; and 1900 = 8.19. An alternate method, *dividing* the North Carolina percentages by their U.S. equivalents (measuring the *percentage* deviation of North Carolina from national structure), yields the following standard deviations: (1) not including chemicals: 1860 = 139.7; and 1900 = 162.8; (2) including chemicals: 1860 = 296.0; and 1900 = 164.2. The electrical machinery group, virtually nonexistent until the end of the nineteenth century, is also excluded from this analysis. The pattern reported here resembles that found by Albert W. Niemi, Jr., "Structural Shifts in Southern Manufacturing, 1849–1899," *Business History Review* 45 (spring 1971): 79–84.

22. Real values are computed using the wholesale price indexes for leather and hides in George E. Warren and Frank A. Pearson, *Prices* (New York, 1933), 26.

23. James Michael Shirley, "From Congregation Town to Industrial City: Industrialization, Class, and Culture in Nineteenth-Century Winston and Salem, North Carolina" (Ph.D. diss., Emory University, 1986), 221–23, 258–65; Douglas De Natale, "Bynum: The Coming of Mill Village Life to a North Carolina County" (Ph.D. diss., University of Pennsylvania, 1985), 74–75, 469–70. John J. Beck dates backwash from the 1850s and the opening of the North Carolina Railroad. John J. Beck, "Development in the Piedmont South: Rowan County, North Carolina, 1850–1900" (Ph.D. diss., University of North Carolina, Chapel Hill, N.C., 1984), 71–72, 74–76, 97–98. On the process in another southern state, see Steven Hahn, *The Roots of Southern Populism: Yeoman Farmers and the Transformation of the Georgia Upcountry, 1850–1890* (New York, 1983), 189; and David F. Weiman, "Petty Commodity Production in the Cotton South: Upcountry Farmers in the Georgia Cotton Economy, 1840 to 1880" (Ph.D. diss., Stanford University, 1983), 411–12.

24. Statistics on towns compiled from U.S. Department of the Interior, Census Office, *Eighth Census, 1860*, vol. 1: *Population of the United States in 1860; Compiled from the Original Returns of the Eighth Census* (Washington, D.C., 1864), 359; U.S. Department of the Interior, Census Office, *Ninth Census, 1870*, vol. 1: *The Statistics of the Population of the United States; Compiled from the Original Returns of the Ninth Census* (Washington, D.C., 1872), 220–26; U.S. Department of the Interior, Census Office, *Statistics of the Population of the United States at the Tenth Census* (Washington, D.C., 1883), 277–84; U.S. Department of the Interior, Census Office, *Report on the Population of the United States at the Eleventh Census: 1890, Part 1* (Washington, 1895), 253–62; U.S. Department of the Interior, Census Office, *Census Reports*, vol. 1: *Twelfth Census of the United States, Taken in the Year 1900: Population, Part 1* (Washington, D.C., 1901), 286–95.

25. On the expansion of commerce and towns in the postbellum South, see Harold D. Woodman, *King Cotton and His Retainers: Financing and Marketing the Cotton Crop of the South, 1800–1925* (Lexington, Ky., 1968), 319–33; Roger L. Ransom and Richard Sutch, *One Kind of Freedom: The Economic Consequences of Emancipation* (New York, 1977), 116–20; Wright, *Old South, New South*, 39–43; Weiman, "Petty Commodity Production in the Cotton South," 400, 411–12; and Carlton, *Mill and Town in South Carolina*, 13–39. On three representative counties in the North Carolina Piedmont, see Beck, "Building the New South," 450–62; Wayne K. Durrill, "Producing Poverty: Local Government and Economic Development in a New South County, 1874–1884," *Journal of American History* 71 (March 1985): 764–81; and De Natale, "Bynum," 74–81.

26. On water-power sites as nodes of economic (and social) life in the rural Piedmont, see De Natale, "Bynum," 12–13. On the Holts, see Beatty, "Edwin Holt Family," 512–13; on Randolph County, see Martha Tune Briggs, "Mill Owners and Mill Workers in an Antebellum North Carolina County" (master's thesis, University of North Carolina, Chapel Hill, 1975), 41–42, 127–31; on the Carpenters, Charles J. Preslar, Jr., *History of Catawba County* (Salisbury, N.C., 1954), 356–58; on the Bynum brothers, De Natale, "Bynum," 134–35.

27. On the links between industrialization and commerce in South Carolina, see Carlton, *Mill and Town in South Carolina*, 40–81. On those links in North Carolina, see Beck, "Building the New South," 462–68; Shirley, "From Congregation Town to Industrial City," 235–48; and Escott, *Many Excellent People*, 213–19. On the role of a persistent planter elite in industrialization, see Billings, *Planters and the Making of a "New South,"* 42–69.

28. On raising capital, see David L. Carlton and Peter A. Coclanis, "Capital Mobilization and Southern Industry: The Case of the Carolina Piedmont," *Journal of Economic History* 49 (March 1989): 73–94. Allan R. Pred, *The Spatial Dynamics of U.S. Urban-Industrial Growth, 1800–1914* (Cambridge, Mass., 1966), esp. 12–142. On "polarization" effects, see Hirschman, *Strategy of Economic Development*, 187–90.

29. Sitterson, "Business Leaders in Post–Civil War North Carolina," 114–18.

30. *Fayetteville Observer*, June 7, 1843; Robert Allison Ragan, "A Short Biographical Sketch of George Washington Ragan," with Caldwell Ragan interview transcript, folder H-285, Southern Oral History Program Collection.

31. On product cycle theory, see Raymond Vernon, "International Investment and International Trade in the Product Cycle," *Quarterly Journal of Economics* 80 (May 1966): 190–207; see also Louis T. Wells, Jr., *The Product Life Cycle and International Trade* (Boston, 1972), esp. 3–33.

32. Basic events in the history of Liddell and Company are documented in George Selden to Walter James Forbes Liddell, April 21, 1875, Walter James Forbes Liddell Papers, Southern Historical Collection; Erie City Iron Works to Walter James Forbes Liddell, June 15, 1875, ibid.; Articles of Co-Partnership, Liddell Engine Company, Dec. 20, 1878, ibid.; Articles of Incorporation, Liddell Company, Dec. 3, 1887, ibid.

33. Articles of Co-Partnership, Liddell Engine Company, Dec. 20, 1878, ibid.; Walter James Forbes Liddell to W. S. Liddell, April 5, 1879, June 16, July 26, 1881, Oct. 30, 1883, ibid.; Selden to

Walter James Forbes Liddell, June 5, 1886, ibid. Unfortunately, Liddell's side of the exchange with Selden is lacking. On the importance of personal service, close relations with customers, and cultivation of a spatially limited market to the success of certain small companies, see James H. Soltow, "Origins of Small Business and the Relationship between Large and Small Firms: Metal Fabricating and Machinery Making in New England, 1890–1957," in *Small Business in American Life,* ed. Stuart Bruchey (New York, 1988), 202–4.

34. Tilley, *Bright-Tobacco Industry,* 536–38, esp. 562. See also J. D. Cameron, *A Sketch of the Tobacco Interests of North Carolina* (Oxford, N.C., 1881), 16–20. Perhaps the greatest regional practitioners of this strategy have been the soft drink makers; a disproportionate number of the major brands have southern origins.

35. J. J. Fariss, *High Point* (High Point, N.C., 1903); North Carolina Bureau of Labor Statistics, *Sixteenth Annual Report, 1902,* 185–93; David Nolan Thomas, "Early History of the North Carolina Furniture Industry, 1880–1921" (Ph.D. diss., University of North Carolina, Chapel Hill, 1964), esp. 6–122. On the concept of the arbiter market and its application to High Point, see James E. Vance, Jr., *The Merchant's World: The Geography of Wholesaling* (Englewood Cliffs, N.J., 1970), 120, 132.

36. On the consequences of the limited southern demand for producers' goods for one heavy industry, see H. H. Chapman, [with the collaboration of W. M. Adamson, H. D. Bonham, H. D. Pallister, and E. C. Wright,] *The Iron and Steel Industries of the South* (University, Ala., 1953), 209–362; and Kenneth Warren, *The American Steel Industry, 1850–1970: A Geographical Interpretation* (Oxford, 1973), 184–85, 190–91, 277–81. Thomas, "Early History of the North Carolina Furniture Industry," 30; *Raleigh News and Observer,* Jan. 2, 1938, sec. M, 1–2.

37. Ragan, "Short Biographical Sketch of George Washington Ragan."

38. On lumbering on the coastal plain, see Howard A. Hanlon, *The Bull Hunchers: A Saga of the Three and a Half Centuries of Harvesting the Forest Crops of the Tidewater Low Country* (Parsons, W.Va., 1970), 225–31, 238–51, 260–62, 279–88, and map between 274 and 275. On Appalachia, see Ronald D. Eller, *Miners, Millhands, and Mountaineers: Industrialization of the Appalachian South, 1880–1930* (Knoxville, Tenn., 1982), 99–112. See also Thomas D. Clark, *The Greening of the South: The Recovery of Land and Forest* (Lexington, Ky., 1984), 14–35.

39 On branding, see Robert, *Tobacco Kingdom,* 218–21; and Tilley, *Bright-Tobacco Industry,* 522–28.

40. On W. T. Blackwell and Company and W. Duke, Sons, and Company, see Tilley, *Bright-Tobacco Industry,* 546–60; Mena Webb, *Jule Carr: General without an Army* (Chapel Hill, N.C., 1987), 30–39, 51–69, 73–80, 138–39; and Robert F. Durden, *The Dukes of Durham, 1865–1929* (Durham, N.C., 1975), 11–25. The emphasis on salesmanship was not limited to the great firms. James E. Scott, a small manufacturer in Hillsboro, devoted nearly half his time to drumming up trade, traveling throughout the eastern United States while his wife mailed circulars, samples, and premiums to prospective jobbers. See the correspondence between James E. Scott and his wife, Mary Belle Mebane Scott, 1886, Mebane Family Papers, Southern Historical Collection.

41. Tilley, *Bright-Tobacco Industry,* 549–50, 552–55; Webb, *Jule Carr,* 51–60; Durden, *Dukes of Durham,* 20–24; James Buchanan Duke to Benjamin Newton Duke, Sept. 29, 1889, James Buchanan Duke Papers, William R. Perkins Library, Duke University, Durham, N.C. "Buck" was commenting on a British offer to purchase the firm at a price based solely on net profit, which was depressed by advertising expenditures. When the offer came, "I promptly refused and laughed at [it]." Cameron, *Sketch of the Tobacco Interests of North Carolina,* 16–20, 52–58; Nannie M. Tilley, *The R. J. Reynolds Tobacco Company* (Chapel Hill, N.C., 1985), 41–46, 64–88.

42. Tilley, *Bright-Tobacco Industry,* 500–502, 568–80; Webb, *Jule Carr,* 63–64, 67–69, 76–78; Durden, *Dukes of Durham,* 26–55; Patrick G. Porter, "Origins of the American Tobacco Com-

pany," *Business History Review* 53 (spring 1969): 59–76. Chandler stresses the role of the high "throughput" resulting from mechanized manufacture in pressing Duke to create his marketing organization. It is arguable, however, that causation was circular, with an expanding market organization demanding higher volumes of cigarettes. Chandler, *Visible Hand,* 241, 249–50, 290–92, 382–91; see also Durden, *Dukes of Durham,* 19–25.

43. Porter, "Origins of the American Tobacco Company," 74–76; Malcolm R. Burns, "Economies of Scale in Tobacco Manufacture, 1897–1910," *Journal of Economic History* 43 (June 1983): 461–74; Tilley, *R. J. Reynolds Tobacco Company,* 64–121; Tilley, *Bright-Tobacco Industry,* 595–607. On High Point's pre-furniture "tobacco strategy," see Fariss, *High Point.*

44. William B. Taylor of Winston-Salem, one of the last small-scale manufacturers, applauded James Buchanan Duke: "You have done more for the tobacco growers of Virginia and North Carolina than anyone else by creating a market for their tobaccos in every part of the world." W. B. Taylor to James Buchanan Duke, Aug. 23, 1922, Duke Papers.

45. Tilley, *Bright-Tobacco Industry,* 632–41; Webb, *Jule Carr,* 80–82, 140, 175–90; Durden, *Dukes of Durham,* 122–51, 177–260. Dale Whittington, "Microelectronics Policy in North Carolina: An Introduction," in *High Hopes for High Tech: Microelectronics Policy in North Carolina,* ed. Dale Whittington (Chapel Hill, N.C., 1985), 5.

46. On the loose-leaf auction system of marketing tobacco, see Tilley, *Bright-Tobacco Industry,* 206–12; on the role of the trust in consolidating production, see Burns, "Economies of Scale in Tobacco Manufacture"; and Tilley, *R. J. Reynolds Tobacco Company,* 104–22.

47. U.S. Department of the Interior, Census Office, *Census Reports,* vol. 8: *Twelfth Census of the United States, Taken in the Year 1900: Manufactures, Part 2: States and Territories* (Washington, D.C., 1902), 666–69; North Carolina Bureau of Labor Statistics, *Twelfth Annual Report, 1898,* 34–40, 189–98. The state bureau counted 173 chewing and smoking tobacco factories; the United States census, the following year, only 80. The difference may be partly due to differing definitions of "manufacturing establishments" (the United States census excluded operations producing less than $500 value); more likely the state's listing was outdated.

48. Questionnaires for report on internal commerce, 1886, box 9, folders 150–53, Calvin H. Wiley Papers, Southern Historical Collection.

49. John S. Hekman, "The Product Cycle and New England Textiles," *Quarterly Journal of Economics* 94 (June 1980): 697–717; Irwin Feller, "The Diffusion and Location of Technological Change in the American Cotton Textile Industry, 1890–1920," *Technology and Culture* 15 (Oct. 1974): 569–93; Melvin T. Copeland, *The Cotton Manufacturing Industry of the United States* (Cambridge, Mass., 1917), 193–219; Reavis Cox, *The Marketing of Textiles* (Washington, 1938).

50. Beatty, "Lowells of the South," 37–63; Woodlawn Mills Day Book, 1874–1875, William R. Perkins Library; questionnaire responses of F. & H. Fries, Thomas H. Gaither, Gwyn and Chatham, John R. Hall, E. J. Lilly, J. Turner Morehead and Company, Charlotte Cotton Mills, Wilmington Cotton Mills, Newton Cotton Mills, Randleman Manufacturing Co., Thomas C. Worth, Franklinville Manufacturing Company, McAden Cotton Mill, Pee Dee Manufacturing Company, Wilson's Cotton Mill, and Thomas H. Holt, in questionnaires for report on internal commerce, 1886, box 9, folders 150–53, Wiley Papers; Alamance Cotton Factory Shipment Book, 1892–1897, Alamance Cotton Mill Records, Southern Historical Collection; Pierpont, "Development of the Textile Industry in Alamance County," 67–71, 97–98, 103–4. By the 1920s the Holts' decline was absolute; Pierpont, "Development of the Textile Industry in Alamance County," 170–220, 278–79.

51. Given the widespread lack of returns for the first years covered in table 6.3, this evidence should be used with caution. Some mills that failed to report an agent had one, according to other evidence.

52. On Worth Street, see Cox, *Marketing of Textiles,* 309–11; and Frank L. Walton, *Tomahawks to Textiles: The Fabulous Story of Worth Street* (New York, 1953), esp. 101–8. Copeland, *Cotton Manufacturing Industry of the United States,* 200–201; on the entrepreneurial culture of Philadelphia textiles, see Philip Scranton, *Proprietary Capitalism: The Textile Manufacture at Philadelphia, 1800–1885* (New York, 1983). Yarn consumption figures appear in U.S. Department of the Interior, Census Office, *Census Reports,* vol. 9: *Twelfth Census of the United States, Taken in the Year 1900: Manufactures, Part 3: Special Reports on Selected Industries* (Washington, D.C., 1902), 64. For examples of commission house solicitations, see Buckingham and Paulson to Mark Morgan, April 2, 1880; Budd and Fuller to Morgan, Aug. 2, 1889; Horace Maxwell to Morgan, Sept. 7, 1889; William E. Hooper and Sons to Morgan, Jan. 27, 1890; H. E. Smith and Company to Morgan, Feb. 12, 1890, all in Malloy-Morgan Cotton Mill Papers, William R. Perkins Library. On aggressive promotion by one house, see H. F. Schenck to J. E. Reynolds and Company, Nov. 2, 9, 1899, H. F. Schenck Letterbooks, William R. Perkins Library.

53. Samuel A. Ashe, *Biographical History of North Carolina,* 8 vols. (Greensboro, N.C., 1905), 3:282–92. See also John Herbert Roper, "Mark Morgan: Personalist Capitalism in a 'Backward' Land" (paper delivered at the meeting of the Southern Regional Science Association, Atlanta, Ga., March 27, 1987), in David L. Carlton's possession.

54. Factory in account with Store, 1881–1884, Malloy-Morgan Cotton Mill Papers; Leonidas L. Polk (the later Populist leader) to Morgan, Feb. 17, 1875, ibid.; Solomon Bear and Bros., Wilmington, to Richmond Cotton Mill, March 17, 1875, ibid.; Thomas S. Memory, Whiteville, to mill, April 1, 1876, ibid.; G. Boney and Sons, Wilmington, to Malloy and Morgan, July 12, 1876, ibid. For complaints, see Claghorn, Herring and Company to Charles Malloy, Aug. 26, 1875, May 31, 1877, March 21, 1879, ibid.; and Buckingham and Paulson to Morgan, July 26, Aug. 5, 27, 1889, Jan. 30, 1891, ibid. For advice, see, for instance, Claghorn, Herring and Company to Malloy, Aug. 26, 1875, ibid.; Joseph H. Coates and Company to Morgan, Sept. 14, 1889, ibid.; Buckingham and Paulson to Morgan, Jan. 3, Feb. 19, 1890, ibid.; Taylor and Longstreth to Morgan, July 5, 1892, Feb. 20, July 14, 1893, ibid.; Eddy and Street to Morgan, Dec. 4, 1901, ibid.; O. H. Sampson and Company to Morgan, Dec. 17, 1894, ibid.; and Charles J. Webb and Company to Morgan, May 18, 21, 1895, ibid.

55. W. A. Erwin to B. N. Duke, May 12, 1892, Benjamin Newton Duke Correspondence, William R. Perkins Library.

56. Pierpont, "Development of the Textile Industry in Alamance County," 97–99, 106–9; Cone Export and Commission Company, *Half Century Book* (n.p., 1941); *Davison's Textile Blue Book, 1894–1895,* 91–99; Agreement between Williamson and Foster, Raleigh, and Cone Export and Commission Company, Sept. 30, 1892, in Moses H. Cone to William H. Williamson, Sept. 30, 1892, Pilot Cotton Mills Correspondence, William R. Perkins Library.

57. Copeland, *Cotton Manufacturing Industry of the United States,* 206; Cone Export and Commission Company, *Half Century Book; Davison's Textile Blue Book, 1894–1895,* 91–99; *1900–1901,* 111–30; *1905–1906,* 126–50.

58. J. H. Erwin to Joshua L. Baily and Company, Feb. 21, March 24, April 4, 1910, Durham Cotton Manufacturing Company Letterpress Book, 1910, Durham Cotton Manufacturing Company Records, William R. Perkins Library. On the importance of selling houses to the "fancy goods" trade, see Copeland, *Cotton Manufacturing Industry of the United States,* 212–13. W. A. Erwin to F. L. Sheldon and Sons, March 3, 1909, Erwin Cotton Mills Company Letterbook, 1908–1909, Kemp P. Lewis Papers, Southern Historical Collection; Woodward, Baldwin and Company to F. W. Poe, June 15, Aug. 2, 8, 1895, and Lockwood, Greene and Company to Poe, Aug. 12, 14, 1895, Francis W. Poe Papers, South Caroliniana Library, University of South Carolina, Columbia.

59. Caldwell Ragan interview by Robert Allison Ragan, p. 31, folder H-285, Southern Oral History Program Collection; Caldwell Ragan interview by Brent Glass, Nov. 15, 1975, transcript, p. 50, folder H-284, ibid.; James Lewis Moore and Thomas Herron Wingate, *Cabarrus Reborn* (Kan-

napolis, N.C., 1940), 68–71, 81; Walton, *Tomahawks to Textiles*, 135–36; *Davison's Textile Blue Book, 1905–1906;* Archibald M. McIsaac, "The Cotton Textile Industry," in *The Structure of American Industry: Some Case Studies*, ed. Walter L. Adams (New York, 1950), 6–7.

60. On labor skill development, see Wright, *Old South, New South*, 78–80, 124–25, 131–33; and Marvin Nelson Fischbaum, "An Economic Analysis of the Southern Capture of the Cotton Textile Industry Progressing to 1910" (Ph.D. diss., Columbia University, 1965), esp. 89–133. On technology, see Feller, "Diffusion and Location of Technological Change in the American Cotton-Textile Industry," 569–93, esp. 588–93. By 1980 an estimated 45 percent of the textile machinery purchased in the United States (mostly in the South) was imported; much of the remainder consisted of spare parts for older American-made equipment. Brian Toyne et al., *The U.S. Textile Mill Products Industry: Strategies for the 1980s and Beyond* (Columbia, S.C., 1983), chap. 3, 22–26.

61. On postwar industrial development programs, see James C. Cobb, *The Selling of the South: The Southern Crusade for Industrial Development, 1936–1980* (Baton Rouge, 1982). On decentralization in North Carolina's development policies, see Wood, *Southern Capitalism*, 163–64. For a critique of those policies, see Brad Stuart, *Making North Carolina Prosper: A Critique of Balanced Growth and Regional Planning* (Raleigh, N.C., 1979); and, from a more explicitly Marxist stance, Joe Persky, "Regional Colonialism and the Southern Economy," *Review of Radical Political Economics* 4 (fall 1972): 70–79.

62. John D. Hekman and Rosalind Greenstein, "Factors Affecting Manufacturing Location in North Carolina and the South Atlantic," in Whittington, *High Hopes for High Tech*, 147–72; Emil E. Malizia, "The Locational Attractiveness of the Southeast to High Technology Manufacturers," ibid., 173–90; Harvey Goldstein and Emil E. Malizia, "Microelectronics and Economic Development in North Carolina," ibid., 225–55; Gregory B. Sampson, "Employment and Earnings in the Semiconductor Electronics Industry: Implications for North Carolina," ibid., 256–95. See also Cobb, "Beyond Planters and Industrialists," 66–68. Edward Atkinson, *Cotton, Articles from the New York Herald* (Boston, 1877), 30, quoted in Fischbaum, "Economic Analysis of the Southern Capture of the Cotton Textile Industry," 204. Atkinson arguably anticipates the critique of the Tennessee Valley Authority and modern economic development policy in Jane Jacobs, *Cities and the Wealth of Nations: Principles of Economic Life* (New York, 1984).

63. Gavin Wright, "Rethinking the Postbellum Southern Political Economy: A Review Essay," *Business History Review* 58 (autumn 1984): 409–16, esp. 415; Karl Marx, *The Eighteenth Brumaire of Louis Bonaparte* (New York, 1963), 15.

64. Albert W. Niemi, Jr., *State and Regional Patterns in American Manufacturing, 1860–1900* (Westport, Conn., 1974), 7, 117, 123; for method, 18.

65. Computed from estimates in E. S. Lee et al., *Population Redistribution and Economic Growth: United States, 1870–1950* (Philadelphia, 1957), 753.

66. *Ibid.*, 753; Niemi, *State and Regional Patterns in American Manufacturing*, 29–67.

67. Regional income estimates come from Richard A. Easterlin, "Regional Income Trends, 1840–1950," in *American Economic History*, ed. Seymour Harris (New York, 1961), 535.

68. Computed from Lee et al., *Population Redistribution and Economic Growth*, 753.

69. Niemi, *State and Regional Patterns in American Manufacturing*, 18.

7. Capital Mobilization and Southern Industry, 1880–1905

"Capital Mobilization and Southern Industry, 1880–1905: The Case of the Carolina Piedmont" first appeared in *Journal of Economic History* 49 (March 1989): 73–94, and is reprinted with permission of the publisher, Cambridge University Press.

Earlier versions of this article were delivered at the annual meeting of the Organization of American Historians, Philadelphia, April 4, 1987, and at the Triangle Economic History Workshop, National Humanities Center, May 6, 1987. The authors wish to thank the OAH commentators, Cathy McHugh and Randall Miller, and members of the audience, particularly Donald Winters and Kenneth Lipartito, for their valuable comments. We wish also to thank members of the Workshop, especially Robert Gallman, Richard Sylla, and Tom Kemp, for their advice. Both the editors and the anonymous referees for the *Journal of Economic History* raised important objections to certain points, which we hope to have clarified. Finally, Robert Korstad supplied valuable suggestions.

1. A recent restatement of this point appears in James C. Cobb, *Industrialization and Southern Society, 1877–1984* (Lexington, Ky., 1985).

2. Different characterizations of this are presented by Fred Bateman and Thomas Weiss, *A Deplorable Scarcity: The Failure of Industrialization in the Slave Economy* (Chapel Hill, N.C., 1981); Gavin Wright, *The Political Economy of the Cotton South: Households, Markets and Wealth in the Nineteenth Century* (New York, 1978), 107–20; and Heywood Fleisig, "Slavery, the Supply of Agricultural Labor, and the Industrialization of the South," *Journal of Economic History* 36 (Sept. 1976): 572–95. It could be argued that the aversion to risk discussed is a continuation of that found by Bateman and Weiss among antebellum planters. There are important differences between our argument and theirs, however. A key difference is that their argument is embedded in the context of the antebellum slave regime; manufacturing was stifled by the relative safety of large-scale slave agriculture and (more speculatively) by the alleged low social status of industrialists in a planter-dominated society. That context, of course, vanished in the 1860s. On this latter point see Bateman and Weiss, *Deplorable Scarcity*, 133–42, 160–63.

3. David L. Carlton, *Mill and Town in South Carolina, 1880–1920* (Baton Rouge, 1982), chaps. 1 and 2; and Gavin Wright, *Old South, New South: Revolutions in the Southern Economy since the Civil War* (New York, 1986), 43–47. For a counterexample from an "underdeveloped" subregion, see Peter A. Coclanis, *The Shadow of a Dream: Economic Life and Death in the South Carolina Low Country, 1670–1920* (New York, 1988), chap. 4.

4. Wright, *Old South, New South*, 60–64; for state-level figures on manufacturing growth, see Everett S. Lee et al., *Population Redistribution and Economic Growth: United States, 1870–1950*, 2 vols. (Philadelphia, 1957), 1:685, 694–95, 697; Donald and Wynelle Dodd, *Historical Statistics of the South* (University, Ala., 1973), 66–73; and U.S. Department of Commerce, Bureau of the Census, *Historical Statistics of the United States, Colonial Times to 1970*, 2 vols. (Washington, 1975), 2:669.

5. Wright, *Old South, New South*.

6. Thomas R. Navin and Marian V. Sears, "The Rise of a Market for Industrial Securities, 1887–1902," *Business History Review* 29 (June 1955): 105–38, esp. 107.

7. On the insurance industry, see Morton Keller, *The Life Insurance Enterprise, 1885–1910: A Study in the Limits of Corporate Power* (Cambridge, Mass., 1963), 131; and B. Michael Pritchett, *Financing Growth: A Financial History of American Life Insurance through 1900* (Philadelphia, 1985), 41–45.

8. Navin and Sears, "Market for Industrial Securities"; Lance E. Davis, "Capital Immobilities and Finance Capitalism: A Study of Economic Evolution in the United States, 1820–1920," *Explorations in Entrepreneurial History*, 2d ser., 1 (fall 1963): 88–105; Lance E. Davis, "The Investment Market, 1870–1914: The Evolution of a National Market," *Journal of Economic History* 25 (Sept. 1965): 355–99; Joseph G. Martin, *A Century of Finance: Martin's History of the Boston Stock and Money Markets, One Hundred Years, from January, 1798, to January, 1898, Comprising the Annual Fluctuations of All Public Stocks and Investment Securities* (Boston, 1898), 125–43; George D. Green,

"Financial Intermediaries," in *Encyclopedia of American Economic History,* 3 vols., ed. Glenn D. Porter (New York, 1980), 2:707–26; and W. Elliot Brownlee, *Dynamics of Ascent: A History of the American Economy* (New York, 1974), 192–95.

9. For finance of manufacturing enterprise through personal savings, see, for example, James H. Soltow, *Origins of Small Business: Metal Fabricators and Machinery Makers in New England, 1890–1957,* (Philadelphia, 1965), 21–23. On the importance of networks in small business finance, see Mansel G. Blackford, "Small Business in America: Two Case Studies," in "Papers Presented at the Twenty-Fifth Annual Meeting of the Business History Conference, 2–3 March 1979," ed. Paul Uselding, *Business and Economic History,* 2d ser., 8 (Urbana, Ill., 1979): 13.

10. Roger L. Ransom and Richard Sutch, *One Kind of Freedom: The Economic Consequences of Emancipation* (New York, 1977), esp. chaps. 1 and 3; Richard A. Easterlin, "Regional Income Trends, 1840–1950," in *American Economic History,* ed. Seymour E. Harris (New York, 1961), 525–47; and Stanley L. Engerman, "Some Economic Factors in Southern Backwardness in the Nineteenth Century," in *Essays in Regional Economics,* ed. John F. Kain and John R. Meyer (Cambridge, Mass., 1971), 279–306. On the problems resulting from the loss of slave wealth, see Gerald D. Jaynes, *Branches without Roots: Genesis of the Black Working Class in the American South, 1862–1882* (New York, 1986), 29–31.

11. On bank deposits, see John A. James, "Financial Underdevelopment in the Postbellum South," *Journal of Interdisciplinary History* 11 (winter 1981): 443–54, esp. 443; on insurance premiums, see Pritchett, *Financing Growth,* 63.

12. On the prominence of migrants, frequently with outside connections, in midwestern manufacturing, see Donald L. Kemmerer, "Financing Illinois Industry, 1830–1890," *Bulletin of the Business Historical Society* 26 (June 1953): 97–111.

13. On the lower market density of the antebellum South, see William N. Parker, "Slavery and Southern Economic Development: An Hypothesis and Some Evidence," *Agricultural History* 44 (Jan. 1970), 115–26; on the resulting low commercial density, see Lewis E. Atherton, *The Southern Country Store, 1800–1860* (Baton Rouge, 1949), 39–42.

14. Davis, "The Investment Market," 388–92; Pritchett, *Financing Growth,* 41–45; and James, "Financial Underdevelopment."

15. On Piedmont entrepreneurs, see Carlton, *Mill and Town,* 43; and Paul D. Escott, *Many Excellent People: Power and Privilege in North Carolina, 1850–1900* (Chapel Hill, N.C., 1985), 217–19. Current research by David L. Carlton on North Carolina entrepreneurs suggests that local machinery makers may be an exception to the rule of native origins. Machine shop owners such as W. J. F. Liddell of Charlotte and O. C. Wysong of Greensboro were northerners who applied skills acquired elsewhere to southern needs. See W. J. F. Liddell Papers, Southern Historical Collection, University of North Carolina, Chapel Hill; on Wysong, see David Nolan Thomas, "Early History of the North Carolina Furniture Industry, 1880–1921" (Ph.D. diss., University of North Carolina, Chapel Hill, 1964), 30–31, 248.

16. U.S. Census Office, *Twelfth Census of the United States, 1900: Manufactures,* pt. 1, 58; hereafter cited as *Census of Manufactures.* "South" is defined here as the states of the Confederacy plus Kentucky; other regions are defined by the usual census groupings, with Maryland and Delaware included in the mid-Atlantic region.

17. *Census of Manufactures,* pt. 1, 58, 224; pt. 3, 54.

18. Stephen J. Goldfarb, "Laws Governing the Incorporation of Manufacturing Companies Passed by Southern State Legislatures before the Civil War," *Southern Studies* 24 (winter 1985), 407–16; and *South Carolina Statutes at Large,* vol. 19 (1886), 540–50. David L. Carlton has examined several hundred corporate charters of manufacturing firms in North Carolina for the years up to 1905; virtually all include limited liability.

19. *Census of Manufactures,* pt. 1, 503. The proportion of manufacturing firms incorporated

was remarkably consistent among most states; the major exceptions were the Rocky Mountain and Pacific states, where the proportion incorporated reached 12 percent.

20. *Census of Manufactures,* pt. 3, 60; on the structure of the Philadelphia textile industry, see Philip Scranton, *Proprietary Capitalism: The Textile Manufacture at Philadelphia, 1800–1885* (New York, 1983).

21. *Census of Manufactures,* pt. 1, 222. The cotton goods and furniture industries are used because they helped lead industrial development in the Carolina Piedmont and were important enough in other regions to permit reasonable comparison. A third important Piedmont industry, tobacco, will be dealt with later.

22. Complaints about the lamentable state of scholarship on small business are recurrent; a recent example is Blackford, "Small Business in America: Two Case Studies," 9.

23. Mansel G. Blackford, *A Portrait Cast in Steel: Buckeye International and Columbus, Ohio, 1881–1980* (Westport, Conn., 1982), 3–45. For another example, that of a Minnesota paper firm, see Donald L. Boese, *Papermakers: The Blandin Paper Company and Grand Rapids, Minnesota* (Grand Rapids, Minn., 1984), 42–43, 73–74. The firm began as the Itasca Paper Company in 1901 with $200,000 in stock issued. Over half its stock was taken by a local banker, with two other men dividing the bulk of the remainder. Scarcely any individual in the Piedmont could command such resources.

24. Lance E. Davis, "Stock Ownership in the Early New England Textile Industry," *Business History Review* 32 (summer 1958): 219, tables 1 and 2. There appear to be some discrepancies in the tables, but the estimate given in the text seems roughly accurate. See also Kenneth Frank Mailloux, "The Boston Manufacturing Company of Waltham, Massachusetts, 1813–1848: The First Modern Factory in America" (Ph.D. diss., Boston University, 1957), 52–53; Robert F. Dalzell, Jr., *Enterprising Elite: The Boston Associates and the World They Made* (Cambridge, Mass., 1987), 26–30.

25. Dalzell, *Enterprising Elite,* appendix; John S. Ewing and Nancy P. Norton, *Broadlooms and Businessmen: A History of the Bigelow-Sanford Carpet Company* (Cambridge, Mass., 1955), 710; John William Lozier, *Taunton and Mason: Cotton Machinery and Locomotive Manufacture in Taunton, Massachusetts, 1811–1861* (New York, 1986), 7–10, 94–108; the quote is on p. 10.

26. Gaston County Clerk of Superior Court, Record of Corporations, vol. 1, 74–76, 81 (microfilm in North Carolina Department of Archives, Raleigh); Trenton Cotton Mills, Stockholders' Minute Book, 1893–1903 (microfilm in North Carolina Department of Archives, Raleigh); Caldwell Ragan interview, Nov. 15, 1975, Southern Oral History Program, H-284, 17–18 (transcript in Southern Historical Collection, University of North Carolina, Chapel Hill. Thanks to Robert Korstad for calling our attention to this). See also the material collected in Robert Allison Ragan, comp., *The Pioneer Cotton Mills of Gaston County, N.C. "The First Thirty" and Gaston County Textile Pioneers* (Charlotte, N.C., 1973).

27. The Spartan Mills stock list is reproduced in Allen H. Stokes, Jr., "John H. Montgomery: A Pioneer Southern Industrialist" (master's thesis, University of South Carolina, 1967), 138–43; the description of Buckeye's stockholders appears in Blackford, *Portrait,* 13.

28. Mooresville Cotton Mills, Stock Ledger A, List of January 1, 1896, William R. Perkins Library, Manuscripts Division, Duke University; Piedmont Manufacturing Company, List of Subscribers, Oct. 3, 1874, typescript in South Caroliniana Library, University of South Carolina, Columbia; Lawrence B. Graves, Jr., "The Beginning of the Cotton Textile Industry in Newberry County" (master's thesis, University of South Carolina, 1947), 78–79; and Cleveland County Clerk of Superior Court, Record of Corporations, vol. 1, 101–3 (microfilm), North Carolina Department of Archives. The Piedmont transcription is incomplete. Ten shares are missing from each of two pages, and fifty from a third; the tally of shareholders falls six short of the official total. The above

figures were calculated assuming that the missing shares on each page were held by a single shareholder, an assumption that overstates the concentration of ownership.

Our definition of "small investor," one whose investment totals $2,500 or less, is intentionally conservative. One could, for instance, use holdings of from $1,000 to $5,000. Alternative estimates using different assumptions are presented for six mills in table 7.3. As one can see, under any of these assumptions the role of the small investor is prominent.

29. Data from Gaston County Clerk of Superior Court, Record of Incorporations, vol. 1 (microfilm), North Carolina Department of Archives. Two firms were excluded, as they were reorganizations of mills in operation before 1880; both were closely held. It should be noted that shareholders' data derived from North Carolina corporate charter records are not nearly as complete or reliable as the shareholders' lists of the corporations themselves. They are offered here for illustrative purposes.

30. Graves, "Newberry County," 78–79; Iredell County Clerk of Superior Court, Record of Incorporations, vol. 2, 28–30 (microfilm), North Carolina Department of Archives; Mooresville Stock Ledger A; and Stock List of the Pacolet Manufacturing Company, Dec. 31, 1895, in Frank E. Taylor Papers, South Caroliniana Library, University of South Carolina, Columbia.

31. By contrast, the median subscribed capital of the twenty-one Gaston County cotton mills mentioned earlier was $25,000. Gaston County mills were, it should be added, abnormally small.

32. Davidson County Clerk of Superior Court, Record of Corporations, vol. 1; and Guilford County Clerk of Superior Court, Record of Incorporations, vols. A, B, and C (all microfilm), North Carolina Department of Archives.

33. Thomas R. Navin, *The Whitin Machine Works since 1831* (Cambridge, Mass., 1950), 227–35; George Sweet Gibb, *The Saco-Lowell Shops: Textile Machinery Building in New England, 1813–1949* (Cambridge, Mass., 1950), 246–49, 272–73, 351–55, 398, 416–19, and appendix 12. Gibb assigns greater importance to the practice than does Navin. In 1896 builders of preparatory machinery concluded an agreement pledging, among other things, not to accept stock in payment for machinery. While the agreement soon broke down because of the need to compete for southern business, it clearly indicates the resistance of machine men to the practice. See Navin, *The Whitin Machine Works,* 246. This is, of course, a special case of the immobility problems of manufacturing capital discussed earlier.

34. Broadus Mitchell, *The Rise of Cotton Mills in the South* (Baltimore, 1921), 237–55; Carlton, *Mill and Town,* 56–59. The quote of South Carolina's H. P. Hammett is from the Anderson, S.C., *Intelligencer,* May 5, 1887.

35. Mitchell, *The Rise of Cotton Mills.*

36. See Carlton, *Mill and Town,* esp. chap. 2.

37. Wright, *Old South, New South,* 87–89; and Harold D. Woodman, *King Cotton and His Retainers: Financing and Marketing the Cotton Crop of the South, 1800–1925* (Lexington, Ky., 1968), 312–14, 348–57.

38. On the traditional reliance of manufacturing firms, especially in textiles, on equity, see Arthur S. Dewing, *The Financial Policy of Corporations,* 2 vols. (New York, 1921), 2:56–60. On the consequences often resulting from resort to leveraged finance, see Arthur S. Dewing, *Corporate Promotions and Reorganizations* (Cambridge, Mass., 1914), 308–9, 340; and Fenelon DeVere Smith, "The Economic Development of the Textile Industry in the Columbia, S.C. Area from 1790 through 1916" (Ph.D. diss., University of Kentucky, 1952), 202–7.

39. Jerome Campbell, "Dave Hall: The ACMI's New President," *Modern Textiles Magazine* (March 1961): 51–52. For more on the Chronicle Mills of Belmont, see Ragan, *Pioneer Cotton Mills.* It should be noted that Hall's father, while described as "maintain[ing] his family . . . with a fair degree of plain, back-country comfort," was able to save enough not only to invest in Chronicle

but also to place another $5,000 in a later mill. Gaston County Clerk of Superior Court, Record of Incorporations, vol. 1, 277–79.

40. On the importance of mill stocks to Charlestonians, see the Langdon Cheves II Papers, South Carolina Historical Society, Charleston. Cheves, an attorney, served as trustee for several relatives. The William Watts Ball Papers, Duke University, contain considerable correspondence concerning mill investments of Ball and his wife. Women represented nearly one-third of Pacolet's stock list (44 of 138), but their median holding was only 15.5; two-thirds held 20 shares or fewer, and they collectively held only one-sixth (942.5, or 16.8 percent) of the shares. Pacolet Manufacturing Company Stock List, Frank E. Taylor Papers, South Caroliniana Library, University of South Carolina, Columbia.

41. Thomas R. Waring to William Watts Ball, March 8, 1912; Lewis W. Parker to Ball, March 11, 1912, both in William Watts Ball Papers, Duke University.

42. LeGette Blythe, *Robert Lee Stowe: Pioneer in Textiles* (Belmont, N.C., 1965), 133; Trenton Stockholders Minute Book; Gaston County Clerk of Superior Court, Record of Incorporations, vol. 1, 277–79. Simon Kuznets, Introduction to Daniel Creamer et al., *Capital in Manufacturing and Mining: Its Formation and Financing* (Princeton, N.J., 1960), xliii–l, notes the primary importance of internal financing to manufacturing growth at the turn of the century.

43. Melvin T. Copeland, *The Cotton Manufacturing Industry of the United States* (Cambridge, Mass., 1912), 143–44; spindleage distributions compiled from *Davison's Textile Blue Book, 1905–1906*. On optimal plant size, see also Mary Josephine Oates, "The Role of the Cotton Textile Industry in the Economic Development of the American Southeast: 1900–1940" (Ph.D. diss., Yale University, 1969), 60–65.

44. Wright, *Old South, New South,* 147–55.

45. Paul F. McGouldrick, *New England Textiles in the Nineteenth Century: Profits and Investment* (Cambridge, Mass., 1968), chap. 5. See also Robert F. Dalzell, Jr., "The Rise of the Waltham-Lowell System and Some Thoughts on the Political Economy of Modernization in Ante-Bellum Massachusetts," *Perspectives in American History* 9 (1975): 229–68.

46. McGouldrick, *New England Textiles,* chap. 7, 135–38.

47. Unlike the New England industry, the southern cotton textile industry scored its first major advances after the American textile machinery industry had reached its maturity, and at a time when the pace of innovation had noticeably slackened. Thus T. Y. Shen's estimates of machine investment/output ratios for selected years from 1840 to 1940 show sharp declines to 1880, with stabilization through World War I. T. Y. Shen, "Job Analysis and Historical Productivities in the American Cotton Textile Industry: A Study in Methodology," *Review of Economics and Statistics* 40 (May 1958): 151. Irwin Feller has noted that the automatic loom was the only major innovation between the 1890s and the 1930s. Irwin Feller, "The Diffusion and Location of Technological Change in the American Cotton Textile Industry, 1890–1970," *Technology and Culture* 15 (Oct. 1974): 569–93.

48. The clearest discussion of this point is in Albert W. Niemi, Jr., "Structural Shifts in Southern Manufacturing, 1849–1899," *Business History Review* 45 (spring 1971): 79–84.

49. See John S. Hekman, "The Product Cycle and New England Textiles," *Quarterly Journal of Economics* 94 (June 1980): 697–717. The classic discussion of "the product cycle" is Raymond Vernon, "International Investment and International Trade in the Product Cycle," *Quarterly Journal of Economics* 80 (May 1966): 190–207. On southern dependence on outside technology, see Feller, "Diffusion"; and Bess Beatty, "Lowells of the South: Northern Influences on the Nineteenth-Century North Carolina Textile Industry," *Journal of Southern History* 53 (Feb. 1987): 37–62.

50. Mena Webb, *Jule Carr: General without an Army* (Chapel Hill, N.C., 1986), 30–85; and Nannie May Tilley, *The Bright-Tobacco Industry, 1860–1929* (Chapel Hill, N.C., 1948), 500–502, 577–79.

51. Robert F. Durden, *The Dukes of Durham, 1865–1929* (Durham, N.C., 1975); Navin and Sears,

"Market for Industrial Securities," 116–19; and Alfred D. Chandler, Jr., *The Visible Hand: The Managerial Revolution in American Business* (Cambridge, Mass., 1977), 290–92, 381–91.

52. Durden, *Dukes of Durham*, 177–98; and Thomas P. Hughes, *Networks of Power: Electrification in Western Society, 1880–1930* (Baltimore, 1983), 265.

53. Thomas C. Cochran, *Frontiers of Change: Early Industrialism in America* (New York, 1981); Diane Lindstrom, *Economic Development in the Philadelphia Region, 1810–1850* (New York, 1978); and William N. Parker, "Native Origins of Modern Industry: Heavy Industrialization in the Old Northwest before 1900" in *Essays on the Economy of the Old Northwest*, ed. David C. Klingaman and Richard K. Vedder (Athens, Ohio, 1987), 243–74. Compare the discussion in Oates, "Role of the Cotton Textile Industry." Numerous counterparts to the Piedmont tobacco magnates emerged at this time in the manufacturing belt; the most obvious examples include Swift and Armour in meat packing, McCormick and Deering in farm machinery, Carnegie in steel, and Rockefeller in oil. See Chandler, *Visible Hand*, pts. 3 and 4.

54. To trace the development of mill securities listings, see the Charleston *News and Courier*, Feb. 3, 1883; Nov. 28, 1885; July 23, 1887; Oct. 7, 1890; Feb. 27, 1891; March 3, 1895; and Jan. 26, 1900. Mill quotations first put in an appearance in the Charlotte *Observer* on June 7, 1900; their source was identified as Hugh MacRae and Company of Wilmington, a leading banking firm.

55. See Hugh MacRae and Company, Bankers, "Data on Important Southern Cotton Mill Stocks, March 1903," broadside in Hugh MacRae Papers, Duke University; and *Security Dealers of North America* (New York, 1927), 68–69, 421–23, 499–501.

56. "Questions Often Asked Us and the Answers," *The Solicitor: A Magazine of Banking* [Wachovia Bank and Trust Company] 9 (March 1917): 7–8; "Report from Bond Department," *The Solicitor* 10 (Sept. 1918): 14–15.

57. *Security Dealers of North America*, 68–69, 421–23, 499–501; "Looking for Investments," *The Solicitor* 10 (Jan. 1918): 10; advertisement, "We Are Prepared to Buy and Sell," *The Solicitor* 12 (Dec. 1919): inside back cover.

58. Albert O. Hirschman, *The Strategy of Economic Development* (New Haven, 1958), 158.

59. U.S. Department of Commerce, *Survey of Current Business* (April 1987), table 2, 34, reports per capita income for North and South Carolina in 1986 at 84.6 and 76.7 percent, respectively, of the U.S. figure, a plateau both states reached in the mid-1970s. U.S. Department of Labor, *Employment and Earnings* (April 1988) reports average hourly earnings for manufacturing production workers in the two states at 83.8 and 85.7 percent respectively of national levels. The four major standard metropolitan statistical areas of the Piedmont all report wage levels beneath the national average, particularly in the southern Piedmont (Charlotte–Gastonia–Rock Hill [86.3] and Greenville-Spartanburg [84.9]), although the more northerly areas (Greensboro–High Point–Winston-Salem [93.3] and Raleigh-Durham [94.9]) approach the national average.

60. See Alice Galenson, *The Migration of the Cotton Textile Industry from New England to the South, 1880–1930* (New York, 1985).

8. The Uninventive South?

"The Uninventive South? A Quantitative Look at Region and American Inventiveness" originally appeared in *Technology and Culture* 36 (April 1995): 220–44, and is reprinted here with permission of Johns Hopkins University Press.

The authors would like to thank Stanley Engerman, Robert Gallman, Robert Higgs, Robert Margo, Paul Rhode, Donald Winters, the panelists and audience attending their session at the Organization of American Historians meeting in Chicago, April 3, 1992, Philip Scranton, and the referees for *Technology and Culture*, for their suggestions.

1. See the collected essays in Naomi R. Lamoreaux, Daniel M. G. Raff, and Peter Temin, eds., *Learning by Doing in Markets, Firms, and Countries,* a National Bureau of Economic Research Conference Report (Chicago, 1999). On the relationship of Lamoreaux and Sokoloff's "markets for inventions" to region, see Naomi R. Lamoreaux and Kenneth L. Sokoloff, "Market Trade in Patents and the Rise of a Class of Specialized Inventors in the Nineteenth-Century United States," *American Economic Review* 91 (May 2001): 39–44.

2. See, e.g., Gavin Wright, *Old South, New South: Revolutions in the Southern Economy since the Civil War* (New York, 1986); Warren C. Whatley, "Southern Agrarian Labor Contracts as Impediments to Cotton Mechanization," *Journal of Economic History* 47 (March 1987): 45–70; Bruce J. Schulman, *From Cotton Belt to Sunbelt: Federal Policy, Economic Development, and the Transformation of the South, 1938–1980* (New York, 1991); James C. Cobb, *Industrialization and Southern Society, 1877–1984* (Lexington, Ky., 1985), and "Beyond Planters and Industrialists: A New Perspective on the New South," *Journal of Southern History* 54 (Feb. 1988): 45–68; Mary Josephine Oates, "The Role of the Cotton Textile Industry in the Economic Development of the American Southeast" (Ph.D. diss., Yale University, 1969); Louis Ferleger, "Capital Goods and Southern Economic Development," *Journal of Economic History* 45 (June 1985): 411–17; Kenneth Lipartito, *The Bell System and Regional Business: The Telephone in the South, 1877–1920* (Baltimore, 1989); David L. Carlton, *Mill and Town in South Carolina, 1880–1920* (Baton Rouge, 1982); David L. Carlton and Peter A. Coclanis, "Capital Mobilization and Southern Industry, 1880–1905: The Case of the Carolina Piedmont," *Journal of Economic History* 49 (March 1989): 73–94; David L. Carlton, "The Revolution from Above: The National Market and the Beginnings of Industrialization in North Carolina," *Journal of American History* 77 (Sept. 1990): 445–75.

3. See Wright, *Old South, New South,* 60–64; and Schulman, *From Cotton Belt to Sunbelt,* 5–6. For state-level figures on manufacturing growth, see Everett S. Lee et al., *Population Redistribution and Economic Growth: United States, 1870–1950,* 2 vols. (Philadelphia, Pa., 1957), 1:685, 694–95, 697; Donald Dodd and Wynelle Dodd, *Historical Statistics of the South, 1790–1970* (University, Ala., 1973), 66–73; U.S. Department of Commerce, Bureau of the Census, *Historical Statistics of the United States: Colonial Times to 1970,* 2 vols. (Washington, D.C., 1975), 2:669; Albert W. Niemi, Jr., *State and Regional Patterns in American Manufacturing, 1860–1900* (Westport, Conn., 1974), 11 and appendix.

4. Clarence H. Danhof, "Four Decades of Thought on the South's Economic Problems," in *Essays in Southern Economic Development,* ed. Melvin L. Greenhut and W. Tate Whitman (Chapel Hill, N.C., 1964), 7–68; William H. Nicholls, *Southern Tradition and Regional Progress* (Chapel Hill, N.C., 1960); Eugene D. Genovese, *The Political Economy of Slavery* (New York, 1965); Jonathan M. Wiener, *Social Origins of the New South* (Baton Rouge, 1978); Dwight B. Billings, Jr., *Planters and the Making of a "New South"* (Chapel Hill, N.C., 1979).

5. See, for instance, Nicholls, *Southern Tradition and Regional Progress;* Allan R. Pred, *The Spatial Dynamics of U.S. Urban-Industrial Growth, 1800–1914: Interpretive and Theoretical Essays* (Cambridge, Mass., 1966), 120–27.

6. See, e.g., Edwin Mansfield, *Statistics for Business and Economics: Methods and Applications,* 2d ed. (New York, 1983), 457–505.

7. Robert Higgs, "American Inventiveness, 1870–1920," *Journal of Political Economy* 79 (May–June 1971): 661–67. Higgs has developed his approach further in two subsequent essays, in which he anticipates the approach we pursue here. See Higgs, "Urbanization and Inventiveness in the United States, 1870–1920," in *The New Urban History: Quantitative Explorations by American Historians,* ed. Leo F. Schnore (Princeton, N.J., 1975), 247–59, and "Urbanization and Invention in the Process of Economic Growth: Simultaneous-Equations Estimates for the United States, 1880–1920," *Research in Population Economics* 2 (1980): 3–20.

8. The reader should note that Higgs's (and our) decision to make the state the unit of analysis implies the validity of what we are investigating, namely, a close association between innovative activity and the culture of a geographic unit. As such, the choice is not above criticism. First, geographic boundaries can be arbitrary and become increasingly so as urban conurbations spill across state lines. Second, over time, innovation arguably becomes increasingly associated not with geographically defined communities but with far-flung institutions such as multi-plant corporations, railroads, and the federal government. Nonetheless, we feel that the state is an appropriate unit. While in some ways arbitrarily defined, states are small enough and numerous enough to allow us to investigate regional characteristics in a way that avoids masking the internal variation within a regional grouping of states. Moreover, the variation among states is wide enough, even in 1920, to suggest that local effects remain important.

9. As with the choice of states as units of analysis, the use of patent statistics as economic indicators poses numerous problems. Too many innovations are never patented; too many patents are unimportant, unrealized, or reflective of legal imperatives rather than technological creativity. Moreover, access to patents involves significant costs, costs that would operate to the disadvantage of people living at a distance from the capital or suffering from disabilities imposed by race or social class; these problems could conceivably affect our own investigations. Finally, the level of patent activity at different times is affected strongly not only by changing costs but also by shifting administrative practice; on this point, see Robert C. Post, "'Liberalizers' versus 'Scientific Men' in the Antebellum Patent Office," *Technology and Culture* 17 (Jan. 1976): 24–54; see also Zvi Griliches, "Patent Statistics as Economic Indicators: A Survey," *Journal of Economic Literature* 28 (Dec. 1990): 1661–1707. Nonetheless, such records provide the best quantitative measure we have or are likely to obtain relating to inventiveness in the past. While most patents are of low quality, it can reasonably be assumed that quality is randomly distributed. Furthermore, it should be borne in mind that our object is to assess not the value of innovation but the propensity to innovate, the level of which need not be reflected in the proportion of major breakthroughs. Barriers to access, particularly those posed by racial discrimination, are more serious, but we think manageable; on race as a factor, see n. 33 below. Finally, changing administrative practices over time can be handled by using, as Higgs does and we do, a series of cross-sectional, or "snapshot," analyses comparing states at the same points in time. Higgs, "American Inventiveness," 664; Simon Kuznets, "Inventive Activity: Problems of Definition and Measurement," in *The Rate and Direction of Inventive Activity*, ed. Richard R. Nelson, Report of the National Bureau of Economic Research, Special Conference Series (Princeton, N.J., 1962), 19–43; Jacob Schmookler, *Invention and Economic Growth* (Cambridge, Mass., 1966), 18–56; Kenneth L. Sokoloff, "Inventive Activity in Early Industrial America: Evidence from Patent Records, 1790–1846," *Journal of Economic History* 48 (Dec. 1988): 813–50, esp. 817. For a recent survey of the literature on patent statistics and their uses, see Griliches, "Patent Statistics as Economic Indicators."

10. Higgs used data from Census reports and patent figures collected from the annual reports of the U.S. Commissioner of Patents. Higgs, "American Inventiveness," 661–64. In order to reduce randomness from his figures for patents, Higgs employed three-year centered averages to obtain figures for each census year; see 664.

11. Pred, *Spatial Dynamics of U.S. Urban-Industrial Growth*, 96.

12. Higgs, "American Inventiveness," 661–64. Higgs defined "South" as the eleven states of the Old Confederacy, plus Oklahoma (after statehood in 1908), Kentucky, and West Virginia, 665.

13. Ibid.

14. Higgs, "Urbanization and Invention in the Process of Economic Growth," reworks his estimating equations in log-linear form for 1880, 1900, and 1920, alternately using as one of his independent variables the ratio of manufacturing and of nonagricultural workers to the total

workforce. Using *MF/LF*, the southern dummy remains insignificant for 1880 and significant for 1900 and 1920.

15. Higgs, "American Inventiveness," 665–66; see also table 8.1.

16. Higgs, "Urbanization and Inventiveness in the United States," 259, n. 18, anticipates this point.

17. For the classic account of the South's early industrialization, see C. Vann Woodward, *Origins of the New South, 1877–1913* (Baton Rouge, 1951), 107–41, 291–320. See also Cobb, *Industrialization and Southern Society*, 17–26; Wright, *Old South, New South*, 124–97.

18. The pioneering work of Gautam Mathur is particularly important in this regard. See Mathur, *Planning for Steady Growth* (Oxford, 1965). For a multinational analysis of the association between investment in machinery and economic growth, see J. Bradford De Long, "Productivity Growth and Machinery Investment: A Long-Run Look, 1870–1980," *Journal of Economic History* 52 (June 1992): 307–24.

19. Nathan Rosenberg, "Capital Goods, Technology, and Economic Growth," *Oxford Economic Papers* 15 (Nov. 1963): 217–27, and *Technology and American Economic Growth* (New York, 1972), esp. 87–116.

20. See W. Paul Strassman, "Creative Destruction and Partial Obsolescence in American Economic Development," *Journal of Economic History* 19 (Sept. 1959): 335–49, and *Risk and Technological Innovation: American Manufacturing Methods during the Nineteenth Century* (Ithaca, N.Y., 1959); Nathan Rosenberg, "Problems in the Economist's Conceptualization of Technological Innovation," in his *Perspectives on Technology* (New York, 1976), 61–84, and *Inside the Black Box: Technology and Economics* (New York, 1982), 3–33.

21. Ferleger, "Capital Goods and Southern Economic Development." In treating the "plantation South," Ferleger essentially follows Jay R. Mandle, whose argument appears in revised form in *Not Slave, Not Free: The African-American Economic Experience since the Civil War* (Durham, N.C., 1992).

22. U.S. Department of Commerce, Bureau of the Census, *U.S. Census, 1920*, vol. 8, *Manufactures, 1919; General Report and Analytical Tables* (Washington, D.C., 1923), 422; *U.S. Census, 1920*, vol. 10, *Manufactures, 1919; Reports for Selected Industries* (Washington, D.C., 1923), 466. On the dearth of machine-tool makers in the South in the early twentieth century, see also U.S. Department of Commerce and Labor, Bureau of the Census, *Census of Manufactures, 1905: Metal Working Machinery*, Bulletin 67, by Fred J. Miller (Washington, D.C., 1907); *American Machinist* 40 (Jan. 29, 1914): 210 (map); Nathan Rosenberg, "Technological Change in the Machine Tool Industry," *Journal of Economic History* 23 (Dec. 1963): 414–43, esp. 421–22.

23. George Sweet Gibb, *The Saco-Lowell Shops: Textile Machinery Building in New England, 1813–1949* (Cambridge, Mass., 1950), 194–95; Rosenberg, "Technological Change in the Machine Tool Industry," 418–19; John William Lozier, *Taunton and Mason: Cotton Machinery and Locomotive Manufacture in Taunton, Massachusetts, 1811–1861* (New York, 1986).

24. John S. Hekman, "The Product Cycle and New England Textiles," *Quarterly Journal of Economics* 94 (June 1980): 697–717; Irwin Feller, "The Diffusion and Location of Technological Change in the American Cotton-Textile Industry, 1890–1920," *Technology and Culture* 15 (Oct. 1974): 569–93; William Mass, "Developing and Utilizing Technological Leadership: Industrial Research, Vertical Integration, and Business Strategy at the Draper Company, 1816–1930," *Business and Economic History*, 2d ser., 18 (1989): 129–39.

25. *U.S. Census, 1920*, vol. 10, *Manufactures, 1919; Reports for Selected Industries*, 186–296; *U.S. Census, 1920*, vol. 8, *Manufactures, 1919; General Report and Analytical Tables*, 486.

26. On the relevant SIC reconstructions, see Niemi (n. 3 above), 105–11. These categories obvi-

ously do not embrace all "capital goods"; transportation equipment is a significant omission. However, engine production, the most "high-tech" branch of transportation equipment, is captured by "machinery," and the behavior of midwestern residuals does not suggest that omission of the integrated automobile industry (a classification first appearing in the 1919 *Census of Manufactures*) poses a significant problem. Another problem is the internal coarseness of the categories, which include, especially among the fabricated metals group, a number of consumer goods industries as well as capital goods producers. The use of SIC categories, however, is designed to standardize definitions of industrial categories over time, and in our view the advantages of standardization outweigh the contamination. In any case, we believe that our results show our approach to be useful.

27. Higgs, "Urbanization and Invention in the Process of Economic Growth," successfully handles Connecticut by transforming his variables into log-linear form; however, we believe that our own approach offers an important insight into the behavior of the state and is thus worth reporting.

28. David M. Potter, *The South and the Sectional Conflict* (Baton Rouge, 1968), 4.

29. In order to minimize overlap and enhance the clarity of the display, the positions of several of the data labels have been shifted slightly, but not so as to materially alter their relationship to each other or to the estimating equation.

30. The concept of the "manufacturing belt" is discussed in Harvey S. Perloff et al., *Regions, Resources, and Economic Growth* (Baltimore, 1960); see esp. the map on 49.

31. Alan L. Olmstead and Paul Rhode, "An Overview of California Agricultural Mechanization, 1870–1930," *Agricultural History* 62 (summer 1988): 86–112.

32. Ann Markusen et al., *The Rise of the Gunbelt: The Military Remapping of Industrial America* (New York, 1991), esp. chaps. 4, 5, and 7.

33. We considered, but rejected, two other approaches. It was suggested that we alter the *dependent* variable, on the premise that the population "at risk" to receive patents was the adult *white* male population. We have our doubts about this suggestion. The geographic variation in age and gender distribution would add little to the variation already observed. The racial factor is obviously more productive of variation; even so, while racial discrimination inhibited blacks' opportunities both to acquire innovative skills and to reap the rewards of innovation, African Americans were hardly shut out from inventive activity altogether. On this point, see Portia P. James, *The Real McCoy: African-American Invention and Innovation, 1619–1930* (Washington, D.C., 1989), esp. 57–99. We nonetheless experimented with this proposition, using the independent variables Percent Urban, *CG/LF*, and the southern dummy for the twentieth-century observations. We found that the new equation effectively accounted for southern regional divergence only in 1900; in 1910 and 1920 the regional effect remained significant. Another, more intriguing, suggestion (from Philip Scranton) was to add a new independent variable, the proportion of the native-born population of a given state born outside that state. Scranton reasoned that such internal migrants probably account for a disproportionate number of patents and thus that their relative scarcity in the South and relative abundance in the West might well account for the observed regional variations. We tested this suggestion for 1920; addition of the new variable for that year did in fact render the southern dummy (though not the western dummy) insignificant. We are uncertain of how to interpret this finding, however, because in-migration is hardly exogenous but is determined largely by the climate of economic opportunity in the given region. Thus the paucity of skilled migrants to the South was, like the region's inventive activity itself, an effect, not a cause.

34. The problematic relationship between the years-of-schooling statistics reported in the 1940

census and the realities of southern rural education in the late nineteenth and early twentieth centuries, especially for blacks, is discussed in Robert A. Margo, "Race, Educational Attainment, and the 1940 Census," *Journal of Economic History* 46 (March 1986): 189–98.

35. Of course, this limitation also allows ample room for criticism of our choice of variables and our own attributions of causation, criticism that we welcome.

36. In recent years, developmental economists in particular have concerned themselves with the ambiguous role of education in the early stages of economic growth. Some have argued that formal education at times can retard innovation and inventiveness. For an introduction to the issues involved, see Michael P. Todaro, *Economic Development in the Third World,* 5th ed. (New York, 1994), 363–99.

37. See, e.g., Alexander J. Field, "Educational Reform and Manufacturing Development in Mid-Nineteenth Century Massachusetts" (Ph.D. diss., University of California, Berkeley, 1974).

38. Marvin Fischbaum, "An Economic Analysis of the Southern Capture of the Cotton Textile Industry to 1910" (Ph.D. diss., Columbia University, 1965), 206–13; Wright, *Old South, New South,* 78–80.

39. On the relationship of broadly diffused commercial opportunity to the rise of literacy in the northern United States, see Gordon S. Wood, *The Radicalism of the American Revolution* (New York, 1992), 313; William J. Gilmore, *Reading Becomes a Necessity of Life: Material and Cultural Life in Rural New England, 1780–1835* (Knoxville, Tenn., 1989).

40. In each state, textiles, wood products (including paper and wood pulp), and, in Vermont, marble and stone quarrying accounted for at least half of all manufacturing employment. It should be noted, though, that Vermont had a significant machine-tool industry, employing over 2,000. U.S. Department of Commerce, Bureau of the Census, *U.S. Census, 1920,* vol. 9, *Manufactures, 1919; Reports for States* (Washington, D.C., 1923), 533, 1505.

41. Further analysis of this point might well cross national boundaries to include Quebec and the Maritime Provinces of Canada, with their well-known "peripheral" characteristics.

42. Wright, *Old South, New South;* Carlton, "Revolution from Above" (n. 1 above). For a variant analysis of the status of the South as a "favored colony" of the North, emphasizing its role as an outlet for northern capital-goods "exports," see Joe Persky, "Regional Colonialism and the Southern Economy," *Journal of Radical Political Economics* 4 (fall 1972): 70–79.

43. Markusen et al., *Rise of the Gunbelt,* 108–12; Jane Jacobs, *Cities and the Wealth of Nations: Principles of Economic Life* (New York, 1984), 93–97.

44. Wright, *Old South, New South,* 273–74; Cobb, "Beyond Planters and Industrialists," 66–68.

9. Unbalanced Growth and Industrialization

"Unbalanced Growth and Industrialization: The Case of South Carolina," first appeared in *Developing Dixie: Modernization in a Traditional Society,* ed. Winfred B. Moore, Jr., Joseph F. Tripp, and Lyon G. Tyler, Jr. (Westport, Conn., 1988), 111–130, and is reprinted here with permission of Greenwood Publishing Group, Inc.

1. For a discussion of New South historiography, see Paul M. Gaston, "The New South," in *Writing Southern History: Essays in Historiography in Honor of Fletcher M. Green,* ed. Arthur S. Link and Rembert W. Patrick (Baton Rouge, 1965), 316–36. A more recent version of the New South approach is David L. Carlton, *Mill and Town in South Carolina, 1880–1920* (Baton Rouge, 1982), chaps. 1 and 2. The most important naysayer is Jonathan M. Wiener, *Social Origins of the New South: Alabama, 1865–1885* (Baton Rouge, 1978); see also James C. Cobb, *Industrialization and Southern Society, 1877–1984* (Lexington, Ky., 1984), esp. chap. 1.

2. The most famous use of 1880 as a turning point is by Broadus Mitchell in *The Rise of Cotton Mills in the South,* Johns Hopkins University Studies in Historical and Political Science, series 39, no. 2 (Baltimore, 1922). C. Vann Woodward, *Origins of the New South 1877–1913* (Baton Rouge, 1951), 140–41, stresses the Civil War, as does Carlton, *Mill and Town,* 15–18. For the use of the 1920s as a takeoff point, see George B. Tindall, "Business Progressivism: Southern Politics in the Twenties," in *The Ethnic Southerners* (Baton Rouge, 1976), 146–47; for World War II, see, for instance, Cobb, *Industrialization and Southern Society,* 51–52.

3. The aggregate performance of southern manufacturing is discussed in David L. Carlton and Lacy K. Ford, Jr., "The 'Colonial Economy' of the Postbellum South: A Reappraisal" (paper delivered at the annual meeting of the Southern Historical Association, Charleston, S.C., Nov. 10, 1983), tables 1–3.

4. Gunnar Myrdal, *Rich lands and Poor: The Road to World Prosperity* (New York, 1957); Albert O. Hirschman, *The Strategy of Economic Development,* Yale Studies in Economics, No. 10 (New Haven, 1958).

5. On the background, see Carlton and Ford, "Colonial Economy."

6. My use of the terms *core* and *periphery* here is loose, since it does not, by and large, involve an economic dependence on the former by the latter. *Both* regions are, in a sense, "peripheral" or (to fudge) "semiperipheral" with regard to the larger national economy. I use the terms here for convenience.

7. U.S. Department of Commerce, Bureau of the Census, *Tenth Census of the United States, 1880: Manufactures,* 2:5, 173–74, 353–55. The Census Office did not calculate "value added by manufacture" for 1880; I have here estimated it by subtracting the value of materials used from the value of manufactured product. The population figures are from *Tenth Census of the United States, 1880: Population,* 1:3, 327–30. On the phosphate industry, see Don H. Doyle and Tom W. Shick, "The South Carolina Phosphate Boom and the Stillbirth of the New South, 1867–1920," *South Carolina Historical Magazine* 86 (Jan. 1985): 1–31; on the upper coast, see David L. Carlton, "The Piedmont and Waccamaw Regions: An Economic Comparison," *South Carolina Historical Magazine* 88 (April 1987): 83–100.

8. *Fifteenth Census of the United States, 1930: Manufactures, 1929, Reports by States,* 3:17, 484. The core counties were Anderson, Cherokee, Chester, Greenville, Greenwood, Lancaster, Laurens, Newberry, Pickens, Spartanburg, Union, and York.

9. Ibid., 488; Doyle and Shick, "Phosphate Boom," 20–24, 30; Howard A. Hanlon, *The Bull Hunchers: A Saga of Logging the Tidewater Low Country* (Parsons, W.Va., 1970), 258–85; Carlton, "Piedmont and Waccamaw Regions"; South Carolina Department of Agriculture, Commerce and Industries *Report, 1930,* 89.

10. Alice Carol Galenson, "The Migration of the Cotton Textile Industry from New England to the South" (Ph.D. diss., Cornell University, 1975), 180–83; *Tenth Census of the United States, 1880, Agriculture,* 3:240.

11. Stephen J. Goldfarb, "A Note on the Limits to the Growth of the Cotton Textile Industry in the Old South," *Journal of Southern History* 48 (Nov. 1982): 545–58; Ernest M. Lander, Jr., *The Textile Industry in Antebellum South Carolina* (Baton Rouge, 1969); *Tenth Census of the United States, 1880, Manufacturers,* 2:505; *Twelfth Census of the United States, 1900,* 9 (pt. 3):69. On the declining historical significance of water power in the late nineteenth century, see Louis C. Hunter, *Water Power: A History of Industrial Power in the United States* (Charlottesville, Va., 1979), 1:chap. 10.

12. *Tenth Census of the United States, 1880, Population,* 1:407; "rural" population as used here excludes those residing in incorporated places of at least 1,000 people; for figures, see ibid., 327–30. Data on county land areas appears in *Twelfth Census of the United States, 1900: Statistics of Popu-*

lation, li. Earlier figures on land areas are available but appear to be crude and unreliable. Use of the 1900 areas poses one problem; one of the 1930 core counties, Greenwood, was created in 1897 from portions of Abbeville and Edgefield, two peripheral counties. In the analyses of 1880 data presented here and below, Greenwood is excluded from the core.

13. See Leonard J. Carlson, "Labor Supply, the Acquisition of Skills, and the Location of Cotton Textile Mills, 1880–1900," *Journal of Economic History* 46 (March 1981): 65–71; Carlton, *Mill and Town,* 114–15, 158–59. See also Allen Heath Stokes, Jr., "Black and White Labor and the Development of the Southern Textile Industry, 1800–1920" (Ph.D. diss. University of South Carolina, 1977), 196–212, 231–61.

14. On the postbellum expansion of cotton cultivation in the South Carolina Piedmont, see Carlton, *Mill and Town,* 18–20; Peter Temin, "Patterns of Cotton Agriculture in Post-Bellum Georgia," *Journal of Economic History* 43 (Sept. 1983): 661–74. Data on stores comes from R. G. Dun and Company, *The Mercantile Agency Reference Book;* for land areas, see n. 12. My counts include stores, artisans' shops, and small manufacturers; they exclude planters and professional men not described as engaging in commercial activity, as well as large-scale manufacturing operations engaging in export production. No estimate of trading density was attempted for the periphery as a whole because shifting county lines and the anomaly of Charleston introduced grave distortions into the results.

15. *Tenth Census of the United States, 1880, Population,* 1:327–30, 407; Carlton, *Mill and Town,* chaps. 1 and 2.

16. Gustavus G. Williamson, "Cotton Manufacturing in South Carolina, 1865–1892" (Ph.D. diss., Johns Hopkins University, 1954), 148–49; Allen Heath Stokes, Jr., "John H. Montgomery: A Pioneer Southern Industrialist" (master's thesis, University of South Carolina, 1967); August Kohn, *The Cotton Mills of South Carolina* (Columbia, S.C., 1907), 21–25.

17. Myrdal, *Rich Lands and Poor,* 33–34; empirical support is offered by Jeffrey G. Williamson in "Regional Inequality and the Process of National Development: A Description of the Patterns," *Economic Development and Cultural Change* 13 (July 1965), pt. 2 (entire issue). Myrdal testifies that his critique of the economic concept of "equilibrium" began to take shape in the course of his study of southern blacks, published as *An American Dilemma: The Negro Problem and Modern Democracy* (2 vols., New York, 1944) (*Rich Lands and Poor,* 13–16).

18. Mary Josephine Oates, *The Role of the Cotton Textile Industry in the Economic Development of the American Southeast, 1900–1940* (New York, 1975); Carlton, *Mill and Town,* 63–64; on textile machinery, see Irwin Feller, "The Diffusion and Location of Technological Change in the American Cotton Textile Industry, 1890–1920," *Technology and Culture* 15 (Oct. 1974): 582–92; John S. Hekman, "The Product Cycle and New England Textiles," *Quarterly Journal of Economics* 94 (June 1980): 699–717.

19. On the negative state in South Carolina, see W. Hardy Wickwar, *Three Hundred Years of Development Administration in South Carolina* (Columbia, S.C., 1970), 115, 118–29; on antebellum political culture see Lacy K. Ford, "Social Origins of a New South Carolina: The Upcountry in the Nineteenth Century" (Ph.D. diss., University of South Carolina, 1983); on the conservative-era assault on manufacturing tax exemptions as "class legislation," see Ford, "Rednecks and Merchants: Economic Development and Social Tensions in the South Carolina Upcountry, 1865–1900," *Journal of American History* 71 (Sept. 1984), 294–318. On Redeemer-era politics and economic development, see Michael Perman, *The Road to Redemption: Southern Politics, 1869–1879* (Chapel Hill, N.C., 1984), chaps. 9 and 10.

20. On the relationship of transportation technology to government or private control, see Alfred D. Chandler, Jr., *The Visible Hand: The Managerial Revolution in American Business* (Cambridge, Mass., 1978), 81–82.

21. The preceding is largely drawn from William L. Suttles, "The Struggle for State Control

of Highways in South Carolina, 1908–1930" (master's thesis, University of South Carolina, 1971), chaps. 1–3.

22. Douglas Summers Brown, *A City without Cobwebs: A History of Rock Hill, S.C.* (Columbia, S.C., 1953), 273–40; Sidney B. Paine, *The Story of the First Electrically Operated Textile Mill* (Schenectady, N.Y., 1930); Robert F. Durden, *The Dukes of Durham, 1865–1929* (Durham, N.C., 1975), 183; Thomas P. Hughes, *Networks of Power: Electrification in Western Society, 1880–1930* (Baltimore, 1983), 265; South Carolina Power Rate Investigating Committee, *Report on the Electric Utility Situation in South Carolina, December 31, 1931*, 52–55, 60–61; A. E. Parkins, *The South: Its Economic-Geographic Development* (New York, 1938), 350–51.

23. *Electric Utility Situation*, 337, 360; on the significance of private ownership in shaping utility systems, see Hughes, *Networks*, 464.

24. *Electric Utility Situation*, 351, 355; Durden, *Dukes*, 177–87. For discussions of load factor and other determinants of utility development strategy, see Hughes, *Networks*, 217–21, 463–65 passim.

25. Columbia *State*, March 20, 1934.

26. *Electric Utility Situation*, 60, 432–42; Wickwar, *Three Hundred Years*, 150; Charleston *News and Courier*, Feb. 27, 1927; Columbia *State*, March 1, 1927; March 20, 1934; Marvin L. Cann, "Burnett Rhett Maybank and the New Deal in South Carolina, 1931–1941" (Ph.D. diss., University of North Carolina, Chapel Hill, 1967), 144–46; a general survey of economic development and power supply on the coastal plain appears in the Murray and Flood "Report on the Santee-Cooper Power Project," Sept. 15, 1934, Exhibit B of South Carolina Public Service Authority, Application for Loan and Grant from U.S. Public Works Administration (on microfilm, Clemson University Library).

27. Columbia *State*, June 27, 1923, clipping in Guignard family scrapbooks, South Caroliniana Library, University of South Carolina, Columbia.

28. *Fourteenth Census of the United States, 1920, Population*, 1:126–27; *Fifteenth Census of the United States, 1930, Population*, 1:985.

29. Note that the periphery includes the relatively developed counties of Richland and Charleston, whose ambitions, unlike those of the central core counties of Greenville and Spartanburg, brought them into alliance with their undeveloped hinterlands.

30. For a sketch of the rise of the modern "positive state," see Wickwar, *Three Hundred Years*, chap. 9; on Maybank, see Cann, "Maybank"; on Brown, see W. D. Workman, Jr., *The Bishop from Barnwell* (Columbia, S.C., 1963). On Jefferies, see Emily Bellinger Reynolds and Joan Reynolds Faunt, *Biographical Directory of the Senate of the State of South Carolina, 1776–1964* (Columbia, S.C., 1964), 245; on his political talents, see "Cordie Page Reminisces," *Independent Republic Quarterly* (Conway, S.C.) 13 (fall 1979): 26–28. See also Anthony Barry Miller, "Palmetto Politician: The Early Political Career of Olin D. Johnston, 1896–1945" (Ph.D. diss., University of North Carolina at Chapel Hill, 1976), 26, 352. A different characterization of this emergent oligarchy appears in V. O. Key, *Southern Politics in State and Nation* (New York, 1949), 153.

31. On the legislative history of the bill, see Suttles, "State Control of Highways," chaps. 5 and 6, and the roll calls in South Carolina House of Representatives, *Journal, 1929*, 897, 1205–6.

32. Miller, "Palmetto Politician," chaps. 1–7; Cann, "Maybank," chap. 6; Key, *Southern Politics*, 139–40, 145–46, 153. Brown expressed open disdain at politics in the large industrial counties, where "there is inevitably a certain amount of demagoguery necessary to insure reelection." His safe seat, he argued, left him "free to think for the best interests of all the people." Workman, *Bishop from Barnwell*, 26–27.

33. *Electric Utility Situation;* Columbia *State*, Feb. 18–28, March 4, 18, 19, April 3, 30, May 2, 8, 9, 10, 1931; Cann, "Maybank," 144. The House vote on final passage, by section, was core, 17 aye, 22 nay; periphery, 45 aye, 32 nay. *South Carolina House of Representatives Journal, 1931*, 2047.

34. Sketches of the early history of Santee-Cooper appear in Cann, "Maybank," chap. 4; Jack

Irby Hayes, "South Carolina and the New Deal, 1932–1938" (Ph.D. diss., University of South Carolina, 1972), 295–308; and Walter B. Edgar, *History of Santee-Cooper, 1934–1984* (Columbia, S.C.: R. L. Bryan, 1984), 4–10.

35. On the legislative history of the creation of the Public Service Authority, see Columbia *State*, Jan.–April 1934; *S. C. House Journal, 1934*, for H. 1186; *S. C. Senate Journal, 1934*, for S. 1701.

36. Edgar, *Santee-Cooper;* Wickwar, *Three Hundred Years*, 152; South Carolina Public Service Authority, *Report, 1939–40*, 12; *1945–46*, 3, 17; *1946–47*, 10–15.

37. Wickwar, *Three Hundred Years*, 158; Jamie W. Moore, "The Lowcountry in Economic Transition: Charleston since 1865," *South Carolina Historical Magazine* 80 (April 1979): 170; South Carolina State Ports Authority, "Summary of Activities, 1942–1955" (n.p.); David R. Peden and Ronald P. Wilder, *Impact of the State Ports Authority upon the Economy of South Carolina*, Occasional Papers, no. 6 (Columbia, S.C., Oct. 1974).

38. Incumbency rates are calculated from Reynolds and Faunt, *Biographical Directory.* Since senators served staggered terms, ratios were calculated by comparing each session list with its predecessor from *two* sessions back. On the postwar oligarchy, see Key, *Southern Politics*, 150–55. The quote is from Charles E. Daniel, cited in Workman, *Bishop from Barnwell*, ix.

39. *U.S. Census, 1980: Population, South Carolina*, 1, (chap. C, pt. 42): 42, 336–40.

10. The American South and the U.S. Defense Economy

1. Gregory Hooks, "Guns and Butter, North and South: The Federal Contribution to Manufacturing Growth, 1940–1990," in *The Second Wave: Southern Industrialization from the 1940s to the 1970s*, ed. Philip Scranton (Athens, Ga., 2001), 255–85.

2. Bruce J. Schulman, *From Cotton Belt to Sunbelt: Federal Policy, Economic Development, and the Transformation of the South, 1938–1980* (New York, 1991); Roger W. Lotchin, ed., *The Martial Metropolis: U.S. Cities in War and Peace* (New York, 1984); Scranton, *Second Wave.*

3. One classic assertion of the South's martial character is John Hope Franklin, *The Militant South* (Cambridge, Mass., 1956); dissents include Marcus Cunliffe, *Soldiers and Civilians: The Martial Spirit in America, 1775–1865* (Boston, 1968), esp. chap. 10; and R. Don Higginbotham, "The Martial Spirit in the Antebellum South: Some Further Speculations in a National Context," *Journal of Southern History* 58 (Feb. 1992): 3–26.

4. The above description is drawn from the following sources: for statistics on defense dependency, *Statistical Abstracts of the United States, 1961*, 238; *Statistical Abstracts, 1971*, 247; *Statistical Abstracts, 1981*, 358; *Statistical Abstracts, 1992*, 388. For description, see Tom Schlesinger with John Gaventa and Juliet Merrifield, *Our Own Worst Enemy: The Impact of Military Production on the Upper South* (New Market, Tenn., 1983), esp. 11.

5. Schlesinger, *Our Own Worst Enemy*, 11–15; Lotchin, *Martial Metropolis;* Roger W. Lotchin, *Fortress California, 1910–1961* (New York, 1992).

6. See Gavin Wright, *Old South, New South: Transformations of the Southern Economy since the Civil War* (New York, 1984); David L. Carlton, chaps. 4 and 6 in this volume; Dewey W. Grantham, *The South in Modern America: A Region at Odds* (New York, 1994), 4–6.

7. David L. Carlton, *Mill and Town in South Carolina, 1880–1920* (Baton Rouge. La., 1982), 13–81; Edward L. Ayers, *The Promise of the New South: Life after Reconstruction* (New York, 1992), 3–131.

8. David R. Johnson, "The Failed Experiment: Military Aviation and Urban Development in San Antonio, 1910–1940," in Lotchin, *Martial Metropolis*, 89.

9. Paolo E. Coletta, ed. *United States Navy and Marine Corps Bases, Domestic* (Westport, Conn., 1985); George W. Hopkins, "From Naval Pauper to Naval Power: The Development of Charleston's Military-Industrial Complex," in Lotchin, *Martial Metropolis*, 2–4; William L.

Tazewell, *Newport News Shipbuilding, the First Century* (Newport News, Va., 1986), 12–66; Benjamin Franklin Cooling, *Gray Steel and Blue-Water Navy: The Formative Years of America's Military-Industrial Complex, 1881–1917* (Hamden, Conn., 1979), 81, 135, 156, 167, 168.

10. George B. Tindall, Jr., *The Emergence of the New South, 1913–1946* (Baton Rouge, 1967), 54; *Fiftieth Anniversary History, 1917–1967, Fort Jackson, S.C.* (n.p., 1967), 1–2; L. Albert Scipio III, *The 24th Infantry at Fort Benning* (Silver Spring, Md., 1986), 3.

11. Tindall, *Emergence of the New South,* 56–60.

12. Margaret Ripley Wolfe, *Kingsport, Tennessee: A Planned American City* (Lexington, Ky., 1987), esp. 58–61.

13.Hopkins, "From Naval Pauper to Naval Power," 8–10; Tazewell, *Newport News Shipbuilding,* 122, 125, 128; Christopher Silver, "Norfolk and the Navy: The Evolution of City-Federal Relations, 1917–46," in Lotchin, *Martial Metropolis,* 114; Tindall, *Emergence of the New South,* 57; Wolfe, *Kingsport,* 70–74.

14. Preston J. Hubbard, *Origins of the TVA: The Muscle Shoals Controversy, 1920–1932* (Nashville, Tenn., 1961); Hopkins, "From Naval Pauper to Naval Power," 8, 10–14; Johnson, "The Failed Experiment," 98–102; Silver, "Norfolk and the Navy," 114–16: Scipio, *24th Infantry at Fort Benning,* 27.

15. David L. Carlton and Peter A. Coclanis, eds., *Confronting Southern Poverty in the Great Depression: The Report on Economic Conditions of the South, with Supplementary Documents* (Boston, 1996).

16. Ralph C. Hon, "The South in a War Economy" *Southern Economic Journal* 8 (Jan. 1942): 291–308.

17. Tazewell, *Newport News Shipbuilding,* 145, 149–50; Robert F. Couch, "The Ingalls Story in Mississippi, 1938–1958," *Journal of Mississippi History* 26 (Aug. 1964): 192–206; Jerry St. Pé, "A Salute to American Spirit: The Story of Ingalls Shipbuilding Division of Litton" (address to meeting of Newcomen Society of the United States, Jackson, Miss., May 10, 1988), 7–8. On BAWI, see James C. Cobb, *The Selling of the South: The Southern Crusade for Industrial Development, 1936–1990,* 2d ed. (Baton Rouge, 1983), 5–34.

18. Hon, "The South in a War Economy," 294–95; U.S. Bureau of the Census, *County Data Book, 1947: Supplement to the Statistical Abstract of the United States* (Washington, D.C., 1947), 7.

19. Hon, "The South in a War Economy," 305; *County Data Book, 1947,* 7; Frederick L. Deming and Weldon A. Stein, *Disposal of Southern War Plants,* National Planning Association, Committee of the South, Report No. 2 (Washington, D.C., 1949), 12–14.

20. Couch, "Ingalls Story in Mississippi," 199–201; Peter Neushul, "Andrew Jackson Higgins and the Mass Production of World War II Landing Craft," *Louisiana History* 39 (spring 1998): 133–66; Jerry E. Strahan, *Andrew Jackson Higgins and the Boats That Won World War II* (Baton Rouge, 1994).

21. John B. Rae, *Climb to Greatness: The American Aircraft Industry, 1920–1960* (Cambridge, Mass., 1968), 122–28, 225–33. The greatest concentration of airframe facilities was in Dallas–Fort Worth, suggesting a major problem with assessing the regional character of defense-industry development. Dallas–Fort Worth was attractive primarily for the characteristics it shared with other Great Plains cities such as Omaha and Wichita: a mid-continent location with good rail links to California, a dry climate, and ample expanses of flat land.

22. Hon, "The South in a War Economy"; Tindall, *Emergence of the New South,* 695–97; Joseph A. Pratt, *The Growth of a Refining Region* (Greenwich, Conn., 1980), 89–90; 94–95, 105, 107, 142; *County Data Book, 1947,* 20–23; Deming and Stein, *Disposal of Southern War Plants,* 57–74.

23. Deming and Stein, *Disposal of Southern War Plants;* Hon, "The South in a War Economy," 306–7.

24. Pratt, *Growth of a Refining Region,* 94, 107; Kenneth Warren, *The American Steel Industry, 1850–1970: A Geographical Interpretation* (Oxford, 1973), 247–48; Schlesinger, *Our Own Worst Enemy,* 101–4; Hon, "The South in a War Economy," 301–4; Rae, *Climb to Greatness,* 181, 188–89.

25. Thomas A. Scott, "Winning World War II in an Atlanta Suburb: Bell Bomber and the Growth of Marietta, Georgia," in Scranton, *Second Wave,* 1–23; Rae, *Climb to Greatness,* 196–97; Jordan A. Schwartz, *The New Dealers: Power Politics in the Age of Roosevelt* (New York, 1993), 293; Martin V. Melosi, "Dallas–Fort Worth: Marketing the Metroplex," in *Sunbelt Cities: Politics and Growth since World War II,* ed. Richard M. Bernard and Bradley R. Rice (Austin, Tex., 1983), 165–66.

26. Hopkins, "From Naval Pauper to Naval Power," 14–15; Silver, "Norfolk and the Navy," 114–16; Johnson, "The Failed Experiment," 102–3; Val L. McGee, *The Origins of Fort Rucker* (Ozark, Ala., 1987), 83–100; Elmer L. Puryear, *Graham A. Barden: Conservative Carolina Congressman* (Buie's Creek, N.C., 1979), 35–39; Grantham, *South in Modern America,* 172.

27. McGee, *Origins of Fort Rucker,* 148–52; *Fiftieth Anniversary History,* 82–84; Deming and Stein, *Disposal of Southern War Plants,* 41.

28. Richard S. Combes, "Aircraft Manufacturing in Georgia: A Case Study of Federal Industrial Investment," in Scranton, *Second Wave,* 24–42, esp. 33; Rae, *Climb to Greatness,* 183, 192–97, 199; McGee, *Origins of Fort Rucker,* 153–56; *Fiftieth Anniversary History,* 104–10.

29. Ann Markusen et al., *The Rise of the Gunbelt: The Military Remapping of Industrial America* (New York, 1991), 30–32.

30. Geoffrey R. Crump, "The Spatial Distribution of Military Spending in the United States, 1941–85" *Growth and Change* 20 (summer 1989): 50–62; Combes, "Aircraft Manufacturing in Georgia," 37–38; Schulman, *From Cotton Belt to Sunbelt,* 139–40; Berkeley Rice, *The C-5A Scandal: An Inside Story of the Military-Industrial Complex* (Boston, 1971), 11–17; St. Pé, "Salute to American Spirit," 16–18.

31. Crump, "Spatial Distribution of Military Spending in the United States"; Tazewell, *Newport News Shipbuilding,* 215–16. Rice, *C-5A Scandal,* 15–16 suggests that the award of the C-5A contract to Lockheed-Georgia may have been motivated primarily by Pentagon concerns with keeping the Marietta facility in operation.

32. John E. Lynch, *Local Economic Development after Military Base Closings* (New York, 1970), 261.

33. Lynch, *Local Economic Development after Military Base Closings,* 69–83.

34. Wright, *Old South, New South,* 239–74, though see also his second thought, "The Persistence of the South as an Economic Region," *Atlanta History* 44 (winter 2001): 69–80; Schulman, *From Cotton Belt to Sunbelt,* 170; Melosi, "Dallas–Fort Worth"; Barry J. Kaplan, "Houston: The Golden Buckle of the Sunbelt," in Bernard and Rice, *Sunbelt Cities,* 196–202; Bradley R. Rice, "If Dixie Were Atlanta," in Bernard and Rice, eds., *Sunbelt Cities,* 31–34.

35. Louis Uchitelle, "Long March of the Arms Contractors," *New York Times,* April 19, 1995, C1, C4.

36. *Statistical Abstracts of the United States,* 1989–2000. Based on 1998 as the most recent year.

37. *New York Times,* June 12, 1997.

38. For a comparative argument using the case of the southern textile industry, see chap. 6 in this volume.

11. The American South and the American Manufacturing Belt

1. Albert O. Hirschman, *The Strategy of Economic Development,* Yale Studies in Economics, 10 (New Haven, 1958), 185–87.

2. On the Agrarian take on regional difference, see, of course, Twelve Southerners, *I'll Take My Stand: The South and the Agrarian Tradition* (New York, 1930). On the southern stereotype as marketing device, see any issue of *Southern Living*, but also see John Shelton Reed, "Instant Grits and Plastic-Wrapped Crackers: Southern Culture and Social Change" in *The American South: Portrait of a Culture*, ed. Louis D. Rubin, Jr. (Baton Rouge, 1979), 27–37. For a classic polemic ascribing southern backwardness to its "traditional values," see William Hord Nicholls, *Southern Tradition and Regional Progress* (Chapel Hill, N.C., 1960). For examples of the ways in which historians have recently manipulated the southern stereotype to explain both the region's pre–World War II underdevelopment and its postwar upsurge, see Marc Egnal, *Divergent Paths: How Culture and Institutions Have Shaped North American Growth* (New York, 1996); and Bruce J. Schulman, *From Cotton Belt to Sunbelt: Federal Policy, Economic Development, and the Transformation of the South, 1938–1980* (New York, 1991).

3. In addition to the works cited in note 2 above, two studies that especially stress the role of repressive elites in shaping post–Civil War southern development are Jonathan M. Wiener, *Social Origins of the New South: Alabama, 1860–1885* (Baton Rouge, 1978); and Dwight B. Billings, *Planters and the Making of a "New South": Class, Politics, and Development in North Carolina, 1865–1900* (Chapel Hill, N.C., 1979).

4. See, for instance, Robert A. Margo, "The South as an Economic Problem: Fact or Fiction" in *The South as an American Problem*, ed. Larry J. Griffin and Don H. Doyle (Athens, Ga., 1995), 164–80; Stanley Engerman, "Some Economic Factors in Southern Backwardness in the Nineteenth Century" in *Essays in Regional Economics*, ed. John F. Kain and John Robert Meyer (Cambridge, Mass., 1971), 279–306; Gavin Wright, *Old South, New South: Revolutions in the Southern Economy since the Civil War* (New York, 1986), 60–64.

5. Schulman, *From Cotton Belt to Sunbelt;* James C. Cobb, *Industrialization and Southern Society, 1877–1984* (Lexington, Ky., 1984).

6. On southern "deindustrialization," see Barry Bluestone and Bennett Harrison, *The Deindustrialization of America: Plant Closings, Community Abandonment, and the Dismantling of Basic Industries* (New York, 1982), 31–40; Jeffrey Leiter, Michael D. Schulman, and Rhonda Zingraff, eds., *Hanging by a Thread: Social Change in Southern Textiles* (Ithaca, N.Y., 1991); Douglas Flamming, *Creating the Modern South: Millhands and Managers in Dalton, Georgia, 1884–1984* (Chapel Hill, N.C., 1992), 307–27.

7. The classic statements of "unbalanced growth" theory are Hirschman, *Strategy of Economic Development*, and Gunnar Myrdal, *Rich Lands and Poor: The Road to World Prosperity* (New York, 1958). The economist Paul Krugman has recently sought to integrate their arguments and those of regional scientists and economic geographers with modern economic theory; see Paul R. Krugman, *Geography and Trade* (Leuven, Belgium, and Cambridge, Mass., 1991) and Paul R. Krugman, *Development, Geography, and Economic Theory* (Cambridge, Mass., 1995). On the importance of communities to industrial development, the work of Philip Scranton is indispensable; see especially his *Endless Novelty: Specialty Production and American Industrialization, 1865–1925* (Princeton, N.J., 1997). See also Jane Jacobs's provocative assertion of the centrality of the urban setting to innovative economic life in *Cities and the Wealth of Nations: Principles of Economic Life* (New York, 1984).

8. That nations coming late to economic development develop "substitutes" for the acquired advantages of earlier comers is an insight commonly associated with Alexander Gerschenkron. See his classic 1952 essay, "Economic Backwardness in Historical Perspective" in *Economic Backwardness in Historical Perspective: A Book of Essays* (Cambridge, Mass., 1962), 5–30.

9. The classic statement of "path dependence" is Paul David, "CLIO and the Economics of QUERTY," *American Economic Review* 75 (May 1985): 332–37.

10. Harvey S. Perloff et al., *Regions, Resources, and Economic Growth* (Baltimore, 1960); David R. Meyer, "Emergence of the American Manufacturing Belt: An Interpretation," *Journal of Historical Geography* 9 (April 1983): 145–74. Patent proportions are calculated from *U.S. Commissioner of Patents Report, 1900*.

11. On Quebec, see Egnal, *Divergent Paths;* on the Maritimes, see Philip J. Wood, "Determinants of Industrialization on the North American 'Periphery,'" in Leiter, Schulman, and Zingraff, *Hanging by a Thread*, 58–78.

12. Jack P. Greene, *Pursuits of Happiness: The Social Development of Early Modern British Colonies and the Formation of American Culture* (Chapel Hill, N.C., 1988); Joyce E. Chaplin, *An Anxious Pursuit: Agricultural Innovation and Modernity in the Lower South, 1730–1815* (Chapel Hill, N.C., 1993); L. Glenn Crothers, "'The Projecting Spirit': Social, Economic, and Cultural Change in Post-Revolutionary Northern Virginia, 1780–1805" (Ph.D. diss., University of Florida, 1997).

13. Robert William Fogel, *Without Consent or Contract: The Rise and Fall of American Slavery* (New York, 1989); Peter A. Coclanis, *The Shadow of a Dream: Economic Life and Death in the South Carolina Low Country, 1670–1920* (New York, 1989).

14. Christopher Clark, *The Roots of Rural Capitalism: Western Massachusetts, 1780–1860* (Ithaca, N.Y., 1990); Thomas Childs Cochran, *Frontiers of Change: Early Industrialism in America* (New York, 1981); Diane Lindstrom, *Economic Development in the Philadelphia Region, 1810–1850* (New York, 1977); David R. Meyer, "Formation of Advanced Technology Districts: New England Textile Machinery and Firearms, 1790–1820," *Economic Geography*, extra issue (1998): 31–45; John W. Lozier, *Taunton and Mason: Cotton Machinery and Locomotive Manufacture in Taunton, Massachusetts, 1811–1861* (New York, 1978).

15. Brian Page and Richard Walker, "From Settlement to Fordism: The Agro-Industrial Revolution in the American Midwest," *Economic Geography* 67 (Oct. 1991): 281–315; Richard C. Wade, *The Urban Frontier: The Rise of Western Cities, 1790–1830* (Cambridge, Mass., 1959); Jon C. Teaford, *Cities of the Heartland: The Rise and Fall of the Industrial Midwest* (Bloomington, Ind., 1993), chap. 1.

16. Teaford, *Cities of the Heartland*, chap. 1; George Rogers Taylor, *The Transportation Revolution 1815–1860;* Albert Fishlow, *American Railroads and the Transformation of the Antebellum Economy* (Cambridge, Mass., 1965), 163–203; Allan Richard Pred, *Urban Growth and the Circulation of Information: The United States System of Cities, 1790–1840* (Cambridge, Mass., 1973); Scranton, *Endless Novelty*, 27–59.

17. Robert S. Starobin, *Industrial Slavery in the Old South* (New York, 1970); Claudia Dale Goldin, *Urban Slavery in the American South, 1820–1860: A Quantitative History* (Chicago, 1976); for a classic statement of an opposing view, see Eugene D. Genovese, *The Political Economy of Slavery; Studies in the Economy and Society of the Slave South* (New York, 1967), 27–59.

18. Coclanis, *The Shadow of a Dream*, 143–54; Robert E. Gallman and Ralph V. Anderson, "Slaves as Fixed Capital: Slave Labor and Southern Economic Development," *Journal of American History* 64 (March 1977): 24–46; Gavin Wright, *The Political Economy of the Cotton South: Households, Markets, and Wealth in the Nineteenth Century* (New York, 1978); Heywood W. Fleisig, "Slavery, the Supply of Agricultural Labor, and the Industrialization of the South," *Journal of Economic History* 36 (Sept. 1976): 572–97; David F. Weiman, "Staple Crops and Slave Plantations: Alternative Perspectives on Regional Development in the Antebellum Cotton South" in *Agriculture and National Development: Views on the Nineteenth Century*, ed. Lou Ferleger (Ames, Iowa, 1990), 119–61; Harold D. Woodman, *King Cotton and His Retainers: Financing and Marketing the Cotton Crop of the South, 1800–1925* (Lexington, Ky., 1968).

19. Morton Rothstein, "The Antebellum South as a Dual Economy: A Tentative Hypothesis," *Agricultural History* 41 (fall 1967): 373–82; Eugene D. Genovese, "Yeoman Farmers in a Slaveholders' Democracy" in *Fruits of Merchant Capital: Slavery and Bourgeois Property in the Rise and Expansion of Capitalism,* ed. Elizabeth Fox-Genovese and Eugene D. Genovese (New York, 1983), 249–64; Fred Bateman and Thomas Joseph Weiss, *A Deplorable Scarcity: The Failure of Industrialization in the Slave Economy* (Chapel Hill, N.C., 1981); on the likely constricting effects of small markets on manufacturing development in the South, see Roger L. Ransom, "Review of Fred Bateman and Thomas Weiss, *A Deplorable Scarcity: The Failure of Industrialization in the Slave Economy,*" *American Historical Review* 87 (June 1982): 856–57.

20. David R. Goldfield, "Pursuing the American Dream: Urban Growth in the Old South" in *The City in Southern History: The Growth of Urban Civilization in the South,* ed. Blaine Brownell and David R. Goldfield (Port Washington, N.Y., 1977), 52–91; Ulrich Bonnell Phillips, *A History of Transportation in the Eastern Cotton Belt to 1860* (New York, 1908).

21. On antebellum southern urbanization, see David L. Carlton, "Urbanization," in *Encyclopedia of the Confederacy,* ed. Richard N. Current (New York, 1993), 1641–48. See also Allan Richard Pred, *Urban Growth and City-Systems in the United States, 1840–1860,* (Cambridge, Mass., 1980), 109–17; David R. Meyer, "The Industrial Retardation of Southern Cities, 1860–1880," *Explorations in Economic History* 25 (Oct. 1988): 366–68. On the southern railroad network, see George Rogers Taylor and Irene D. Neu, *The American Railroad Network, 1861–1890* (Cambridge, Mass., 1956). On the exceptional case of Richmond, see Sally Ann Flocks, "'In the Hands of Others': The Development of Dependency by Richmond's Manufacturers on Northern Financiers" (Ph.D. diss., Yale University, 1983).

22. Robert W. Fogel and Stanley L. Engerman, *Time on the Cross: The Economics of American Negro Slavery,* 2 vols. (Boston, 1974), 1:147–57; Fogel, *Without Consent or Contract,* chaps. 1 and 4; Richard Graham, "Slavery and Economic Development: Brazil and the United States South in the Nineteenth Century," *Comparative Studies in Society and History* 23 (Oct. 1981): 620–55.

23. Richard A. Easterlin, "Regional Income Trends, 1840–1950," in *The Reinterpretation of American Economic History,* ed. Robert William Fogel and Stanley L. Engerman (New York, 1971), 38–49; Engerman, "Southern Backwardness in the Nineteenth Century"; Roger L. Ransom and Richard Sutch, *One Kind of Freedom: The Economic Consequences of Emancipation* (New York, 1977), 1–55.

24. John F. Stover, *The Railroads of the South, 1865–1900: A Study in Finance and Control* (Chapel Hill, N.C., 1955); Maury Klein, "The Strategy of Southern Railroads," *American Historical Review* 73 (April 1968): 1052–68; Maury Klein, *The Great Richmond Terminal: A Study in Businessmen and Business Strategy* (Charlottesville, Va., 1970). Two good case studies of the shift (treating the same company) are Cecil Kenneth Brown, *A State Movement in Railroad Development: The Story of North Carolina's First Effort to Establish an East and West Trunk Line Railroad* (Chapel Hill, N.C., 1928), and Allen W. Trelease, *The North Carolina Railroad, 1849–1871, and the Modernization of North Carolina* (Chapel Hill, N.C., 1991).

25. Scranton, *Endless Novelty,* 81–160; Alfred Dupont Chandler, *The Visible Hand: The Managerial Revolution in American Business* (Cambridge, Mass., 1977), 240–344.

26. John J. Beck, "Development in the Piedmont South: Rowan County, North Carolina, 1850–1900" (Ph.D. diss., University of North Carolina at Chapel Hill, 1984), 74–76, 97–98; Nicholls, *Southern Tradition and Regional Progress;* Herman Hollis Chapman, *The Iron and Steel Industries of the South* (University, Ala., 1953), 98–110, 27, 29–30; Myrdal, *Rich Lands and Poor,* 27–29.

27. Lozier, *Taunton and Mason;* David J. Jeremy, *Transatlantic Industrial Revolution: The Diffusion of Textile Technologies between Britain and America, 1790–1830s* (Cambridge, Mass., 1981);

George Sweet Gibb, *The Saco-Lowell Shops: Textile Machinery Building in New England, 1813–1949* (Cambridge, Mass., 1950); Thomas R. Navin, *The Whitin Machine Works since 1831: A Textile Machinery Company in an Industrial Village* (Cambridge, Mass., 1950).

28. David L. Carlton, "The Revolution from Above: The National Market and the Beginnings of Industrialization in North Carolina," *Journal of American History* 77 (Sept. 1990): 445–75; David L. Carlton, "Paternalism and Southern Textile Labor: A Historiographical View" in *Race, Class, and Community in Southern Labor History,* ed. Gary M. Fink and Merl Elwyn Reed (Tuscaloosa, Ala., 1994), 17–26; David L. Carlton and Peter A. Coclanis, "The Uninventive South? A Quantitative Look at Region and American Inventiveness," *Technology and Culture* 36 (April 1995): 302–26. On the "family labor" system, see Cathy McHugh, *Mill Family: The Labor Systems in the Southern Cotton Textile Industry, 1880–1915* (New York, 1988). On the "skill-saving" character of southern textile industrialization, see Marvin Fischbaum, "An Economic Analysis of the Southern Capture of the Cotton Textile Industry Progressing to 1910" (Ph.D. diss., Columbia University, 1965).

29. Robert Franklin Durden, *The Dukes of Durham, 1865–1929* (Durham, N.C., 1975); Nannie M. Tilley, *The R.J. Reynolds Tobacco Company* (Chapel Hill, N.C., 1985).

30. Carlton, "The Revolution from Above"; Kenneth Warren, *The American Steel Industry, 1850–1970: A Geographical Interpretation* (Oxford, 1973), 65–73, 182–94. A major exception to this rule is the Texas Gulf Coast, which developed a petroleum-based complex that diverges from this story in so many respects that to deal with them would overwhelm the present paper. I honestly regard the Texas story, at least from the turn of the century forward, as more properly part of the history of the West than that of the South. A good discussion of the rise of the Texas Gulf industrial complex is Joseph A. Pratt, *The Growth of a Refining Region* (Greenwich, Conn., 1980).

31. On the dearth of machine tool makers in the South in the early twentieth century, see also U.S. Department of Commerce and Labor, Bureau of the Census, *Census of Manufactures, 1905: Metal Working Machinery,* Bulletin 67, by Fred J. Miller (Washington, D.C.: U.S. Government Printing Office, 1907); *American Machinist* 40 (Jan. 29, 1914): 210 (map). On the early southern automobile industry, see Craig Steven Pascoe, "Manufacturing a New South: The Business Biography of John Gary Anderson" (Ph.D. diss., University of Tennessee, Knoxville, 1999); Karsten Hülsemann, "Greenfields in the Heart of Dixie: How the American Auto Industry Discovered the South," in *The Second Wave: Southern Industrialization from the 1940s to the 1970s,* ed. Philip Scranton (Athens, Ga., 2001), 219–54. On the contrasting experience of the Midwest, see Page and Walker, "From Settlement to Fordism," 304–10; David A. Hounshell, *From the American System to Mass Production, 1800–1932: The Development of Manufacturing Technology in the United States* (Baltimore, 1984), 189–261; Michael Schwartz, "Markets, Networks, and the Rise of Chrysler in Old Detroit, 1920–1940," *Enterprise and Society* 1 (March 2000): 63–99.

32. Robert Higgs, "American Inventiveness, 1870–1920," *Journal of Political Economy* 79 (May–June 1971): 661–67; see also chap. 8 in this volume.

33. David M. Potter, "The Historical Development of Eastern-Southern Freight-Rate Relationships," *Law and Contemporary Problems* 12 (summer 1947): 416–48; William H. Joubert, *Southern Freight Rates in Transition* (Gainesville, Fla., 1949).

34. Chandler, *The Visible Hand;* Scranton, *Endless Novelty,* 297–343; Philip Scranton, "'Have a Heart for the Manufacturers!': Production, Distribution, and the Decline of American Textile Manufacturing," in *World of Possibilities: Flexibility and Mass Production in Western Industrialization,* ed. Charles F. Sabel and Jonathan Zeitlin (New York, 1997), 310–43; Ann Markusen, "Sticky Places in Slippery Space: A Typology of Industrial Districts," *Economic Geography* (July 1996): 293–313.

35. Naomi R. Lamoreaux and Kenneth L. Sokoloff, "Inventors, Firms, and the Market for Technology," in *Learning by Doing in Markets, Firms, and Countries,* ed. Naomi R. Lamoreaux, Daniel M. G. Raff, and Peter Temin (Chicago, 1999), 19–60.

36. Potter, "Eastern-Southern Freight-Rate Relationships"; Joubert, *Southern Freight Rates in Transition,* 349–55.

37. Hülsemann, "Greenfields in the Heart of Dixie"; Perloff et al., *Regions, Resources, and Economic Growth;* Cobb, *Industrialization and Southern Society;* Wright, *Old South, New South,* 147–55, 263–64; Pete Daniel, *Breaking the Land: The Transformation of Cotton, Tobacco, and Rice Cultures since 1880* (Urbana, Ill., 1985); Jack Temple Kirby, "The Southern Exodus, 1910–1960: A Primer for Historians," *Journal of Southern History* 49 (Nov. 1983): 585–600; Teaford, *Cities of the Heartland,* 189–97, 230–39.

38. Steve Fraser and Gary Gerstle, *The Rise and Fall of the New Deal Order, 1930–1980* (Princeton, N.J., 1989); Lizabeth Cohen, *Making a New Deal: Industrial Workers in Chicago, 1919–1939* (New York, 1990); Teaford, *Cities of the Heartland,* 183–86.

39. Teaford, *Cities of the Heartland,* 210–30; the "conspiracy" argument is offered in different variants by Kirkpatrick Sale, *Power Shift: The Rise of the Southern Rim and Its Challenge to the Eastern Establishment* (New York, 1975), and Schulman, *From Cotton Belt to Sunbelt.* Schulman in particular emphasizes the role of defense spending in redistributing resources from the manufacturing belt to the South, but the role of federal defense spending in postwar southern economic growth has been grossly exaggerated; see Gregory Hooks, "The Federal Contribution to Manufacturing Growth, 1940–1990" in Scranton, *Second Wave,* 255–85 and chap. 10 in this volume. See also Ann R. Markusen, *Regions: The Economics and Politics of Territory* (Totowa, N.J., 1987), 183–88.

40. Gavin Wright, "The Civil Rights Revolution as Economic History," *Journal of Economic History* 59 (June 1999): 267–90.

41. Gavin Wright suggests a similar point; see Wright, *Old South, New South,* 273–74.

42. Margaret Levenstein made this point in her commentary on an earlier version of this paper, delivered at the Annual Meeting of the Organization of American Historians on March 31, 2000. See also Markusen, "Sticky Places in Slippery Space." For another view of midwestern resurgence, stressing the "creative destruction" of the earlier industrial culture and the widespread adoption by Michigan firms of Japanese techniques, see Richard Florida, "Regional Creative Destruction: Production Organization, Globalization, and the Economic Transformation of the Midwest," *Economic Geography* 72 (July 1996): 314–34.

43. See chap. 6 in this volume.

Index